CHANGING MEN

OTHER RECENT VOLUMES IN THE
SAGE FOCUS EDITIONS

CHANGING MEN

New Directions in Research on Men and Masculinity

Edited by

Michael S. Kimmel

SAGE PUBLICATIONS
The International Professional Publishers
Newbury Park   London   New Delhi

to

Edwin H. Kimmel and Martin Bauml Duberman
with gratitude and love

For information address:

SAGE Publications, Inc.
2455 Teller Road
Newbury Park, California 91320

SAGE Publications Ltd.
6 Bonhill Street
London EC2A 4PU
United Kingdom

SAGE Publications India Pvt. Ltd.
M-32 Market
Greater Kailash I
New Delhi 110 048 India

Printed in the United States of America

Library of Congress Cataloging-in-Publication Data

Main entry under title:

Changing men.

(Sage focus editions ; v. 88)
Includes bibliographies.
1. Men. 2. Masculinity (Psychology) 3. Sex
role. 4. Men's studies. I. Kimmel, Michael S.
HQ1090.C467 1987   305.3'1   86-29754
ISBN 0-8039-2996-X
ISBN 0-8039-2997-8 (pbk.)

92 93 94 10 9 8 7 6

Contents

Acknowledgments

This volume assembles innovative and exciting research on men and masculinity. As such, it contributes to the demarcation of a new field called *men's studies*, as well as to the examination of masculinity within traditional academic disciplines. Such work, of course, does not take place in a vacuum, but assumes the pioneering work on gender already accomplished by women's studies. Inspired by these insights, scholars have begun to examine men's lives and experiences, not simply as normative assumptions, but as gendered and socially and historically variable.

My own work in editing this volume has benefited greatly from colleagues and friends who have provided intellectual support, academic guidance, and searching criticism. If "the personal is political," as a motto of the women's movement would have it, then surely it is also professional, and it would be virtually impossible to disentangle what types of contributions each of these colleagues and friends made to the whole. I am grateful to Angela Aidala; Claire August; Jeff Beane; Bob, Joann, and Liz Brannon; Carol Briggs; Barbara and Herb Diamond; Kate Ellis; John Gagnon; Judith Gerson; Cathy Greenblat; Wray Herbert; Sandi Kimmel; Martin Levine; Iona Mara-Drita; Dorothy Sloboda; Catharine Stimpson; and Cooper Thompson.

Joseph Pleck has advised me at every stage of this project, as senior scholar, researcher, and editorial collaborator. His remarkable intellectual range helped to locate these diverse essays within their respective literatures, and his comments on many of the chapters resulted in significantly improved arguments. And my editors at Sage—first, Lisa Freeman-Miller, and later Terry Hendrix and Mitch Allen—have been exemplary in their responsiveness, competence, and genuine warmth.

I have received some financial support for the final preparation of the manuscript from a Faculty Research Grant at Rutgers University, and my own research was supported in part by a Summer Faculty Fellowship at Rutgers University.

Finally, the two men to whom this collection is dedicated have been among the most important influences on my own development—personal, political, and intellectual—as a man. It seems fitting that this volume be for them.

—Michael S. Kimmel
New York City

1

Rethinking "Masculinity"

New Directions in Research

MICHAEL S. KIMMEL

Men are changing—not, perhaps, with the bang of transformation, but also not simply with a whispered hint of a slight nudge in a new direction. New role models for men have not replaced older ones, but have grown alongside them, creating a dynamic tension between ambitious breadwinner and compassionate father, between macho seducer and loving companion, between Rambo and Phil Donahue. Men today are doing far more housework and spending more time with their children, yet the proportion of domestic time is still skewed heavily toward women (see Pleck, 1986). Men are today exploring new options in their work environments, and paying more attention to their physical and emotional health, yet continue to evidence far higher rates of stress-related diseases and deaths. Men are today developing a wider repertoire of emotions, seeking to express their feelings more deeply and with a wider range of women and men, and yet violence against women (rape, sexual assault, battery) and homophobia both seem to be increasing. Surely, then, we live in an era of transition in the definition of masculinity—what it means to be a real man—not, as some might fantasize, in which one mode comes to replace another mode, but in which two parallel traditions emerge, and from the tension of opposition between them a new synthesis might, perhaps, be born.

If men are changing at all, however, it is not because they have stumbled upon the limits of traditional masculinity all by themselves. For at least two decades, the women's movement (and also, since 1969, the gay liberation movement) has suggested that the traditional enactments of masculinity were in desperate need of overhaul. For some men, these critiques have prompted a terrified retreat to traditional constructions; to others it has inspired a serious reevaluation of traditional worldviews, and offers of support for the social, political, and economic struggles of women and gays.

As men have been changing, so too has the study of men and masculinity. Social scientific research on gender has mushroomed in the past two decades, in part a response to the dramatic gains made by the women's movement and also the gay movement. Feminist scholarship has placed gender in the center of discourse on social organization, has retrieved significant women from historical obscurity, and, following the new social history, has assembled a portrait of the daily life of working women in other areas. So dramatic has been this work on gender by feminist scholars that today few universities have no courses on women's studies, few scholarly presses have no women's studies series, and few social scientists deny the centrality of gender as an independent variable in social organization.

And now comes "men's studies." Though it has not had (nor will it have) the impact of women's studies, men's studies has already become a visible presence among teachers and scholars. Newspaper and magazine articles have heralded its arrival (Petzke, 1986; Saholz, 1986; Yoshihashi, 1984) and a growing number of courses are being offered at universities and colleges across the nation (see Femiano, 1984). Several academic journals have devoted special issues to studies of men and masculinity (*Family Coordinator*, 1979; *Journal of Social Issues*, 1978; and *American Behavioral Scientist*, 1986) and several scholarly monographs (Komorovsky, 1976; Pleck, 1981, 1986), popular books (Ehrenreich, 1983; Fasteau, 1975; Gerzon, 1982; Tolson, 1977), and anthologies (Brannon & David, 1976; Brod, 1987; Gary, 1981; Lewis, 1982; Pleck & Pleck, 1980; Pleck & Sawyer, 1974) have demarcated the field. Although it is still young, men's studies already has introductory-level college textbooks (Doyle, 1983; Franklin, 1984) and a published annotated bibliography with over 1,000 entries (August, 1985). This anthology is a contribution to this new field.

Men's studies responds to the shifting social and intellectual contexts in the study of gender and attempts to treat masculinity not as the normative referent against which standards are assessed but as a problematic gender construct. Inspired by the academic breakthroughs of women's studies, men's studies addresses similar questions to the study of men and masculinity. As women's studies has radically revised the traditional academic canon, men's studies seeks to use that revision as the basis for its exploration of men and masculinity. Men's studies seeks neither to replace nor to supplant women's studies; quite the contrary. Men's studies seeks to buttress, to augment women's studies, to complete the radically redrawn portrait of gender that women's studies has begun (see also Brod, 1987; and his chapter in this volume).

Such is the rationale for courses about men and masculinity. Often, when asked about men's studies, scholars have responded initially with suspicion. "Aren't all courses that don't have the word 'women' in the title about men? Why do we need a separate course about men?" was the way one colleague put it to me. And this is surely true: Men have been the normative gender, and those courses not specifically about some other group have always been de facto about men. Yet these courses have also been about men within the context of specific public functions: We study men as scientists, as authors, as presidents or other government officials, as soldiers or kings. But rarely, if ever, do we study men as men; rarely do we make masculinity the object of inquiry as we examine men's lives. If men have been traditionally the benchmark gender (and women the "other"), then studies of men and masculinity have never made masculinity itself the object of inquiry. Men's studies takes masculinity as its problematic, and seeks to explore men's experiences as men not in some social roles. While our experience is structured by its social structural location—social roles define individual enactments of them— it is also equally true that gender structures the dimensions of those roles. Other factors such as race, class, ethnicity, and age will mediate the generalizability of our explorations, but masculinity as problematic opens up entirely new areas for social scientific study.

Such study is increasingly interdisciplinary, drawing on research from social and behavioral sciences as well as the humanities and even the natural and biological sciences. While most of the essays in this collection are written by social and behavioral scientists, there are also works by researchers in departments of history, urology, philosophy, urban affairs, and communications. They employ methods from quantitative survey analysis to in-depth interviews and hermeneutic interpretation; other research in men's studies is employing methodologies from the humanities such as deconstruction of literary texts, comparative and historical analysis, and comparative cultural methods drawn from anthropology. This interdisciplinary quality will only increase as other disciplines begin to reexamine conventional wisdoms as gender-based ideologies.

Beyond "Sex Roles": Gender as a Social Construction

This interdisciplinary perspective developing within men's studies echoes the interdisciplinary perspective developed by women's studies in the last two decades. It does so for reasons of both form and content. As I mentioned above, men's studies requires the reinterpretation of conventional wisdoms as gender-based ideologies, a formulation it gratefully borrows from women's studies. Formally, then, this reinterpretation slowly encompasses the different academic disciplines—at differing rates of speed, to be sure—but the sweep of the compass can cover all academic fields. More important, however, men's studies is beginning to follow women's studies' lead in the content of its inquiry into the structure of gender in the United States.

For several decades, the study of gender has used a "sex-role" model, a model that specified the ways in which biological males and biological females became socialized as men and women in a particular culture. But this sex-role paradigm has come under increasing criticism for being ahistorical, psychologically reductionist, and apolitical. (See Pleck, 1981, for the most comprehensive critique of the male sex-role model, and see Stacey & Thorne, 1985, and Gerson & Peiss, 1985, for comparable critiques of sex-role research in general.) Because many of the articles collected here move beyond this paradigm—and because transcending the sex-role paradigm is essential to maintaining the strongly interdisciplinary perspective of men's studies—it may be useful to spell out this critique in a bit more detail.

The sex-role paradigm posits a historically invariant model, a kind of static sex-role container into which all biological males and females are forced to fit. This process of fitting into preexisting roles is called "socialization." As such, the paradigm ignores the extent to which our conceptions of masculinity and femininity—the content of the male or female sex role—is relational; that is, the product of gender relations that are historically and socially conditioned. Masculinity and femininity are relational constructs, the definition of either depends upon the definition of the other. Although "male" and "female" may have some universal characteristics (and even here the research on biological dimorphism suggests a certain fluidity), one cannot understand the social construction of either masculinity or femininity without reference to the other.

Further, the sex-role paradigm is based upon the traits associated with the role—a kind of laundry list of behavioral characteristics—rather than their enactments. This makes sex roles not only more static than they might otherwise be but posits an ideal configuration that bears little, if any, relation to the ways in which sex roles are enacted in everyday life. In addition, the sex-role paradigm minimizes the extent to which gender relations are based on power. Not only do men as a group exert power over women as a group, but the historically derived definitions of masculinity and femininity reproduce those power relations. Masculinity becomes associated with those traits that imply authority and mastery, femininity with those traits that suggest passivity and subordination. By undervaluing the historical and social bases for gender relations, then, the sex-role paradigm reproduces the very problems it seeks to understand. If, as Harrison (1978) remarks, the "male sex role is dangerous to your health," then the sex-role paradigm is equally dangerous to successful academic inquiry.

Once we posit that the notions of masculinity or femininity are relational, and that both genders are socially constructed, new areas are opened for empirical research. And this is precisely the direction of such interdisciplinary work in both women's studies and men's studies. Some scholars are reinterpreting the literary canon, others revealing the ways in which gender constructed the meanings derived from everyday life, others exploring the contemporary construction of gender relations.

My own empirical research on male responses to the emergence of feminism, and especially on "profeminist" men, is strongly influenced by a social constructionist perspective on gender relations. Because the sex-role paradigm posits two fixed, static, and mutually exclusive role containers, with little or no interpenetration, one could hardly understand the emergence of profeminist men in the late nineteenth-century United States. Yet there were substantial numbers of men who believed that the solution to the "crisis of masculinity" observed by many lay in embracing the feminist model of social reconstruction. One could, of course, simply question the appropriateness of fit between these men and the male sex role, which is precisely what many antagonists of profeminist men actually did. But such an example gives evidence of the inadequacy of such a sex-role model, for it cannot explain the historical emergence of numbers of such men at specific historical junctures and not at others (see Kimmel, 1987).

What's more, the sex-role paradigm is equally hard-pressed to interpret different responses to feminism by men who were not sympathetic to women's causes. Resting on an individual psychological model, the sex-role paradigm cannot adequately grasp shifting structural possibilities of the definition of gender, or the institutional strategies devised in response to shifting gender relations. But two other male responses to feminism in the late nineteenth century—what we might call "antifeminist" and "promale"—rested precisely on these institutional changes, either at the level of policy formation or through voluntary associations. Antifeminist men sought to return women to the private, domestic sphere, whereas promale men ignored women's increased public participation and sought to develop only distinctly male organizations from which women would be excluded. This ranged from craft guilds and athletic organizations to a revamped military and the Boy Scouts of America.

In fact, such historical research suggests an additional element of the social construction of masculinity, one that is also suggested in several of the chapters in this book. Put quite simply, this research suggests that although both masculinity and femininity are socially constructed within a historical context of gender relations, definitions of masculinity are historically reactive to changing definitions of femininity. Here is the argument in brief: Social changes such as changes in the organization of work, the shifting of the geographic frontier, and demographic shifts create the structural parameters for changes in family structure and the relationships of family to economy and society. For example, structural changes led to changes in fertility and morality, to increased participation by women in the labor force and in the public sphere in general. These changes in family organizations in turn structure changes in gender relations, as women begin to move from domestic to public spheres and define an ideology that justifies such movement. In a sense, then, feminist women sought to redefine femininity to include active public participation, including (although not limited to) education, religious institutions, and social reforms. The "New Woman" redefined femininity—to which the "cult of true womanhood" was a reactionary backlash—and this redefinition called into question the definition of masculinity, given that the two are relational constructions. (Such an argument counters Riesman's assertion in *The Lonely Crowd* that "characterological change in the West seems to occur first with men"; quoted in Ehrenreich & English, 1979, p. 239.)

Masculine "reactivity" has a political component as well, not unnoticed by feminist scholars; in a society based upon the institutional power of men over women, men benefit from inherited definitions of masculinity and femininity and would be unlikely to change them— indeed, unlikely even to call them into question. Men, as a group, have historically exhibited a smug satisfaction with existing gender relations. In fact, I would argue that men have, as a group, benefited from the sex-role paradigm that has governed behavioral science's treatment of gender, as it uses masculinity as the normative standard of reference and maximizes the distance between the two genders while minimizing the extent to which these definitions reproduce existing power relations, vary historically, and therefore are open to challenge.

New Perspectives on Masculinity

The chapters in this volume move beyond the sex-role formulation and explore the components of masculinity as it has been socially and historically constructed through a process of gender relations. The first four chapters—"The Structure of Male Role Norms" by Edward Thompson and Joseph Pleck, "The Embodiment of Masculinity" by Marc Mishkind, Judith Rodin, Lisa Silberstein, and Ruth Striegel-Moore, "The Life of a Man's Seasons" by Michael Messner, and "On Heterosexual Masculinity" by Gregory Herek—directly explore the structure of masculinity in the contemporary United States.

Although several scholars have explored the structure of the male role, few have examined it empirically, disaggregating its several constituent elements and specifying the relationships among these variables. Such research is especially important to underscore the ways in which such dimensions are contingent upon and interact with notions of femininity. Thompson and Pleck, for example, measure several related components of masculinity in a population of college-age males. They find some support for the normative structure of male roles but imply that the strength of these norms among college-age males may be less than we might have thought originally, which suggests slight shifts in the normative orientation of contemporary college-age men.

Although longitudinal research will be required to demonstrate such social shifts, these data support the theoretical assumptions above that changing gender relations, and especially changes in definitions of femininity, will prompt reevaluations of masculinity. Interestingly, although Thompson and Pleck argue that male roles "appear distinct from attitudes toward women," the normative aspect of masculinity remains a perceived differentiation from femininity. This suggests a cognitive gap between attitudes about women and attitudes about the structure of masculinity. A man, it would appear, can hold any attitude about women he likes, but his masculinity is still bound up with behaving differently from women.

One fascinating contradiction that emerges between traditionally stereotypical behavior for males and females concerns the relationship of men and women to their bodies. Popular wisdom often has it that women are preoccupied with their bodies, expending tremendous energies in fitting them into normative models of femininity. (This is evident in studies of dieting and eating disorders, and self-perception, and in historical treatments of women's fashion.) So although "Dislike of Own Body Found Common Among Women" as a headline in a recent *New York Times* article proclaimed, men "tend to see themselves as just about perfect" (Goleman, 1985). (And this article was in the "science" section of the newspaper!) Marc Mishkind and his colleagues at Yale suggest a very different pattern among men, one that contrasts with perceptions of uniquely feminine preoccupation with body image.

Mishkind et al. insist that men are quite preoccupied with body image and maintain an idealized image of the perfect body type to which they aspire: the "muscular mesomorph." Not only do men see themselves in terms of perceived distance from the mesomorphic ideal (instead of "just about perfect"), but such bodily preoccupation with body image has been increasing in recent years. And their suggestions about the origins and trajectory of this increase are suggestive and interesting. First, they argue, the decreasing stigmatization of gay men as "failed men"—the replacement of the old stereotype of the limp-wristed "sissy" with the new stereotype gay macho bodybuilder—has increased men's overall concerns with body image. Second, they argue that women's increased participation in the public sphere has led to a kind of "muscular backlash" given that cognitive, occupational, and life-style differences between men and women are decreasing; therefore body image emerges as one of the few areas in which men can differentiate themselves from women. (I would add a third element to this, following Barbara Ehrenreich's, 1983, suggestions that increased body awareness among men is also an artifact of the decrease in men's drawing identity from their breadwinner role in a consumer capitalist society and perceiving their bodies as, in part, a reflection of their role as autonomous consumers.)

Michael Messner's research on the "life course of the jock" suggests the ways in which athletic competition expresses a set of behaviors associated with masculinity. He argues that "from boyhood through adulthood, sports often acts as a central aspect of the individual life structure of the male." Thus the transition from being an athlete as a primary source of identity to athletics as simply one of several recreational aspects of one's life is difficult for men, especially as it occurs so early in the life course. Messner argues that within athletics, men experience a sense of public glory as well as a locus for the legitimate expression of strong emotion, and that leaving athletics requires that they find alternative sources for each. Thus the world of sports is "an important context within which to confront the need for a humanization of men."

As noted above, masculinity is constructed in part by differentiating it from femininity, which is what we mean when we say that the social construction gender is a relational construct. Gregory Herek extends this argument to its logical next step by arguing that heterosexual masculinity is also constructed from its perceived differentiation from homosexuality. Because homosexuality was understood to be "feminized" for so many years—that is, men who are like women—heterosexual masculinity (normative masculinity) is also defined by its distance from homosexuality. Herek's review of the literature and his suggestions for empirical research suggest that homophobia is a vital component of heterosexual masculinity. Here Herek echoes Helen Hacker's (1957, p. 231) assessment that "masculinity is more important to men than femininity is to women," because men have so much more at stake, having to differentiate themselves from both women and homosexual men.

Herek explores some of the psychic consequences for heterosexual men that such terrified distancing can produce, but one can only speculate about the future direction for heterosexual masculinity in light of the increasingly traditional masculine construction of homosexuality.

Men in Domestic Settings

One of the major arenas in which changes in the definition of masculinity have been occurring has been the domestic sphere. How has fatherhood changed historically, both as behavior and as ideology? What are contemporary married couples doing to implement these new definitions of the father? These are the questions addressed by the chapters in this section.

Joseph Pleck, for example, explores the ways in which fatherhood has changed through the course of American history. In the colonial era, fathers were a source of moral teaching, and the notion of "duty" of father to children and of children to fathers was the overriding frame of father-child relations. By the mid-twentieth century, however, this reciprocally dutiful relationship was replaced by an image of father as "distant breadwinner," fueled by early psychoanalytic elevations of the maternal role and new work patterns that removed the father from the home for most daylight hours. However, Pleck suggests that this distance reached its own limits after World War II, as overprotective motherhood was blamed for the enervation of American manhood (which often was a code for fear of homosexuality) and fathers were reasserted as "sex-role model." This new model borrowed images from the colonial model, but also, as Pleck indicates, differed significantly from it as well, as new theories about gender came to dominate behavioral science discourse.

The relative balance of fathers' and mothers' participation in child care is a subject of negotiation among contemporary couples. Teresa Jump and Linda Haas present evidence from their empirical study of dual-career couples in "Fathers in Transition." In their sample, Jump and Haas find fathers providing 38% of the total child care, which is a significant increase over other estimates. While the sharing of work and family obligations within a dual-career relationship expands opportunities both for women in the career world and for men in the domestic world, traditional childhood experiences make the integration of these new roles difficult. Jump and Haas suggest that dual-career fathers find themselves in a "state of transition," caught between traditional and nontraditional understandings of their new roles.

Men and Women

Since definitions of masculinity are constructed in relation to definitions of femininity, one crucial area of research remains male-female relations. The three articles in Part III—"What Do Women Want . . . from Men?" by Kathleen Gerson, "One of the Boys" by Gary Alan Fine, and "The Fraternal Bond as a Joking Relationship" by Peter Lyman—employ different analytic strategies to understand the shifting bases for male-female relations, to explore how men and women are renegotiating the traditional scripts they have inherited. After exploring how structural changes, such as women's increased labor force participation, have led to changes within the family and in the roles played by women and men within the family, Gerson asks how the relations between men and women shape women's efforts to balance the demands of family, children, and career. The changing relations between men and women create new conditions for women's choices, which, in turn, further transform gender relations. Her current research on this topic will unravel the effect of these changes on men's lives and assess how men are responding to the changing structure of women's choices.

Gary Alan Fine takes a novel approach in exploring the structure of masculinity. He suggests that we can make visible the norms that govern male institutions when we observe how women are treated in such institutions; the presence of women will reveal their "otherness" and consequently provide an articulation of the normative structure of masculinity. His participant observation in three restaurant kitchens led him to conclude that "gender roles are socially emergent and grounded in behavior" so that the "ability of women to become 'one of the boys' demonstrates that these styles of behavior can be learned, and are not fixed and static." Yet acceptance in the social world of men requires that women negotiate their way through a set of difficult and sensitive issues. Most important, women must learn to respond appropriately to intimations of sexuality, either through sexual innuendo or by sexual joking. It is through sexuality, Fine suggests, that men demarcate their social world, and keep women out.

Peter Lyman explores the relationship between sexual humor and masculinity in another innovative essay based on a remarkable series of events. When a fraternity's traditional sexist joke on a neighboring sorority resulted in women's anger and affront, these two groups asked Lyman to mediate their discussions of the appropriate place of sexual humor in the organization of their ongoing relationship. Whereas Fine specifies what women need to negotiate their way through a male world as a way of exploring what that world actually looks like, Lyman explores how the joking relationship cements male-male relationships within the fraternity, and suggests how the homosocial component of these relationships almost requires (for the preservation of heterosexual masculinity) the strongly heterosexual element of the male joker and female audience dynamic.

Deconstructing Male Sexuality

Masculinity is tied intimately to sexuality. Sexuality is organized around a gender axis; gender is perhaps the key organizing principle of sexuality. Gender informs sexuality, sexuality confirms gender. It makes sense, therefore, to include studies of male sexuality in this collection. Because sexual performance is one of the crucial arenas in which masculinity is socially constructed and enacted, and because, as Herek notes, heterosexual masculinity hinges on demonstrable sexual orientation and distancing from perceived femininity, performance failure can challenge the essence of masculinity, can confront men with the possibility that they are not "real men." In "In Pursuit of the Perfect Penis," Leonore Tiefer describes two related themes in the medical treatment of erectile disorders, both of which combine to assuage the potentially damaged masculine identity. First, Tiefer describes a growing tendency to treat erectile disorders as physiologically based problems. Here she explains the array of medical and surgical procedures currently employed to treat these disorders. But, Tiefer argues, the data that suggest such a large number of physiologically based problems are seriously flawed because the sample is only those men who present themselves for penile implant surgery in the first place. That only 50% of this highly self-selected sample may have some physiologically based impairment indicates that psychologically based etiologies are far more likely. But men with erectile disorders, of course, also prefer a physiological to a psychological explanation because it relieves them of conscious responsibility—that is, it preserves their masculine identity. The medicalization of male sexuality through the development of penile implant surgery is thus an instance of the broader process of identity management.

It is also an example of the trivialization of sexuality. Tiefer follows historians of the psychological treatments of sexuality—especially Robinson (1973), who argued that the emergence of sexology from Havelock Ellis to Alfred Kinsey and his associates to the sex therapy of William Masters and Virginia Johnson has reduced sexuality to a surface phenomenon that can be treated by a host of "quick-fix" techniques. Such techniques avoid longer-term therapeutic interventions, which unravel the often complicated and deeply embedded relationships among sexual performance, gender identity, and individual life history. In this sense, sex therapy—of which implant surgery is only a more recent and especially medicalized version—is as American as apple pie, applying a shallow dab of technical know-how to a deep-rooted problem. To really "cure" these cases of erectile disorder would perhaps require some individual therapeutic intervention as well as a social therapeutic reevaluation of the social construction of masculinity in the United States.

Arthur Shostak's research on men's responses to abortion has been revealing about the organization of male sexuality. In his chapter, Shostak asks about men's experiences when they accompany their sexual partners to obtain abortions. From surveys and detailed interviews, Shostak suggests unmet emotional needs on the part of male partners, who often experience a great deal of confusion and ambivalence about sexuality and abortion. His suggestion that abortion is "fatherhood glimpsed" reveals how it may evoke men's fantasies and ambivalences about fatherhood, as well as about sexuality. By exploring why men attend the procedure, what their experience is, and what services are available to them in the clinic, Shostak argues that men's unmet needs remain an important unexplored area of the abortion experience. However, it is important to stress that Shostak does not oppose abortion as an option for women, nor does he believe that men's needs in any way outstrip or even equal those of the women who are seeking abortions.

Given that gender is socially constructed, research can specify the materials from which it is constructed and suggest how it is organized. Images of gender in the media become texts on normative behavior, one of many cultural shards we use to construct notions of masculinity. In "Mass-Media Sexual Violence and Male Viewers," Edward Donnerstein and Daniel Linz, two of the foremost researchers on the effect of mass media representations of violence and sexuality on attitudes and behavior, survey the literature to assess the effect of mass-media sexual violence on male viewers. They find that images of sexual violence lead to an increase in men's beliefs of rape myths, their reported willingness to commit acts of sexual violence themselves, and a decrease in sympathies with women victims. However, when images of sexual violence are disaggregated into their component parts—violence, sexual violence, and sexuality—the authors find that almost identical results obtain for both violence and sexual violence, but virtually no significant change in attitudes is evident from repeated viewings of explicitly sexual scenes in which coercion and violence are not present.

Obviously, the policy implications of such research findings are enormous, especially in light of recent feminist and right-wing attempts to introduce legislation against pornography. Donnerstein and Linz imply that such feminist efforts, which have the important goal of protecting women from male violence and sexual assault, may be misdirected and that images of violence, not sexuality, ought to be the targets of their legislative efforts.

Finally, Mrinalini Sinha explores male sexuality as a weapon employed in the service of colonial domination. Her compelling historical analysis of the ideology of British imperialism in nineteenth-century Bengal, "Gender and Imperialism," explains the development of certain British legal innovations within Bengal as a continuing British emasculation of Bengali men. While the Age of Consent Act has been seen traditionally by historians as the extension of more "modern" conceptions of women and marriage to a "backward" population, Sinha provides an ingenious use of gender as a historical category to suggest that the act was more motivated by continuing efforts to explain backwardness by an enervated manhood, enervated precisely by the practice of early intercourse and the practice of child brides. Thus she concludes that "the commitment to the Victorian ideal of manliness, and the belief in Bengali 'unmanliness' were vital features of the rationalization of colonial rule." This, she speculates, dovetailed with nineteenth-century concern about British masculinity at home, and especially with the emergence of the homosexual as a distinct social category.

Race and Gender

The next two chapters—Lawrence Gary's "Predicting Interpersonal Conflict Between Men and Women" and Noel Cazenave and George Leon's "Men's Work and Family Roles and Characteristics"—remind us that the social construction of masculinity varies along class, race, age, and ethnic lines, even if masculinity is always constructed in relation to femininity, independent of these other sociocultural dimensions. Gary argues that the structure of conflict between black men and black women appears somewhat different from that between white women and white men. He also argues that such findings are often obscured by applying white-generated notions of what constitutes a "family" to black relational and residential patterns, where they are less likely to fit as neatly and may, in fact, skew the data. These different male-female relationship patterns mean that some issues—child care and family income, for example—may emerge as less salient, and others, such as personal habits, may emerge as more salient causes of interpersonal conflict between black men and black women. These differences suggest important issues for mental health practitioners who draw their cases from racially varied populations.

Cazenave and Leon explore the projected relation between family and work roles among college students. By controlling for race, class, and gender of the students, Cazenave and Leon find how black and white women and men expect these two roles will interact in their lives. They find that students are motivated variously by desire either to maintain or to attain social status, and that the structure of status attainment and status maintenance vary by class, race, and gender in predictable ways. For example, blacks—both men and women—"place greater emphasis on the salience of the provider role for married men than do white respondents." It is interesting that with some variations, they find that both career and family involvement are seen by all groups as essential components of masculinity, and that college students may not see the antagonism between these two roles that has often been assumed.

Toward Men's Studies

The final three chapters in this volume—"A Case for Men's Studies," by Harry Brod; my own "Teaching a Course on Men"; and "The Men's Movement," by Michael Shiffman—explore future directions in the study of men and masculinity from several related angles. Brod's statement is an eloquent articulation of a kind of programmatic for men's studies, a demarcation of the field. Clearly, in this formulation, men's studies takes as its point of departure the new feminist scholarship, and Brod makes clear his debt to that scholarship. Brod argues that there is a genuine area to be delineated that discusses men and masculinity as its object of study, and therefore his article is a fine theoretical summation of many of the underlying premises that inform the compilation of this volume. One would hope, with its clear acknowledgment that men's studies does not seek to replace women's studies, that Brod's argument could become the theoretical foundation for future programs and courses in this growing field.

My chapter picks up these themes in a discussion of a course I have been regularly teaching called "The Sociology of the Male Experience." The chapter's subtitle poses the question about the motivation for courses about men and masculinity: Do they represent "masculinist reactions" against the gains of feminist scholarship and women's studies, or are they a "gentlemen's auxiliary" to that scholarship? As does Brod, I argue that men's studies must remain accountable to women's studies, both as intellectual discipline and course offering.

Finally, Michael Shiffman presents an exploratory empirical profile of the "men's movement," an organized political effort to reformulate the male role and also to lend organized support for the struggles of women and gay people. Locating his analysis squarely in the sociological literature on social movement organizations, Shiffman paints a fascinating portrait of this movement, a loose network of scholars, activists, and others who are politically committed to transformation of masculinity. One particularly interesting element of this movement is how gay, bisexual, and heterosexual men participate together. Since, as Lyman and Fine had earlier pointed out, male-male relations are often mediated by a high degree of heterosexual joking, the ability of these men to develop new mechanisms for working relationships seems especially promising.

These chapters suggest a portion of the range of the new scholarship on men and masculinity. But the terrain is much larger, and these articles are, I believe, substantively interesting as specific studies and suggest some of the unexplored territory that remains to be charted. As an interdisciplinary field, men's studies will draw its objects of study and its methodologies from social and behavioral sciences as well as from the humanities and the natural and biological sciences. As an academic enterprise, it regroups conventionally drawn studies within a new framework and suggests new areas for research. And as a corollary to women's studies, it supports the radical redefinitions of the social construction of gender relations that underlie the field demarcated by its "older sister."

REFERENCES

August, E. (1985). *Men's studies: A selected and annotated interdisciplinary bibliography.* Littleton, CO: Libraries Unlimited.

Brannon, R., & David, D. (Eds.). (1976). *The forty-nine percent majority.* Reading, MA: Addison-Wesley.

Brannon, R., & Pleck, J. (Eds.). (1978). Special issue on men. *Journal of Social Issues.*

Brod, H. (1987). *Men's studies: From Achilles' heel to Damocles' sword.*

Doyle, J. (1983). *The male experience.* Dubuque, IA: William C. Brown.

Ehrenreich, B. (1983). *The hearts of men.* Garden City, NY: Doubleday.

Ehrenreich, B., & English, D. (1979). *For her own good.* Garden City, NY: Doubleday.

Fasteau, M. (1975). *The male machine.* New York: Delta.

Femiano, S. (Ed.). (1984). *Men's studies course outlines.* (private printing)

Franklin, C. (1984). *The changing definition of masculinity.* New York: Plenum.

Gary, L. (Ed.). (1981). *Black men.* Newbury Park, CA: Sage.

Gerson, J. & Peiss, K. (1985). Boundaries, Negotiation, Consciousness: Reconceptualizing Gender Relations. *Social Problems 32.*

Gerzon, M. (1983). *A choice of heroes.* Boston: Houghton Mifflin.

Goleman, D. (1985, March 19). Dislike of own bodies found common among women. *New York Times.*

Gould, M., & Kern-Daniels, R. (1977). Toward a sociological theory of gender and sex. *American Sociologist, 12.*

Hacker, H. (1957). The new burdens of masculinity. *Marriage and Family Living, 19.*

Harrison, J. (1978). Warning: The male sex role may be hazardous to your health. *Journal of Social Issues, 34*(1).

Kimmel, M. S. (1986). *Male responses to feminism at the turn of the century.* Working paper, Rutgers University, Department of Sociology.

Kimmel, M. S. (1987). The "crisis" of masculinity in historical perspective. In H. Brod (Ed.), *Men's studies: From Achilles' heel to Damocles' sword.*

Komorovsky, M. (1976). *Dilemmas of masculinity.* New York: Norton.

Lewis, R. (Ed.). (1982). *Men in difficult times.* Englewood Cliffs, NJ: Prentice-Hall.

Lewis, R., & Pleck, J. (Eds.). (1979, October). Special issue on men. *Family Coordinator.*

Lopata, H. Z., & Thorne, B. (1978). On the term "sex roles." *Signs, 3.*

Petzke, D. (1986, February 11). "Men's studies" catches on at colleges, setting off controversy and infighting. *Wall Street Journal.*.

Pleck, J. (1981). *The myth of masculinity.* Cambridge: MIT Press.

Pleck, J. (1986). *Working wives/working husbands.* Newbury Park, CA: Sage.

Pleck, J., & Pleck, E. (Eds.). (1980). *The American man.* Englewood Cliffs, NJ: Prentice-Hall.

Pleck, J., & Sawyer, J. (Eds.). (1974). *Men and masculinity.* Englewood Cliffs, NJ: Prentice-Hall.

Robinson, P. (1973). *The modernization of sex.* New York: Harper & Row.

Saholz, E. (1986, April 28). The Book on Men's Studies. *Newsweek.*

Thorne, B. (1985). The missing feminist revolution in sociology. *Social Problems, 32.*

Tolson, A. (1977). *The limits of masculinity: Male identity and women's liberation.* New York: Harper & Row.

Yoshihashi, P. (1984). The new boy on campus: Men's studies. *New York Times Educational Supplement.*

PART I

Reformulating the Male Role

2

The Structure of Male Role Norms

EDWARD H. THOMPSON, Jr.
JOSEPH H. PLECK

Although numerous studies have investigated social attitudes toward the appropriate sex roles for women (Bayer, 1975; Cherlin & Walters, 1981; Mason, Czajka, & Arber, 1976; Powell & Steelman, 1982; Thornton & Freedman, 1979), considerably less research has examined public attitudes toward the male sex role. With the exception of studies examining stereotypes and sex-role behavior (e.g., Davidson, 1981; Hacker, 1981; Moore & Nuttall, 1981; Narus & Fischer, 1982; Skelly & Lundstrom, 1981), researchers have not charted specifically the norms governing the male role. This chapter analyzes the structure of the norms of the male role as defined by college men and their relation to selected attitudes toward women.

The Male Role

Before continuing, a caveat is in order. There is some ambivalence in the sex-role literature on the distinction between descriptive norms (the characteristics individual men are perceived as actually having) and sociocultural norms (the attributes and behavior men should have ideally). Much of the research has addressed the former and is based on explicit comparisons between men and women; however, male sex-role norms are operationalized properly by the latter. We use the term *male role* to refer to the social norms that prescribe and proscribe what men should feel and do. It is a sensitizing concept that summarizes the general social expectations men face, and these norms can be assessed operationally by examining attitudes toward the array of prescriptions and proscriptions men encounter because of their sex.

Early formulations summarized the male sex role according to two sets of social norms. Zelditch (1955), Hartley (1959), Turner (1970), and Komarovsky (1976) reasoned that the standards for "being a man" comprised two orthogonal themes: Men should cultivate an independent style of achievement, and they should cultivate incompetency in all feminine activities. Hartley (1959) and Turner (1970) believed that the antifemininity standard was the more dominant social norm governing the male role. A similar two-dimensional model formulated by Sawyer (1970; Pleck & Sawyer, 1974) identified the core imperatives of the male role as seeking achievement ("getting ahead") and suppressing emotion ("staying cool").

In Cicone and Ruble's (1978) review, studies of sex-role attributes and stereotypes (descriptive norms) suggested that three dimensions underlie people's perceptions of males. That is, if we assume that the threefold categorization of attributes perceived to be characteristic of the typical or average male also synthesizes the dominant social norms governing the male role, then men should be active and achievement oriented, dominant in their interpersonal relationships, and level-headed and self-contained. This three-dimensional model of the male role makes no mention of the avoidance of femininity norm.

Brannon (1976; Brannon & Juni, 1984) postulates four clusters of norms that define the male role. The most salient, he believes, is the proscriptive norm against anything feminine: "no sissy stuff." The other three elaborate on positive prescriptions for activity and an instrumental orientation: achieving status ("the big wheel"), cultivating independence and self-confidence ("sturdy oak"), and developing the penchant for aggressiveness ("give 'em hell").

Collectively, these different conceptual models suggest a range of normative standards defining the traditional male sex role. Making use of data collected for other purposes, the present study investigates empirically the structure of norms governing the traditional male role, as reflected in the attitudes held in a collegiate male sample.

We also briefly investigate the relation between men's endorsement of traditional male role norms and their attitudes toward the appropriate role for women. Some individuals may exhibit conservative attitudes toward the role of both sexes; others may hold liberal attitudes regarding the appropriate standards for one sex while, at the same time, holding traditional attitudes toward permissible behavior for the other; and some express liberal attitudes about the roles of both sexes.

Method

Sample

Data used for the investigation come from a 20% random sample (N = 400) of the men attending two liberal arts colleges (one Catholic, one other) in the New England area. The sample was drawn from the same colleges Rosenkrantz, Vogel, Bee, Broverman, and Broverman (1968) used a decade earlier to define the male stereotype. Questionnaires were hand-delivered to the students who live in campus housing and were mailed to the remainder, providing a 58% overall response rate. An analysis comparing students recruited by the two sampling methods showed no significant differences across sociodemographic characteristics or response patterns. Of the 233 respondents, 24% were freshmen, 29% sophomores, 28% juniors, and 19% seniors. The vast majority of the subjects were under 25 years old, and no student was over 30. The sample is predominantly white (96%), Catholic (84%), and middle to upper class. Almost three-quarters of the respondents' fathers had completed an undergraduate degree, and half had completed some type of graduate or professional training. Of the respondents' mothers, 45% completed college and 20% held an advanced degree.

Measures

Male role norms were assessed by respondents' agreement or disagreement with 57 belief statements about men's expected behavior. Each statement was scored on a 7-point Likert scale. The items were taken directly from Brannon and Juni (1984) and were interpreted to measure clusters of male role norms. The clusters address the beliefs that men should avoid anything feminine, conceal emotions and feelings that make men appear vulnerable, dedicate themselves to work and supporting a family, acquire skills that warrant respect and admiration, become mentally and physically tough, become self-reliant, and be willing to take risks and engage in violence.[1] High scores denote traditional attitudes.

In the data available for this analysis, traditional attitudes toward sex roles for women were assessed by two single-item agree/disagree measures: the respondent's disagreement with the Equal Rights Amendment ("The Equal Rights Amendment is a sorely needed addition to the constitution"; see Bayer, 1975), and desire to marry a virgin ("When I marry, I would prefer that my wife be a virgin"; see Reiss, 1981). For both items, scores were adjusted to have high scores indicate traditional attitudes. Measures of a number of standard social and demographic variables were available as controls.

Results

Factorial Structure

A principal-factor solution with iterative estimate of commonalities was performed initially on the 57 brief statements. The criteria for factor extraction were based on Cattell's scree test. On the basis of the eigenvalues and interpretability, three common factors were extracted initially that accounted for 28% of the variance of the items. The factor matrix was then rotated twice, to provide an orthogonal solution and an oblique solution in order to test the argument that obliquely defined factors are more appropriate and make more psychological sense (Brannon, 1978). Both the factor loading and factor pattern matrices were found to satisfy simple structure principles (Thurston, in Harman, 1976, p. 98) and are presented in Table 2.1. For purposes of clarity, only the items having significant weights (either factor loadings of 0.40 or greater on the orthogonal factors, or a factor coefficient greater than 0.40 on the oblique factors) were retained and used to identify the common factors.

Results indicate that the structure of male role norms for college men is threefold. The first common factor is a cluster of items underscoring men's need to achieve status and others' respect. This cluster will be identified as the "Status" norm. The second factor reflects the expectations that men should be mentally, emotionally, and physically tough and self-reliant; the factor is labeled "Toughness." The third factor identifies a set of items that refer to the belief that men should avoid stereotypically feminine activities and occupations; this factor can best be interpreted as an "Antifemininity" factor. The oblique solution (see Table 2.1) shows the extent to which the three clusters of norms covary with one another: The Status and Toughness factors are moderately correlated ($r = .27$), as are the Status and Antifemininity factors ($r = .22$)

TABLE 2.1
Factor Loadings for Belief Items

Item Content (abbreviated)	Orthogonal Rotation			Oblique Rotation		
	Factor 1	Factor 2	Factor 3	Factor 1	Factor 2	Factor 3
1. Success at work has to be a central goal	.506			.507		
2. Young man earns respect by working hard	.531			.538		
3. A man must earn high income for family	.612			.609		
4. A man should work overtime	.470			.483		
5. A man always deserves family's respect	.465			.466		
6. It's essential for man to be respected	.576			.575		
7. A man should never back down	.428		.309	.404		
8. I like a man who's sure of himself	.490			.503		
9. A man should be rational	.526			.542		
10. A man should always be self confident	.464	.303		.422		
11. A man must stand on his own two feet	.445			.421		
12. I like a guy who does not complain		.454	.335		.396	
13. A man should not disclose pains		.441			.423	
14. Nobody likes a man who discloses worries		.449			.427	
15. I like a man to look somewhat tough	.356	.441		.309	.413	
16. When the going gets tough, the tough . . .		.567			.534	
17. Young man should be physically tough	.324	.555			.531	
18. It disgusts me to see a man show weakness	.402	.443		.341	.386	
19. Fists are sometimes necessary		.605			.637	

(continued)

TABLE 2.1 Continued

Item Content (abbreviated)	Orthogonal Rotation			Oblique Rotation		
	Factor 1	Factor 2	Factor 3	Factor 1	Factor 2	Factor 3
20. A real man enjoys a bit of danger	.309	.501			.483	
21. A man should be ready to fight		.663			.681	
22. A man should refuse to fight		-.473			-.509	
23. Bothers me if man does something feminine		.308	.538			.546
24. A man who cooks, sews is not appealing			.619			.630
25. It's embarrassing to have a woman's job			.451			.435
26. A man shouldn't work as a secretary			.587			.586
27. Hairdresser and cook not very masculine			.497			.503
28. It's disgusting for man to dye hair			.411			.393
29. A boy should be taught to cook, sew			-.450			-.477
30. It's embarrassing for man to cry at movie			.428			.406
Eigenvalue	9.91	3.73	2.60			
Percentage of igem variance	17%	6%	5%			
Criterion, initial value				21.60		
Criterion, final value (39 iterations)				13.747		
Correlation among factors				1.000	.272	.222
					1.000	.285
						1.000

NOTE: For clarity of presentation, the 27 items that had loadings < 0.40 on the three factors were excluded; and for the 30 items in the table, loadings of < 0.30 have not been presented. A completed presentation of loadings for both solutions can be obtained from the authors.

and the Toughness and Antifemininity factors (r = .28).

Although the orthogonal and oblique factor solutions yielded quite similar results, the oblique solution eliminated some "noise," as Brannon (1978) anticipated. It specifies more clearly which items have both unambiguous and significant weights above 0.40 on the common factors. Eleven items unambiguously load on the first oblique factor (Status); six had coefficients in excess of 0.50, and five had loadings between 0.40 and 0.49. Because of the exceptional clarity of the factor, it was decided that all eleven items would be retained for the development of a measure of the norms prescribing status achievement. The second oblique factor (Toughness) identified eight unambiguous marker items, five with coefficients above 0.50 and three between 0.40 and 0.49. However, three other items (12, 15, 18) failed to meet the required loading criteria or were ambiguous as to which factor they best represented. To construct a measure of Toughness, the three items were therefore excluded from consideration. Examination of the last oblique factor shows that eight items loaded unambiguously, but one item (28) failed to meet the a priori loading criteria. Seven items were therefore retained for the development of an Antifemininity measure. The means and standard deviations for the 26 retained items are shown in Table 2.2.

The status factor draws equally from the separate clusters of items Brannon and Juni (1984) classified as assessing the "big wheel" and "sturdy oak" dimensions. The Toughness factor includes items from the clusters assessing proscriptions against emotional vulnerability ("no sissy stuff"), prescriptions for being mentally and physically tough ("sturdy oak"), and prescriptions for a willingness to be aggressive ("give 'em hell"). The present antifemininity factor is composed of other items from the "no sissy stuff" dimension.

Traditional Male Role Norms

Scale scores were constructed by averaging the raw scores of the items on each extracted factor. Averaging raw scores was considered preferable to computing exact factor scores, which would differ from study to study and which would leave problematic any comparison of results from different groups (Nunnally, 1978). The coefficient alpha for the Status scale was 0.81, for the Toughness scale 0.74, and for the Antifemininity scale 0.76, which suggest that the three scales have moderate to good reliability. On the average, respondents scored near the midpoint of the Status norms, somewhat agreed with the toughness norms, and somewhat disagreed with the antifemininity norms (see

TABLE 2.2

Means and Standard Deviations for Male Role Norm Scales

Scales and Items (Exact Wording)	Mean	S.D.
Status Norm Scale	3.90	0.99
1. Success in his work has to be man's central goal in this life.	2.82	0.12
2. The best way for a young man to get the respect of other people is to get a job, take it seriously, and do it well.	4.74	1.59
3. A man owes it to his family to work at the best-paying job he can get.	3.61	1.70
4. A man should generally work overtime to make more money whenever he has the chance.	3.50	1.62
5. A man always deserves the respect of his wife and children.	4.31	2.09
6. It is essential for a man to always have the respect and admiration of everyone who knows him.	3.65	1.62
7. A man should never back down in the face of trouble.	4.13	1.53
8. I always like a man who's totally sure of himself.	4.78	1.55
9. A man should always think everything out coolly and logically, and have rational reasons for everything he does.	4.18	1.80
10. A man should always try to project an air of confidence even if he really doesn't feel confident inside.	4.21	1.62
11. A man must stand on his own two feet and never depend on other people to help him do things	3.09	1.64
Toughness Norm Scale	4.29	1.09
1. When a man is feeling a little pain he should try not to let it show very much.	4.33	1.76
2. Nobody respects a man very much who frequently talks about his worries, fears, and problems.	4.16	1.74
3. A good motto for a man would be "When the going gets tough, the tough get going."	4.97	1.49

(continued)

Table 2.2). Paired t-tests indicated that scale means differ significantly from one another at the 0.001 level (1 versus 2, t(231) = 4.73; 1 versus 3, t(231) = 4.22; 2 versus 3, t(232) = 9.24).

Table 2.3 presents the product-moment and partial correlation coefficients (controlling respondent's age, race, religion, father's education, and mother's education) for the three male role norms scales and two attitudes toward women measures. Results indicate that the three male role norm scales are moderately intercorrelated, but the two attitudes concerning women are related only negligibly and likely measure different beliefs. The two attitudes toward women also are differentially correlated with endorsement of the three male norms. Men who opposed ERA more readily endorsed the Toughness and Antifemininity norms. Preference for a virgin wife is associated with endorsing the Status and Antifemininity norms.

TABLE 2.2   Continued

Scales and Items (Exact Wording)	Mean	S.D.
4. I think a young man should try to become physically tough, even if he's not big.	3.91	1.74
5. Fists are sometimes the only way to get out of a bad situation.	3.78	1.95
6. A real man enjoys a bit of danger now and then.	4.30	1.63
7. In some kinds of situations a man should be ready to use his fists, even if his wife or his girlfriend would object.	4.44	1.87
8. A man should always refuse to get into a fight, even if there seems to be no way to avoid it.*	2.51	1.85
Anti-femininity Norm Scale	3.57	1.10
1. It bothers me when a man does something that I consider "feminine."	4.00	1.61
2. A man whose hobbies are cooking, sewing, and going to the ballet probably wouldn't appeal to me.	3.78	1.93
3. It is a bit embarrassing for a man to have a job that is usually filled by a woman.	3.95	1.61
4. Unless he was really desperate, I would probably advise a man to keep looking rather than accept a job as a secretary.	3.76	1.77
5. If I heard about a man who was a hairdresser and a gourmet cook, I might wonder how masculine he was.	3.43	1.82
6. I think it's extremely good for a boy to be taught to cook, sew, clean the house, and take care of younger children.*	4.45	1.38
7. I might find it a little silly or embarrassing if a male friend of mine cried over a sad love scene in a movie.	3.61	1.84

NOTE: Items and the norm scale are 7-point Likert scales anchored at 7 with "very strongly agree."
*These items were reversed scored.

Discussion

The factorial structure of the male role, as defined by college-aged men, is three-dimensional. The trio of Status, Toughness, and Anti-femininity norms were identified by both orthogonal and oblique factor solutions and convey a strong impression of face validity. Each cluster of items forms a profile of a normative standard mentioned frequently in the sex-role literature. The three empirically derived factors appear quite similar in content to the dimensions of the male role proposed in several of the early, intuitively derived typologies. However, none of the earlier typologies parallels exactly the findings of this research.

As a group, the men in this sample did not fully endorse traditional male role norms. The Toughness norm was supported only slightly; the

TABLE 2.3

Correlations Among Male Role Norm Scales
and Attitudes Toward Women

	(1)	(2)	(3)	(4)	(5)
Male Role Norms					
(1) Status	–	.299**	.327**	.103	.187*
(2) Toughness	.315**	–	.418**	.343**	.044
(3) Antifemininity	.346**	.414**	–	.262**	.232**
Attitudes Toward Women					
(4) Opposition to ERA	.103	.346**	.250**	–	.057
(5) Preference for virgin wife	.192*	.032	.232**	.067	–

NOTE: The upper half of the matrix presents product-moment correlation coefficients. The lower half presents partial correlation coefficients controlling for respondent's age, father's education, other's education, religion, and race.
*p < .01; **p < .001.

Status norm was, on average, neither supported nor rejected; and the Antifemininity norm was slightly rejected. It thus seems that this collegiate sample readily recognized the presence of the traditional norms but did not concur with or reject them. Of course, these findings about the presence and salience of traditional male role norms are not necessarily generalizable to other groups. Sex-role norms perhaps vary by age (Brim, 1976; Moreland, 1980), socioeconomic status (Rubin, 1976; Turner, 1970), and birth cohort (Pleck, 1976).

Individuals within the sample who endorsed/rejected one of the traditional male role norms were also likely to endorse/reject the other two. The three norms showed direct covariation beyond chance. Nonetheless, it is noteworthy that the male role norm scales are more strongly intercorrelated than they are correlated with the two measures of attitudes toward women. These differences in the strength of associations may be only a methodological artifact, as the male norms were assessed by multi-item scales and the attitudes toward women were assessed by single items. However, the observed pattern is consistent with our view that some individuals can endorse traditional attitudes toward men and, at the same time, endorse modern attitudes toward women. Similarly, others can reject the traditional expectations men face while holding liberal attitudes toward women. If patterns of endorsing/rejecting sex-role norms are not necessarily parallel, then the changes in the direction of liberal (or modern) attitudes toward women may not predict similar changes in attitudes toward men (see Pleck, 1981; Scanzoni & Fox, 1980).

The three male role norms show differential association to measures of attitudes toward women. Men's endorsement of the norm proscribing feminine activities was related significantly to both an anti-ERA stance and a preference for a virgin wife. Support for the Antifemininity standard may therefore predict a traditional view of women. However, support for the other two male role norms is less predictive of attitudes toward women. Each predicted only one of the two attitudes surveyed here.

In conclusion, the traditional male role is a three-dimensional standard, but the strength of this normative orientation is weak in a contemporary collegiate sample. Male role norms appear distinct from attitudes toward women. Research is needed to examine which men endorse/reject which male role standards. Further work is also necessary to assess how women view the male role and how these attitudes covary with women's judgments about their own role.

NOTE

1. Several other available scales assessing attitudes toward the male role (e.g., Allen, 1954; Doyle & Moore, 1978; Fiebert, 1983; Moreland & Van Tuinen, 1978; Villimez & Touhey, 1977) have the weakness that most of their items make explicit comparisons between the sexes. These scales are operationally indistinguishable from those assessing descriptive norms. Thus it is difficult to argue that the scales concern social attitudes toward the male role norms per se.

REFERENCES

Allen, D. A. (1954). Antifemininity in men. *American Sociological Review, 19*, 591-593.

Bayer, A. E. (1975). Sexist students in American colleges: A descriptive note. *Journal of Marriage and the Family, 37*, 391-397.

Brannon, R. (1976). The male sex role: Our culture's blueprint for manhood, what it's done for us lately. In D. David & R. Brannon (Eds.), *The forty-nine percent majority: The male sex role.* Reading, MA: Addison-Wesley.

Brannon, R. (1978). Measuring attitudes toward women (and otherwise): A methodological critique. In J. Sherman & F. Denmark (Eds.), *The psychology of women: New directions in research.* New York: Psychological Dimensions.

Brannon, R., & Juni, S. (1984). A scale for measuring attitudes about masculinity. *Psychological Documents, 14*, 6-7.

Brim, O. G., Jr. (1976). Theories of the male mid-life crisis. *The Counseling Psychologist, 6*, 2-9.

Cherlin, A., & Walters, P. B. (1981). Trends in United States men's and women's sex-role attitudes: 1972 to 1978. *American Sociological Review, 46*, 453-460.

Cicone, M. V., & Ruble, D. N. (1978). Beliefs about males. *Journal of Social Issues, 34*(1), 5-16.

Davidson, I. R. (1981). Pressures and pretense: Living with gender stereotype. *Sex Roles, 7*, 331-347.

Doyle, J., & Moore, R. (1978). Attitudes toward the male's role scale (AMR): An objective instrument to measure attitudes toward the male's sex role in contemporary society. *JSAS Catalog of Selected Documents in Psychology, 8,* 35-36.

Fiebert, M. (1983). Measuring traditional and liberated males' attitudes. *Perceptual and Motor Skills, 56,* 83-86.

Hacker, H. M. (1981). Blabbermouths and clams: Sex differences in self-disclosure in same-sex and cross-sex friendship dyads. *Psychology of Women Quarterly, 5,* 385-401.

Harman, H. (1976). *Modern factor analysis* (3rd ed.). Chicago: University of Chicago Press.

Hartley, R. (1959). Sex-role pressures in the socialization of the male child. *Psychological Reports, 5,* 457-468.

Komarovsky, M. (1976). *Dilemmas of masculinity: A study of college youth.* New York: Norton.

Mason, K. O., Czajka, J. L., & Arber, S. (1976). Changes in U.S. women's sex role attitudes, 1964-1974. *American Sociological Review, 41,* 573-596.

Moore, D., & Nuttall, J. R. (1981). Perceptions of the male sex role. *Personality and Social Psychology Bulletin, 7,* 320-325.

Moreland, J. (1980). Age and change in the adult male sex role. *Sex Roles, 6,* 807-818.

Moreland, J., & Van Tuinen, M. (1978). *The attitudes toward masculinity transcendence scale.* Ohio State University, Department of Psychology.

Narus, L. R., & Fischer, J. L. (1982). Strong but not silent: A reexamination of expressivity in the relationships of men. *Sex Roles, 8,* 159-168.

Nunally, J. C. (1978). *Psychometric theory.* New York: McGraw-Hill.

Pleck, J. H. (1976). The male sex role: Definitions, problems, and sources of change. *Journal of Social Issues, 32*(3), 155-164

Pleck, J. H. (1981). *The myth of masculinity.* Cambridge: MIT Press.

Pleck, J. H., & Sawyer, J. (1974). *Men and masculinity.* Englewood Cliffs, NJ: Prentice-Hall.

Powell, B., & Steelman, L. C. (1982). Testing an undertested comparison: Maternal effects on son's and daughter's attitudes toward women in the labor force. *Journal of Marriage and the Family, 44,* 349-355.

Reiss, I. (1981). Some observations on ideology and sexuality in America. *Journal of Marriage and the Family, 43,* 272-283.

Rosenkrantz, P., Vogel, S., Bee, H., Broverman, I., & Broverman, D. (1968). Sex-role stereotypes and self-concepts in college students. *Journal of Consulting and Clinical Psychology, 32,* 287-295.

Rubin, I. (1976). *Worlds of pain.* New York: Basic Books.

Sawyer, J. (1970). On male liberation. *Liberation, 15,* 32-33.

Scanzoni, J., & Fox, G. L. (1980). Sex roles, family and society: The seventies and beyond. *Journal of Marriage and the Family, 42,* 743-756.

Skelly, G. U., & Lundstrom, W. J. (1981). Male sex roles in magazine advertising, 1959-1979. *Journal of Communication, 31,* 52-57.

Thornton, A., & Freedman, D. S. (1979). Changes in the sex role attitudes of women, 1962-1977. *American Sociological Review, 44,* 831-842.

Turner, R. (1970). *Family interaction.* New York: John Wiley.

Villimez, W., & Touhey, J. (1977). A measure of individual differences in sex stereotyping and sex discrimination: The "macho" scale. *Psychological Reports, 41,* 411-415.

Zelditch, M. (1955). Role differentiation in the nuclear family: A comparative study. In T. Parsons & F. Bales (Eds.), *Family, socialization and interaction process.* New York: Free Press.

3

The Embodiment of Masculinity

Cultural, Psychological, and Behavioral Dimensions

MARC E. MISHKIND
JUDITH RODIN
LISA R. SILBERSTEIN
RUTH H. STRIEGEL-MOORE

Women have been traditionally concerned with their appearance. Indeed, the pursuit of and preoccupation with beauty are central features of the female sex-role stereotype (Rodin, Silberstein, & Striegel-Moore, 1985). Perhaps because of this, we have ignored the significant role that physical appearance and body image play for men. Certainly, examination of current magazines and other media strongly suggests that bodily concern is strong for men. Advertisements celebrate the young, lean, muscular male body, and men's fashions have undergone significant changes in style both to accommodate and to accentuate changes in men's physiques toward a more muscular and trim body (Gross, 1985). Today men serve as marketing targets for products such as diet sodas and cosmetics that would have been considered too feminine only a few years ago.

The changes in society's attitudes toward men's bodies, along with the changes in men's behaviors regarding their appearance, have prompted us to examine the role of body image in men's lives. How does body image figure into men's sense of masculinity in particular and their

AUTHORS' NOTE: Address requests for reprints to Marc E. Mishkind, Department of Psychology, Box 11A Yale Station, New Haven, CT 06520.

self-concept in general? We suggest that men arrange themselves along a continuum, from unconcerned with body at one end to extremely concerned at the other. This conceptualization may help predict the type and degree of behavior in which individuals engage to change their physical appearance and come closer to the masculine ideal.

This article addresses several issues. First, how do men feel about their bodies? Given that these feelings often are assessed in comparison to some ideal body type, we consider what this ideal is and what benefits accrue to someone who more closely represents the ideal body type. We then ask how this ideal body type relates to current conceptions of masculinity and the male sex role. We next examine various efforts that men undertake to achieve the ideal, and we evaluate the positive and negative consequences of these efforts. Following this we try to identify behaviors associated with increased levels of concern. Finally, we ask why at this historical moment men are paying increased attention to their appearance and are striving in growing numbers to achieve the male body ideal. Our thesis is that the male body ideal, and various pressures for men to conform to it, may be producing psychological and physical ill effects at the present time, effects that will increase because they reflect a historical trend.

How Men Feel About Their Bodies

One index of men's bodily concern is their degree of satisfaction with their physical appearance. Of college-age men we surveyed, 95% expressed dissatisfaction with some aspect of their bodies. Studies suggest that men carry with them images of both their own body and also their ideal body, and that these two images are nonidentical. For example, when shown line drawings depicting seven body types, more than 70% of undergraduate men saw a discrepancy between their own body and their ideal body type (see also Tucker, 1982b).[1]

This dissatisfaction is not general and diffuse but highly specific and differentiated. Men consistently express their greatest dissatisfaction toward chest, weight, and waist. Other areas have also elicited dissatisfaction, most notably arms, hips, nose, stomach, shoulders, and height (Berscheid, Walster, & Bohrnstedt, 1973; Calden, Lundy, & Schlafer, 1959; Clifford, 1971; Miller, Coffman, & Linke, 1980; Secord & Jourard, 1953).

Given that men experience significant body dissatisfaction because they see themselves as deviating from the ideal, it becomes crucial to determine the ideal male body type. When asked about physique preferences, the overwhelming majority of males report that they would prefer to be mesomorphic (i.e., of well-proportioned, average build) as opposed to ectomorphic (thin) or endomorphic (fat). This preference is expressed by boys as young as 5 and 6 (Lerner & Gellert, 1969; Lerner & Schroeder, 1971) and also by college-age men (Dibiase & Hjelle, 1968; Tucker, 1982b). Within the mesomorphic category, a majority select what we shall refer to as the hypermesomorphic or muscular mesomorphic body as preferred (Deno, 1953; Tucker, 1982b). This physique is the "muscle man"-type body characterized by well-developed chest and arm muscles and wide shoulders tapering down to a narrow waist. Men indicate greater body satisfaction to the extent that their self-reported (Tucker, 1982b) or actual (Jourard & Secord, 1954; Sugerman & Haronian, 1964) body shape resembles this ideal.

That many men feel bodily dissatisfaction because they do not resemble the mesomorphic or hypermesomorphic ideal might not in itself be particularly distressing. The discrepancy between self and ideal is problematic only if men believe that those closest to the ideal reap certain benefits not available to those further away. Research strongly suggests that this is true, both because physical appearance is so important generally in our society and because of the specific benefits that accrue to mesomorphic men.

It is axiomatic in Western culture that "what is beautiful is good" (Dion, Berscheid, & Walster, 1972; Hatfield & Sprecher, in press). This stereotype is already evident in preschoolers, who view attractive peers as friendlier and smarter than unattractive peers (Dion, 1973) and for whom physical attractiveness is correlated significantly with popularity (Vaughn & Langlois, 1983). Teachers treat attractive children more favorably and perceive them as more intelligent than less attractive children (Adams & Cohen, 1976a, 1976b; Clifford, 1975; Clifford & Walster, 1973; Felson, 1980; Martinek, 1981).

Attractive adults are believed to live happier and more successful lives (Berscheid & Walster, 1974). There is surely some truth to this; attractive people enjoy distinct advantages in interpersonal situations (see Hatfield & Sprecher, in press). For example, an attractive person is more likely to receive help (Benson, Karabenick, & Lerner, 1976; West & Brown, 1975), to elicit cooperation in conflict situations (Sigall, Page, & Brown, 1971), and to experience more satisfying interpersonal relationships (Blumstein & Schwartz, 1983; Reis, Nezle, & Wheels, 1980). Attractive applicants have a better chance of getting jobs and receive higher starting salaries (Cann, Siegfried, & Pearce, 1981; Dipboye, Fromkin, & Wibach, 1975).

By contrast, obese people are stigmatized and punished by adults and children alike (see Rodin et al., 1985). Children have more negative attitudes toward obese children than toward children with a wide range of handicaps, such as being in a wheelchair, missing a hand, or having a facial disfigurement (Goodman, Richardson, Dornbusch, & Hastorf, 1963; Richardson, Hastorf, Goodman & Dornbusch, 1961). Adults expect obese individuals to have more negative personality traits and lead less happy lives than lean individuals (Hiller, 1981), and negative attitudes are expressed particularly strongly when obese persons are perceived as being personally responsible for their condition (DeJong, 1980).

Because physical appearance is so important in our culture, we want to ask if the mesomorphic male body is considered the most attractive body type, and if there is any evidence to suggest that the mesomorphic individual gains the various benefits that accrue to attractive individuals. Mesomorphic physiques are considered better looking and more attractive than nonmesomorphic physiques (Horvath, 1981; Kirkpatrick & Sanders, 1978; Staffieri, 1967), and mesomorphic males do receive numerous social benefits. Studies demonstrate that people assign overwhelmingly positive personality traits to drawings or photographs of mesomorphic males and mostly negative traits to ectomorphic and endomorphic males (Brodsky, 1954; Kirkpatrick & Sanders, 1978; Lerner, 1969; Staffieri, 1967; Wells & Siegel, 1961; Wright & Bradbard, 1980). For example, Kirkpatrick and Sanders found that the positive traits ascribed to mesomorphs by young adults were strong, best friend, has lots of friends, polite, happy, helps others, brave, healthy, smart, and neat. By contrast, the endomorph was characterized by a preponderance of negative traits, including sloppy, dirty, worries, lies, tired, stupid, lonely, and lazy. The ectomorph was also described negatively, though not to the extent of the endomorph: quiet, nervous, sneaky, afraid, sad, weak, and sick.

These stereotypes exist in both middle and lower classes (Wells & Siegel, 1961), in blacks as well as whites (Brodsky, 1954; Wright & Bradbard, 1980), and they gain increasing strength with age until young adulthood (Lerner, 1972; Lerner & Korn, 1972) but may decrease thereafter (Kirkpatrick & Sanders, 1978). Personality descriptions consistent with these stereotypes have been elicited when boys of varying physiques are given personality ratings by peers (Hanley, 1951), parents (Washburn, 1962), teachers (Hendry & Gillies, 1978), and "objective" judges (Walker, 1963).

Males may behave in accord with these stereotypes. Early research sought to demonstrate an inborn relationship between body build and personality (e.g., Sheldon, 1942); however, it is now generally agreed that such relationships are learned (McCandless, 1960) and have no or minimal genetic determinants (see Montemayor, 1978). The research we

reviewed reveals deeply entrenched cultural preferences toward mesomorphic males and aversions to endomorphic and ectomorphic males.
Given this preference and the demonstrated importance of physical
appearance in our society, it is no wonder that men aspire to resemble
the mesomorphic ideal and feel dissatisfied to the extent that they do
not.

Mesomorphy and Masculinity

We have seen that men care a great deal about their body build and
that they aspire to a widely held ideal of physical attractiveness, the
muscular mesomorph. The muscular male probably enjoys social
advantages that are yet undocumented. But why has it become so? We
believe that the muscular mesomorph is the ideal because it is intimately
tied to cultural views of masculinity and the male sex role, which
prescribes that men be powerful, strong, efficacious—even domineering
and destructive. For example, Rosenkrantz et al. (1968) found strong
agreement that the masculine stereotype included items such as
aggressive, independent, dominant, self-confident, and unemotional.
Masculinity on the Spence and Helmreich (1978) Personal Attributes
Questionnaire is represented by high scores on items such as independent, active, competitive, persistent, self-confident, and feels superior. A muscular physique may serve as a symbolic embodiment of
these personal characteristics.

Writers who have made a connection between muscles and these
"ideal" masculine qualities describe men as making their bodies an
"instrument of their power" (Reynaud, 1983), "armoring" themselves
(Nichols, 1975), or adopting the "soldier archetype" of masculinity
(Gerzon, 1982). These assertions are substantiated empirically by
Darden (1972), who found that people rate mesomorphically propor-
tioned bodies as the most masculine. The embodiment of masculinity,
the muscular mesomorph, is seen as more efficacious, experiencing
greater mastery and control over the environment, and feeling more
invulnerable. Indeed, research suggests that people apply such stereotypically masculine traits as "active," "daring," and "a fighter" to mesomorphic boys but not to endomorphic or ectomorphic boys (Hanley,
1951; Hendry & Gillies, 1978). Males also view their own bodies
primarily along these active and functional dimensions, in contrast to
women, who evaluate themselves primarily along an aesthetic dimension
(Kurtz, 1969; Lerner, Orlos, & Knapp, 1976; Story, 1979), and men
consider physical attractiveness virtually equivalent to physical potency

(Lerner et al., 1976). Hence they experience an intimate relationship between body image and potency—that is, masculinity—with the muscular mesomorph representing the masculine ideal. A man who fails to resemble the body ideal is, by implication, failing to live up to sex-role norms, and may thus experience the consequences of violating such norms.

A Man's Body and His Sense of Self

How important is a man's body to his sense of self? How connected to a man's self-worth are his feelings about his body? Studies have revealed consistently a significant correlation between men's body satisfaction and self-esteem, the average correlation of these studies being around 0.5. Although some studies have found a stronger relationship between body-esteem and self-esteem for women than for men (Lerner, Karabenick, & Stuart, 1973; Martin & Walter, 1982; Secord & Jourard, 1953), others have found comparable or even greater relationships between body satisfaction and measures of self-esteem, anxiety, and depression for men than for women (Franzoi & Shields, 1984; Goldberg & Folkins, 1974; Lerner et al., 1976; Mahoney, 1974). How a man feels about himself is thus tied closely to how he feels about his body. It remains for researchers to examine the relative importance of body image to a man's sense of self when compared with other variables such as career achievement, but the data already available suggest that feelings about body play a significant role in self-esteem.

Efforts to Decrease the Gap
Between Actual and Ideal Body Shape

We have seen that a great number of men acknowledge a gap between their actual and ideal body types, and that the greater this gap, the lower their self-esteem. As a result, men feel motivated to close this gap. This often depends upon which parts of the body are the foci of dissatisfaction.

In a large-scale factor-analytic study, Franzoi and Shields (1984) found three primary dimensions along which men's bodily satisfaction and dissatisfaction occur. The first factor, "physical attractiveness," includes the face and its constituent features, such as cheekbones, chin, ears, and eyes. These features contribute to making a man appear "handsome" or "good-looking." The second factor, dubbed "upper-body strength," contains muscle groups that men typically want to build up in order to improve their physique: biceps, shoulder width, arms, and chest. The third factor, "physical conditioning," contains items that reflect a man's concern with being physically "fit" or in "good shape," such as physical stamina, energy level, physical condition, stomach, and weight.

Each of these three dimensions—facial attractiveness, upper-body strength, and physical conditioning—suggests specific ways in which men could attempt to narrow the distance between their real and ideal selves. A man who wishes to improve his facial attractiveness may perhaps modify his hairstyle or undertake cosmetic surgery. However, we believe that men pursue this kind of self-improvement less frequently. First, facial appearance is viewed typically as less malleable than one's body: "Good looks" are seen as something with which one is or is not endowed. Second, this dimension seems more closely tied to aesthetic dimensions of attractiveness than functional dimensions, and the latter are more central to masculine physical attractiveness.

A man who desires to increase his muscle size and strength—that is, to embody the muscular mesomorphic ideal—may engage in weight lifting or use weight-training machines. Physical conditioning is most likely to be achieved through long workouts of running, swimming, aerobic exercising, or other activities that build stamina and endurance while decreasing body fat. Given that the physical effects of endurance workouts may be less readily visible than the effects of body building, we surmise that men who want to be widely recognized for their physical masculinity are more likely to opt for muscle building as their form of physical exercise. There is evidence that weight-lifting men, compared with those who engage in other athletic activities, are more likely attempting to compensate for a lowered sense of masculinity (Harlow, 1951; Thune, 1949), but replications with current samples are needed.

A different route to altering one's body shape involves dieting. Although women continue to be the largest consumers of diet books and diet products, men constitute a rapidly increasing market. Light beers and diet sodas are promoted by male athletes in order to establish a masculine association to products with formerly feminine connotations. The "drinking-man's diet" was an effort to capture a relatively untapped male market, and the businessman's lunch is being replaced now by salad bars and lighter fare. Our clinical experience suggests that men are entering diet programs in increasing numbers for both appearance and health.

Increased efforts expended on exercise and dieting are reinforced by a societal attitude that everyone can improve himself or herself through sufficient effort. People believe that body size and shape are almost totally under volitional control (Bennett, 1984). In fact, this is largely a myth. Individual differences in body build have a large genetic component. Identical twins, for example, even when reared apart, are significantly more similar in weight than fraternal twins or siblings (see Stunkard, Foch, & Hrubec, 1985). Adopted children resemble their biological parents in weight, far more than their adoptive parents (Stunkard et al., 1985), For those men who are genetically disposed to deviate from the muscular mesomorphic ideal, the costs of attempting to achieve this ideal may be considerable.

A man who strives to bridge the self-denial gap will experience a heightened attentiveness to and focus on his body. This may render his standards more perfectionistic (and hence perhaps more out of reach) and enhance his perceptions of his shortcomings. Both his limitations and the gap itself can become increasingly salient. To the extent that he feels that he falls short, he will experience the shame of failure. He also may feel ashamed at being so focused on his body, presumably because this has been associated traditionally with the female sex-role stereotype.

There may also be physical costs of trying to bridge the gap between self and ideal. Studies investigating the physiological changes that result from dieting suggest that dieting is an ineffective way to attain long-term weight loss; it may, in fact, contribute to subsequent weight gain and binge eating (Herman & Polivy, 1975; Rodin et al., 1985; Wooley & Wooley, 1984). A substantial decrease in daily caloric intake will result in a reduced metabolic rate, which thus impedes weight loss (Apfelbaum, 1975; Garrow, 1978). Upon resuming normal caloric intake, a person's metabolic rate does not rebound immediately to its original pace; in fact, a longer period of dieting will prolong the time it takes for the metabolic rate to regain its original level (Evan & Nicolaidis, 1981). Thus even normal eating after a period of dieting may promote weight gain. Food restriction produces other physiological changes that contribute to maladaptations in food utilization and an increased proportion of fat in body composition (Bjorntorp & Yang, 1982; Fried, Hill, Nickel, & DiGirolamo, 1983; Miller, Faust, Goldberger, & Hirsch, 1983). Dieting may ultimately produce effects the opposite of those intended. In addition to these biological ramifications, dieting also produces psychological results that are self-defeating. Typically, a dieter feels deprived of favorite foods and, when "off" the diet, is likely to overeat (Polivy & Herman, 1985).

Body-building attempts may also carry hazards. Men tend to see an overdeveloped muscular body as the most masculine physique (Darden, 1972), and many body builders ingest male hormones and steroids in their efforts to attain this exaggerated hypermesomorphic look (Todd, 1983). These represent only a minority of body-conscious men, but the health ramifications for them may be significant.

Thus far we have focused only on the negative consequences of trying to attain the masculine body ideal. There are potentially powerful positive consequences. The more a man experiences himself as closing the self-ideal gap—for example, through exercising—the more positive he will feel toward body and self. Higher frequencies of exercise have been associated with greater body satisfaction (Joesting, 1981; Joesting & Clance, 1979), and programs of physical activity have led to more positive feelings toward one's body (McGlenn, 1980; Tucker, 1982a). The more a man works toward attaining his body ideal and the closer he perceives himself as approximating it, the greater his sense of self-efficacy.

Some men opt not to involve themselves in the deliberate pursuit of the mesomorphic ideal, which can also have both positive and negative effects. Lack of concern with changing one's physical appearance may protect a man from intense bodily preoccupation and its ramifications, but those who experience dissatisfaction but do not strive to change their physiques are likely to suffer from guilt and self-criticism. A recent Gallup survey reports that many people who refrain from exercising feel that their lives would be better if they were to do so (Harris & Gurin, 1985).

Subcultures of High Bodily Concern

The increased cultural attention given to the male body and the increasing demands placed on men to achieve the mesomorphic build push men further along the continuum of bodily concern. Men are likely experiencing more body dissatisfaction, preoccupation with weight, and concern with their physical attractiveness and body shape now than they did even two decades ago. Fashion designers currently are broadening the chest and tapering the waist of men's clothing lines in order to fit their male customers (Gross, 1985). However, research is needed to document these current trends.

At the extreme, such concerns could lead to excessive attention to one's body and to an obsessive preoccupation with body-altering behavior such as weight lifting, exercising, and dieting. With women, extreme bodily concern, coupled with difficulties in achieving the ideal body type, portends disregulated eating patterns such as bulimia—frequent and compulsive binge eating, sometimes followed by purging (Striegel-Moore, Silberstein, & Rodin, 1986). Those subcultures of women that amplify the sociocultural emphasis on appearance and weight (e.g., dancers, models) manifest higher rates of eating disorders (Crago, Yates, Beutler, & Arizmendi, 1985; Druss & Silverman, 1979; Garner & Garfinkel, 1978). Similarly, we might expect that subgroups of men that place relatively greater emphasis on physical appearance would be at greater risk for excessive weight control behaviors and even eating disorders.

An illustrative group is the gay male subculture, which places an elevated importance on all aspects of a man's physical self—body build, grooming, dress, handsomeness (Kleinberg, 1980; Lakoff & Scherr, 1984). We predicted that gay men would be at heightened risk for body dissatisfaction and for eating disorders. In a sample of heterosexual and homosexual college men, gay men expressed greater dissatisfaction with body build, waist, biceps, arms, and stomach. Gay men also indicated a greater discrepancy between their actual and ideal body shapes than did "straight" men and showed higher scores on measures of eating disregulation and food and weight preoccupation.[2] If the increased focus on appearance continues for men in general, such concerns and eating disorders may begin to increase among all men.

Why Now?

We have argued that men are moving further along the continuum of bodily concern. But why do men at this time in history appear to be pursuing the muscular mesomorphic ideal to a greater extent than ever before? Western society currently places an unprecedented emphasis on life-style change and self-management as the major health-promoting activities (Surgeon General's Report, 1984). The burden of illness has shifted from infectious diseases to cardiovascular disorders, automobile accidents, and cancers, many of which are considered preventable through behavior change (Hamburg, Solomon, & Parron, 1983). Looking healthy is the external manifestation of the desired healthy state, so the body symbolizes the extent of one's self-corrective behavior. Further, what were once considered exclusively male abilities and domains are decreasingly so. Whereas once a man could be assured of his masculinity by virtue of his occupation, interests, or certain personality characteristics, many women now opt for the same roles. Gerzon (1982) writes that the five traditional archetypes of masculinity—soldier, frontiersman, expert, breadwinner, and lord—are now archaic artifacts, although the images remain. The soldier archetype conveys the image of the strong, muscle-armored body. The frontiersman and lord are no longer viable roles for anyone, and the expert and breadwinner are no longer exclusively male. Thus men may be grasping for the soldier archetype—that is, building up their bodies—in an exaggerated attempt to incorporate what possible options remain of the male images they have held since youth. One of the only remaining ways men can express and preserve traditional male characteristics may be by literally embodying them.

It is worth considering whether this ubiquitous interest in achieving the maleness-as-soldier ideal is a reflection of the conservative militaristic trends in our society. Is it a coincidence that men are opting for muscle building at a time of greater U.S. military intervention in foreign governments, and increased xenophobic patriotic media events such as *Rambo,* which features an overly muscled mesomorph who returns to Vietnam to avenge American pride and honor for a war we "lost"? Perhaps, also, the current ideal of thinness for women represents the flip side of this phenomenon. The thin female body connotes such stereotypically feminine traits as smallness, weakness, and fragility, which are the mirror opposite of the strength and power represented by the muscular male body. The current female body ideal may be considered the "last bastion of femininity."

We therefore propose a second, "polarization" hypothesis: The male and female body ideals, which are physically and symbolically opposite extremes, may be a reaction against sexual equality, an expression of a wish to preserve some semblance of traditional male-female differences. Lippa (1983) found that what people considered the "ideal" male and "ideal" female body shapes were more different from each other than what people believed to be the "typical" male and female body shapes. Even these typical body shapes were more differentiated than men's and women's actual body shapes.

Conclusions

The body plays a central role in men's self-esteem, and men are striving in growing numbers to achieve the male body ideal. This may have a profound impact on their psychological and physical health. We suspect that the causes and consequences of bodily concern reviewed here represent a growing cultural trend, attributable to increased emphasis on self-determination of health and the ambiguity of current male and female sex roles. Surprisingly little research of any type has addressed these issues, and developmental studies in particular are greatly needed. Perhaps we have failed to focus more scholarly attention on body and bodily esteem because, as Blumstein and Schwartz (1983) have noted, "since most scholars overvalue the power of the mind, they tend to denigrate or even ignore the power of the body." It is also possible that society's effort to relegate bodily concern exclusively to the female sex-role stereotype has deflected attention from the major role it plays for men and may contribute to men's conflicts in acknowledging concern with their appearance. Answers to these and other scientific questions regarding the role of the body in men's lives will be fundamental to our understanding of the male experience.

NOTES

1. A recent study may appear to contradict this assertion that a large percentage of men experience a discrepancy between their actual and ideal body shapes. Fallon and Rozin (1985) report no such discrepancy. However, these researchers averaged their data, not taking into account that some men wish to increase their body size and other men wish to decrease their body size, and that both are expressions of bodily dissatisfaction. If we were to average our own data we would be led to the same erroneous conclusion.

2. Subjects were 47 undergraduate males recruited from introductory psychology classes (assumed to be predominantly heterosexual) and 71 homosexual male undergraduates and graduate students recruited from gay student organizations. Compared with the heterosexual men, the homosexual men showed a greater self-ideal discrepancy on both the Fallon and Rozin (1985) figures (1.3 versus .9, t = 2.9, p < .01) and Tucker (1982b) figures (1.4 versus .9, t = 3.1, p < .01). The homosexual men scored higher on the Dieting subscale of the Garner, Olmsted, Bohr, and Garfinkel (1982) Eating Attitudes Test (5.0 versus 2.4, t = 3.6, p < 001), the Drive for Thinness subscale of the Garner, Olmsted, and Polivy (1982) Eating Disorders Inventory (3.4 versus 1.1, t = 3.36, p < .01), and the Bulimia subscale of the Eating Disorders Inventory (.7 versus .2, t = 2.8, p < .01).

REFERENCES

Adams, G. R., & Cohen, A. S. (1976a). An examination of cumulative folder information used by teachers in making differential judgments of children's abilities. *Alberta Journal of Educational Research, 22,* 216-225.

Adams, G. R., & Cohen, A. S. (1976b). Characteristics of children and teacher expectancy: An extension to the child's social and family life. *Journal of Educational Research, 70,* 87-90.

Apfelbaum, M. (1975). Influence of level of energy intake on energy expenditure in man: Effects of spontaneous intake, experimental starvation and experimental overeating. In G. A. Brey (Ed.), *Obesity in perspective* (Vol. 2) (OBHEW Publication No. NIH 75-708). Washington, DC: Government Printing Office.

Bennett, W. I. (1984). Dieting: Ideology versus physiology. *Psychiatric Clinics of North America, 7,* 321-334.

Benson, P. L., Karabenick, S. A., & Lerner, R. M. (1976). Pretty pleases: The effects of physical attractiveness, race, and sex on receiving help. *Journal of Experimental Social Psychology, 12,* 409-415.

Berscheid, E., & Walster, E. (1974). Physical attractiveness. In L. Berkowitz (Ed.), *Advances in experimental social psychology* (Vol. 7). New York: Academic Press.

Berscheid, E., Walster, E., & Bohrnstedt, G. (1973). The happy American body—survey report. *Psychology Today, 7,* 119-123, 126, 128-131.

Bjorntorp, P., & Yang, M. U. (1982). Refeeding after tasting in the rat: Effects on body composition and food efficiency. *American Journal of Clinical Nutrition, 36*, 444-449.

Blumstein, P. W., & Schwartz, P. (1983). *American couples*. New York: William Morrow.

Brodsky, C. M. (1954). A study of norms for body form-behavior relationships. *Anthropological Quarterly, 27*, 91-101.

Calden, G., Lundy, R. M., & Schlafer, R. J. (1959). Sex differences in body concepts. *Journal of Consulting Psychology, 23*, 378.

Cann, A., Siegfried, W. D., & Pearce, L. (1981). Forced attention to specific applicant qualifications: Impact on physical attractiveness and sex of applicant biases. *Personnel Psychology, 34*, 65-75.

Clifford, E. (1971). Body satisfaction in adolescence. *Perceptual and Motor Skills, 33*, 119-125.

Clifford, M. M. (1975). Physical attractiveness and academic performance. *Child Study Journal, 5*, 201-309.

Clifford, M. M., & Walster, E. (1973). The effect of physical attractiveness on teacher expectations. *Sociology of Education, 46*, 248-258.

Crago, M., Yates, A., Beutler, L. E., & Arizmendi, T. G. (1985). Height-weight ratios among female athletes: Are collegiate athletics the precursors to an anorexic syndrome? *International Journal of Eating Disorders, 4*, 79-87.

Darden, E. (1972). Masculinity-femininity body rankings by males and females. *Journal of Psychology, 80*, 205-212.

DeJong, W. (1980). The stigma of obesity: The consequences of name assumption concerning the causes of peripheral deviance. *Journal of Health and Social Behavior, 21*, 75-87.

Deno, E. (1953). Self-identification among adolescent boys. *Child Development, 24*, 269-273.

Dibiase, W. J., & Hjelle, L. A. (1968). Body image stereotypes and body type preferences among male college students. *Perceptual and Motor Skills, 27*, 1143-1146.

Dion, K. K. (1973). Young children's stereotyping of facial attractiveness. *Developmental Psychology, 9*, 183-188.

Dipboye, R. L., Fromkin, H. L., & Wibach, K. (1975). Relative importance of applicant sex, attractiveness and scholastic standing in evaluations of job applicant resumes. *Journal of Applied Psychology, 60*, 39-43.

Druss, R. G., & Silverman, J. A. (1979). Body image and perfectionism of ballerinas: Comparison and contrast with anorexia nervosa. *General Hospital Psychiatry, 1*, 115-121.

Evan, P., & Nicolaidis, S. (1981). Changes in efficiency of ingestants are a major factor of regulation of energy balance. In L. A. Cioffi, W.P.T. James & T. B. Van Itallie (Eds.), *The body weight regulatory system: Normal and disturbed mechanisms*. New York: Raven.

Fallon, A. E., & Rozin, P. (1985). Sex differences in perceptions of desirable body shape. *Journal of Abnormal Psychology, 94*, 102-105.

Felson, R. B. (1980). Physical attractiveness, grades and teachers' attributions of ability. *Representative Research in Social Psychology, 11*, 64-71.

Franzoi, S. L., & Shields, S. A. (1984). The body esteem scale: Multidimensional structure and sex differences in a college population. *Journal of Personality Assessment, 48*, 173-178.

Fried, S. K., Hill, J. O., Nickel, M., & DioGirolamo, M. (1983). Prolonged effects of fasting-refeeding on rat adipose tissue lipoprotein lipaseactivity: Influence of caloric restriction during refeeding. *Journal of Nutrition, 113*, 1861-1869.

Garner, D. M., & Garfinkel, P. E. (1978). Sociocultural factors in anorexia nervosa. *Lancet, 2,* 674.

Garner, D. M., Olmsted, M. P., & Polivy, J. (1982). The eating disorder inventory: A measure of cognitive/behavioral dimensions of anorexia nervosa and bulimia. In P. L. Darby, P. E. Garfinkel, D. M. Garner & D. V. Coscina (Eds.), *Anorexia nervosa.* New York: Allan R. Liss.

Garner, D. M., Olmsted, M. P., Bohr, Y., & Garfinkel, P. E. (1982). The eating attitudes test: Psychometric features and clinical correlates. *Psychological Medicine, 48,* 173-178.

Garrow, J. (1978). The regulation of energy expenditure. In G. A. Bray (Ed.), *Recent advances in obesity research* (Vol. 2). London: Newman.

Gerzon, M. (1982). *A choice of heroes: The changing faces of American manhood.* Boston: Houghton Mifflin.

Goldberg, B., & Folkins, C. (1974). Relationship of body-image to negative emotional attitudes. *Perceptual and Motor Skills, 39,* 1053-1054.

Goodman, N., Richardson, S. A., Dornbusch, S. M., & Hastorf, A. H. (1963). Variant reactions to physical disabilities. *American Sociological Review, 28,* 429-435.

Gross, M. (1985, September 8). The impact of fitness on the cut of clothes: Men's fashions of the Times. *New York Times.*

Hamburg, D., Solomon, F., & Parron, D. (1983). *Health and behavior.* Washington, DC: National Academy Press.

Hanley, C. (1951). Physique and reputation of junior high school boys. *Child Development, 22,* 247-260.

Harlow, R. (1951). Masculine inadequacy and the compensatory development of physique. *Journal of Personality, 19,* 312-333.

Harris, T. G., & Gurin, J. (1985, March). The new eighties lifestyle: Look who's getting it all together. *American Health,* pp. 42-47.

Hatfield, E., & Sprecher, S. (in press). *Mirror, mirror: The importance of looks in everyday life.* New York: SUNY Press.

Hendry, L. B., & Gillies, P. (1978). Body type, body esteem, school, and leisure: A study of overweight, average, and underweight adolescents. *Journal of Youth and Adolescence, 7,* 181-195.

Herman, C. P., & Polivy, J. (1975). Anxiety, restraint, and eating behavior. *Journal of Abnormal Psychology, 84,* 666-672.

Hiller, D. V. (1981). The salience of overweight in personality characterization. *Journal of Psychology, 108,* 233-240.

Horvath, T. (1981). Physical attractiveness: The influence of selected torso parameters. *Archives of Sexual Behavior, 10,* 21-24.

Joesting, J. (1981). Comparisons of students who exercise with those who do not. *Perceptual and Motor Skills, 53,* 426-466.

Joesting, J., & Clance, P. R. (1979). Comparison of runners and nonrunners on the body-cathexis and self-cathexis scales. *Perceptual and Motor Skills, 48,* 1046.

Jourard, S. M., & Secord, P. F. (1954). Body size and body-cathexis. *Journal of Consulting Psychology, 18,* 184.

Kirkpatrick, S. W., & Sanders, D. M. (1978). Body image stereotypes: A developmental comparison. *Journal of Genetic Psychology, 132,* 87-95.

Kleinberg, S. (1980). *Alienated affections: Being gay in America.* New York: St. Martin's.

Kurtz, R. M. (1969). Sex differences and variations in body attitudes. *Journal of Consulting and Clinical Psychology, 33,* 625-629.

Lakoff, R. T., & Scherr, R. L. (1984). *Face value, the politics of beauty.* Boston: Routledge & Kegan Paul.

Lerner, R. M. (1969). The development of stereotyped expectancies of body-build relations. *Child Development, 40*, 137-141.

Lerner, R. M. (1972). "Richness" analysis of body build stereotype developments. *Developmental Psychology, 7*, 219.

Lerner, R. M., & Gellert, E. (1969). Body build identifications, preference, and aversion in children. *Developmental Psychology, 1*, 456-462.

Lerner, R. M., & Korn, S. J. (1972). The development of body build stereotypes in males. *Child Development, 43*, 912-920.

Lerner, R. M., & Schroeder, C. (1971). Physique identification, preference, and aversion in kindergarten children. *Developmental Psychology, 5*, 538.

Lerner, R. M., Karabenick, S. A., & Stuart, J. L. (1973). Relations among physical attractiveness, body attitudes, and self concept in male and female college students. *Journal of Psychology, 85*, 119-129.

Lerner, R. M., Orlos, J. B., & Knapp, J. R. (1976). Physical attractiveness, physical effectiveness, and self-concept in late adolescents. *Adolescence, 11*, 313-326.

Lippa, R. (1983). Sex typing and the perception of body outlines. *Journal of Personality, 51*, 667-682.

Mahoney, E. R. (1974). Body-cathexis and self-esteem: The importance of subjective importance. *Journal of Psychology, 88*, 27-30.

Martin, M., & Walter, R. (1982). Korperselbstbild und neurotizismus bei Kindern und Jugendichen. *Praxis der Kinderpsychologie und Kinderpsychiatrie, 31*, 213-218.

Martinek, T. J. (1981). Physical attractiveness: Effects on teacher expectations and dyadic interactions in elementary age children. *Journal of Sports Psychology, 3*, 196-205.

McCandless, B. R. (1960). Rate of development, body build and personality. *Psychiatry Research Reports, 13*, 42-57.

McGlenn, R. L. (1980). Relationship of personality and self image change of high and low fitness adolescent males to selected activity programs (Doctoral dissertation, United States International University, 1976). *Dissertation Abstracts International, 40*, 1410B-1411B.

Miller, T. M., Coffman, J. G., & Linke, R. A. (1980). Survey on body image, weight, and diet of college students. *Journal of the American Dietetic Association, 77*, 561-566.

Miller, W. H., Faust, I. M., Goldberger, A. C., & Hirsch, J. (1983). Effects of severe long-term food deprivation and refeeding on adipose tissue cells in the rat. *American Journal of Physiology, 245*, E74-E80.

Montemayor, R. (1978). Men and their bodies: The relationship between body type and behavior. *Journal of Social Issues, 34*, 48-64.

Nichols, J. (1975). *Men's liberation: A new definition of masculinity.* New York: Penguin.

Polivy, J., & Herman, C. P. (1985). Dieting and binging: A causal analysis. *American Psychologist, 40*, 193-201.

Reis, H. T., Nezle, K. J., & Wheels, L. (1980). Physical attractiveness in social interaction. *Journal of Personality and Social Psychology, 38*, 604-617.

Reynaud, E. (1983). *Holy virility: The social construction of masculinity.* London: Pluto.

Richardson, S. A., Hastorf, A. H., Goodman, N., & Dornbusch, S. M. (1961). Cultural uniformity in reaction to physical disabilities. *American Sociological Review, 26*, 241-247.

Rodin, J., Silberstein, L. R., & Striegel-Moore, R. (1985). Women and weight: A normative discontent. In T. B. Sonderegger (Ed.), Nebraska Symposium on Motivation, 1984: Psychology and gender. Lincoln: University of Nebraska Press.

Rosenkrantz, P., Vogel, S., Bee, H., Broverman, I., & Broverman, D. (1984). Sex-role stereotypes and self-concepts in college students. *Journal of Consulting and Clinical Psychology, 32*, 287-295.

Secord, P. F., & Jourard, S. M. (1953). The appraisal of body-cathexis: Body cathexis and the self. *Journal of Consulting Psychology, 17*, 343-347.

Sheldon, W. H. (1942). *The varieties of temperament.* New York: Harper & Row.

Sigall, H., Page, R., & Brown, A. C. (1971). Effort expenditure as a function of evaluation and evaluator attractiveness. *Representative Research in Social Psychology, 2*, 19-25.

Spence, J. T., & Helmreich, R. L. (1978). *Masculinity and femininity.* Austin: University of Texas Press.

Staffieri, J. (1967). A study of social stereotypes of body image in children. *Journal of Personality and Social Psychology, 7*, 101-104.

Story, M. D. (1979). Factors associated with more positive body self-concepts in preschool children. *Journal of Social Psychology, 108*, 49-56.

Striegel-Moore, R., Silberstein, L. R., & Rodin, J. (1986). Toward an understanding of risk factors for bulimia. *American Psychologist, 41*, 246-263.

Stunkard, A. J., Foch, T. T., & Hrubec, Z. (1985). *A twin study of human obesity.* Unpublished manuscript, University of Pennsylvania.

Stunkard, A. J., Sorenson, T.I.A., Hanis, C., Teasdale, T. W., Chakraborty, R., Schull, W. J., & Schulsinger, F. (1985). *An adoption study of human obesity.* Unpublished manuscript, University of Pennsylvania.

Sugerman, A. A., & Haronian, F. (1964). Body type and sophistication of body concept. *Journal of Personality, 32*, 380-394.

Surgeon General's Report. (1984). *The health of the nation.* Washington, DC: U.S. Department of Health and Human Services.

Thune, J. (1949). Personality of weight lifters. *Research Quarterly of the American Physical Education Association, 20*, 296-306.

Todd, T. (1983, August 1). The steroid predicament. *Sports Illustrated, 39*, 62-78.

Tucker, L. A. (1982a). Effect of a weight-training program on the self-concepts of college males. *Perceptual and Motor Skills, 54*, 1055-1061.

Tucker, L. A. (1982b). Relationship between perceived somatotype and body cathexis of college males. *Psychological Reports, 50*, 983-989.

Vaughn, B. E., & Langlois, J. H. (1983). Physical attractiveness as a correlate of peer status and social competence in preschool children. *Developmental Psychology, 19*, 561-567.

Walker, R. N. (1963). Body build and behavior in young children, II: Body build and parents' ratings. *Child Development, 34*, 1-23.

Washburn, W. C. (1962) The effects of physique and intrafamily tensions on self-concept in adolescent males *Journal of Consulting Psychology, 27*, 460-466.

Wells, W. D., & Siegel, B. (1961). Stereotyped somatotypes. *Psychological Reports, 8*, 77-78.

West, S. C., & Brown, T. J. (1975). Physical attractiveness, severity of emergency and helping. Field experiment and interpersonal stimulation. *Journal of Experimental Social Psychology, 11*, 531-538.

Wooley, S. C., & Wooley, O.W. (1984). Should obesity be treated at all? In A.J. Stunkard & E. Stellar (Eds.), Eating and its disorders New York: Raven.

Wright, D.C. & Bradbard, M. R. (1980). Body build-behavioral stereotypes, self-identification, preference and aversion to black preschool children. *Perceptual and Motor Skills, 51*, 1047-1050.

4

The Life of a Man's Seasons

Male Identity in the
Life Course of the Jock

MICHAEL MESSNER

In 1983-1984 I conducted interviews with 30 men who had at one time identified themselves as athletes. When I explained to one man in his late 30s that I was "pursuing an understanding of the lives of ex-athletes," he winced. When asked about his reaction, he replied, "I'm *not* an *ex*-athlete. Just because my career is over doesn't mean I'm no longer an athlete." His statement only begins to give us an appreciation of the *depth* of the sense of identification that many men develop with their roles as athletes: It's almost as though by calling him an "ex-athlete," I had called him an "ex-*man*."

How do we begin to understand the intensity of this sense of identification that many males get from their status as athletes? First, since men have not at all times and places related to sports the way they do currently, it is important to examine this reality through a historical prism. In the first two decades of this century, men feared that the closing of the frontier and changes in the workplace, family, and schools were "feminizing" society (Filene, 1975). The Boy Scouts of America was founded in 1910 to provide a separate sphere of social life where "true manliness" could be instilled in boys *by men* (Hantover, 1978). The

AUTHOR'S NOTE: Portions of this essay appeared in *Arena Review*, Vol. 9, No. 2 (1985), and will appear in H. Brod (Ed.), *Men's Studies: From Achilles' Heel to Damocles' Sword* (forthcoming).

contemporaneous rapid rise of organized sports can be attributed largely to the same phenomenon. As socioeconomic and familial changes eroded traditional bases of male identity and privilege, sport became an increasingly important cultural expression of traditional male values—organized sport became a "primary masculinity-validating experience" (Dubbert, 1979, p. 164).

In the post-World War II era, the bureaucratization and rationalization of work, along with the decline of the family wage and women's gradual movement into the labor force, further undermined the "breadwinner role" as a basis for male identity, resulting in a "defensive insecurity" among men (Tolson, 1977). Both on a personal/existential level for athletes and on a symbolic/ideological level for spectators and fans, sport has become one of the "last bastions" of male power and superiority over—and separation from—the "feminization" of society. The rise of football as "America's number-one game" is likely the result of the comforting *clarity* it provides between the polarities of traditional male power, strength, and violence and the contemporary fears of social feminization.

But these historical explanations for the increased importance of sports, despite their validity, beg some important questions: Why do men fear the "feminization" of their world? Why do men appear to need a separate male sphere? And why do organized sports appear to be such an attractive means of expressing those needs? To answer these questions, it is helpful to listen to athletes' voices and examine their lives within a social-psychological perspective. Daniel Levinson (1978. p. 195) has argued that a male's continual development and change throughout his life course is centered around the process of individuation, the struggle to separate, to "decide where he stops and where the world begins."

> In successive periods of development, as this process goes on, the person forms a clearer boundary between self and world.... Greater individuation allows him to be more separate from the world, to be more independent and self-generating. But it also gives him the confidence and understanding to have more intense attachments in the world and to feel more fully a part of it.

This dynamic of separation and attachment provides a valuable social-psychological framework[1] for examining motivations, experiences, and problems in the life course of the athlete.

Boyhood: The Promise of Sports

How do organized sports come to play such a central role in boys' lives?[2] Jackie Ridgle, once a star high school, college, and professional basketball player, explained his early motivations:

My principal and teachers said, "Now, if you work at this you might be pretty damned good." So it was more or less a community thing—everybody in the community said, "Boy, if you work hard and keep your nose clean, you gonna be *good*." 'Cause it was *natural instinct*.

"It was natural instinct." "I was a natural." Several athletes used words such as these to explain their early attraction to sports. But certainly there is nothing "natural" about throwing a ball through a hoop, hitting one with a bat, or jumping over hurdles. A youth, for instance, may have amazingly dexterous inborn hand-eye coordination, but this does not predispose that person to a career of hitting baseballs any more than it predisposes the person to a career as a brain surgeon. What is significant is that a disproportionately high percentage of "natural" male athletes from poor, working-class, and ethnic minority communities end up pouring their hopes and dreams almost entirely into sports (Edwards, 1973, 1984). For instance, with a different socioeconomic background, MacArthur Lane may have become a great musician instead of a great running back. But he didn't. When he was a child, he told me, he was most interested in music:

I wanted to be a drummer. But we couldn't afford drums. My dad couldn't go out and buy me a drum set or a guitar even—it was just one of those things, that, uh, he was just trying to make ends meet.

But Lane *could* afford, as can so many young black males in this society, to spend countless hours at the local park, where he was told by the park supervisor,

. . . that I was a natural—not only in gymnastics or baseball—whatever I did, I was a natural. He told me I shouldn't waste this talent, and so I immediately started watching the big guys then.

Thus if a youth was "good," he received attention from family, peers, and community, which soon became his primary motivation, as he poured more time and energy into achieving athletic excellence. But given how few actually "make it" through sports, how can the intensity with which millions of boys and young men throw themselves into sports be explained? Are young males simply pushed, socialized, or even *duped* into putting so much emphasis on athletic success? It is important here to examine just what it is that young males hope to get out of the athletic experience. And in terms of *identity,* it is crucial to examine the ways in which the structure and experience of sports activity meets the developmental needs of young males. The story of Willy Rios sheds light on what these needs are. Rios was born in Mexico and moved to the United States at a young age. He never knew his father, and his mother died when he was 9 years old. He felt rootless, and threw himself into sports, but his initial motivations do not appear to be based upon a need to compete and win:

> Actually, what I think sports did for me is—it brought me into kind of an instant family. By being on a Little League team, or even just playing with all kinds of different kids in the neighborhood, it brought what I really wanted, which was some kind of closeness.,

Rios's story suggests that the underlying motivational factor behind young males' sports strivings is a need for connection, "closeness" with others. But why do so many boys see *sports* as an attractive means of establishing connection with others? Chodorow (1978) argues that the process of developing a gender identity yields insecurity and ambivalence in males. Males develop "rigid ego boundaries" that ensure separation from others, yet they retain a basic human need for closeness and intimacy. Consequently, the young male, who both seeks and fears attachment to others, finds the rule-bound structure of games and sports to be a psychological "safe" place in which he can get (nonintimate) connection with others within a context that maintains clear boundaries, distance, and separation. For the successful boy, some of these ambivalent needs can be met temporarily. But there's a catch: For Willy Rios, it was only after he learned that he would get attention from other people for being a good athlete—indeed, that this attention was contingent upon his being good—that performance and winning became important to him. It took him years to realize that no matter how well he performed, how successful he became, he would not get the closeness that he craved through sports.

> It got to be a product in high school. Before, it was just fun, and having acceptance, you know. Yet I had to work for my acceptance in high school that way, just being a jock. So it wasn't fun any more. But it was my

self-identity, being a good ballplayer. I was realizing that whatever you excel in, you put out in front of you. Bring it out. Show it. And that's what I did. That was my protection. . . . It was rotten in high school, really.

This conscious striving for successful achievement becomes the primary means through which the young athlete seeks connection with other people. But it is sadly ironic that what they seek from sports is something that sports cannot deliver; and the pressure to achieve strips them of the ability to receive what sports really can offer: fun. The establishment of a public masculine identity is concerned more with *doing,* with *achieving,* than it is with fun. With no clear cultural rite of passage into adult manhood—indeed, with no clear cultural *definition* of masculinity—the achievement of masculine status is truly problematic. And if it is difficult to define masculinity in terms of what it *is,* it is at least clear to boys what it is *not*: A boy is not considered masculine if he is feminine. In sports, being told by coaches, fathers, or peers that you "throw like a girl" or play like a "sissy" or a "woman" is among the most devastating insults a boy can receive, and this can act as a powerful force in shaping his actions and his self-image.

Adolescent Male Identity and "The Crowd"

The crowd—immediate family, friends, peers, teammates, and the more anonymous fans and media—appears to be a crucially important part of the process of establishing and maintaining the self-images of young athletes. By high school, most of the men interviewed for this study had found sports to be a primary means through which to establish their manhood. If they were good athletes, the expectations of the crowd became very powerful and were internalized within the young man's own expectations. As one man stated, by the time he was in high school, "it was expected of me to do well in all of my contests—I mean, by my coach and my peers and my family. So I in turn expected to do well, and if I didn't do well, then I'd be very disappointed." When so much is tied to performance, the dictum that "you are only as good as your last game" is a powerful judgment. The young man must continually prove, achieve, and then *re*-prove, and *re*achieve his status. As a result, many young athletes learn to seek and *need* the appreciation of the crowd to feel that they are worthy human beings. But the internalized values of masculinity along with the insecure nature of the sports world mean that the young man does not need the crowd to feel *badly* about himself. In fact, if one is insecure enough, even "success" and the compliments and attention of other people can come to feel hollow and meaningless.

In his youth, 48-year-old Russ Ellis shared the basic insecurity common to young males, in his case, compounded by being a poor black in an unstable family. Athletics emerged early as the primary arena in which he and his peers competed to establish a sense of self. For Ellis, his small physical stature made it difficult for him to compete successfully in most sports, thus feeding his insecurity—he just never felt as though he belonged with "the big boys." Eventually, though, he became a respected middle-distance runner. But:

> Something began to happen [in high school] that later plagued me quite a bit. I started doing very well and winning lots of races and by the time the year was over, it was no longer a question for me of *placing*, but *winning*. That attitude really destroyed me, ultimately. I would get into the blocks with worries that I wouldn't do well—the regular stomach problems—so I'd often run much less well than my abilities—that is, I'd take second or third.

It is interesting that his nervousness, fears, and anxieties—as far as he knows—were not visible to "the crowd":

> I know in high school, certainly, they saw me as confident and ready to run. No one assumed I could be beaten, which fascinated me, because I had never been good at understanding how I was taken in other people's minds—maybe because I spent so much time investing myself in their regard in my own mind. I was projecting my fear fantasies on them, and taking them for reality.

In 1956, Ellis surprised everyone by taking second place in a world-class field of quarter-milers. But since they ran in world record time, it only seemed to raise the ante and increase the pressure:

> Up to that point I had been a nice zippy kid who did good, got into the [UCLA] *Daily Bruin* a lot, and was well-known on campus. But now an event would come up and the papers would say, "Ellis to face so-and-so." So rather than my being *in* the race, I *was* the race, as far as the press was concerned. And that put a lot of pressure on me that I never learned to handle. What I did was to internalize it, and then I'd sit there and fret and lose sleep, and focus more on not winning than on how I was doing. And in general, I didn't do badly—like one year in the NCAA's I took fourth— you know, in the *national finals*. But I was focused on winning. You know, later on, people would say, "Oh, wow, you took *fourth* in the

NCAA?—you were *that good?*" Whereas I thought of these things as *failures*, you know?

Ellis's years of training, hopes, and fears converged at the 1956 Olympic trials, where he failed to qualify. A rival whom he had routinely defeated won the event in the Melbourne Olympics as Ellis watched on TV:

> That killed me. Destroyed me. I had the experience many times after that of digging down and finding that there was infinitely more down there than I ever got—I mean, I know that more than I know anything else. Sometimes, I would really feel like an eagle, running. Sometimes in practice at UCLA, running was just exactly like flying—and if I could have carried that attitude into events, I would have done much better. But instead, I'd worry. Yeah, I'd worry myself sick.

In a very real sense, young males like Russ Ellis are set up for disappointment—or worse—by the values and structure of the sports world. The Lombardian ethic teaches males that "winning isn't everything; it's the only thing." Yet, very few ever reach this mythical "top"—though those who do are made ultra-visible through the media. It is tempting, therefore, to view this system as a "structure of failure," and, given the dominant values, the participants are apt to blame themselves for their "failure," leading to what Schafer (1975, p. 50) calls feelings of "widespread conditional self-worth."

But the athlete's sense of identity established through sports is insecure and problematic *not* simply because of the high probability of "failure," but because *success itself* in the sports world involves the development of a personality that *amplifies* many of the most ambivalent and destructive traits of traditional masculinity. Within this hierarchical world, to survive and avoid being pushed off the ever-narrowing pyramid of success, the athlete must develop certain kinds of relationships—to himself, to his body, to other people, to the sport itself. The successful athlete must develop a highly goal-oriented personality that encourages him to view his body as a tool, a machine, or even a weapon that is used to defeat an objectified opponent. He is likely to have difficulty with establishing intimate and lasting friendships with other males because of low self-disclosure, homophobia, and cutthroat competition. And he is likely to view his public image as a "success" as far more basic and fundamental than any of his interpersonal relationships.

For most of the men interviewed the quest for success was not as grim as it was for Russ Ellis. Most seemed to get, at least for a time, a positive sense of identity (and even some "happiness") out of athletic accomplishments. Crowd attention, for many, affirmed their existence as males. One respondent, 42-year-old Gary Affonso, now a high school coach, spoke of his "intense desire to practice and compete" during his high school years:

> I used to practice the high jump by myself for hours at a time—only got up to 5'3"—scissor! [laughs] But I think part of it was, the track itself was in view of some of the classrooms, and so as I think back now, maybe I did it for the attention, to be seen. In my freshman year, I chipped my two front teeth in a football game, and after that I always had a gold tooth, and I was always self-conscious about that. Plus I had my glasses, you know, I felt a little conspicuous.

It is this simultaneous shyness, self-consciousness, and conspicuousness *along with* the strongly felt need for attention and external validation (attachment) that so often characterizes athletes' descriptions of themselves in boyhood and adolescence. The crowd, within this context, becomes a distant, nonthreatening source of validation and attention for the insecure male. But what sports *promise* the young male—affirmation of self and connection with others—is often *undermined* by the youth's actual experience in the sports world. The athletic experience also "sets men up" for another serious problem: the end of a career at a very young age.

Disengagement Trauma: A Crisis of Male Identity

For some, the end of an athletic career approaches gradually, as an unwanted houseguest whose eventual arrival can be anticipated to limit the inevitable inconvenience. For others, an athletic career ends with the shocking suddenness of a violent thunderclap that rudely awakens one from a pleasant dream. But whether it approaches gradually or emerges suddenly, the end of a playing career represents the termination of what has often become the *central aspect* of a young male's individual life structure, thus initiating change and transition in his life course.

Previous research on the disengagement crises faced by many retiring athletes has focused on the health, occupational, and financial problems frequently faced by retiring professionals (Hill and Lowe, 1978; McPherson, 1978). These problems are especially severe for retiring black athletes, who often have inadequate educational backgrounds and fewer opportunities within the sports world for media or coaching jobs (Edwards, 1984). But even for those retiring athletes who avoid the pitfalls of financial and occupational crisis, substance abuse, obesity, and ill health, the end of a playing career usually involves a certain crisis of identity. This identity crisis is probably most acute for retiring professional athletes, whose careers are coming to an end exactly when most men's careers are just beginning to take off. As retired pro football player Marvin Upshaw stated:

> You find yourself just scrambled. You don't know which way to go. Your light, as far as you're concerned, has been turned out. You miss the roar of the crowd. Once you've heard it, you can't get away from it. There's an empty feeling—you feel everything you wanted is gone. All of a sudden you wake up and you find yourself 29, 35 years old, you know, and the one thing that has been the major part of your life is gone. It's gone.

High school and college athletes also face serious and often painful adjustment periods when their careers end. Another respondent, 26-year-old Dave Joki, had been a good high school basketball player, and had also played in college:

> These last few months I've been trying a lot of different things, thinking about different careers, things to do. There's been quite a bit of stumbling—and I think that part of my tenuousness about committing myself to any one thing is I'm not sure I'm gonna get strokes if I go that way [embarrassed, nervous laugh]. It's scary for me and I stay away from searching for those reasons. I guess you could say that I'm stumbling in my relationships too—stumbling in all parts of life [laughs]. I feel like I'm doing a lot but not knowing what I want.

Surely there is nothing unusual about a man in his mid-20s "stumbling" around and looking for direction in his work and his relationships. But for the former athlete, this stumbling is often more confusing and problematic precisely because he has lost the one activity through which he had built his sense of identity. The accolades he received from being a good athlete were his major psychological foundation. This interaction between self and other, through which the athlete attempts to solidify his identity, is akin to what Cooley called "the looking-glass self." If the athletic activity and the crowd can be viewed as a mirror into which the athlete gazes and, in Russ Ellis's words, "invents himself," we can begin to appreciate how devastating it can be when that looking glass is suddenly and permanently shattered, leaving the young man alone, isolated, and disconnected. And since young men often feel comfortable exploring close friendships and intimate relationships only after they have established their separate work- (or sports-) related positional identity, relationships with other people are likely to become more problematic than ever during disengagement.

Work, Love, and Male Identity
After Disengagement

The former athlete inevitably must face a painful truth: At a relatively young age, he has to start over. "Now I gotta get on with the rest of it," former major league baseball player Ray Fosse put it. How is "the rest of it" likely to take shape for the athlete after his career as a player is over? How do men who are "out of the limelight" for a few years redefine themselves as men? And how do their definitions of "success" and their relationships with friends and family change?

Many retired athletes seek to retain the relationship with the crowd that earlier served as the primary basis for their identity. Some throw themselves wholeheartedly into a new vocation—or a confusing series of vocations—in a sometimes pathetic attempt to recapture the "high" of athletic competition as well as the status of the successful athlete in the community. Jackie Ridgle, 35 years old, is experiencing what Daniel Levinson (1978, p. 140) calls a "surge of masculine strivings" common to men in their mid-30s. Once a professional basketball player, Ridgle seems motivated now by a powerful drive to be seen once again as "somebody" in the public eye. When interviewed, he had been hired recently as an assistant college basketball coach, which made him feel once again that he had a chance to "be somebody":

> When I say "successful," that means somebody that the public looks up to just as a basketball player. Yet you don't have to be playing basketball. You can be anybody: You can be a senator or a mayor, or any number of things. That's what I call successful. Success is recognition. Sure, I'm always proud of myself. But there's that little goal there that until *people* respect you, then [snaps fingers]—anybody can say, "Oh, I know I'm the greatest thing in the world," but *people* run the world, and when *they* say you're successful, then you *know* you're successful.

It is common in early adulthood for men to define themselves primarily in terms of their position in the public world of work. And since the man's quest to establish himself in the (mostly) male work world is often accompanied by his frequent physical absence from the home and his emotional distance from his family, his closest interpersonal relationships often suffer. Tragically, it is only at midlife, when the children have already "left the nest" and the woman is often ready to go out into the public world herself that some men "discover" the importance of connection and intimacy.

Yet the interviews indicate that there is not always such a clean polarity in the lives of men between work/success and care/intimacy. The "breadwinner ethic" does serve to sustain male privilege and the subordination and economic dependence of women as mothers and housekeepers. Yet my interviews also indicate that men's strivings to achieve are rooted more in an ethic of responsibility and *care* for their families. For instance, 36-year-old Ray Fosse, whose own father left his family when he was quite young, has a strong sense of commitment and responsibility as a provider of income and stability in his own family:

> I'm working an awful lot these days, and trying not to take time away from my family. A lot of times I'm putting the family to sleep, and working late hours and going to bed and getting up early and so forth. I've tried to tell my family this a lot of times: The work that I'm doing now is gonna make it easier in a few years. That's the reason I'm working now, to get that financial security, and I feel like it's coming very soon . . . but, you know, you go a long day and you come home, and it's just not the quality time you'd like to have. And I think when that financial security comes in, then I'm gonna be able to forget about everything.

Jackie Ridgle's words mirror Fosse's. His two jobs mean that he has little time to spend with his wife and three children:

> I plan to someday. Very seldom do you have enough time to spend with your kids, especially nowadays, so I don't get hung up on that. The wife do sometimes, but as long as I keep a roof over their heads and let'em know who's who, well, one day they'll respect me. But I can't just get bogged down and take any old job, you know, a filling station job or something. Ah, hell, they'll get more respect, my kids for me, right now, than they would if I was somewhere just a regular worker.

For men who had been successful athletes, the move from sports to work/career as a means of establishing connection and identity in the world is a "natural" transition. Breadwinning becomes a man's socially learned means of seeking attachment, both with his family and, more abstractly, with "society." Thus, whereas the care that a woman gives her family usually puts her into direct daily contact with her family's physical, psychological, and emotional needs, a man's care usually is expressed more abstractly, often in his absence, as his work removes him from day-to-day, moment-to-moment contact with his children. A man may want—even crave—more direct connection with his children, but that connection, and the time it takes to establish and maintain it, may cause him to lose the competitive edge he needs to win in the work world, and that is the arena in which he feels he ultimately will be judged. While Ray Fosse wants to stay with his children when his wife works as a substitute teacher, he finds actually doing so "frustrating" because it impinges upon his ability to be flexible in his business dealings.

Men at Midlife and Beyond

This intense, sometimes obsessive, early adulthood striving for work and career success often changes in midlife, when many men begin to experience what Levinson (1978, p. 242) calls "detribalization." Here the man

> becomes more critical of the tribe—the particular groups, institutions, and traditions which have the greatest significance for him, the social matrix to which he is most attached. He is less dependent upon tribal rewards, more questioning of tribal values. . . . The result of this shift is not normally a marked disengagement from the external world, but a greater integration of attachment and separateness.

This detribalization—putting less emphasis on how one is defined by others and becoming more self-motivated and self-generating—is often accompanied by a growing sense of "flawed" or "qualified" success. A man's early-adulthood dream of success begins to tarnish, appearing increasingly illusory. Or, the success that a man has achieved begins to appear more and more hollow and meaningless, possibly because it has not delivered the closeness that he craves. The fading or loss of the dream involves a process of mourning, but as Levinson (1978, pp. 248-249) points out, it can also open the man to new experiences, new kinds of relationships, and new dreams.

Now 48, Russ Ellis states that a few years ago he experienced a "midlife crisis" where he came to the realization that "I was never going to be on the cover of *Time*." His wife had a T-shirt made for him emblazoned with the message, "Dare to Be Average":

> And it doesn't really *mean* dare to be average—it means dare to take the pressure off yourself, you know? Dare to be a normal person. It gets a

funny reaction from people. I think it hits at that place where somehow we all think that we're going to wind up on the cover of *Time,* or something, you know? Do you have that? That some day, somewhere, you're gonna be *great,* and everyone will know, everyone will recognize it? Now, I'd rather be great because I'm *good*—and maybe that'll turn into something that's acknowledged, but not at the headline level. I'm not racing so much; I'm concerned that my feet are planted on the ground and that I'm good.

To the question of whether he's running now as opposed to racing, he replied:

I guess—but running and racing have the same goals. [Laughs, pauses, then more thoughtfully]—But maybe you're right—that's a wonderful analogy. Pacing myself. Running is more intelligent—more familiarity with your abilities, your patterns of workouts, who you're running against, the nature of the track, your position, alertness. You have more of an internal clock.

Russ Ellis's midlife "detribalization"—his transition from a "racer" to a "runner"—has left him more comfortable with himself, with his abilities and his limitations. He has also experienced an expansion of his ability to experience intimacy with a woman, and, in his words, "I feel more fully inducted into the human race by knowing about that."

Toward an Understanding of Men and Sport

This research has suggested that from boyhood through adulthood, sports often acts as a central aspect of the individual life structure of the male. For boys who experience early success, the attention they receive becomes a convenient and attractive means of experiencing attachment with other people within a social context, which allows the young male to maintain firm ego boundaries and, thus, his separation from others. But often, athletic participation exacerbates the already problematic, insecure, and ambivalent nature of males' self-images, and thus their ability to establish and maintain close and intimate relationships. Some men,[3] as they reach midlife, achieve a level of individuation—often through a "midlife crisis"—which leads them to redefine success and expand their ability to experience intimate attachments.

If many of the problems faced by men (not just athletes) today are to be dealt with, class, ethnic, and sexual preference divisions must be confronted. This would necessarily involve the development of a more cooperative and nurturant ethic among men, as well as a more egalitarian and democratically organized economic system. And since the sports world is an important cultural arena that serves partly to socialize boys and young men to hierarchical, competitive, and aggressive values, it is also an important context within which to confront the need for a humanization of men.

Yet, as this research has suggested, the developing psychology of young boys is already predisposed to be attracted to the present structure and values of the sports world, so any attempt to *simply* infuse cooperative and egalitarian values into sports is likely to be an exercise in futility. In a society with equal parenting, as well as greater equality in the public realm, boys and men could grow up with an earlier balance between separation and attachment. And a young male with a more balanced personality would be able to enjoy athletic activities for what they ultimately do have to offer: the opportunity to engage in healthy exercise, to push oneself toward excellence, and to bond with other people in a challenging and fun activity.

NOTES

1. The social psychological approach used in this study contains a dangerous pitfall: In focusing on real people's lives and the changes they experience through their life course, we risk reifying the social structure. Despite Levinson's (1978) and my own insistence that a social psychological approach must take into account the interaction between self and world, the focus on development changes in the life structure of the individual tends to relegate structural factors, such as class and ethnicity, to the role of a fixed and unchanging "backdrop" in front of which the individual changes, adjusts, adapts, and plays out the drama of his or her personal existence.

2. This chapter focuses on boys who became "athletes"—those who at some point became closely identified with their athletic role. Of course, there are also millions of males who at an early age were rejected by, became alienated from, or lost interest in the sports world. This important topic is outside the scope of this study.

3. Farrell and Rosenberg (1981) conclude from their research that only a portion of men experience a "midlife crisis" that results in the man transcending his instrumental personality in favor of a more affective generativity. Put another way, there is no assurance that Jackie Ridgle, as he ages, will transform himself from a "racer" to a "runner" as Russ Ellis has done. Thus the fundamental questions in future examinations of men's lives should focus on building an understanding of just what the keys are to such a shift at midlife. How are individual men's changes, crises, and relationships affected, shaped, and sometimes contradicted by the social, cultural, and political context in which they find themselves? And, perhaps more important, what social changes might make it more likely that boys and men might develop more balanced and secure personalities at an early age?

REFERENCES

Chodorow, N. (1978). *The reproduction of mothering.* Berkeley: University of California Press.

Dubbert, J. L. (1979). *A man's place: Masculinity in transition*. Englewood Cliffs, NJ: Prentice-Hall.

Edwards, H. (1973). *Sociology of sport*. Homewood, IL: Dorsey.

Edwards, H. (1984). The collegiate athletic arms race: Origins and implications of the "Rule 48" controversy. *Journal of Sport and Social Issues, 8*(1).

Farrell, M. P., & Rosenberg, S. D. (1981) *Men at midlife*. Boston: Auburn House.

Filene, P. G. (1975). *Him/her/self: Sex roles in modern America*. New York: Harcourt Brace Jovanovich.

Gilligan, C. (1982) *In a different voice: Psychological theory and women's development*. Cambridge, MA: Harvard University Press.

Hantover, J. (1978). The Boy Scouts and the validation of masculinity. *Journal of Social Issues, 34*(1).

Hill, P., & Lowe, B. (1978). The inevitable metathesis of the retiring athlete. *International Review of Sport Sociology 9*(3-4).

Levinson, D. J. (1978). *The seasons of a man's life*. New York: Ballentine.

McPherson, B. D. (1978, August). Former professional athletes' adjustment to retirement. *Physician and Sports Medicine*.

Rubin, L. B. (1983). *Intimate strangers*. New York: Harper & Row.

Schafer, W. E. (1975, Fall). Sport and male sex role socialization. *Sport Sociology Bulletin, 4*.

Tolson, A. (1977). *The limits of masculinity*. New York: Harper & Row.

5

On Heterosexual Masculinity

Some Psychical Consequences of the Social Construction of Gender and Sexuality

GREGORY M. HEREK

This chapter considers the proposition that to be "a man" in contemporary American society is to be homophobic—that is, to be hostile toward homosexual persons in general and gay men in particular. Starting from some empirical observations of links between homophobia and gender, I shall discuss heterosexual masculinity as a culturally constructed identity and how it has been affected by the recent emergence of gay identities. Then I shall consider how heterosexual masculine identity is constructed by individuals, and how expressing hostility toward gay people enhances such an identity. Finally, I shall propose some strategies for disentangling homophobia from heterosexual masculinity and will consider prospects for changing both.

Throughout this chapter I will describe explicit hostility or prejudice toward gay men and lesbian women as *homophobia*. This term usually is defined as an irrational fear or intolerance of homosexuality or homosexual persons (Herek, 1984; Lehne, 1976; Morin & Garfinkle, 1978; Weinberg, 1972). Of the many words that describe prejudice against lesbians and gay men, it is currently the most popular. It is not an ideal label, however, for many reasons. It overly psychologizes the concept of prejudice against lesbians and gay men. Although it is sometimes used to describe a cultural ideology (Morin & Garfinkle, 1978), it usually is interpreted as a psychological phenomenon, focusing more on what is wrong with individuals than on social-structural problems. Homophobia, however, is manifest at both individual and societal levels. Just as the distinction between individual and institutional racism has been important to the Black movement in the United States (Carmichael & Hamilton, 1968), so it is important to distinguish psychological homophobia from its institutional manifestations. Examples of institutional homophobia are laws that prohibit two consenting people of the same sex from making love in the privacy of their bedroom or that require dismissal of teachers who say that such laws should be abolished.

Another problem with this term is that its -phobia suffix suggests that individual prejudice is based primarily on fear and that this fear is irrational and dysfunctional. I have argued elsewhere (Herek, 1984) that homophobia is tenacious partly because it is very functional for individuals who manifest it. Later I will discuss the functions homophobia serves in connection with the male sex role.

Starting Points:
Some Empirical Observations

It is a common observation that heterosexual men are more homophobic than heterosexual women. Empirical data, however, suggest qualifications for this assertion: Men are more homophobic than women in some respects but not in others. National opinion polls typically find no significant difference between males' and females' responses to questions about homosexuality (Glenn & Weaver, 1979; Irwin & Thompson, 1977; Levitt & Klassen, 1974; Nyberg & Alston, 1976-1977; Scheneider & Lewis, 1984). Smaller-scale experimental and questionnaire studies, in contrast, generally have found more negative attitudes among males than among females, especially with attitudes toward gay men (Herek, 1986a; Kite, 1984).

We can reconcile the different findings of public opinion polls and social psychological studies if we recognize each method's strengths and weaknesses. Poll data obtained from more or less representative samples allow generalization to the larger population, but they rely on only one or two items to assess attitudes concerning sexual orientation. Such single-item measures are less reliable than the multiple-item scales and behavioral measures used in more intensive psychological studies. The latter, however, are conducted with highly select samples—usually college students—and so do not produce readily generalizable results.

More important for the present context, there are differences in content. Polls focus on a single facet of attitudes, usually a question of morality or civil liberties. A frequently used item, for example, reads, "What about relations between two adults of the same sex—do you think it is always wrong, wrong only sometimes, or not wrong at all?" (Nyberg & Alston, 1976-1977). Disregarding the possible bias introduced by framing the topic so negatively, such an item addresses a broad moralistic evaluation. Longer questionnaires of the sort used in laboratory studies include similar topics, but they also tap personal affective issues—personal comfort or discomfort, liking for gay persons, and general emotions associated with the topic of homosexuality. This is apparent in an item such as this: "I think male homosexuality is disgusting" (Herek, 1986a). Both sets of data are revealing. Males and females probably hold roughly similar positions on general questions of morality and civil liberties, but males are more homophobic in their emotional reactions to homosexuality.

Several other empirical observations are relevant to a discussion of this gender difference in affective reactions to gay people. First, heterosexuals' negative attitudes toward lesbians and gay men are correlated consistently with traditional views of gender and family roles. This pattern undoubtedly is related to widespread stereotypes that gay people violate the demands of such roles: Gay men commonly are perceived as effeminate and lesbian women as masculine (Herek, 1984). Although such images are not the sole source of hostility toward gay people, they are an important contributing factor for both men and women (Laner & Laner, 1979, 1980). Even controlling statistically for gender differences in sex-role attitudes (women tend to hold less traditional views than men), this variable remains an important predictor of homophobia for heterosexuals, both female and male (Herek, 1986a).

Another relevant set of empirical findings concerns the role of defensiveness in homophobia. In psychodynamic terms, defensiveness involves an unconscious distortion of reality as a strategy for avoiding recognition of some unacceptable part of the self. One mode of defense is externalization of unacceptable characteristics through projection and other strategies. This externalizing defensive style, as measured by Gleser and Ihilevich's (1969) Defense Mechanisms Inventory (DMI) may affect homophobia in heterosexual males more than in heterosexual females (Herek, 1986a).

In a study of the psychological functions served by homophobia (to be discussed in detail later), I observed that attitudes toward gay people served an entirely defensive function for 20% of the men (n = 81) and 5% of the women (n = 123). This evaluation was based on content analysis of an essay written by respondents to describe their attitudes toward lesbians and gay men. Persons classified as holding defensive attitudes toward gay people also showed a general tendency to externalize, as measured by the DMI. Defensive males showed the highest externalization scores of any respondents (Herek, 1986b).

It is interesting that persons with defensive attitudes manifest greater conformity to what they perceive as gender-appropriate characteristics. Using a semantic differential technique with adjective pairs pretested for their relevance to gender stereotypes (e.g., hard-soft), respondents rated themselves "men in general" and "women in general." Difference scores between ratings of self and of men and women provided a measure of self-perceptions. Defensive males perceived greater similarity between themselves and men in general and greater differences between themselves and women in general than did other males. Similarly, defensive females perceived themselves to be more like women and less like men than did other females (Herek, 1986b).

This pattern suggests that the defensiveness associated with homophobia is linked to gender issues. Defensive attitudes appear to result from insecurities about personal adequacy in meeting gender-role demands. These insecurities may lead to hyperconformity to perceived standards of gender-appropriate traits (Pleck, 1981). Although the sample was not systematically selected, the higher concentration of males in the defensive category suggests that such conflicts may be associated with homophobia more for heterosexual males than for females.

These findings suggest that some males' homophobia is primarily based on anxieties associated with the male role. But it would be a mistake to assume a link between homophobia and the male sex role only for overtly defensive males. Defenses are employed only when more common measures fail. The defensive males I observed probably were not qualitatively different from other homophobic males; they simply were experiencing greater difficulty in maintaining a heterosexual masculine identity. Their strategy for reducing the anxiety that ensued was to exaggerate the "normal" level of homophobia associated with the male role.

This analysis points toward a hypothesis that heterosexual men have more negative reactions to gay people than do women, on the average, because such hostility is inherent in the cultural construction of heterosexual male role and identity; this is less true for heterosexual female role and identity. This process works at a social level, where heterosexual males are pressured by peers and societal standards to conform to certain behavioral patterns, and at a psychological level, where heterosexual males internalize those standards and experience anxiety that they will fail to measure up to their role. The source for this anxiety is fear of losing one's sense of self, or identity, as a heterosexual man (which is equivalent to a male's identity as a person). Conformity to social standards and defense against anxiety push heterosexual men to express homophobic attitudes and provide rewards in the form of social support and reduced anxiety, both of which increase self-esteem. In other words, heterosexual men reaffirm their male identity by attacking gay men.

The Social Construction of Heterosexual Masculinity

Social roles and their attendant psychological identities are not "given" by nature. Variables such as race, class, gender, and sexual orientation are human creations, based on certain observable phenomena that come to be defined in certain ways through social interaction over time. The social constructionist position holds that what most people call reality is a consensus worldview that develops through social interaction (see Berger & Luckmann, 1966; Foucault, 1978; Gergen, 1985; Plummer, 1981). In this perspective gender and sexual orientation must be understood within historical, sociological, and social psychological contexts, rather than in exclusive individualistic terms. By highlighting human plasticity, the constructionist view also allows for the possibility of change. What has been constructed can be reconstructed, albeit with considerable effort. Gender and sexual orientation thus should be understood as changeable ideologies rather than as biological facts.

The Cultural Construction of Gender

Being a man is a crucial component of personal identity for males in our society, stemming from the early experience of gender as a self-defining characteristic. Although personal conceptions of masculine identity in contemporary America vary according to race, class, age, and other social variables (Cazenave, 1984), there remains a stable common core, which I have called "heterosexual masculinity."

As an identity, heterosexual masculinity is defined both positively and negatively. Heterosexual masculinity embodies personal characteristics such as success and status, toughness and independence, aggressiveness and dominance. These are manifest by adult males through exclusively social relationships with men and primarily sexual relationships with women. Heterosexual masculinity is also defined according to what it is not—that is, not feminine and not homosexual. Being a man requires not being compliant, dependent, or submissive; not being effeminate (a "sissy") in physical appearance or mannerisms; not having relationships with men that are sexual or overly intimate; and not failing in sexual relationships with women (Brannon & David, 1976; Pleck, 1981).

In recent years writers have pointed out the maladaptive aspects of heterosexual masculinity in terms of physical health, personal happiness, and psychological adjustment (Fasteau, 1974; Harrison, 1978; Jourard, 1971; Pleck, 1981). Additionally, to the extent that heterosexual masculinity dominates politics and international relations, it may increase the likelihood of interstate warfare and thereby be maladaptive for the entire human species (Fasteau, 1974). Although heterosexual masculinity may have been adequate or at least harmless in former times, historical change has rendered it today an outmoded identity seriously in need of transformation. Despite its dysfunctional aspects, it continues to meet some needs for individuals and will remain entrenched until those needs can be met in some other way.

The Cultural Construction of Sexual Orientation

The historical development of our cultural ideology about sexuality is clearest in what cultural constructionists call the "making of the modern homosexual" (Plummer, 1981). Over the last few centuries, the view developed that what a person does sexually defines who the person is, and negative evaluations were attached to people who did not do what they were supposed to do and who thus were not what they were supposed to be. Not being what one is supposed to be receives many labels, including criminal, wicked, and sick (see Boswell, 1980; Katz, 1983; Weeks, 1977).

To analyze this process requires distinguishing sexual behavior from socioerotic identity. Sexual behavior is any observable action that involves sexual arousal and its continuation or satisfaction. This circular but adequate working definition emphasizes that sexual behavior is something one does. Barring some sort of injury or disability, all human beings can engage in sexual behavior, as can most other animal species. But what makes behavior sexual? What is sexually arousing? Here we make use of Freud's (1905/1961) assumption that humans are born with an amorphous, unformed sexuality—we are polymorphously perverse. Our behavioral repertoire is ambisexual.

Over the course of individual development, the principal source of sexual arousal becomes located in the genitals for most people, and they find that they are aroused by a relatively limited range of things in the world—typically by human beings of a particular gender with fairly specific physical and psychological qualities. In other words, people acquire preferences for certain sexual partners, acts, and situations. Obviously, people are attracted to each other for a host of reasons other than gender—for example, physical appearance, intellect, personality, sense of humor, and religious and political values. But gender is a basic consideration for most people, whether or not it is conscious.

Development of sexual behavioral preferences is common across human cultures and in other species as well. But humans differ from other species (and among cultures) in their personal and social identities based in large part on sexual preferences. In our culture, we summarize those identities with the label *sexual orientation*, defined as a pattern of sexual and affectional preferences for persons of a particular sex. In contemporary American society, those preferences and their associated identities have settled on two categories: heterosexuality and homosexuality.[1]

There is an important difference between *heterosexual* and *homosexual* when they are used as adjectives, describing sexual behavior of which anyone is capable, and when they are used as nouns, describing identity. As nouns *homosexual* and *heterosexual* are mutually exclusive socioerotic identities. Given this dichotomy, our society clearly approves of one identity and not the other.

The significance of this construction for human experience can better be appreciated by considering alternative forms of sexuality. In many New Guinea societies, for example, becoming a man requires incorporating the semen of other men into one's own body through homosexual acts. Once manhood is achieved, heterosexual behavior is socially prescribed (Herdt, 1981, 1982; Williams, 1937). In some indigenous American societies, biological males could assume women's occupations and be recognized socially as women; some men in this "berdache" role married (biological and social) males. In some tribes, a comparable role was available to biological females (Blackwood, 1984; Whitehead, 1981). To the extent that the concept of "sexual orientation" can be applied to such societies, it must be modified considerably.

Such cross-cultural comparisons show us that our notions of heterosexuals and homosexuals are part of a particular historically derived knowledge system. As socioerotic identities, homosexuality and heterosexuality have been created within our culture, starting from the raw material of humans' inherent ambisexuality and inevitable development of erotic and affectional preferences.

This is not to minimize the reality of homosexual or heterosexual identities or to claim that they are simply figments of our imagination that can be easily dismissed. Culturally constructed identities are not easily changed. But it is important to realize that "heterosexuals" and "homosexuals" do not exist in nature; they are constructs, ways of giving meaning to particular patterns of sexual behavior and inter-personal relationships. Understanding the roots of institutional homo-phobia requires learning how our cultural sense of erotic reality developed historically—how we came to be a society of heterosexuals and homosexuals, rather than people whose sexual behavior is shaped by other influences. This historical process of defining socioerotic identities must have been very closely tied to seeing one identity as natural and preferable and seeing the other as unnatural, criminal, wicked, or sick (see Chauncey, 1983; D'Emilio, 1983; Katz, 1983; Plummer, 1981; Weeks, 1977).

Through intense political struggle, lesbians and gay men have made considerable progress in shifting the realm of discourse on sexual orientation from medicine to civil liberties (e.g., see Altman, 1982; D'Emilio, 1983). In many cities, being a homosexual person today is more like belonging to an ethnic minority than it is like sharing a psychiatric diagnosis with other deviants. Being heterosexual un-doubtedly has changed as well in that it has become a more salient identity. Members of dominant groups typically think of themselves not as elites but as "normal"—for example, white men think of themselves as "people" until confronted by Blacks or women (Miller, 1976). As more lesbians and gay men publicly assert their identities, sexual normalcy begins to include both homo- and heteroeroticism, and more people in the dominant majority must consciously label themselves as heterosexual rather than taking it for granted.

Thus although past American notions of masculinity have implicitly included the component of heterosexuality, that component is now more salient and often must be explicitly avowed as part of one's identity. Pressures to define (rather than assume) one's status as a heterosexual man are likely to intensify in the near future for at least two reasons. First, the epidemic of acquired immune deficiency syndrome (AIDS) is likely to lead to more overt discrimination against gay men than has been evident in the recent past. Single males in particular now are being confronted with publicly labeling themselves as heterosexual to avoid such stigma. Second, it appears that the mainstream American conception of masculinity is currently changing in some respects, with some men adopting superficially more flexible behavior patterns. This may be a continuation of the social shift from traditional to modern male roles (Pleck, 1981), or it may reflect a new shift to a "postmodern" definition of masculinity. In either case, recent changes in the "masculine" component of heterosexual masculinity seem to be offset by fortification of the heterosexual component. Thus the man who is "secure" in his masculinity (heterosexuality) may be gentle and may eat quiche.

These cultural and historical patterns provide an appropriate context for understanding heterosexual masculinity. They uncover its roots in social organization of interpersonal relations rather than in biological predispositions to be either heterosexual or masculine. Males in our society grow up in this context, and their identity develops through involvement with family, neighborhood, school, and society. I shall discuss this social psychological level, where cultural ideologies become a part of personal identity, in the next section.

The Personal Construction of Heterosexual Masculinity

Personal identity (self-concept) involves what we are not at least as much as what we are (McGuire, 1984). Boys may learn to be men primarily through learning not to be women, while girls can learn directly how to be women through observing readily available female role models (Lynn, 1969). The negative definition of heterosexual masculinity is at least as important as its positive definition. Homophobia is thus an integral component of heterosexual masculinity, to the extent that it serves the psychological function of expressing who one is not (i.e., homosexual) and thereby affirming who one is (heterosexual). Further, homophobia reduces the likelihood that heterosexual men will interact with gay men, thereby ruling out opportunities for the attitude change that often occurs through such contact (Schneider & Lewis, 1984). When such interactions occur, accidentally, heterosexual masculinity prevents individuation of the participating gay man; instead he is treated primarily as a symbol. These assertions can be clarified best by explaining the psychological functions served by homophobia.

Heterosexual Masculinity and the Functions of Homophobia

Our sense of self is established through social interaction (Mead, 1934). Expressing our opinions, beliefs, values, and attitudes toward others plays a major role in constructing our personal identities. This view derives from a particular perspective on attitudes, the functional approach, which proposes that people hold their opinions because they get some psychological benefit from doing so. In other words, attitudes and opinions serve psychological functions (Katz, 1960; Smith, Bruner, & White, 1956; Herek, in press).

There are two major categories of such functions. One includes attitudes that derive their benefit directly from characteristics of the attitude object; these include heterosexual males' attitudes based on utilitarian considerations of whether gay men have been (or are likely to be) a source of reward or punishment. Such considerations can be based upon past interactions with individual gay men as well as benefit or detriment from gay men as a group (e.g., a merchant who has many gay customers, a renter who must move because gentrification by gay speculators has inflated rents in his neighborhood).

A second category includes attitudes whose function is not directly related to perceived characteristics of gay men but instead results primarily through the attitude's expression. By expressing the attitude, individuals affirm their sense of self in relation to others and increase self-esteem. It is when homophobia serves an expressive function of this kind that it is integrally related to heterosexual masculinity in at least three specific ways. First, homophobia may serve a defensive-expressive function, a way of preventing anxiety that results from intrapsychic conflicts concerning one's own heterosexual masculinity. Gay men symbolize parts of the self that do not measure up to cultural standards; directing hostility at them is a way of externalizing the conflict. This is the function most likely served by homophobia for the defensive males described earlier. Second, homophobia may serve a social-expressive function. In this case, a heterosexual man expresses prejudice against gay men in order to win approval from important others and thereby increase self-esteem. Third, homophobia may serve a value-expressive function. A heterosexual man may express homophobia as part of a larger ideology that is self-defining—for example, a conservative religious ideology that prescribes strict behavioral guidelines for men and women in all facets of life.

For each of these expressive functions, homophobia helps to define what one is not and direct hostility toward that symbol. With the defensive-expressive function, homophobia serves to deny one's own homoerotic attractions and "feminine" characteristics; with the social-expressive function, it defines group boundaries (with gay men on the outside and the self on the inside); for the value-expressive function, it defines the world according to principles of good and bad, right and wrong (with oneself as good and gay men as bad).

To the extent that homophobia serves an expressive function, it is self-perpetuating. Under normal circumstances, homophobic men will not give up their prejudice as long as it continues to be functional. And their prejudice makes it unlikely that they will interact personally with gay men; rather, friendly interaction with gay men is likely to increase anxiety, incur the disapproval of friends, and call into question a man's virtue. There is hope, however, for reducing homophobia and for challenging the ideology of heterosexual masculinity.

The Way Out:
Changing Attitudes and Identities

Given that heterosexual masculinity and homophobia exist at both societal and individual levels, change must also come at both levels. This means changing institutions (the organization of family, work, child care, marriage) as well as people. Here I will briefly address the latter.

The functional approach suggests some strategies for changing attitudes, all based on the assumption that we must render the current attitude dysfunctional in some way while providing benefit from the target attitude. With direct functions, this usually involves arranging pleasant interactions with the attitude target (that is, gay men). With expressive attitudes, however, this is not a simple task for reasons already mentioned. Additional steps must be taken with each of the expressive functions.

With social-expressive functions, new norms must be created. One strategy is to solicit personal statements from significant role models of heterosexual masculinity that their own attitudes toward gay men are not hostile. Another approach is to provide direct social support for men whose homophobia is being challenged; this might be achieved most effectively in the context of a therapeutic or men's group. Attacking value-expressive attitudes does not necessarily require dismantling an entire value system. Instead, it can involve making competing values salient. For example, values of justice and fair play may be raised, or values of open-mindedness or charity toward one's neighbor.

Defensive-expressive attitudes probably are the most difficult to challenge because, as with any defense mechanism, they work at an unconscious level. Any attempt to make them conscious (which threatens to make conscious the repressed anxiety) is likely to be met by great resistance. To some extent, this can be used favorably by "short-circuiting" the prejudice through arousal of insight. Simply persuading a man that excessive hostility toward gay men is a sign of latent homosexuality may at least lead that man to avoid expressing his hostility. Unfortunately, it will not resolve the conflict underlying the prejudice and could, in fact, exacerbate it. One strategy might be attempting to change attitudes incrementally, starting with attitudes toward lesbians, who may be less anxiety-arousing.

My suggestions on this point have focused on changing attitudes toward gay men without changing the identity of heterosexual masculinity that underlies them. A long-term strategy for eradicating homophobia, however, must focus on heterosexual masculinity. Although a detailed consideration of how to change contemporary male roles is beyond the scope of this chapter, two promising avenues of inquiry deserve mention.

First, it will be useful to explore systematically how gay men deal with their own internalized homophobia in the process of coming out. As males in this culture, gay men are taught the ideal of heterosexual masculinity. When they acknowledge their own sexual preferences to themselves, however, they must discard this ideology in order to maintain their self-esteem. Although gay men often adhere to many components of the male sex role, their understanding of masculinity must somehow change in the course of accepting their homoeroticism. Research on this topic may provide insight for changing heterosexual males as well (see Nungesser, 1983).

Second, this perspective will lead to a functional analysis of heterosexual masculinity. Gay men usually renounce their internalized homophobia only when its costs outweigh its benefits. Similarly, individuals will renounce heterosexual masculinity only when it becomes clearly dysfunctional to them. Although the male sex role is hazardous to the health of those who adhere to it (Harrison, 1978), it also meets some basic psychological needs in much the same way that homophobic attitudes do. Approximating the ideal of heterosexual masculinity can help a man's career, attract friends and admirers, increase his self-esteem, and give him a sense of doing his duty as a man. Of course, the career also may be damaging to his physical and psychological health, the friendships may lack intimacy, and the self-esteem may be based on a general inability for critical introspection and emotional expression. In addition, doing his duty may preclude pursuing his own goals. Until men become aware of these costs, change is unlikely. They will become what Pleck calls "martyrs for the male role" (J. Pleck, personal communication, 1985). And through the homophobia inherent in heterosexual masculinity, they will take many gay men and lesbians with them.

Even realizing how dysfunctional the male role can be does not make change the inevitable. Men cannot change without clear alternative ways of living. Formulating such alternatives must constitute an agenda for all who hope to improve our society—gay, lesbian, and heterosexual.

NOTE

1. Although the category of bisexuality exists, its status as a true identity is suspect; regardless of its accuracy, most people seem to hold the view that a person is either heterosexual or homosexual (Klein & Wolf, 1985; Ruitenbeek, 1973).

REFERENCES

Altman, D. (1982). *The homosexualization of America, the Americanization of the homosexual.* New York: St. Martin's.

Berger, P. L., & Luckmann, T. (1966). *The social construction of reality.* Garden City, NY: Doubleday.

Blackwood, E. (1984). Sexuality and gender in certain Native American tribes: The case of cross-gender females. *Signs, 10*(1), 27-42.

Boswell, J. (1980). *Christianity, social tolerance, and homosexuality: Gay people in western Europe from the beginning of the Christian era to the fourteenth century.* Chicago: University of Chicago Press.

Brannon, R., & David, D. (1976). The male sex role: Our culture's blueprint for manhood and what it's done for us lately. In D. Davis & R. Brannon (Eds.), *The forty-nine percent majority: The male sex role.* Reading, MA: Addison-Wesley.

Carmichael, S., & Hamilton, C. V. (1968). *Black power: The politics of liberation in America.* New York: Random House.

Cazenave, N.A. (1984). Race, socioeconomic status, and age: The social context of American masculinity. *Sex Roles, 11,* 639-656.

Chauncey, G. (1983). From sexual inversion to homosexuality: Medicine and the changing conceptualization of female deviance. *Salmagundi, 58/59,* 114-146.

D'Emilio, J. (1983). *Sexual politics, sexual communities: The making of a homosexual minority in the United States, 1940-1970.* Chicago: University of Chicago Press.

Fasteau, M. F. (1974). *The male machine.* New York: McGraw-Hill.

Foucault, M. (1978). *The history of sexuality: Vol. 1. An introduction.* New York: Pantheon. (Original work published 1976)

Freud, S. (1961). Three essays on the theory of sexuality. In J. Strachey (Ed. and Trans.), *The standard edition of the complete psychological works of Sigmund Freud.* London: Hogarth. (Original work published 1905)

Gabay, E. D., & Morrison, A. (1985, August). *AIDS-phobia, homophobia, and locus of control.* Paper presented at the meeting of the American Psychological Association, Los Angeles.

Gergen, K. J. (1985). The social constructionist movement in modern psychology. *American Psychologist, 40,* 266-275.

Glenn, N. D., & Weaver, C. N. (1979). Attitudes toward premarital, extramarital, and homosexual relations in the U.S. in the 1970s. *Journal of Sex Research, 15,* 108-118.

Gleser, G. C., & Ihilevich, D. (1969). An objective instrument for measuring defense mechanisms. *Journal of Consulting and Clinical Psychology, 33,* 51-60.

Harrison, J. (1978). Warning: The male sex role may be hazardous to your health. *Journal of Social Issues, 34*(1), 65-86.

Herdt, G. (1981). *Guardians of the flutes: Idioms of masculinity.* New York: McGraw-Hill.

Herdt, G. (Ed.). (1982). *Rituals of manhood: Male initiation in Papua New Guinea.* Berkeley: University of California Press.

Herek, G. (1984). Beyond "homophobia": A social psychological perspective on attitudes toward lesbians and gay men. *Journal of Homosexuality, 10*(1/2), 1-21.

Herek, G. (1986a). *The gender gap in attitudes toward lesbians and gay men: Its measurement and meaning.* Paper submitted for editorial review.

Herek, G. (1986b). *Can functions be measured? A new perspective on the functional approach to attitudes.* Paper submitted for editorial review.

Herek, G. (in press). The instrumentality of ideologies: Toward a neofunctional theory of attitudes and behavior. *Journal of Social Issues.*

Irwin, P., & Thompson, N. L. (1977). Acceptance of the rights of homosexuals: A social profile. *Journal of Homosexuality, 3*(2), 107-121.

Jourard, S. M. (1971). *The transparent self.* Princeton, NJ: Van Nostrand.

Katz, D. (1960). The functional approach to the study of attitudes. *Public Opinion Quarterly, 24,* 163-204.

Katz, J. N. (1983). *Gay/lesbian almanac.* New York: Harper & Row.

Kite, M. E. (1984). Sex differences in attitudes toward homosexuals: A meta-analytic review. *Journal of Homosexuality, 10*(1/2), 69-81.

Klein, F., & Wolf, T. J. (Eds.). (1985). Bisexualities: Theory and research. *Journal of Homosexuality, 11*(1/2).

Laner, M. R., & Laner, R. H. (1979). Personal style or sexual preference: Why gay men are disliked. *International Review of Modern Sociology, 9,* 215-228.

Laner, M. R., & Laner, R. H. (1980). Sexual preference or personal style? Why lesbians are disliked. *Journal of Homosexuality, 5*(4), 339-356.

Lehne, G. K. (1976). Homophobia among men. In D. David & R. Brannon (Eds.), *The forty-nine percent majority: The male sex role* (pp. 66-88). Reading, MA: Addison-Wesley.

Levitt, E. E., & Klassen, A. D. (1974). Public attitudes toward homosexuality: Part of the 1970 national survey by the Institute for Sex Research. *Journal of Homosexuality, 1*(1), 29-43.

Lynn, D. B. (1969). *Parental and sex-role identification.* Berkeley, CA: McCutchan.

McGuire, W. J. (1984). Search for the self: Going beyond self-esteem and the reactive self. In R. A. Zucker, J. Aronoff & A. Rabin (Eds.), *Personality and the prediction of behavior* (pp. 73-102). New York: Academic Press.

Mead, G. H. (1934). *Mind, self, and society.* Chicago: University of Chicago Press.

Miller, J. B. (1976). *Toward a new psychology of women.* Boston: Beacon.

Morin, S. F., & Garfinkle, E. M. (1978). Male homophobia. *Journal of Social Issues, 34*(1), 29-47.

Nungesser, L. (1983). *Homosexual acts, actors, and identities.* New York: Praeger.

Nyberg, K. L., & Alston, J. P. (1976-1977). Analysis of public attitudes toward homosexual behavior. *Journal of Homosexuality, 2*(2), 99-107.

O'Donnell, C. R., O'Donnell, L., Pleck, J. H., Snarey, J., & Rose, R. M. (1985). *Psychosocial responses of hospital workers to the Acquired Immunodeficiency Syndrome (AIDS).* Paper submitted for editorial review.

Pleck, J. H. (1981). *The myth of masculinity.* Cambridge: MIT Press.

Plummer, K. (Ed.). (1981). *The making of the modern homosexual.* London: Hutchinson.

Ruitenbeek, H. M. (1973). The myth of bisexuality. In H. M. Ruitenbeek (Ed.), *Homosexuality: A changing picture* (pp. 199-204). London: Souvenir.

Schneider, W., & Lewis, I. A. (1984, February). The straight story on homosexuality and gay rights. *Public Opinion,* pp. 16-20, 59-60.

Smith, M. B., Bruner, J. S., & White, R. W. (1956). *Opinions and personality.* New York: John Wiley.

Weeks, J. (1977). *Coming out: Homosexual politics in Britain, from the nineteenth century to the present.* London: Quartet.

Weinberg, G. (1972). *Society and the healthy homosexual.* New York: St. Martin's.

Whitehead, H. (1981). The bow and the burden strap: A new look at institutionalized homosexuality in native North America. In S. B. Ortner & H. Whitehead (Eds.), *Sexual meanings: The cultural construction of gender and sexuality* (pp. 80-115). Cambridge: Cambridge University Press.

Williams, F. E. (1937). *Papuans of the trans-fly.* London: Oxford University Press.

PART II

Men in Domestic Settings

6

American Fathering in Historical Perspective

JOSEPH H. PLECK

In American society, there has been an explosion of interest in fathers and fatherhood today. One can hardly watch television, open a national magazine, or go to a movie without seeing themes of father-child relationships, fatherhood, or fatherlessness—from *Star Wars*'s Luke Skywalker's search for his true father, to a recent cover story in the Sunday supplement *Parade* about the actor James Caan as a father, tellingly titled "The Only Role That Matters." In the last decade and a half, calls for greater father involvement have become increasingly insistent.

Yet, in spite of this contemporary interest, and signs of widespread support for an enlarged father role, the pace of change has been slow. While men are doing more child care and housework than they used to, women still perform the bulk of these activities (Pleck, 1985). Beneath

AUTHOR'S NOTE: Research reported in this article was conducted as part of the Fatherhood Project, supported by the Ford, Levi Strauss, Ittelson, and Rockefeller Family Foundations. Earlier versions have benefited from comments by Harris Dienstfrey, Michael Kimmel, Michael Lamb, James Levine, and Elizabeth H. Pleck.

the apparent contemporary support for greater father involvement lies a deep-seated ambivalence about what the role of the father really should be, rooted in the complex historical legacy of American culture's perceptions of fathering. Contradictory images of fatherhood from the past have left their mark on contemporary attitudes. This chapter analyzes the dominant images of fatherhood in earlier periods of U.S. history,[1] and considers their impact today.

Eighteenth and Early Nineteenth Centuries: Father as Moral Overseer

There is no question that colonial mothers, as their counterparts today, provided most of the caretaking that infants and young children received. But fathers were nonetheless thought to have far greater responsibility for, and influence on, their children. Prescriptions for parents were addressed almost entirely to fathers; the responsibilities of mothers were rarely mentioned (Degler, 1980).

Fathers were viewed as the family's ultimate source of moral teaching and worldly judgments. The father was viewed as a moral pedagogue who must instruct children of both sexes what God as well as the world required of them. A diary entry by Cotton Mather when he was still young and in good health, provides a perhaps extreme illustration:

> I took my little daughter Katy into my study and there I told my child that I am to die shortly, and she must, when I am dead remember everything that I said unto her. I set before her the sinful and woeful condition of her nature, and I charged her to pray in secret places every day without ceasing that God for the sake of Jesus Christ would give her a new heart . . . I gave her to understand that when I am taken from her she must look to meet with more humbling afflictions than she does now [when] she has a careful and tender father to provide for her. (in Demos, 1982: 426)

When ministers and others wrote about fatherhood, they emphasized a variety of responsibilities. Fathers ought to concern themselves with the moral and religious education of the young. If literate himself, he should teach reading and writing. He was responsible for guiding his sons into a occupational "calling." He played a key role in the courtship and marriage making of both his sons and daughters, by approving a proposed match and alloting family property to the couple.

Notions of the "duty" of fathers to their children, and of children to their fathers, were central to father-child relationships (Rotundo, 1982). One expression of the family hierarchy, viewed as ideal during this period, appears in *The Token of Friendship, or Home, The Center of Affections* (1844):

> The father gives his kind command,
> The mother joins, approves;
> The children all attentive stand,
> Then each obedient moves. (in Ewen, 1976: 152)

This emphasis on the paternal role was rooted in this period's conception of the differences between the sexes, and the nature of children. Men were thought to have superior reason, which made them less likely than women to be misled by the "passions" and "affections" to which both sexes were subject. Children were viewed as inherently sinful, ruled by powerful impulses as yet ungoverned by intellect. Because of women's weakness of reason and inherent vulnerability to inordinate affections, only men could provide the vigorous supervision needed by children. Fathers had to restrain their children's sinful urges and encourage the development of sound reason. Mothers were less able to provide these needed influences because of their own tendency to "indulge" or be excessively "fond" of their children. Consistent with these conceptions, common law assigned the right and obligation of child custody to the father in cases of marital separation.

Some descriptions of actual father-child interactions appear in diaries, letters, and other personal accounts: a father and his 10-year-old son carting grain to the mill; a father counseling his adult daughter on her impending marriage; a father and son "discoursing" on witchcraft; a son and daughter joining their father in an argument with neighbors. From such records emerges a "picture, above all, of active, encompassing fatherhood, woven into the whole fabric of domestic and productive life. . . . Fathers were a visible presence, year after year, day after day. . . . Fathering was thus an extension, if not a part, of much routine activity." (Demos, 1982: 429) This integration of fatherhood in daily life derived in large part from the location of work, whether farming or artisanship and trade, in the family context. It was natural and even necessary for children to be involved.

Relationships between fathers and children, especially sons, often had strong emotional components. Sons were often regarded as extensions of their fathers; young or newly born sons were commonly described by their fathers as "my hope" or "my consolation" (Demos, 1982:428). However, since fathers believed they could and should restrain their emotions, fathers "tended to express approval and disapproval in place of affection and anger" (Rotundo, 1985: 9).

Another indicator of the strength of father-son relationships is that boys serving apprenticeships, and young men on their own, maintained contact with their family primarily through letters to and from their fathers. In contrast to the large volume of letters from children to their fathers that have survived, there are few letters written directly to mothers. Sons would often ask to be "remembered" to their mothers, but in terms that seem formal or even perfunctory. For example, a man whose father had just died who included the following message for their mother when he wrote home to a brother: "I sincerely condole with her on the loss of her husband; please tender my duty to her" (Demos, 1982: 428).

Early Nineteenth to Mid-Twentieth Centuries: Father as Distant Breadwinner

New conceptions of parent-child relationships began to appear during the nineteenth century. A gradual and steady shift toward a greater role for the mother, and a decreased and more indirect role for the father is clear and unmistakable. Whereas in the earlier period fathers were the chief correspondents of their adolescent and adult children, mothers played that role at least as often in the nineteenth century. To the extent that either parent was involved in the marital choices of their children, it was now usually the mother. In contrast to the earlier period when mothers showed little concern with any aspect of their sons' lives after childhood, letters and diaries now indicated they were emotionally entangled with sons well into adulthood. Where it had been common earlier to give blame or credit for how children turned out as adults entirely to their fathers, now the same judgment was made about mothers (Demos, 1982).

This shift paralleled a new ideology about gender. While social historians do not agree on its ultimate structural sources, they have documented its centrality to social thought during the nineteenth century. This gender ideology emphasized the purity of the female "sphere" (i.e., the home) and feminine character as unselfish and nurturant. Women's "purity" elevated her above men, making her particularly suited for "rearing" the young. At the same time, infancy and early childhood (as opposed to middle childhood and adolescence) received greater emphasis; mothers were thought to have a special influence in these earlier periods. The belief in maternal influence extended even to the period before birth: the mother's experience during pregnancy, it was thought, might literally shape the destiny of her child (Demos, 1982).

This period saw the development of the contemporary presumption of maternal custody following divorce. It is difficult to define with precision when all vestiges of the earlier practice of awarding custody to fathers disappeared. Increasingly, the interests of the child were interpreted as justifying if not requiring maternal custody. In the latter part of the nineteenth century, court decisions more often promulgated the notion that women have a unique right and obligation to take custody (Grossberg, 1983).

Consistent with these trends, educators during the nineteenth century came to view children as needing a "feminine" influence in their schooling (Suggs, 1977). It is little remembered today that among the foremost "reforms" of nineteenth century educational innovators such as Horace Mann and Ichabod Crane was their introduction of female teachers in the elementary schools.

It took some time for this shift in parental patterns to become fully reflected in all areas of American social thought. Until well into the twentieth century, psychology continued to be dominated by European theorists, grounded in quite different conceptions of family life. To both Jung and the early Freud, the father was unquestionably the towering figure in the life of the child. Freud, it is true, gave a role to the mother, but primarily as the object of the male child's libidinous drives, not as the molder of his character. To the early Freud at least, the mother was psychologically important primarily because the male child's love for her brought him into competition with his father, in an Oedipal drama whose outcome (identification with the father and consolidation of the superego) creates adult male character structure.

Freudian and other psychodynamic theories began to change in the early twentieth century, reflecting an increasing emphasis on the child's primary affectional tie to the mother. Led by Freud himself, psychoanalysis in the 1920's began to focus on pre-Oedipal issues (the psychoanalytic code word for the mother). Central to the many variant formulations was a clear theme: the Oedipal conflict is the key to the clinically less serious neurotic disorders, but the more severe and less treatable forms of psychopathology (the psychoses and personality disorders) result from earlier, more fundamental problems with the mother.

Harry Stack Sullivan, one of the most influential figures in modern clinical psychiatry, also gave almost exclusive attention to the mother: She transmits anxiety and irrational societal expectations to the child, potentially leading to personality "warps" of varying severity. Sullivan's writings hardly ever mention the father. The same is true for John Watson, the founder of "behaviorism," whose advice to parents not to give too much affection to the child was addressed almost entirely to mothers.

While the elevation of the maternal role was the dominant theme from the mid-nineteenth to mid-twentieth centuries, some observers expressed reservations about it. Bronson Alcott wrote in 1845 that "I cannot believe that God established the relation of father without giving the father something to do" (in Demos, 1982: 432). At the turn of the century, cultural critics attacked rising maternal influence, along with urbanization and immigration, as having a feminizing effect on American political, cultural, and religious institutions (Kimmel, 1986). In the first decade of the twentieth century, J. McKeen Cattell, an early founder of American psychology, criticized the "vast horde of female teachers" to whom children were exposed (in O'Neil, 1967: 81).

A major structural source of the decline in the father's role and increased maternal influence was the emergence of new paternal work patterns away from the family, brought about by industrialization.[2] "For the first time, the central activity of fatherhood was sited outside one's immediate household. Now being fully a father meant being separated from one's children for a considerable part of each working day" (Demos, 1982: 434). As geographical distance between the workplace and the home increased, so too did the father's direct involvement with his children. "The suburban husband and father is almost entirely a Sunday institution," noted a writer in *Harper's Bazaar* in 1900 (Demos, 1982: 442).

This new kind of father focused entirely on breadwinning was depicted in early twentieth century advertisements. Mothers were shown as the general purchasing managers of the household, while fathers were portrayed primarily as breadwinners whose wages made family consumption and security possible. Life insurance promotions reminded fathers of their primary function as breadwinners. A 1925 Prudential ad showed a widowed mother visiting her children in an orphan asylum. The child in the ad says the asylum authorities told him "father didn't keep his life insurance paid up" (Ewen, 1976: 153-154). The mark of a good father had become a good insurance policy.

In his new role, father's authority was reduced. In a well-known passage, Alexis de Tocqueville described how weak paternal authority seemed when he visited the United States in the 1830s:

A species of equality prevails around the domestic hearth. . . . I think that in proportion as manners and laws become more democratic, the relation of father and son becomes more intimate and more affectionate; rules and authority are less talked of, confidence and tenderness are often increased. . . . The father foresees the limits of this authority . . . and surrenders it without a struggle. (in Degler, 1980, p. 75)

The father continued to set the official standard of morality and to be the final arbiter of family discipline, but he did so at more of a remove than before: He stepped in only when the mother's delegated authority failed. "The father . . . was kicked upstairs, as they say in industry, and was made chairman of the board. As such, he did not lose all his power—he still had to be consulted on important decisions—but his wife emerged as the executive director or manager of the enterprise which is called the family" (LeMasters, in Sebald, 1976, p. 19).

A potential consequence of this indirect authority was that fathers lost touch with what was actually going on in the family. Clarence Day's portrayal of a turn-of-the-century middle-class family, *Life with Father* (1935), was a popular comic expression of this hazard: In spite of his high-status job and the elaborate deference he appears to receive from his wife and children, he is in fact easily manipulated by them. Contemporary concerns about "declining" paternal authority find many of their roots in this period.

Lynd and Lynd's (1929/1956) study of Middletown in the 1920s documents the results of these trends. One resident says: "It is much more important for children to have a good mother than it is for them to have a good father because the mother not only establishes their social position, but because her influence is the prepotent one." A business-class mother says: "My husband has to spend time in civic work that my father used to give to us children." Lynd and Lynd observed little difference in the amount of fathers' involvement between the working-class and business-class fathers; however, business-class wives more often accepted the low involvement, while the working-class wives more often expressed resentment about it.

Middletown notes a "busy, wistful uneasiness" about not being a better parent among many elite fathers: "I'm a rotten dad. If our children amount to anything it's their mother who'll get all the credit. I'm so busy I don't see much of them and I don't know how to chum up with them when I do." Another remarked: "You know, I don't know that I spend any time having a good time with my children. . . . And the worst of it is, I don't know how to. I take my children to school in the car each morning; there is some time we could spend together, but I just spend it thinking about my own affairs and never make an effort to do anything with them." This emotional gap led children to long for greater father involvement. Middletown high school students chose "spending time with his children" among a list of 10 possible desirable qualities in a father far more often than any of the others (Lynd & Lynd, 1929/ 1956, p. 148-149).

1940-1965: Father as Sex Role Model

During and following World War II, the criticisms that had accompanied the rise of maternal influence in the earlier period became increasingly powerful. At the turn of the century, excessive mothering had been one of a cluster of social transformations creating concern. Now, while other discomfiting trends such as urbanization and immigration had either been accepted or brought under control, mothers stood more alone as objects of social unease (Kimmel, 1986). During the postwar years, this heightened critique of mothering helped usher in a new perception of the father's direct importance in child rearing as a sex role model. This new view derived from negative perceptions of mothers, and encouraged paternal participation of only a limited sort. The new conception did not become dominant; the distant father-breadwinner still prevailed. Nonetheless, the sex role model interpretation of fathering is historically important as the first positive image of involved fatherhood to have a significant impact on the culture since the moral overseer model of the colonial period.

The intensified critique of mothers' influence is particularly evident in Philip Wylie's (1942) popular *A Generation of Vipers*:

> Megaloid momworship has got completely out of hand. Our land, subjectively mapped, would have more silver cords and apron strings criss-crossing it than railroads and telephone wires. Mom is everywhere and everything and damned near everybody, and from her depends all the rest of the U.S. Disguised as good old mom, dear old mom, sweet old mom, your loving mom, and so on, she is the bride at every funeral and the corpse at every wedding. (p. 185)

In academic psychology, David Levy's *Maternal Overprotection* argued that contemporary mothers took too dominant a role in the lives of their children because they were not fully satisfied in their relationships with their husbands. "The child must bear the brunt of the unsatisfied love life of the mother." (Levy 1943, p. 121) Following the war, military psychiatrists blamed the battle breakdowns and other problems of the American fighting man on the American mother (Strecker, 1948). Even the early feminist critiques of the traditional housewife role, written during the early 1960s, sounded a similar theme. Betty Friedan's *The Feminine Mystique* prominently features the argument that the housewife-mother has too close a relationship with her sons, resulting in the "rampant homosexuality" which she described as "spreading a murky smog throughout every area of American life, especially the arts" (1963, p. 265).

New attention to the father's direct role was first manifested not in research on normal father-child relationships, but rather in studies of what happened when the father was absent. The post-war father was seen as a towering figure in the life of his child not so much by his presence as by his absence. Many of the social factors contributing to this enormous post-war interest in father absence directly or indirectly derived from the events of the war. Most obviously, fathers had gone away to the war en masse, and many had not returned. The first studies of the effects of paternal separation were in fact conducted with children of wartime-absent fathers (e.g., Bach, 1946). In addition, wartime induced changes in women's roles. Wives entered paid employment on a large scale, and learned greater independence from men through having to live without their husbands for the duration. Partly as a result, the divorce rate immediately following demobilization was high. Further, the war's economic boom stimulated an enormous and historically unprecedented migration of rural dwellers, especially blacks, to the older cities of the Northeast and Midwest and the newer cities of the West. Traditional family structure broke down, at least among many of these new urban migrants. Rates of father absence rose.

Parallel to the cultural concern about father absence was a more general concern about fathers' weakness and passivity even when they were technically "present." Mass culture expressed it in parody. "The domesticated Dad, who was most entertaining when he tried to be manly and enterprising, was the butt of all the situation comedies. Danny Thomas, Ozzie Nelson, Robert Young, and (though not a father in the role) Jackie Gleason in 'The Honeymooners,' were funny as pint-sized caricatures of the patriarchs, frontiersmen, and adventurers who once defined American manhood" (Ehrenreich and English, 1979, p. 240).

Father absence and father passivity became linked in the public mind with a perceived epidemic of juvenile delinquency in the 1950s. A dramatic expression of this connection occurs in the film *Rebel Without a Cause*. In one of the film's most powerful scenes, the delinquent son finally seeks out his father for advice during a crisis. But when he finds his father wearing an apron while washing dishes in the kitchen, the son recoils in disgust.

A new theory about gender came to dominate developmental psychology which theoretically articulated an extremely significant role for the father, particularly with sons. This theory held that boys face a terrible problem in developing male identity: Developing masculinity is absolutely essential to psychological health, but contemporary child rearing practices make it difficult for boys to do it. Male identity is thwarted by boys' initial identification with their mothers, and by high rates of father absence and the relative unavailability of fathers even when "present." According to the theory, the combination of too much mothering and inadequate fathering lead to insecurity in male identity. This insecure masculinity is manifested directly in homosexuality, as well as more indirectly in delinquency and violence, viewed as "overcompensations" or "defenses" against it (Pleck, 1981, 1983). As this theory evolved, fathers came to be seen as essential for the sex role development of their daughters as well. This conception of father as sex role model served as the equivalent of the much earlier view of the father as moral pedagogue. Healthy sex role identification replaced salvation as the moral imperative.

This new view of the father's role encouraged paternal involvement with children, but also drew a clear distinction between paternal and maternal roles. "The mother has a primarily expressive relationship with both boys and girls; in contrast, the father rewards his male and female children differently, encouraging instrumental behavior in his son and expressive behavior in his daughter. The father is supposed to be the principal transmitter of culturally based conceptions of masculinity and femininity" (Biller, 1971, p. 107).

This new interpretation of the role of the father gave the father a direct but limited role with his children. Some academic authorities expressed great concern about the father being over-involved, or having a role too similar to the mother, particularly if combined with the mother taking a "masculine" role. A standard anthology on the family states that "severe personality problems in one spouse may require the wife to become the wage-earner, or may lead the husband to perform most maternal activities." It further suggests that "a child whose father performs the mothering functions both tangibly and emotionally while the mother is preoccupied with her career can easily gain a distorted image of masculinity and femininity" (Bell and Vogel, 1968, p. 32, 586).

Nor was it thought that fathers should be directly involved in the birth of their children. An obstetrician asserted in 1964 that whether he is "short, thin or fat, of any race, color, or creed," an expectant father "tends to pace, chain smoke, and talk to himself out loud." The doctor went on to observe that "a prospective father behind the wheel is more dangerous than a drunk on the Fourth of July." A guide for the expectant father of the same era suggested that all fathers-to-be learn from the model of an accountant who passed the time in the hospital waiting room by "determining how much tax money would be saved over the years as a result of the new dependency claim that was on the way" (in Gerzon, 1982, p. 203).

Some Implications for the Present

There is no question that the father-breadwinner model established in the nineteenth and early twentieth centuries remains culturally dominant today, both in fathers' actual behavior and its media representation. It is important to recognize that this model has a specific history. To become dominant, it had to supplant an earlier view in which fathers had the ultimate responsibility for, and influence on, their children. The conception of father as moral overseer was promulgated and reinforced by the paramount colonial social institution, the church. It is perhaps difficult for us today to appreciate the power and depth of this past cultural mentality in which fathers' role was considered so important.

As the influence of the church declined, the changing nature and increasing importance of the economy promoted a new model of father as distant breadwinner, paired with a new view of mother's role. Even as this model arose and became dominant, some criticized it or promoted other views. At the turn of the century, their objections appeared to focus at least as much on mothers' influence being too strong as fathers' being too weak. In the 1950s and 1960s, such reservations attained a new level of cultural influence. In particular, academic psychology absorbed and systematized these criticisms in its sex role theory, and then used its own growing influence to disseminate it throughout the culture. Thus the sex role model of fatherhood became a strong though still secondary counterpoint to the dominant father-breadwinner image.

Today, the critique of the distant father-breadwinner is intensifying further. A new image, summed up in the term "the new father," is clearly on the rise in print and broadcast media. This new father differs from older images of involved fatherhood in several key respects: he is present at the birth; he is involved with his children as infants, not just when they are older; he participates in the actual day-to-day work of child care, and not just play; he is involved with his daughters as much as his sons.

The new father represents the further extension of the sex role model and other counter-images challenging the dominant breadwinner model over the last century. Several other phenomena parallel or contribute to the new father image. The increase in postwar wives' employment, and the postwar feminism associated with it, have been its greatest impetus. These led mothers to demand that fathers become more involved. Further, feminist scholars generated new developmental theories of gender (Chodorow, 1978; Dinnerstein, 1976) which support a much broader father role than the older sex-role-model theory. Some feminist analyses imply or directly hold that men are impoverished by not being more active as fathers. This argument has been adopted and highly elaborated as one of the central ideas of the contemporary men's movement, and diffused through the culture more broadly.

It is important to recognize that alongside the "new father," the older alternatives to the father-breadwinner model still have considerable cultural force. The theory of paternal sex role modeling remains the most widely expressed formal argument (that is, the one expressed in most college courses, newspaper articles, popular psychology literature) for greater father involvement. (In recent years, I have been asked repeatedly to testify in support of the Boy Scouts' argument to exclude women as scoutmasters because "boys need male models.")

The moral overseer model of fatherhood also continues to influence a large and probably growing number of fathers today. Its earlier decline coincided with the waning of organized religion as a paramount social institution. One component of the fundamentalist Christian resurgence of recent decades is a revival of Christian fatherhood as an ideal. Today's Christian-father movement is accompanied by its own literature of books (see Benson, 1977; MacDonald, 1977) and periodicals.[3]

The fathers' rights movement is also a significant force on the cultural scene. This movement reflects a complex amalgam of fathers driven by antifeminist backlash (echoing the critics of maternal influence earlier in this century) with other fathers motivated by an actual denial of their genuine desire to remain involved as fathers after divorce. The "new father" coexists somewhat uneasily with this as well as the other profathering ideologies having an impact today. Seifert (1974), for example, describes the problems for men working in child-care centers when some staff and parents want greater male involvement to help break down traditional sex roles, but others want it to help reinforce them.

The discrepancy between the actual pace of change in men and the profusion of profathering imagery has led some to dismiss the image of the new, involved father as only media "hype." While this element clearly exists, it is also important to recognize that the new father is not *all* hype. This image, like the dominant images of earlier periods, is ultimately rooted in structural forces and structural change. Wives *are* more often employed, and do less in the family when they are; men *are* spending more time in the family, both absolutely and relative to women (husbands' proportion of the total housework and child care rose from 20% to 30% between 1965 and 1981; see Pleck, 1985b). If the distant father-breadwinner has a social-structural base, so too does the new father.

The historical legacy of American culture's images of fatherhood includes both the distant father-breadwinner model and a variety of alternatives to it. While the father-breadwinner model is under increasing attack, it is still unquestionably dominant. The tensions among these competing models will continue to be expressed in both American social institutions and in the lives of American fathers. In the future, tension between the breadwinner model and more involved conceptions of fatherhood will continue, if not increase.

Such tensions are reflected directly in the current debate about improving parental leave policies in the workplace, including broadening them to apply to fathers (Pleck, 1986). Although the actual cost of offering paternity leave is minimal compared to the cost of parental leave for mothers (simply because fathers use it much less), paternity leave receives a highly disproportionate share of attention as a frivolous and exorbitantly expensive consequence of gender-neutral parental leave policies. (A 1986 national conference on work and family issues [co-sponsored by the U.S. Department of Labor, the AFL-CIO, and the National Association of Manufacturers] at which I was scheduled to speak on paternity leave had to be canceled because labor contract negotiations between the conference vendor and one of its unions had come to an impasse over the issue of paternity leave, and the union threatened to picket the conference!) Paternity leave, and other policies to reduce work-family conflict for fathers, evoke negative responses; not so much because of their actual cost, but because they so directly challenge the father-breadwinner model.

NOTES

1. My analysis is especially indebted to Demos (1982) and Rotundo (1985). Both of these rely heavily on Rotundo (1982).

2. There was, of course, considerable diversity in the ways in which industrialization affected patterns of work and family life in the United States and Europe, and diversity in work and family patterns both before and after whatever benchmarks are used to date industrialization (Pleck, 1976).

3. For example, *For Dads Only: A News and Creative Ideas Resource for Christian Dads and Husbands,* PO Box 340, Julian, CA 92036.

REFERENCES

Bach, G. (1946). Father-fantasies and father typing in father-separated children. *Child Development, 17,* 63-80.

Bell, N., & Vogel, E. (Eds.). (1968). *A modern introduction to the family* (rev. ed.). New York: Free Press.

Benson, D. (1977). *The total man.* Wheaton, IL: Tyndale House.

Bernard, J. (1981). The good-provider role: Its rise and fall. *American Psychologist, 36,* 1-12.

Biller, H., (1971). *Father, child, and sex role.* Lexington, MA: Heath.

Bloom-Feshbach, J. (1981). Historical perceptions of the father's role. In M. E. Lamb (Ed.), *The role of the father in child development* (2nd Ed., pp. 71-112). New York: Wiley-Interscience.

Chodorow, N. (1978). *The reproduction of mothering: Psychoanalysis and the sociology of gender.* Berkeley: University of California Press.

Day, C. (1935). *Life with father.* New York: Knopf.

Degler, C. (1980). *At odds: Women and the family in America from the Revolution to the present.* New York: Oxford University Press.

Demos, J. (1982). The changing faces of fatherhood: A new exploration in American family history. In S. Cath, A. Gurwitt & J. Ross (Eds.), *Father and child: Developmental and clinical perspectives* (pp. 425-450). Boston: Little, Brown.

Dinnerstein, D. (1976). *The mermaid and the minotaur: Sexual arrangements and the human malaise.* New York: Harper & Row.

Ehrenreich, B., & English, D. (1979). *For her own good: 150 years of the experts' advice to women.* Garden City, NY: Anchor/Doubleday.

Ewen, S. (1976). *Captains of consciousness: Advertising and the social roots of the consumer culture.* New York: McGraw-Hill.

Friedan, B. (1963). *The feminine mystique.* New York: Norton (pagination in citations from 1970 Dell paperback edition).

Gerzon, M. (1982). *A choice of heroes.* Boston: Houghton Mifflin.

Grossberg, M. (1983). Who gets the child? Custody, guardianship, and the rise of judical patriarchy in nineteenth-century America. *Feminist Studies, 9,* 235-260.

Kimmel, M. (1986). *From separate spheres to sexual equity: Men's responses to feminism at the turn of the century.* Working paper #2, Rutgers University, Department of Sociology.

Levy, D. (1943). *Maternal overprotection.* New York: Norton.

Lynd, R., & Lynd, H. M. (1956). *Middletown: A study in modern American culture.* New York: Harcourt, Brace. (Original work published 1929)

MacDonald, G. (1977). *The effective father.* Wheaton, IL: Tyndale House.

O'Neill, W. (1967). *Divorce in the progressive era.* New Haven, CT: Yale University Press.

Pleck, E. (1976). Two worlds in one: Work and family. *Journal of Social History, 10,* 178-195.

Pleck, J. (1981). *The myth of masculinity.* Cambridge: MIT Press.

Pleck, J. (1983). The theory of male sex role identity: Its rise and fall, 1936-present. In M. Lewin (Ed.), *In the shadow of the past: Psychology views the sex* (pp. 205-225). New York: Columbia University Press.

Pleck, J. (1985a). *Working wives, working husbands.* Newbury Park, CA: Sage.

Pleck, J. (1985b). American fatherhood: A historical perspective. *American Behavioral Scientist, 29*(1), 7-23.

Pleck, J. (1986). Employment and fatherhood: Issues and innovative policies. In M. E.

Lamb (Ed.), *The father's role: Applied perspectives* (pp. 385-412). Boston: Little, Brown.

Rotundo, A. (1982). *Manhood in America: The northern middle class, 1770-1920* (Doctoral dissertation, Brandeis University). (University Microfilms No. 82-20,111).

Sebald, H. (1976). *Momism: The silent disease of America.* Chicago: Nelson-Hall.

Seifert, K. (1974). Some problems of men in child care center work. In J. Pleck & J. Sawyer (Eds.), *Men and masculinity* (pp. 69-73). Englewood Cliffs, NJ: Prentice-Hall.

Strecker, E. (1946). *Their mothers' sons.* Philadelphia: Lippincott.

Suggs, R. (1978). *Motherteacher: The feminization of American education.* Charlottesville: University of Virginia Press.

Wylie, P. (1942). *A generation of vipers.* New York: Rinehart.

7

Fathers in Transition

Dual-Career Fathers
Participating in Child Care

TERESA L. JUMP
LINDA HAAS

The traditional image of fatherhood is changing. Beyond his biological contribution, the traditional perspective of the father's role has been limited to protecting and providing for his family (Giveans & Robinson, 1985; Lutwin & Siperstein, 1985). In the home, fathers were often respected but feared and remained invisible, distant, and aloof in their parenting roles (Giveans & Robinson, 1985; Margolis, 1984).

In the last decade, the arenas of social science, education, law, medicine, and the media have rediscovered and embraced the expanding role of the modern father (Langway, Whitman, Zabarsky, & Cary, 1981). A new model of fatherhood has emerged that calls for fathers to join with mothers as equal partners in child care (Fein, 1978). According to Backett (1982, p. 104), this means that both fathers and mothers cater to the child's needs, are available to him or her where possible, and their care is viewed as equivalent—it means that both parents should have equal choices about their freedom to carry out their own individual pursuits with the overall *feeling* of responsibility for the organization of child care being shared between them.

Such a model is regarded as having benefits for women, men, and

AUTHORS' NOTE: This is a revised version of a paper presented at the annual meeting of the National Council on Family Relations, held in San Francisco, October 17-20, 1984. The authors wish to thank Ain Haas, David Clark, and anonymous reviewers for helpful comments.

children. As summarized by Ehrensaft (1983), the benefits for the mother include increased opportunity to seek fulfillment in occupational pursuits and a closer relationship with her husband as they deal jointly with child-care problems. For the father, the benefits include enhanced opportunities to enjoy the development of the child, to experience genuine human interaction, often lacking in the alienating workplace, and to develop the nurturant side of his personality. For children, the benefits include a "richer, more complex emotional milieu," new role models, and freedom from an overinvolved parent. Some experts assert, based on research findings, that fathers can establish as close and intimate bonds with their children as mothers can, and that they can be as competent as mothers are at providing nurturance, affection, and stimulation (see, Gilbert, 1985; Giveans & Robinson, 1985; Kotelchuck, 1976; Lamb, 1981; Parke & Tinsley, 1981; Pleck, 1981; Sawin & Parke, 1979).

Although some studies indicate an increased acceptance of men's participation in child-care tasks (Gilbert, 1985; Haas, 1982; Lein, 1978; Mason & Arber, 1976; Scanzoni, 1978), others emphasize how far we remain from an equitable division of parenting (Gilbert, 1985; Szinovacz, 1984). Even when they "help out" with child care, research suggests that "fathers do what they like with children, while mothers do what has to be done with them" (Bird, 1979). Women usually spend time on physical care, such as cooking, feeding, and bathing, while men's time more often involves play and discipline (Belsky, 1980; Berk, 1979; Clark-Stewart, 1980; Gecas, 1976; Jones, 1985; Kamerman, 1980; Katsh, 1981 Lamb, 1980; Robinson, 1977).

It is within the setting of the dual-career family that equal participation of fathers in child care would seem likely to first appear. Well-educated, middle-class men have been found to have less stereotypical sex-role attitudes than do lower-class, less-educated males (Bloom-Feshbach, 1981; Farkas, 1976; Lamb, 1982; Mason & Arber, 1976; Radin & Goldsmith, 1983). A wife's income, education, and occupational status have been found to be associated with greater paternal involvement (Haas, 1980; Hoffman, 1977; Hood, 1983; Ybarra, 1982). Wives in dual-career families also seem to be willing to relinquish primary responsibility for child rearing and to request greater assistance from their husbands. Research does suggest that fathers in dual-career families tend to assist more in child care than do other fathers (Bird, 1979; Eversoll, 1979; Hill & Stafford, 1980; Hood, 1983; Russell, 1982; Walker & Wallston, 1986), but fall short of egalitarian parenting.

This chapter describes the findings from a study of the extent of participation of fathers in a dual-career setting. Also described are factors associated with fathers in this setting experiencing greater satisfaction with parenting and encountering fewer problems.

Methodology

A snowball sampling technique was employed to select 50 dual-career couples in Indianapolis who had at least one child 5 years of age or younger in 1983. Names of potential respondents for the study were obtained through professional associations, employers, women's groups, day-care centers, colleagues, and friends. In all, 86 couples were located, but 36 of these refused to participate in the study because of severe time constraints. A strict career definition was applied to the sample: a job that is highly salient personally, has a developmental sequence, and requires a high degree of commitment (Rapoport & Rapoport, 1971). The sample of 50 dual-career couples was composed of highly visible professional leaders and role models in the city.

In terms of demographic characteristics of the sample, the fathers had extremely high educational levels, with 40% holding undergraduate degrees, 40% master's degrees, and 20% doctorate degrees. Representing a wide range of professional careers, the fathers worked in the following fields: business management (24%), medicine (22%), law (18%), art and music (10%), accounting (6%), engineering (6%), dentistry (4%), with the rest employed in architecture, education, social work, government administration, and journalism. The income range for the fathers varied between $19,000 and $175,000, with the average being $49,000. All but three were white, despite an aggressive attempt to recruit minority couples for the study. Ages ranged from 29 to 43 years old.

The average number of children in the families was two, although one couple had five children. Ages spanned 20 weeks to 15 years, with only those 5 years old or younger being focused on in the study.

Data Collection Methods

Fathers and mothers participated in separate 90-minute semistructured interviews in their homes. The interview verified the dual-career couple's authenticity and family status and administered a 150-item questionnaire. The survey explored an individual's attitudes toward child care, perceptions of the division of labor regarding housework and children, feelings about the extent of support they had for a dual-career life-style, and background socialization variables. Instructions were also given for an open-ended time/task log that individuals were to complete during a week, recording actual participation in child care. Follow-up intensive interviews were conducted with each partner among five couples who, from time-log data, appeared to have a more egalitarian approach to the sharing of child rearing. These two-hour interviews probed the transition from a traditional to a nontraditional family life-style, and views on parenting, child care, and careers.[1]

Analysis Strategy

To find significant differences between responses of fathers and mothers, t-tests were employed; Pearson product moment correlation coefficients were used to discover noteworthy associations between fathers' satisfaction and problems and variables thought to be related to these. Two-tailed tests were applied because plausible arguments for either direction could be made in most cases.[2]

Findings

Participation in Child Care by Fathers in Dual-Career Families

Time analysis. The fathers in the study were active participants in child care, spending between 8 and 49 hours in child care and averaging 27 hours per week. Past studies of father-participation in child care reported traditional fathers spending as few as 6 hours a week (Gilbert, 1985), while fathers in dual-career families spent 20 hours in child care (Haas, 1982), and role-sharing fathers 10.4 hours (Haas, 1980). Mothers in the study averaged 42 hours a week in child care, with their hours ranging from 20 to 84. The difference for fathers and mothers was statistically significant ($T = 7.53$, $p \leq .001$). Similar to other findings, fathers accounted for 38% care done by the couples (Defrain, 1979; Haas, 1982; Jones, 1985).

Patterns of sharing. From the time-analysis data, three categories of child-care sharing were distinguished: *egalitarian*—father/mother participation 40-60%; *transitional*—father participation 20-39%/mother participation 61-80%; and *traditional*-father participation 0-19%/mother participation 81-100%. Time analysis revealed the sample was composed of 27 egalitarian couples (54%), 20 transitional couples (40%), and 3 traditional couples (6%). A higher percentage of fathers in this study appeared to be more equitable partners in child care than were fathers in previous studies (Gilbert, 1985; Haas, 1982).

Task analysis. Fathers spent significantly less time than mothers did in all major dimensions of child care: physical caregiving (that is, routine tasks related to a child's physical care—diapering, bathing, feeding, and so on); social development (social interaction, entertaining, talking, disciplining); cognitive development (tasks related to nurturing a child's intellectual growth—reading, counting, playing games); affective needs (meeting child's emotional needs, comforting, nurturing); and miscellaneous needs (arranging child care, shopping, transportation). (See Table 7.1)

Although mothers had the primary responsibility for child care in each major dimension, further time-log analysis showed many fathers to be equally involved in specific child-care tasks within each dimension. (See Table 7.2)

Tasks with equal father participation[3] included not only traditional father-oriented activities (for example, discipline and decision making), but also ones that are more nontraditional for men (such as assisting with toileting, teaching developmental concepts, and general child supervision).

Fathers' most time-consuming tasks were related to physical caregiving (58%), cognitive development (15%), social development (14%), miscellaneous needs (10%), and affective needs (3%).[4] These percentages were very similar to those for mothers. Fathers' and mothers' most time-consuming activities were identical within the dimensions of cognitive, social, affective, and miscellaneous needs; these included playing, social interaction, holding, and providing transportation (see Table 7.2). Only in the area of physical caregiving were there some differences in parenting styles. General supervision was a much more time-consuming activity for fathers than it was for mothers, while food preparation demanded the most time from mothers. Both parents, however, devoted considerable time to feeding and developing their children's motor skills.

Fathers spent relatively less time than mothers did at indirect (nonpersonalized) child care, compared to direct (personal) child care. Indirect child care included activities such as cleaning up after, food preparation, laundry, making child-care arrangements, sewing, shopping, decision making, and cleaning the child's room. Only 13% of the time fathers spent in child care was taken up with these types of tasks, compared to 21% for mothers. From another perspective, fathers provided 40% of the total personal child-care time in the family, while

TABLE 7.1

Time Analysis of Dual-Career Parental Roles

Child-Care Dimensions	Percentage Fathers Did	Time (in hours) During One Week		
		Mothers	Fathers	Both Parents
Physical needs	38	24.77	15.35	40.12
Social needs	40	5.65	3.76	9.41
Cognitive needs	43	5.33	4.02	9.35
Affective needs	38	1.35	.81	2.16
Miscellaneous needs	34	5.28	2.74	8.02
Total	38	42.38	26.68	69.06

NOTE: All differences between mothers and fathers were statistically significant, according to two-tailed t-tests, at the .05 level of probability.

they were responsible for 28% of the nonpersonal time.

Perceptions of paternal involvement. Interview data allowed a comparison between fathers' self-reports and the time-budget findings. Fathers were fairly accurate at predicting their participation in child care, relative to that of their wives, for only one of the five dimensions of child care: cognitive development. They overestimated their share of time spent in social development and affective needs, and underestimated their time in providing physical care. Fathers' tendency to downplay their participation in physical caregiving suggests that some fathers might not fully recognize and feel comfortable in their expanding nontraditional roles.

In summary: (a) The majority of fathers in the study were active participants in child care; (b) over half of the couples shared child care in an egalitarian-type marriage; (c) fathers spent significantly less time in overall child care than did their wives; (d) fathers actively participated in nontraditional caregiving tasks (such as physical care); (e) the children's physical care was the most time-consuming child-care dimension for fathers; (f) fathers were more likely to provide child care that involved personal contact with children; (g) there were often discrepancies between the perceptions of fathers in dual-career families and actual practices in their paternal roles.

**Dual-Career Fathers'
Satisfaction with Parenting**

Of interest in the study were fathers' *feelings* about their participation in parenting. Nearly all fathers (94%) reported being quite satisfied with their caregiving responsibilities. Over one-third (35%) of the fathers said

TABLE 7.2
Task Analysis of Dual-Career Parental Roles

| | Time (in minutes) During One Week | | |
Tasks	Fathers' Mean	Mothers' Mean	t-Value
Physical needs			
bathing	44.52	76.58	−3.93*
cleaning up after	46.86	116.10	−4.03*
dressing	41.60	93.18	−5.56*
diapering	15.14	37.34	−3.86*
helping with toileting	10.66	10.38	0.96
feeding	202.00	341.76	−4.33*
food preparation	66.36	197.58	−7.18*
putting to bed	66.50	118.38	−2.49*
health needs	12.74	24.44	−2.10*
laundry	17.56	49.60	−2.19*
motor development	185.42	243.28	−2.07*
going to the doctor	3.50	13.12	−2.17*
general supervision	208.38	164.66	1.22
Affective needs			
relating to feelings	.04	2.60	−2.32*
comforting	9.42	18.38	−2.49*
holding	25.44	36.66	−2.09*
nurturing	13.10	21.76	−2.04*
relating to others	0	.30	−1.00
other affection activities	.60	1.50	−1.00
Cognitive needs			
reading	39.92	50.14	−2.24*
counting	2.14	.50	0.99

(continued)

they were dissatisfied with the *time* they spent in child care. Most fathers felt they didn't spend enough time with their children. Mothers' responses were similar to fathers in the above items. Although some fathers wished they spent more time with their young children, the majority felt they spent sufficient time in child care.

When fathers were asked which caregiving tasks they liked, the most frequently given answers were in the dimension of social development. Affection-related activities were mentioned rarely as a favorite activity. The pattern was different for mothers, whose favorite activities were in the cognitive development dimension, while their least favorite involved physical caregiving. When asked which specific child-care tasks they did not like, only one-third of fathers could name a least favored task. Over half of the mothers could name responsibilities they disliked (for exam-

TABLE 7.2   Continued

Tasks	Time (in minutes) During One Week		
	Fathers' Mean	Mothers' Mean	t-Value
giving information	8.98	5.66	0.86
teaching	3.68	5.16	−0.67
playing	154.10	210.82	−2.33*
rhymes/songs	1.76	13.80	−3.65
learning activities (i.e., puzzles, games, computer)	22.06	16.76	0.67
other cognitive activities (i.e., educational TV—Sesame Street, Mr. Rogers, etc.)	8.34	6.82	0.47
Social needs			
talking	43.14	91.82	−3.17*
discipline	13.46	14.98	−0.38
moral development	.24	.94	−1.73
social interaction (i.e., parties, leisures, outings, entertainment, visits)	140.48	183.50	−1.33
other social needs (i.e., TV, movies, videogames)	28.16	47.90	−2.05*
Miscellaneous needs			
child-care arrangements	6.54	24.32	−3.19*
mending	3.90	2.74	0.28
shopping	57.70	127.72	−3.68*
spiritual activities	13.80	20.38	−1.69
transportation	79.78	137.96	−3.72*
decision making	.70	2.84	−1.05
cleaning child's room	2.20	1.00	1.00

*$p < .05$.

ple, physical care). Negative responses from fathers focused in physical caregiving also.

In summary: (a) The majority of fathers in the study were satisfied both with the time they spent in child care and with the responsibilities they assumed in child care; (b) many fathers wished they could spend even more time with their children; (c) fathers had different likes and dislikes than mothers had among child-care tasks, with fathers disliking fewer tasks.

Fathers' Perceptions of Problems

Life-style demand and coping strategies. One disadvantage of the dual-career life-style is that it can be very demanding. Almost half (46%) of the fathers felt their life-style was very demanding (5 on a 1-5 scale), while the rest rated their life-style a 4. Mothers found it even more demanding ($\overline{X} = 4.7$) than their husbands did ($\overline{X} = 4.3$), perhaps because they assumed primary responsibility for child care. Overall, husbands in dual-career families ($\overline{X} = 3.5$) related a mostly positive coping ability for their demanding life-styles (wives $\overline{X} = 4.2$). Compared to their wives (22%), though, only a small percentage of husbands (2%) reported feeling they were coping very well (5-high in a 1-5 scale). Fathers described using the following coping techniques (in descending order of use): lowering expectations, sharing child care and household tasks, making time for oneself, using informal support networks, hiring outside help, organization and planning, family conferences, scheduling family leisure/recreation activities, maintaining a sense of humor, and eating out often.

Life-style problems. Discomfort with assuming a nontraditional social role was a problem for many fathers in the study. When asked if it bothered them to participate in child-care tasks, which are defined traditionally as inappropriate for men, half (48%) said it was difficult for them. (A similar percentage of mothers said it was difficult for them to relinquish their traditional authority over child rearing.)

When asked if they had disagreements with their spouses about child-care responsibilities, two-thirds of the fathers said no, one-fifth (22%) reported occasional disagreements, and 12%, frequent disagreements. (Slightly more mothers reported disagreements, but the difference was not statistically significant.) When asked what the disagreements were about, one-third of fathers (and mothers) said they concerned the husband's not doing his fair share. Other problems mentioned were scheduling conflicts, different priorities, and the wife being unwilling to relinquish her traditional authority for child care. Only 16% of the fathers reported having sought counseling for marital or parenting problems.

In summary: (a) Fathers in the study felt their life-style to be a demanding one; (b) overall, husbands were coping positively with the demands of their life-styles, although only a few felt they were coping very well; (c) fathers employed a variety of coping strategies to manage their life-styles, (d) fathers were bothered by taking on nontraditional role responsibilities; and (e) sharing child care was not a frequent cause of marital disagreements or reason to seek counseling.

Determinants of Satisfaction and Problems Associated with Parenting

What factors influence fathers' experience with parenting in dual-career families? Several categories were examined, including the amount of fathers' participation in child care; aspects of the fathers' and mothers' work and career orientations; husbands' attitudes toward wives working; extent of social support fathers received for pursuing their life-styles; and fathers' childhood socialization.

Fathers' participation in child care. Are those fathers who come closest to the new ideal of the active father more satisfied with the time and share of tasks they do, as well as with the life-style, than are those fathers who participate less in child rearing?

To investigate the effects of paternal involvement on levels of satisfaction and problems, the absolute and relative amounts of time fathers spent in overall child care, and within dimensions of child care, were correlated with the various measures of satisfaction and problems. Only one of the possible 24 relationships between time variables and satisfaction variables was found to be statistically significant. Fathers who spent more time in social development tasks, relative to their wives, reported being more satisfied with the time they spent on child care (r = .25). More active fathers did not appear to experience different levels of satisfaction with parenting than did less active fathers.

Fathers who spent more time in overall child care, and within the physical caregiving dimension, were significantly more likely to feel bothered by taking on a nontraditional parenting role (r = .34 and r = .30, respectively). However, other dimensions were not related significantly to feeling bothered, perhaps because they can be more easily regarded as men's traditional parenting role. Fathers who spent relatively more time with their children were much less likely to report that they and their wives had sought counseling (r = .24). Fathers who spent relatively more time on social development tasks also reported having fewer disagreements and attending counseling less often (r = .27 and r = .33, respectively), while those who spent more time on social development reported higher coping levels (r = .36). Fathers who spent relatively more time at miscellaneous tasks (chauffeuring, arranging child care, and so on) were also less likely to seek counseling (r = .28). This suggests that spending more time at child care yields benefits to fathers in dual-career marriages in terms of improving relationships with their wives.

Fathers' work. Several aspects of mens' careers and orientation to work were examined for their possible effects on experiences with parenting. These included career demands and job flexibility and men's experience of job fulfillment, career satisfaction, and career commitment.

Fathers' jobs were on the whole rather demanding ($\overline{X}$ = 3.96 on a 1-5 scale), and characterized by limited flexibility ($\overline{X}$ = 3.52). Fathers with less demanding careers reported significantly more satisfaction with time spent in child care (r = .26). The demanding nature of the job, however, had no effect on fathers' satisfaction with their responsibility for child care. Job flexibility was not associated significantly with either measure of fathers' satisfaction with parenting. Fathers with less demanding careers reported the dual-career life-style to be less demanding (r = .24). Fathers whose jobs were more flexible also reported higher coping levels (r = .26). The demanding and inflexible nature of the father's job was not found to be associated significantly with feeling bothered by assuming a nontraditional role, experience of marital disagreements, or seeking counseling.

Overall, fathers in the study were fulfilled in their jobs ($\overline{X}$ = 3.94 out of 5), quite committed to their careers ($\overline{X}$ = 4.18), and generally satisfied with the careers they had chosen ($\overline{X}$ = 4.02). Fathers whose jobs were less fulfilling reported significantly higher levels of satisfaction with the time they spent in child care (r = .26), but not greater satisfaction with their responsibilities in child care. Career satisfaction and career commitment had no significant associations with satisfaction variables. Fathers with higher levels of career satisfaction and career commitment reported the dual-career life-style to be significantly more demanding (r = .24 and r = .26, respectively). Having a satisfying career was also related to seeking marriage counseling (r = .28). Thus study findings give some support to the idea that a demanding career is difficult to manage when both parents have careers.

Husband's attitude toward wife's career. Husbands' commitment to their wives' careers was found to be very high, with a mean of 4.42, and did not have a significant effect on their satisfaction with child care or with the time they spent in caregiving. Only one significant association was found between husbands' attitude toward their wives' careers and problem variables; husbands who were positive about their wives' careers were strongly likely to report that the dual-career life-style was demanding (r = .56).

Wife's career. There was only one significant relationship found for a wife's variables (that is, career satisfaction, career fulfillment, and career commitment) and a husband's satisfaction and problems with parenting. Husbands who had wives with high career commitments were less likely to report that the couple had sought counseling (r = .29). This is the opposite of what was found for husbands' career commitments; when a husband's career commitment was high, the couple was more likely to seek counseling.

Extent of support received. The majority (58%) of fathers said community services were deficient. Day care was, by far, the service described as the most deficient, and the one fathers were likely to say they needed most. (Similar responses were given by mothers.) Fathers who reported community services as being plentiful or adequate reported that they were coping with the dual-career life-style better (r =

.37). No other measures of problems or satisfaction with dual-career parenting were related to this aspect of social support.

Most fathers (90%) said they were satisfied with their particular day-care arrangements (about the same percentage as mothers). However, almost one-third could still name changes they would like to see in their child-care situation. Most wished their arrangement would be "higher quality." However, dissatisfaction with one's own day-care situation was not found to be related significantly to any of the satisfaction or problem measures.

Only 10% of fathers (and mothers) reported that their workplaces offered support services for dual-career families. Fathers whose workplaces did offer support services (such as flextime, special counseling, or on-site day care) reported significantly higher levels of satisfaction with time spent in child care (r = .36). No other measures of satisfaction or problems were associated with having support from one's workplace.

Fathers were asked if other organizations they belonged to, such as professional associations, unions, churches, or community organizations, offered support services for dual-career families. Most fathers (83%) could not name any available support service. Three-fourths of the fathers also said their employers offered no support services for working families. Only a few workplaces offered counseling, on-site day care, or alternative schedules. Fathers who did report receiving support from other organizations held higher levels of satisfaction with the time they spent in child care (r = .28). No other measures of satisfaction or problems were related to this support variable.

When asked to gauge the level of emotional support they received from their own parents, fathers reported a mean of 3.02 (out of 5; wives $\overline{X}$ = 3.57). The more support from parents, the less likely husbands were to report marital disagreements (r = .26). Otherwise, satisfaction levels and experience of problems were not affected by parental support levels.

Few relationships between social support variables and measures of satisfaction and experiencing of problems were found. Support from institutions and individuals does not seem to be an important prerequisite of successful fathering in a dual-career family.

Childhood socialization. Most of the men in the study perceived their upbringing to be fairly traditional (1.9 on a scale where 5 was egalitarian). However, this measure of parental socialization did not have any significant association with any of the satisfaction or problem measures. The parents of the men in the study were also very traditional regarding attitudes toward sex roles, with most of their mothers (91%) and fathers (80%) being described as holding traditional sex-role attitudes. Men whose mothers had held egalitarian sex-role attitudes found the dual-career life-style less demanding and were bothered less by assuming a nontraditional family role (r = .23, r = .27, respectively). Men whose fathers were more egalitarian also felt less bothered about assuming a nontraditional family role (r = .38).

For 90% of the men in the study, their mothers had been the ones entirely responsible for child care when they were growing up. However, men whose fathers had been more involved in child care were found to be significantly less bothered about assuming an active parenting role than were men whose own fathers had not participated in child care (r = -.32). No other measure of satisfaction or problems were significantly related to fathers' participation in child care.

Another survey item examined the family/work orientation of the parents of the dual-career fathers. The majority reported their mothers to be very family-oriented. As traditional, the previous generation of fathers were perceived to be somewhat more work-oriented than family-oriented (X = 3.7), where five were work-oriented and one was family-oriented. Having a family-oriented father was significantly related to the respondent's feeling that the life-style was not demanding (r = .39). Other measures of satisfaction and problems were not affected.

In summary: (a) Overall, father participation in child care was not associated with satisfaction levels in parenting, but did appear to improve marital relationships; (b) fathers' work demands and flexibility were not found to be related to frequency of marital disagreements, marital counseling, or feeling bothered by assuming nontraditional roles; (c) fathers with high levels of career satisfaction and career commitment felt their life-style to be significantly more demanding, while fathers with less fulfilling jobs were more satisfied with time spent in child care; (d) husbands in the study who were positive about their wives' careers were more likely to feel their life-style was exceptionally demanding; (e) the work variables (career satisfaction, career fulfillment, career commitment) for wives in the study were not generally associated with their husbands' satisfaction or problems in parenting; (f) social support from institutions and individuals didn't appear to be important for successful fathering in a dual-career family; and (g) having parents who had fairly egalitarian attitudes and behaviors seemed to have a moderate effect on fathers experiencing fewer problems with their dual-career life-style.

Summary and Conclusions

The dual-career family life-style challenges the traditional perspective of fatherhood. The father in a dual-career family has a wife who is a co-provider, emancipating him from the strains of total economic responsibility for the family. One of the major sociological consequences of dual-career families is the breaking down of rigid sex roles for males and females. The life-style rewards fathers with opportunities to share work and family roles, and experience a more human, balanced existence.

However, the newly expanded freedoms for such fathers are not totally free from the chains of tradition. "These fathers come to their unique life-style with social scripts which are based on traditional values which associate masculinity with aggressive, instrumental, dominant and powerful behavior" (Gilbert, 1985, p. 9). "Moreover, men typically look to their breadwinning role, and not their roles as husband and father to confirm their manliness" (Brenton, 1966). A wife also helps to validate her husband's sense of masculinity by playing prescribed roles that boost his ego, power, and self-esteem. Thus the dual-career life-style can present a dilemma for a husband with a professional wife who is gaining power and status in the workplace, while demanding her husband's participation in housework and child care. For some men, the clash of their traditional upbringing with the contemporary changes in men's roles may yield distressed "future shock" and marital dissolution. Other husbands in dual-career families will require a revised self-image with new sources for self-esteem and masculinity (Gilbert, 1985).

The findings of this study suggest that fathers in dual-career families are operating in a state of transition—moving from the traditional perspective of fatherhood toward a more egalitarian model. The fathers in the sample remain entrenched in the norms of traditional masculinity in the following ways: (a) They are often bothered by participating in nontraditional child-care tasks (for example, the physical care they provide); (b) they are involved in more personal, direct child-care activities than domestic work associated with child rearing (such as cooking or laundry); (c) they rarely mentioned favorite tasks related to the affective dimension of child care (for example, nurturing and comforting); and (d) they seemed quite satisfied with their paternal roles in child care (both time and tasks).

From a positive view, the findings reveal that the majority of fathers in the study were pursuing an active parenting role. The fathers, overall, provided 38% of the total child care in the family and one-third of the fathers related a desire to spend even more time with their young children. Tasks analysis showed many fathers participating in physical caregiving tasks (such as diapering, feeding, and toileting), which was unheard of in an earlier generation of fathers. Also, the fathers were quite committed to their dual-career life-style and to their wives' careers. They were coping well and had developed individual coping strategies to manage their life-style. Without social supports and role models, they were attempting to make their way (with their spouses) as pioneers in an uncharted frontier.

Society could do much to help the transition of the father in dual-career families toward a more equal parenting role. The structures of the workplace are steeped in the traditional values of masculinity and totally ignore a man's family life (the reverse is true for women). The media give little direction to the "new father" and his concerns for "having it all." The need for quality and dependable day-care services can no longer be viewed as simply a women's issue. Fathers in the study were as concerned as their wives were over the deplorable day-care alternatives for working families. Nonexistent social supports (such as parent education, counseling, paternity leaves) leave the dual-career family alone (without mentors or social scripts) to survive in an unresponsive society. Finally, social science research itself often focuses exclusively on women in dual-career or work/family studies, giving little recognition to the significant role of men in the family.

NOTES

1. This chapter focuses mainly on responses from fathers, but occasionally includes information gathered on mothers for comparison purposes.

2. A conventional level of .05 was used for determining significance, though tests of significance are not entirely appropriate here, since the sample was not a random one. They still serve as a technique for eliminating arbitrariness in the process of deciding which findings were noteworthy and which were not.

3. "About as much time" was defined as fathers spending 40-60% of all time spent by the couple.

4. The time logs may have shown low figures for affection because they may have been ineffective measures of the time parents spent meeting children's needs for affection. Logging all kisses and hugs could become a bit difficult.

REFERENCES

Backett, K. (1982). *Mothers and fathers*. London: Macmillan.

Belsky, J. (1980). A family analysis of parental influence. In F. Pedersen (Ed.), *The father-infant relationship*. New York: Praeger, 1980.

Berk, S. (1979). Husbands at home. In K. Feinstein (Ed.), *Working women and families*. Newbury Park, CA: Sage.

Bird, C. (1979). *The two paycheck marriage*. New York: Rosen & Wade.

Bloom-Feshbach, J. (1981). Historical perspectives on the father's role. In M. Lamb (Ed.), *The role of the father in child development*. New York: John Wiley.

Clark-Stewart, K. (1980). A father's contribution to children's cognitive and social development. In F. Pedersen (Ed.), *The father-infant relationship*. New York: Praeger.

Defrain, J. (1979, April). Androgynous parents tell who they are and what they need. *Family Coordinator, 28*(2), 237-244.

Ehrensaft, D. (1983). When women and men mother. In J. Trebilcot (Ed.), *Mothering: Essays in feminist theory* (pp. 237-244). Totowa, NJ: Rowman & Alanheld.

Eversoll, D. (1979, October). A two generational view of fathering. *Family Coordinator, 28*(4), 503-507.

Farkas, G. (1976). Education, wage rates and the division of labor between husband and wife. *Journal of Marriage and the Family 38,* 473-483.

Fein, R. A. (1978). Research in fathering: Social policy and an emergent perspective. *Journal of Social Issues 34,* 122-135.

Gecas, V. (1976). The socialization and child care roles. In I. Nye (Ed.), *Role structure and analysis of the family.* Newbury Park, CA: Sage.

Gilbert, L. (1985). *Men in dual-career families: Current realities and future prospects.* Hillsdale, NJ: Lawrence Erlbaum.

Giveans, D., & Robinson, M. (1985). Fathers and the preschool-age child. In S. S. Hanson & F. Bozett (Eds.), *Dimensions of fatherhood.* Newbury Park, CA: Sage.

Haas, L. (1980, July). Role-sharing couples: A study of egalitarian marriages. *Family Relations, 29*(3).

Haas, L. (1982). *Dual-earner couples: Sharing housework and child care.* Paper presented at the meeting of the National Women's Studies Association, Arcata, CA.

Hill, R., & Stafford, F. (1980, Spring). Parental care of children. *Journal of Human Resources 15*(2), 219-239.

Hoffman, L. (1977). Changes in family roles. *American Psychologist, 34,* 646-657.

Hood, J. (1983). *Becoming a two-job family.* New York: Praeger.

Jones, L. C. (1985). Father-infant relationships in the first year of life. In S. Hanson & F. Bozett (Ed.), *Dimensions of fatherhood.* Newbury Park, CA: Sage.

Kamerman, S. (1980). *Parenting in an unresponsive society.* New York: Free Press.

Katsh, B. (1981, September). Fathers and infants. *Journal of Family Issues, 2*(3), 275-296.

Kotelchuck, M. (1976). The infant's relationships to the father. In M. Lamb (Ed.), *The role of the father in child development.* New York: John Wiley.

Lamb, M. (Ed.). (1976). *The role of the father in child development.* New York: John Wiley.

Lamb, M. (1980). The development of parent-infant attachments. In F. Pedersen, (Ed.), *The father-infant relationship.* New York: Praeger.

Lamb, M. (1981). The development of father-infant relationships. In M. Lamb (Ed.), *The role of the father in child development* (2nd ed., pp. 459-488). New York: John Wiley.

Lamb, M. (1982). *Nontraditional families: Parenting and child development.* Hillsdale, NJ: Lawrence Erlbaum.

Langway, L., Whitman, L., Zabarsky, M., & Carey, J. (1981, November 30). A new kind of life with father. *Newsweek,* pp. 93-97.

Lein, L., & Working Family Project. (1978). Parenting. In R. Rapoport & R. Rapoport. *Working couples.* New York: Harper/Colophon.

Lutwin, D., & Siperstein, G. (1985). Househusband fathers. In S. Hanson & F. Bozett, *Dimensions of fatherhood.* Newbury Park, CA: Sage.

Margolis, M. (1984). *Mothers and such.* Berkeley: University of California Press.

Mason, C., & Arber, S. (1976). Change in U.S. women's sex-role attitudes 1964-1974. *American Sociological Review, 41,* 573-596.

Parke, R., & Tinsley, B. (1981). The father's role in infancy. In M. Lamb (Ed.), *The role of the father in child development* (2nd ed., pp. 429-451). New York: John Wiley.

Pleck, J. (1981). *The myth of masculinity.* Cambridge: MIT Press.

Pleck, J. (1981). Men's power with women, other men and society: A men's movement analysis. In R. A. Lewis (Ed.), *Men in difficult times: Masculinity today and tomorrow*. Englewood Cliffs, NJ: Prentice-Hall.

Radin, N., & Goldsmith, R. (1983). *Predictors of father involvement in child care*. Paper presented at the meeting of the Society for Research in Child Development, Detroit.

Rapoport, R., & Rapoport, R. (1971). *Dual-career families*. Baltimore: Penguin.

Robinson, J. (1977). *How Americans use time: A social-psychological analysis of everyday behavior*. New York: Praeger.

Russell, G. (1982). Highly participant Australian fathers. *Merrill-Palmer Quarterly, 28*, 137-156.

Sawin, D., & Parke R. (1979, October). Fathers' affectionate stimulation. *Family Coordinator, 28*(4), 509-513.

Scanzoni, J. (1978). *Sex roles, women's work & marital conflict*. Lexington, MA: D. C. Heath.

Szinovacz, M. (1984, Fall-Winter). Changing family roles and interaction. *Marriage & Family Review, 27*, 163-201.

Walker, L., & Wallston, B. (1986). Social adaptation: A review of dual-career family literature. In L. L'Abate (Ed.), *Handbook of family psychology*. Homewood, IL: Dow Jones-Irwin.

Ybarra, L. (1982). When wives work. *Journal of Marriage and the Family, 44*(1), 169-178.

PART III

Men and Women

8

What Do Women Want From Men?

Men's Influence on Women's Work and Family Choices

KATHLEEN GERSON

Women's expectations of men pose important and perplexing questions for social research. What tensions and contradictions develop when hierarchical power relations are intertwined with sexual intimacy and emotional attachment? What strategies of adjustment make it possible for heterosexual commitment to coexist with power inequality? Under what conditions do women resist gender inequality, and what are the consequences for their relationships with men?

This chapter will attempt to clear away some conceptual and empirical misconceptions that shroud these questions by placing women's needs and desires in a larger social context. It will examine the relationship between women's changing social position and changes in their expectations of and relationships with men. I argue that women's views of men and men's influences on women develop out of a rapidly

AUTHOR'S NOTE: I am grateful to Michael Kimmel, Joseph Pleck, and an anonymous reviewer for their helpful responses to an earlier draft.

changing social context that is rearranging the opportunities and constraints faced by both sexes and altering the balance of power between them.

Few theorists have addressed these questions convincingly, often implying that the question cannot be answered, that women's needs are too contradictory or irrational to lend themselves to coherent analysis. Traditional psychoanalytic and functional theories argue that women are biologically predisposed and/or socialized as children to develop nurturant and dependent personalities. Although this view may have been tenable when most men were breadwinners and most women homemakers, current variations in family patterns call into question any analysis that stresses women's uniform commitment to nurturance and dependence on men. Traditional theories have become trapped by an empirical dilemma: If women are both biologically and psychologically predisposed to be dependent and nurturing, why are so many currently rejecting traditional heterosexual commitments in favor of economic, social, and emotional independence from men?

Dramatic changes in gender relations have prompted social theorists to reconsider the question of what women want from men and why. Although most have criticized traditional approaches, they have not been united in their conclusions. Some maintain that women today, like women in the past, remain emotionally dependent on men and continue to develop a set of psychological needs in childhood that lead them to want to be economically and emotionally cared for as adults (Dowling, 1981). Others argue that women are frustrated by men's less developed empathic capacities and turn to childbearing to create the intimacy men cannot provide (Chodorow, 1978). Still others postulate that, were it not for male dominance, women would neither desire nor choose heterosexual alliances; in a world that men do not control, they argue, women would prefer and "naturally" seek sexual, emotional, and economic alliances with other women (Rich, 1980; Rubin, 1975).

Unfortunately, feminist approaches, like traditional ones, have tended to view women as a homogeneous group with shared interests, viewpoints, and desires. Whether they posit biological (Rossi, 1977, 1984), psychodynamic (Chodorow, 1978), or social structural causes (Ehrenreich, 1983; Polatnik, 1973), these analyses have stressed uniformity among men as well, assuming that all, or certainly most, men share an aversion to child-rearing involvement and emotional commitment. In all of these accounts, whether traditional or feminist, women are viewed as pursuing relational intimacy and family security while men remain the reluctantly pursued.

This analysis makes two assumptions that have generally been absent in the debate over what women want from men. First, women's needs and desires are rooted in social-historical contexts that are variable and present different groups of women with different dilemmas and constraints. Second, this structural variation produces not only significant diversity in women's experiences with men but also deep divisions among women in terms of what they want and define as their interests in heterosexual relationships. To understand fully what women want from men and why, we must first ask, Which women? What is their social context?

I will analyze the social context and worldviews of domestic and nondomestic women by comparing full-time homemakers, women committed to childlessness, and women attempting to combine work and motherhood. These comparisons are based on 63 in-depth interviews conducted with working-class and middle-class women who were young adults in the 1970s. These women came of age in a period of rapid social change in gender relations and are thus especially well situated to illuminate how and why women's relationships with men are changing. (See Gerson, 1985, for a full description of the sample and procedure.)

Men's Influences on Women's Work and Family Decisions

Although men can never control women completely, their structural power gives them considerable leverage in heterosexual relationships. But, like women, men are not a homogeneous group and vary in the kinds and degrees of power they possess, their personal orientations toward parenthood and family life, and the kinds of pressures they exert on and supports they offer to the women in their lives. Social structural differences among men produce important differences among women. Because women differ in the kinds of relationships they have (or have not) developed with men and in the kinds of pressures and supports they have experienced from men, they differ in their orientations toward work and motherhood and in their outlooks on heterosexual commitment. Men play a critical role in the development of domestic versus nondomestic orientations among women.

Domestic Women

Virtually all the domestically oriented women interviewed had established long-term, committed heterosexual partnerships that either immediately or gradually assumed the shape of a traditional marriage. In this context, even those who initially held high work ambitions relinquished independent pursuits in favor of preserving relationships with male partners. Over 60% entered adulthood with nondomestic aspirations, only to become traditional over time. How did this process of turning toward domesticity occur?

First, even for those who worked, commitment to a traditional heterosexual partnership meant commitment to the male career. Because the male career took precedence, women in traditional marriages often relinquished advancement opportunities. They perceived their interests as lodged in their husbands' jobs, which consistently paid more, and often feared that work success would threaten personal relationships and undermine security at home. They thus chose interpersonal commitment over work commitment.

Second, domestic women did not experience severe economic squeezes in their households. Their husbands' earnings were judged sufficient to provide a "comfortable" standard of living without a second earner. Even those with histories of economic independence before marriage came to accept economic dependence on a male income as part of the larger bargain struck with husbands.

Third, almost 90% of those oriented toward domesticity encountered blocked mobility at work, where male employers refused to advance female employees. These women were employed in heavily female-dominated occupations and professions, often against their wishes. When faced with the frustrations of ill-rewarded, dead-end work, they turned to domestic pursuits for the autonomy and fulfillment paid work promised but did not deliver.

Finally, domestic women experienced pressures both within and outside their marriages to bear and rear children. Male partners were often eager to become fathers, and children came to be seen as a "natural" expression of the relationship's value. As workplace frustration mounted, children offered an alternative occupation and a means of escape from the paid labor force. Although almost half of this group planned to work part-time or intermittently over the course of their lives, all placed commitments to husbands and children over strong work ties.

In sum, domestically oriented women were exposed to a traditional package of constraints and incentives that has historically promoted female economic and social dependence on men. They were insulated from the structural forces that are leading other women to reject traditional heterosexual partnerships.

Nondomestic Women

Nondomestic women had a contrasting set of experiences with men. They were exposed to a different package of opportunities and constraints that encouraged and sometimes forced them to alter the terms of the bargain women and men have traditionally struck. Two-thirds of this group began adulthood with domestic aspirations, only to find themselves leading very different lives as adults.

Almost two-thirds of this group experienced unstable, often dissatisfying heterosexual partnerships. Some never built a relationship in which marriage was seen as possible or desirable. Others entered traditional marriages but divorced when these relationships became stultifying or conflict-ridden. Still others remained married but experienced periods of discord or separation that transformed their perceptions of their choices and their definitions of marital commitment. This instability had profound effects on women's work and family commitments. The recognition that a man would not always be there to depend on prompted the development of increased self-reliance through work and the postponement (and occasionally rejection) of marriage and motherhood.

For some, the move away from domesticity occurred in the context of a stable marriage, when men's earnings failed to meet the family's perceived needs. An erosion of male economic resources pushed these women into the work force to generate income for the whole family, including the husband. This produced unanticipated consequences, as some developed increased commitment to paid jobs and parallel ambivalence toward parenting and dependence on men. Nondomestic women generally lacked male economic and social support for domesticity. Despite childhood expectations, they were thus forced to reject traditional commitments to men in favor of economic independence and committed work ties.

As they lost traditional sources of male support through marriage, nondomestic women gained new and independent sources of support at work. Three-fourths experienced expanded work opportunities, often because male employers offered unanticipated upward mobility out of female-dominated jobs. This unexpected support from men at work promoted the development of nontraditional orientations toward work, parenthood, and men.

In sum, contrasting experiences with men at home and at work led domestic and nondomestic women to make different life choices and reach different conclusions about the value of heterosexual commitment.

Coping Strategies and
Views of Men

Domestic and nondomestic women faced a set of contradictions and dilemmas in their relationships with men. In the context of rapid social change, all experienced uncertainty about what to expect and demand from male partners. Depending on their orientation toward work and the specific constraints of their situations, they developed different coping strategies and different outlooks on the sexual division of labor.

Domestic Responses

Domestically oriented women found themselves in the unenviable position of defending the legitimacy and viability of the domestic option against the incursions of social change. Behaviorally and ideologically, they supported traditional male privileges and obligations and struggled to keep men economically responsible. They were happy to provide homemaking services in return and, indeed, excluded men from domestic duties, which they wished to preserve for themselves. They thus became unwittingly involved in a defense of a way of life once considered sacrosanct but increasingly devalued and insecure.

Domestic women thus supported and reproduced a strict sexual division of labor in breadwinning and caretaking responsibilities. They carefully subordinated work commitments to family commitments; they looked to husbands to provide the economic support that made their domesticity possible; and, given limited options in the paid labor force, they had little or no desire to trade places with their husbands. A disillusioned ex-schoolteacher and full-time mother of two stated:

> I have met guys who were housepersons, but I can't see any logical reason [for it]. It would turn it all crazy for me to come home around 5:30, and he'd have to have things ready for me. I think if I thought that [bringing in a paycheck] was my role for the rest of my life, I would hate it. I don't want to be him, then I would have to go and fight the world. [I don't want] the pressures he has to bear—supporting a family, a mortgage, putting in all those hours at the office. Ugh!

Domestic women also clung tightly to beliefs about men's, women's, and children's proper places to justify their domestic choice. When asked, for example, how housework should be divided between husbands and wives, 67% said the wife should do most or all of it (compared to only 30% of the nondomestic group). Similarly, when asked about a woman with young children working outside the home, even if her family did not need the money, 53% felt it was "not a good idea" (compared to only 24% of the nondomestic group).

Domestic women argued that biological mothers, but not fathers, are uniquely qualified to rear children and that other arrangements are dangerous and selfish; that men are morally responsible for providing economic support to their families; and that children will suffer if women try to be like men by combining parenthood with committed work. This homemaker and mother of two summed up the group's outlook:

> I have a neighbor with young children who works just because she wants to. I get sort of angry. . . . I think I resent the unfairness to the child. I don't know how to answer the argument that men can have families and work but women can't. Maybe it's not fair, but that's the way it is.

Domestic women developed a set of political responses to the changes taking place around them. They feared the erosion of traditional domestic supports, such as permanent marriage and a male "family wage." They opposed nontraditional family patterns and larger social changes, such as rising rates of divorce and an increased acceptance of sex outside marriage, that make it easier for men to reject breadwinning responsibilities. They believe that reliable men, who are good providers, were preferable to more glamorous but less dependable men. One homemaker explained:

> There's this mystique about the charismatic, not decent, and dependable sort of man. They're movie types. . . . My husband goes to work at eight and comes home at five, and [people] say, "Isn't that boring?" And I say, "No, not at all," because it gives me time to do what I want.

These conservative reactions grew out of a context of insecurity. Faced with the erosion of traditional domestic supports but without access to viable, satisfying work outside the home, domestic women struggled to preserve the "protections" of traditional marriage amid rapid social changes. (Both Ehrenreich, 1983, and Luker, 1984, argue that female antifeminism stems in large part from traditional women's fears that new options for women make it easier for men to shirk their traditional responsibilities.) As marriages around them dissolved and neighbors departed for the workplace, they feared that the loss of a male breadwinner would leave them bereft and force them back into dead-end jobs they disliked. A 27-year-old ex-clerk expressed this fear:

[Having a child] has made me more dependent on my husband. I think he was attracted to me because I was very independent, and now I'm very dependent. I don't know what I would do if things didn't work out between him and me, and we had to separate, and I had to go to work to support my child. I think I'd be going bananas. It's scary to me.

Domestic women also disapproved of nondomestic women, who challenge traditional patterns by "trying to be like men." They argued that career women and working mothers are "selfish, unfulfilled, and very much in competition with men." By "fighting their way up the ladder," work-committed women take on traits that are desirable in men but corrupting to women. As this ex-saleswoman put it:

Women can [take on men's jobs], but it's a blood and guts type of thing. Those who make it are witches because they found out what they had to do to get there. I wouldn't have liked the person I would have become.

Nondomestic Responses

Nondomestic women faced different alternatives and responded with different beliefs and behaviors. They struggled to build a personal life that was satisfying and did not undermine their hard-won work accomplishments. Their responses depended largely on their experiences with men and the pressures and supports men provided. These experiences, in turn, influenced their beliefs about men and the possibilities for gender equality.

First, women with a history of unsatisfactory relationships with men developed a profound distrust toward marriage and concluded that commitment to marriage and motherhood was a risk they could not afford to take. These women viewed heterosexual partnerships as fragile and temporary, they decided that it was no longer possible to create the preconditions deemed necessary for childbearing. A divorced, 35-year-old administrator explained:

I have a tremendous skepticism about men and the permanence of relationships, which makes me want to say, "Don't give up anything, because you're going to lose something that you're going to need later on, because [the man] won't be there."

In the context of such marital fragility, childless women concluded that their careers and would-be offspring would suffer from the lack of male economic, social, and emotional support. Because men could not be relied on to be responsible fathers, motherhood threatened to be an unpleasant and potentially disastrous experience that might lead to work failure, disturbed children, mental breakdown, and financial collapse. A businesswoman in her mid-30s concluded:

[Having children] probably would set my career back irretrievably. . . . The real thing that fits in here is my doubts about men and marriage, because if I had real faith that the marriage would go on, and that we would have two incomes, and be providing for these children, being set back in my career wouldn't be that big a deal.

Childless women found it preferable to preserve their independence than to risk everything without the promise of continued male support. They also took comfort in the freedom from men that childlessness afforded them. A divorced clerical worker explained:

One thing about being divorced is you don't have to answer to anybody for anything. If you're miserable, you're miserable because you yourself are miserable. You aren't miserable because somebody else is making you that way.

Paradoxically, some women in committed relationships concluded that children threatened to undermine not only work commitments but intimate relationships as well. Male partners either did not want or refused to help rear potential offspring, making motherhood appear as risky and dangerous as if no partner were present. Indeed, because children threatened both work achievements and relationships with spouses or lovers, motherhood appeared even more hazardous. A childless librarian married to a fireman feared:

[If we had a child,] I'm sure we'd fight all the time. He's told me over and over again if I had a child, it would be my responsibility; that's one of his threats. I'm not even sure we'd stay married.

Whether their views resulted from the absence of a male partner or the presence of one, childless women did not challenge the traditional sexual division of parenting responsibilities or the beliefs that justify this system. Ironically, they espoused many of the principles held by domestic women. They agreed that children will suffer if their mothers pursue careers and could not envision a strategy that challenged traditional arrangements. An office worker in her late 20s declared:

> I just think [children are] a responsibility, and you have to be willing to devote all your time to them, and if you can't do that, I don't think you should have them. I know that's really old-fashioned, but I tend to believe it.

They also agreed that men can have careers and children but women cannot. A childless interior designer in her mid-30s concluded:

> You could have children and work, but you would also be working on a certain level, wouldn't really be a very senior or involved person. Although men can be presidents of companies and have children, women can't.

And, like their domestic counterparts, both single and married childless women felt men were untrustworthy. However, their concern was not about male economic support but rather the difficulty of getting men to be reliable, involved parents. According to a 29-year-old childless secretary:

> Equal sharing sounds good, but I don't think it would work. I can't see [my husband] fixing supper, and I can't see him staying home and doing the domestic chores. He'd be more likely to stay home all morning and play with the baby rather than wash the clothes and cook dinner.

Childless women's reactions were, however, the opposite of their domestic counterparts. Instead of opting for domesticity, they chose childlessness as the only acceptable response to a set of structural arrangements that relieves men of child-rearing responsibility (beyond breadwinning) and a set of beliefs that pits the interests of the work-committed mother against the interests of the child. Like the childless secretary who announced, "I came into this world alone, and I'm going out alone," they emphasized the value of self-reliance and took pride in their independence from men and children.

Those women who decided to combine work and motherhood found male partners who both wanted children and supported female partners' work careers. These women were thus better positioned to ease the cross-pressures of their situations by bringing men into the job of parenting and demanding greater equality in their private lives. Their husbands' dependence on economic contributions coupled with their husbands' desires to become fathers gave work-committed women the power to change the sexual division of labor at home. This situation also led them to change their beliefs about men's, women's, and children's natural needs and abilities. Work-committed mothers reached different conclusions than both domestic and childless women about the proper way to rear children, the proper place of men in family life, and the possibilities for gender equality in the modern world.

First, work-committed mothers concluded that men, like women, are capable of and morally responsible for the care and nurturance of their offspring. Indeed, these women often judged their spouses to be more nurturant and oriented toward parenthood than they. As one secretary preparing for a child put it:

> Children can really be a job, but I miss the times Steve is with other children, and I watch him. He's really good with them. I think he would be a very, very good [parent]. That would be a major thing for me. I would feel a lot of satisfaction for him to have that satisfaction in that type of relationship.

Second, those who planned to combine work and motherhood viewed male partners as supportive and trustworthy. A professor thus stated:

> [My husband] respects my accomplishments. He wants me to keep doing something I enjoy. He wants me to be fairly independent, and he also wants his own independence ... as long as he can support himself and half a child, or half of whatever goes on between us.

Work-committed women, moreover, were willing to become mothers only in the context of equal parenting. Otherwise, they reasoned, everyone would suffer. They thus engaged in a protracted but at least partially successful struggle to bring their male partners into household work. Although few expected or achieved complete equality, all made participatory fatherhood a precondition to childbearing:

> I want [equal] participation, and without it I don't want children. I want it for the children, for myself. Without two people doing it, I think it would be a burden on one person. It's no longer a positive experience, it has a lot of negative aspects to it. (lawyer in her early 30s)

> I think that eventually it's going to come to the point that if we're willing to have children, we work things out pretty much [equally] between ourselves. And I think he would rather help out than to not have [children] at all. It's a two-way thing. (office manager in her late 20s)

In the context of male pressure and support, work-committed mothers concluded that their children would benefit, not suffer, from a nontraditional arrangement. They rejected ideologies inherited from their mothers, which domestic and childless women still espoused. As one upwardly mobile office worker reasoned:

> I liked my mother being home, but I think it's okay for a mother to work. As long as she doesn't make her children give things up, and I don't think I'd make my children give anything up by me working.

Finally, these changes in their beliefs and in their male partners' behavior gave work-committed mothers a means to escape from the double-binds their childless counterparts experienced. They rejected the belief that women have to choose between work and motherhood in favor of an ideology of gender equality in work and parenthood. An aspiring office worker noted,

> I don't think I'd even consider having [children] if they [affected my work plans]. It's only when I think of them as something that can easily be handled with a little money and [my husband's] help.

Theoretical Implications:
The Changing Structure of Gender Relations

For individual women, the pressures men exerted in their lives seemed private and idiosyncratic. Similarly, the beliefs and expectations these women developed about men—whether traditional or nontraditional—appeared natural and given. At an aggregate level, however, these pressures and responses were neither accidental nor disorderly, but rooted in a set of contrasting structural situations.

Most (white, middle-class) women coming of age 30 years ago could assume they would marry for life; that their husbands would be willing and able to support them economically; that male employers would deny them upward mobility and bar them from well-rewarded work in male-dominated fields; and that men as a group would support female domesticity and aggressively oppose other alternatives. Men provided the economic, social, and ideological support for female domesticity even as they undermined other options for women. Women, and men, face a very different situation today. A changing structure of gender relations has eroded the structural supports for female domesticity and uncontested male dominance, it has also changed the role men play in women's lives.

First, the decline in the stability of heterosexual partnerships—rising rates of divorce, separation, cohabitation, postponed marriage, and even permanent singlehood—means that a growing proportion of women now find themselves outside the structure of permanent, legal marriage (Cherlin, 1981; Glick & Norton, 1977; Norton & Glick, 1976). This change represents a chance for increased independence from male dominance within traditional marriage, but it also means that fewer women can depend on men for lifetime economic and emotional security.

Second, there has been a decline in the ability of a single breadwinner to support an entire family (Blumberg, 1980; Vickery, 1979), forcing even stably married women into the labor force to bring home wages on which the whole family depends. Although a sizable earnings disparity persists between male and female workers, and economic equality between spouses remains a rare occurrence, working wives in dual-earner households bring increased economic and social power to heterosexual relationships (Berk, 1980; Blumstein & Schwartz, 1983; Huber & Spitze, 1983). The rise of the female worker and her independent earnings has done more than provide women with increased leverage in their negotiations with male partners, although this alone is significant; economic independence has also given women a means of escape from relationships judged unduly oppressive.

Third, although significant barriers to workplace equality remain, male employers can no longer blatantly discriminate with impunity against women workers. As women have entered the work force in unprecedented numbers and begun to join male-dominated occupational preserves, they have placed increased pressure on male employers, colleagues, and legislators to secure their equal rights as workers.

Fourth, the rise of the woman worker has eroded the ideological supports for male dominance and female domesticity. As the predominance of the so-called traditional family has given way to a variety of family and household forms, it has become increasingly difficult to assert that the traditional division of sexual labor is natural, inevitable, and morally superior. Although many still defend this family form, it now must compete with other alternatives, such as equality in parenting and freedom from family commitments. No single ideology of family life predominates; instead, a diversity of opposing beliefs increasingly vie for ideological hegemony.

Although an increasing proportion of men and women—especially among younger age cohorts—have been exposed to changes in the structure of gender relations, a significant proportion have remained insulated from the changes taking place around them. Those who have not been exposed to structural changes have been motivated, if not forced, to reproduce the domestic patterns of an earlier period. Those women exposed to a shifting set of structural arrangements, however, have faced compelling reasons to reject domesticity and resist male dominance. Because their structural situations differ, domestic and nondomestic women have been influenced in different ways by men and have developed different expectations of men.

Whatever the form or content, women's relationships with men are neither the result of universal, unchanging psychological predispositions nor passive reactions to male dominance. Rather, a changing structure of gender relations is creating new possibilities—for cooperation and conflict—in male-female relationships. Larger social changes are providing women with new sources of power, but they are also creating new insecurities and vulnerabilities. Only in this context of altered constraints and opportunities can women's varied views of men be understood.

Outlook for the Future

As new life patterns for women become more widespread and deeply anchored, emerging divisions among women ensure continued disagreement about what women want from men. Domestic women, who fear the loss of the "protections" traditional marriage once provided, will argue that men should support women economically and stay clear of women's domestic preserves. They will cling to traditional notions of manhood, including men's right to superior economic and political power, as tightly as they cling to traditional notions of womanhood, including women's duty to support their husbands and nurture their children. Nondomestic women, unable or unwilling to depend on male economic support, will search for security and fulfillment at the workplace and will fight for greater gender equality in male-dominated work institutions. Those who conclude that men are not dependable and permanent partnership is no longer possible or desirable, will reject heterosexual commitment altogether, opting instead for independence from men. Others, wishing to combine work and motherhood, will push for gender equality in family as well as work arrangements—not only in parenting and breadwinning responsibilities but also in redefinitions of what it means to be a man or a woman. These women will increasingly look to men as sexual partners and work colleagues for support in the struggle to achieve equality and to ease the integration of work and family life for both sexes.

How are men likely to respond to the disparate, sometimes contradictory stances women take? Men's responses will also reflect diverse structural situations. Men, like women, occupy varied social positions that structure not only their alternatives but also their willingness to support and ability to resist demands for gender equality. Whether a man supports or opposes nontraditional demands from women will depend largely on what he stands to lose or gain from social change. Many men will vigorously oppose the mounting assaults on male power and privilege; others may find unexpected benefits in sharing the burdens of breadwinning and the pleasures of parenthood. (Of the few studies on men's reactions to changes in women's lives, see Barnet & Baruch, 1984; Gerson, 1984; Pleck, 1984.)

Whatever their situation, men will not and cannot remain insulated from the changes currently taking place in women's lives. They will be forced to develop strategies of adjustment to new social circumstances. Men's reactions to women's emerging demands and desires will greatly affect the fortunes of both sexes. As divisions continue to develop among women concerning what they want from men, differences between traditional and nontraditional individuals of both sexes may well become as socially and politically significant as the historic but diminishing differences between women and men.

REFERENCES

Bane, M. J. (1976). *Here to stay: American families in the twentieth century.* New York: Basic Books.

Barnet, R. C., & Baruch, G. K. (1984). *Men at home: Fathers' participation in family life* (Research Report No. 4, Fall). Wellesley, MA: Wellesley College, Center for Research on Women.

Berk, S. F. (1980). *Women and household labor.* Newbury Park, CA: Sage.

Blumberg, P. (1980). *Inequality in an age of decline.* New York: Oxford University Press.

Blumstein, P., & Schwartz, P. (1983). *American couples: Money, work, sex.* New York: William Morrow.

Cherlin, A. J. (1981). *Marriage, divorce, remarriage.* Cambridge, MA: Harvard University Press.

Chodorow, N. (1978). *The reproduction of mothering: Psychoanalysis and the sociology of gender.* Berkeley: University of California Press.

Dowling, C. (1981). *The Cinderella complex: Women's hidden fear of independence.* New York: Summit.

Ehrenreich, B. (1983). *The hearts of men: American dreams and the flight from commitment.* Garden City, NY: Doubleday.

Gerson, K. (1984). *Explaining patterns of parenthood among young adult men.* New York: New York University Presidential Fellowship.

Gerson, K. (1985). *Hard choices: How women decide about work, career, and motherhood.* Berkeley: University of California Press.

Glick, P. C., & Norton, A. J. (1977). Marrying, divorcing, and living together in the U.S. today. *Population Bulletin, 32,* 2-39.

Huber, J., & Spitze, G. (1983). *Sex stratification: Children, housework, jobs.* New York: Academic Press.

Luker, K. (1984). *Abortion and the politics of motherhood.* Berkeley: University of California Press.

Masnick, G., & Bane, M. J. (1980). *The nation's families: 1960-1990.* Cambridge, MA: Joint Center for Urban Studies of MIT and Harvard University.

Norton, A. J., & Glick, P. C. (1976). Marital instability: Past, present, and future. *Journal of Social Issues, 32,* 5-20.

Pleck, J. H. (1984). *Men at work: A new focus for fatherhood activists* (Research Report No. 4, Fall). Wellesley, MA: Wellesley College Center for Research on Women.

Polatnik, M. (1973). Why men don't rear children: A power analysis. *Berkeley Journal of Sociology, 18,* 45-86.

Rich, A. (1980). Compulsory heterosexuality and lesbian existence. *Signs: Journal of Women in Culture and Society, 5,* 631-60.

Rossi, A. S. (1977). A biosocial perspective on parenting. *Daedalus, 106,* 1-31.

Rossi, A. S. (1984). Gender and parenthood. *American Sociological Review, 49,* 1-19.

Rubin, G. (1975). The traffic in women. In R. R. Reiter (Ed.), *Toward an anthropology of women.* New York: Monthly Review Press.

Smith, R. E. (Ed.). (1979). *The subtle revolution: Women at work.* Washington, DC: Urban Institute.

Vickery, C. B. (1979). Women's economic contribution to the family. In R. E. Smith (Ed.), *The subtle revolution: Women at work.* Washington, DC: Urban Institute.

9

One of the Boys

Women in Male-Dominated Settings

GARY ALAN FINE

The number of social locales from which women are completely excluded is rapidly diminishing in American society. Yet, the mere fact that women have access to a male-dominated setting does not mean they will be fully accepted or treated with respect. Ethnographic research in restaurant kitchens suggests that women can be accepted by male colleagues, but this acceptance comes at a cost. Women who wish to be part of a male-dominated group typically must accept patterns of male bonding and must be able to decode male behavior patterns. They must be willing to engage in coarse joking, teasing, and accept male-based informal structure of the occupation—in other words, become "one of the boys." While some women find this behavioral pattern congenial, others do not, and they become outcasts or marginal members of the group. Through an examination of restaurant kitchens I describe the conditions and implicit rules that influence the acceptance or rejection of females in male groups.

As women increasingly move into worlds previously inhabited only by men, the question arises: How do they adjust? How can women become full and equal partners in work worlds in which men predominate? One approach to this question is to examine the informal norms that govern the world of male work. What options are open to women who wish to enter this world?

Rosabeth Kanter (1977) has argued that the numerical composition of a work force has profound implications for the behaviors of these men and women. A work force with a large majority of men and a few token women has a very different structure and set of behavioral expectations than does a work force that is balanced. When women are in a minority they are more likely to have to adjust their behavior to that of their male co-workers than to try to change that behavior or to behave in their own preferred style, without regard to the consequences. This may not be the most desirable situation, but, as a general rule, it is difficult to alter.

These issues have been addressed in ethnographic studies of occupations and organizations. Few should be surprised that most of these studies have been conducted by women, and that the issues generally have been ignored by male researchers. As a consequence most of the studies that have examined the role of females in largely male organizations have focused on the perspective of the female employee. Since the researchers were female, it was difficult for them to obtain rich data from the male majority—at least in informal settings (see Kanter, 1977, p. 319). The sexual dynamics of participant observation have been noted by others (for instance, Easterday, Papademas, Schorr, & Valentine, 1977; Hunt, 1984; Wax, 1979); gender as a "master status" limits and directs the types of information likely to become available. In research by women, it is inevitable that the male perspective on "token" or "minority" women will be deemphasized. This is significant because many of the research findings are grounded in what women think "must" cause the behavior of their male colleagues (e.g., Lorber, 1984).

In this analysis I shall explain how males view those few women in their midst and how they treat them. I argue that to be accepted women must choose to be "one of the boys" and this act must be accepted by the males. In general, males have consensual informal arrangements; those women who can and do choose to accept these normative standards may be treated well, whereas those who fail to accept these informal rules by choice or lack of experience are more likely to experience difficulties and discrimination.

In studies of three predominantly male settings (Little League baseball, fantasy role-play gaming, and restaurant kitchens) I have found little hostility per se against women (discriminating against women simply because they were women); rather, difficulties arose from the fact that these women did not share the informal work values of men. Often, I suspect, these difficulties derived from unknowing behaviors by the women. In the work setting, men found it was not "fun" being with women, or at least it was not as much fun as being with men. The "clubby" atmosphere, characteristic of all-male groups, is threatened even—I might say especially—with the presence of a sole woman.

Research settings. In this article I draw upon my research in restaurant kitchens in the Twin Cities. I spent one month observing the kitchens of four restaurants. I supplemented this qualitative observation with interviews with the full-time cooks and chefs to examine how cooks constructed aesthetic products in the context of an industrial occupation. In addition to this research focus, because all of these restaurants had a majority of male cooks, I was able to observe the relationship between the sexes among cooks, and between cooks and waitresses (who were lower status, but often higher paid—including tips—than the cooks). Being a male researcher, obviously I attained closest rapport with the male cooks (at least on these sex-role issues); thus my emphasis is on their attitudes and behavior in the kitchen.

I selected the four restaurants to provide a reasonable range of cooking environments in the Twin Cities metropolitan area. I make no claim that these four restaurants are representative of all restaurants: They represent upper-status Minnesota restaurants, and none could be described as an "ethnic" restaurant. (1) La Pomme de Terre is an haute cuisine French restaurant, by all accounts one of the best and most innovative restaurants in the Upper Midwest. The restaurant employs five male and two female cooks (and a female pastry chef who works mornings). All but one of the wait staff are male. (2) The Owl's Nest is a continental-style restaurant best known for its fresh fish. Its primary luncheon clientele consists of businessmen and politicians, and the restaurant is a multiyear Holiday Award winner. The restaurant employs seven male cooks and one female cook. Approximately 75% of the servers are female. (3) Stan's Steakhouse, a family-owned and -operated establishment, has received several metropolitan awards for the quality of its beef. Stan's employs seven male and two female cooks; waitresses only are employed. (4) The Twin Cities Blakemore Hotel is part of a chain of hotels—a chain not known particularly for the quality of its cuisine. The hotel is modern, catering especially to business travelers. The hotel has a banquet service, and operates a moderately expensive "Continental" restaurant and a coffee shop. The wait staff is entirely female. Of the cooks, seven are male and two are female.

In all four restaurants, the managers and/or owners, head chefs, and assistant chefs are male. These social worlds are primarily male in terms of their status structure. Using Kanter's (1977, p. 209) terms, women constitute a "minority group" rather than "tokens." I separate the cooks from the wait staff, who have a lower status than the cooks in the status hierarchy of these restaurants, even though through tips they may be better paid.

In none of these restaurants were women co-workers rejected out of hand. Individual women might be rejected, and certainly some female cooks were not fully accepted, but it did not appear that women *could not* be accepted. All male informants denied discrimination against women. The questions are: What obstacles must women overcome to be accepted? How can women overcome these obstacles? What are the costs of this acceptance? What alternatives are there to accepting the male world as given? To describe some of the obstacles women must overcome to become accepted in a "male world," I shall focus on three themes. Specifically, I shall analyze (1) "off-color" humor and obscene language, (2) sexual talk directed at women, and (3) the need for cooperation in accomplishing the informal side of work.

Off-Color Humor and Obscene Language

A common practice when men gather is to trade obscene stories (see Fine, 1976). Trading stories is a pleasant diversion, and breaks from mundane work are considered desirable—whether these breaks constitute a secondary involvement while work continues or reflects a full break from work. Studies of women in male-dominated environments have recognized the difficulty many women have in adjusting to this brutal humor and rough talk (Valentine, 1985). For some women these off-color stories and language may exclude them from male gatherings (Kirkpatrick, 1974, p. 109); for some men it is an excuse for excluding women from these male settings because men just would not be "themselves" with a female present (Easterday et al., 1977, p. 338). Kanter (1977, p. 229) notes in her study of women in a large corporation:

> Indsco women faced constant pressure to allow jokes at the expense of women, to accept "kidding" from the men around them. When a woman objected, the men denied any hostility or unfriendly intention, instead accusing the woman, by inference, of "lacking a sense of humor."

It is reasonable to assume that most men felt no unfriendly intent in their joking. They were, after all, only having a good time, and building a work community in the process (Mechling & Mechling, 1985).

I found obscene joking in all these restaurants. Simply put, men are endlessly fascinated with sex and its variations (which is, of course, not unique to them), and are willing to comment on it publicly. Younger males are testing their maturity (Fine, 1976, 1981); for older males, the test is more subtle, but it is also a judgment of "macho" beliefs and willingness to talk about those beliefs. Of course, different standards for appropriate talk and action exist among groups—not all male groups emphasize "masculine" themes equally (e.g., college professors tend not to have a robust macho culture, even when women are a distinct minority). At the restaurants comments such as the following were common:

> A male cook turns to his male co-worker, eating a banana, and announces: "I saw my girlfriend sucking on something like that last night." His co-worker grins. (Field notes, Owl's Nest)

> At the Owl's Nest, rainbow trout is served with its head on. Gene jokes to me: "Some people think it's a little gross, but everyone needs a little head once in a while." The men in the kitchen chuckle. (Field notes, Owl's Nest)

Such examples could be multiplied, and they underlie a problem with cross-sex interaction. Males enjoy this banter, and yet it is likely that many women would find remarks about oral sex to be offensive. Either the sexual joking must go, or the women must go—or must adjust.

In fact, males do make similar remarks to females in their work environment—remarks that could be perceived as offensive:

> A waitress comes into the kitchen and says to the chef: "A lady would like the tail of an ivory salmon." The chef jokes: "We'll give her some tail." (Field notes, Owl's Nest)

An even more graphic example is presented in a study of a prosecutor's office. The office director performed a comic routine about the pretrial questioning of a rape victim, directing his questions to the female participant observer:

> Now, I just want to ask you a few questions before we go into court and I want you to feel free to be open in your answers because I've heard it all before. Now, did you enjoy it? Come on, you can tell me. Did you like it? Now, you say that you were standing at the bus stop when this guy pulled over and grabbed you. What did you do to make him do that? What were you doing, huh? You must've done something to make him do that? Now, what was it? (Gurney, 1985, p. 54)

The author reports that all the men found this little playlet immensely amusing, but she was made so uncomfortable she made an excuse to leave the meeting shortly thereafter. The men involved probably did not consider this joking sequence to be offensive. Indeed, we might imagine that, if asked, the joker would claim (with some justice) that the butt of the joke was the "macho prosecutor" and not the female victim. The claim of the joke could be defined as the belief of *other* males that women are guilty, even though *we* know this belief is silly. Yet, elementary role-playing should emphasize that the joke might be taken as being directed at the woman. The same joke may have two quite different messages. Of course, at the least the men enjoyed this humor because it was risque, even if they didn't consider it politically offensive. Such jokes might lead women to avoid those settings in which such comments regularly occur—lunches, after-hours parties, and the like (Epstein, 1970; Kirkpatrick, 1974)—in these settings some real work is accomplished and a sense of community is built.

Some women find such joking to be quite congenial, and they are successful in such interaction:

> Bill, a waiter, returns to the kitchen with an order of veal medallions Madeira with morels. The female customer didn't want them because they were not what she expected—often veal medallions are thinner than those from a veal chop. Bill explains to Don, the sous chef who cooked them, "She's wrong, but I'm not going to argue." This begins a long discussion of the difficulty of pleasing female customers, who are seen as more demanding than men. Bill finally jokes: "She doesn't like it because it's big and fat and pink." Diane, a female cook, adds: "She must have had an awful experience as a child." Don, still annoyed, jokes: "I'd like to to go out and give her something that's big and fat and pink." Since they can't use the veal, Don offers it to the others in the kitchen. Diane refuses the veal, at which Don jokes: "I thought you liked things that were big, fat, and pink." Diane jokes back: "I'm trying to quit." (Field notes, La Pomme de Terre)

Later Don and Diane tell each other dirty jokes, and talk about auto mechanics and the physique of female customers. As Rosabeth Kanter (1977, p. 229) notes:

> Some tokens managed to adapt very well. They used the same kind of language as many of the men. One woman loved fishing, she said, so when she came on as a manager and her office was concerned that she would end fishing trips, she could show them they had nothing to fear. . . . A professional woman joined the men on "women hunts," taking part in conversations in which the pros and cons of particular targets were discussed. There were women known to be able to "drink the men under the table."

The relationship between men and women depends very much on the woman and her attitudes—perhaps more than on the community of men, where norms are already set and unlikely to change rapidly. It is up to the men to decide what kind of woman their female co-worker is and how much trust she should be accorded. The two other women who worked nights at La Pomme de Terre with Diane both complained about their exclusion from the male subculture, and they disliked this joking. The other cook was a quiet woman, not as competent as Diane, who rarely joked with her male colleagues, although on the surface relations were pleasant. She noted:

> There's a kind of comaraderie that hasn't included me since I've been here. . . . This is the first job where I've really felt outside of things. (Field notes, La Pomme de Terre)

The only female waiter was offended by what she considered sexist joking in the kitchen. When I asked her whether she found any discrimination in the kitchen, Diane commented:

> I find that I really have to prove myself. There's a period of adjustment for everybody, and they put you through a test that's mostly emotional. They want to see if you have a breaking point; they just want to see how far they can push you. It happens just about everywhere. (Personal interview, La Pomme de Terre)

When I asked the head chef at La Pomme de Terre what he felt a layperson would be most upset by in his kitchen, he responded:

> I would have to say if they were a woman, probably the behavior that goes on in the kitchen sometimes. Sexism and crude jokes. There's all kinds of things going on. Well, Diane, she's almost like one of the guys. . . . Either she should be detested for it or she's quite admirable because she's always let everybody know that they don't have to tread light steps around her. It's amazing how when you get a woman in the kitchen the attitude changes totally. Everybody clams up a little bit and they are careful about what they say. (Personal interview, La Pomme de Terre)

Women seem to be likely to attribute deliberate intention to their male co-workers, whereas the males appeal to the "atmosphere," "the natural crudeness" of their environment to justify their joking. These relationships remind one of the practice of "binging" (Haas, 1972), in which the more established workers in the construction industry "test" the new recruits to see how far they can push them without cracking; construction work being based on the assumption of trust, an absence of "cool" could prove fatal. Outsiders (in this case women) especially must be tested to determine whether they can be counted on by the other employees (Hughes, 1971). As a result, Epstein (1970, p. 979) suggests that women professionals are more successful when the work environment is formal. The more informality and discretion in a setting, the harder it is for men and women to adjust smoothly. To the extent that males perceive the work environment as "homosocial," it is difficult for a woman to be accepted because she disrupts this atmosphere (Lipman-Blumen, 1976). The special characteristics of a work environment in which one is associated with like-minded others (see Weston & Rofel, 1984) can be threatened by the introduction of those who are presumed not to identify with the basis of community. Since joking is a traditional way by which unofficial, unstated, but crucial values are expressed, the joking culture of a workplace underlies the gender/sexual character of that workplace. By removing sexual joking from the workplace, some worry that the sense of community that is built by it might diminish as well with the consequences of making work less satisfying and efficient—at least for male workers (Mechling & Mechling, 1986).

Sexual Talk

Men frequently treat women as sex objects, and often seem unable to refrain from making sexually charged remarks. Obviously such sexual talk and action is socially situated. Not every woman gets "propositioned" or "hustled" by every man at every time. The likelihood of such behavior is related to the personality of the male, the physical attractiveness and personality of the woman, the implicit expectations of the setting, and the immediate circumstances in which the men and women find themselves. Many women are propositioned at some time in their working lives, so even though on most occasions they are not, a single incident may cast a pall over the work environment.

In most instances sexual remarks are not *designed* to make a woman's life unpleasant, although that may be their effect. However, they are aimed typically at those of less status or at those new in the environment. Men may not realize that what they are doing is offensive, recognizing variation in intent, circumstances, and responses. There may be a sharp difference between the perspectives of males and females.

I divide this sexual banter into two categories. The first is the "hustle" or the "pickup," in which the male is trying to establish a sexual relationship with the woman. The second is (from the point of view of the male) playful sexual joshing. In both cases, the female and her embodiment are the target of the remark.

Hustling

Particularly when a female target is young and attractive, a male may attempt to "come on" to her—sometimes using his power or position. This is relatively rare in absolute frequency, and is hard to observe since seductions and harassments typically occur in private, as in this case reported by a female participant observer attempting to interview a male morgue attendant.

> I was in the midst of industriously questioning the attendant about his job at the morgue and he came back with, "Are you married?"
>
> Observer: "No. How long have you worked here?"
>
> Attendant: "Three years. Do you have a steady boyfriend?"
>
> Observer: "No. Do you find this work difficult?"
>
> Attendant: "No. Do you date?"
>
> Observer: "Yes. Why isn't this work difficult for you?"
>
> Attendant: "You get used to it. What do you do in your spare time?" (Easterday et al., 1977, p. 339)

The circumstances that the two are alone and that the attendant has something the observer needs (information) make this extended hustle possible. At the beginning of a relationship such interactions are most common. Martin (1978, p. 56) describes the reaction of a new policewoman about her first days on the job:

> They [the male police officers] all tried to hit on us when we arrived, to see who could be the first to get one of us. When we had the_____detail (and had to remain at a fixed post), they'd line up their cars trying to get our phone numbers.

Some women do accept these invitations, and some male-female liaisons at work are not unwelcome by the females who have been "hustled" (see Collins, 1983; Skeen & Nielson, 1983).

The problem and the dilemma in this situation is how can those women who object to these hustles reject them while still maintaining a congenial work relationship with these men? Women must judge the situation and handle it (a problem men do not face). Unlike at dating bars, these individuals will continue to interact, whatever the outcome of their encounter. The woman must be firm without insulting. Martin's sample of policewomen included one who talked endlessly about her boyfriend, another who pointedly wore a wedding ring, and a third who stated the problem baldly:

> If I'm unfriendly, I get labeled a snob . . . which you can't be. If I'm friendly, some of them think "she's looking at me." If I act as I generally am (warm and friendly) there are some who figure "she's an easy catch." What you have to do is catch it on the first remark and let them know where you stand. If you laugh it off, it doesn't do any good. . . . They take it as encouragement. (p. 57)

Women often define themselves as victims, and also see themselves being blamed for being victims. Some men, on the other hand, are convinced that they have been led on, and are being condemned for what are normal behaviors in other settings. Because of sexual relationships between men and women, the presence of men and women at work inevitably produces sexual tensions. This is complicated when women workers are a minority; they feel they have little support when hustled by their male co-workers.

Sexual Teasing

Sexual teasing is more common and more public. Because of its public nature it is both easier and harder to handle than private forms of hustling. Its public character means that males will not push this joking beyond the consensual limits of good taste—as defined by men. Simultaneously, for the woman not to lose face she must respond so as to present herself as a colleague—enjoyable to be with, yet not a butt for jokes. Ideally, the woman must give as good as she gets. This rests on the personality and style of the woman (see Kirpatrick, 1974, pp. 115-118). The woman's behavior is key for establishing the tone of her work relation with the majority of men—another problem that men typically do not face.

Some of these joking sequences are not particularly offensive:

> Phil, the head day cook, notes that Amy, a young pantry worker, is left-handed. He jokes to her: "I finally found out what's the matter with Amy after all this time. She's left-handed. No wonder you can't keep a boyfriend." Amy replies, smiling: "Shut up." (Field notes, The Owl's Nest)

> Arnie, the chef at the Blakemore says to a coffee shop waitress: "What's up with you, blue eyes?" She jokes back. (Field notes, Blakemore Hotel)

Other sequences are more offensive:

> Karen, one of the waitresses at the Owl's Nest, asks Jim, the head chef, for
> an order of scallops for her lunch, even though waitresses are rarely given
> such expensive food. Jim makes the scallops and Phil, the day cook, jokes
> to him: "You can tell who's sleeping with the chef." Jim jokes back: "You
> guys are just jealous." (Field notes, The Owl's Nest)

Some joking involves physical contact—although nothing that could
be fairly described as an attack. The touching is of a playful nature,
although it is touching that would be inappropriate if done by a female
to a male or by a male to another male, such as when Ken, a cook at the
Owl's Nest, playfully slapped a waitress's buttocks. Most women can
handle themselves and their male colleagues, and interviews suggest no
major problems with sexual teasing. If the woman can banter in return,
interaction is smooth:

> Carl, a male cook at the Blakemore, is joking with Kate, a female cook at
> approximately the same rank, about how handsome he is: "I was walking
> down the street and this woman came up to me and said 'What's your
> name? I want your body.'" Kate replies humorously: "Carl, shut up." Carl
> says with irony: "Don't you like my sad jokes?" Kate responds: "They are
> *sad.*" (Field notes, Blakemore Hotel)

> Ted, a head waiter at the Owl's Nest, rubs the back of Cheri's neck (Cheri
> is an attractive waitress in her 20s). Later Ted puts his hand around her
> waist and on her shoulder. Cheri pats Ted's somewhat bulging stomach
> and asks about his pants size. (Field notes, The Owl's Nest)

None of these instances can be truly defined as an advance or as
harassment, but they represent a challenge to which female employees
must respond if they are not to be thought cold and unfriendly. The
woman must accept this male sensual play and sexual talk, and do so in
terms of the male norms of the workplace. The rules are given by the
majority, and women have little choice if they wish to be accepted. For
some women this arrangement is reasonable, but for others it poses
obstacles to their advancement. Some of the excesses of male activity
may be curbed by sexual harassment guidelines, which particularly
affect larger, more bureaucratic organizations:

> Arnie, the chef at the Blakemore, has just finished mildly criticizing a new
> waitress. He turns to Sue, a veteran waitress: "I used to chase after new
> waitresses at my last place. But I'm respectable." Sue, laughing, asks:

"What happened?" Arnie, joking but serious, replies: "This company told
me that they frown on harassment cases." (Field notes, Blakemore Hotel)

Stateways change folkways, although these changes may create unin-
tended consequences (such as greater formality), as well as those that are
intended.

Teamwork and Maleness

Men sometimes believe that a woman would not make as good a
co-worker as would another man. It is not only that women are not able
to "take a joke" or be kidded, but that they are not really part of the
team. In a small industrial organization like the kitchen, in which
harmonious relations depend on teamwork and cooperation, trust in
co-workers may be crucial. Women may see this as discrimination
against women because they are women:

> Kate explains to me that she thinks Tom Devine, the manager of the hotel,
> doesn't like her or Dana, the two female cooks at the Blakemore. She says
> that sometimes he doesn't say hello to her in response to her greeting. Kate
> insists: "I haven't done anything." I ask her if she thinks Devine's attitude
> is based on the fact she is a woman; she agrees: "He's the type that a
> kitchen's no place for a woman. He doesn't give us credit. You're nothing.
> He automatically just judged me." (Field notes, Blakemore Hotel)

Devine insisted he had nothing against women, per se; what
objections he had were to the two cooks and their attitudes, which
undermined the authority structure of the kitchen. Although there was
some justification for this claim, it is difficult to judge such matters in
objective terms. In the period I observed, there was resentment to
cutbacks in staff and to the way the kitchen was run, and these female
cooks were among the least satisfied, claiming they would not exert
themselves to help beyond their job requirements. This attitude is not
representative of all female cooks; however, when it occurs it may be
used to typify the minority group, rather than being defined as
idiosyncratic—at least as viewed by the female employees.

That this discrimination against women is not omnipresent can be
seen in the near-total acceptance of Diane at La Pomme de Terre:

> Diane tells me that tonight she's "third man" working the broiler and oven
> with Howard, the head chef, and Don, the sous chef. She adds: "I'll be

helping salads if Claude gets busy." She willingly worked hard for the sake of the restaurant (including unpaid overtime) and enjoyed being part of the team. Don later complimented her as "tough." (Field notes, La Pomme de Terre)

Part of the problem in the relationship between men and women is that females are not deemed able to do everything males can, and are unable to be full members of the kitchen community. Although men sometimes see women as more careful in the preparation of food (their food looks nicer), men often assume women can't work as rapidly. Many women are unable to lift large vats of stock or some packages of food, requiring them to ask their male co-workers for assistance. Some men see this as significant.

The differentiation of women from the rest of the work community is particularly evident in those jobs or portions of jobs that involve danger. For example, at Stan's Steakhouse, the men do all the frying and cutting of meat. Women are more likely to work on salads, in the pantry, and on pastries and desserts, but not with hot foods. Support for this is also found in the lack of acceptance of women in police departments. Many male police officers believe women do not belong on the streets, and women rarely are put in charge of dangerous situations. As one male officer commented:

> Most of the ones I've met honestly and sincerely try to do a good job, but they just don't belong on the street. Most, because of their emotional background, are too unstable in high pressure situations . . . there are exceptions to every rule. (Remmington, 1983, p. 123)

Men claimed they were overprotective of female officers on the street, putting themselves at risk. Because of the reluctance of male officers to trust female officers to fight, and perhaps because of a reluctance by the females, they are not fully initiated. In the words of a male policeman:

> You're not really a "police" until you get your butt beat . . . and beat one in return . . . and the women in this department make sure that they don't ever get into a good fight. (Remmington, 1983, p. 125)

Women who are seen as "real" police officers and those willing to rough up suspects demonstrate that they accept the underside, the informal structures and rules, of the male occupation. As Hughes notes, it may take an especially lengthy time for a minority co-worker to become trusted:

In order that men may communicate freely and confidentially, they must be able to take a good deal of each other's sentiments for granted. They must feel easy about their silences as well as about their utterances. These factors conspire to make colleagues, with a large body of unspoken understandings, uncomfortable in the presence of what they consider odd kinds of fellows. (Hughes, 1971, p. 146)

When a woman declines to participate in the informal underside of the occupation, all women are tarred and all employees are made uncomfortable. When a woman (such as Diane) is willing to do so, only she is praised—often as an exception to her group (Hughes, 1971).

Being One of the Boys

My analysis suggests that a woman who wishes to be accepted in a largely male work group must play by the rules of the game already set by males. Before she plays this game, she may have to decipher the rules (Harragan, 1977). This does not mean the game is not "winnable," but it argues that female players are at a disadvantage. This is evident in the fact that we speak of female workers as a group with special problems, whereas we do not do the same for males.

Men do not object to female co-workers out of mysogynistic urge. It is not gender per se that is the problem, but rather the cultural traditions surrounding gender. Women have the potential to disrupt patterns of male interaction, possibly without realizing they are doing so. Specifically, males may feel constrained in what they may say in front of women: Joking and cursing are seen as outside the chivalrous pale. Males may be criticized for teasing these female co-workers in ways seen as suitable in other settings in which males and females interact. Even the mating rituals of males and females must be curtailed. Further, women may be perceived as being unable to perform tasks involved in a cooperative work relationship because of physical limitations.

These features together cause females to be seen as a potentially disruptive influence. The female starts with obstacles males do not have to face. Although women can overcome these obstacles, their success is often treated as a personal success, not as a success for their group: they are seen as exceptions. In parallel, a sexist male (or one who harasses women) may be seen by feminist critics as representing all men, rather than representing an idiosyncratic role response by one man. Some women are successful and some men are offensive. Most men and women operate as best they can within their role restrictions, producing a somewhat uncertain, partially successful adjustment between the sexes.

Given current rules, women (and all minorities) who wish to be successful must decipher the rules of the game and play by them. While some suggest that women need not be "one of the boys" (Kirkpatrick, 1974, p. 118), they must accept the boys' rules. One need not go out drinking, but one must establish friendly, nonjudgmental relationships with those who do. In the short run the informal rules and objectives of the occupation must be preserved, even when these rules and objectives are contrary to women's socialization. The woman must reach some kind of modus operandi, without rocking the delicately balanced boat.

In doing this, the woman must quickly acquire a sense of what is expected of her—the games that mother never taught (Harragan, 1977). These rules are unstated by men and typically not even realized by them. But they are quite real—they have an ethnomethodological reality. By accidentally breaking the rules surrounding male bonding, they underline the existence of these rules and their incompetence (culturally). This represents adult socialization through trial and error. Women in these work situations are, in Garfinkel's (1967) terms, "cultural dopes." If they are to succeed, they must smarten up quickly.

We must distinguish between the biological and the social. The male orientation I have described in this chapter can be adopted by women, although whether that is desirable is a matter of opinion. The underlying point is that gender roles are socially emergent and grounded in behavior. The ability of women to become "one of the boys" demonstrates that these styles of behavior can be learned, and are not fixed and static. To date, the ability of women to move into male occupational preserves has indicated that women are capable of adapting to the behavioral styles practiced by men, not the other way around.

Such acceptance is accompanied by interpersonal negotiation on a set of "sensitive" issues. Many of the obstacles women face specifically have to do with sexuality. The expressive component of social life can never be disentangled from the instrumental component. Work is not divorced from leisure. Women find it easy to succeed on the instrumental component, but male expressive behaviors prove more intractable. Somehow the two sexes must establish an adequate modus operandi for the "nonwork" side of work. Part of the problem with this negotiation is that neither party may be aware that there is a need for negotiation. Something is wrong, but no one may be quite certain what the problem is—other than that people feel uncomfortable. This may lead to ascriptions being made to the new (female) workers as the cause of the problem, rather than to a recognition that it is the "relationship" between the two that needs to be adjusted.

Each sex, like different cultures, has its own standards for comfortable interaction. Of course, this does not mean that each person—male or female—will share these views, but that these represent the standard expectations. These forms of behavior require little explanation or justification within the group—they are normative standards. For males, these expectations involve a rough and rowdy exterior, in which tenderness and the softer emotions are excised. Machismo, while not always present, need not be justified among males. The presence of female equals threatens to alter these standards, changing a relatively unambiguous setting into one fraught with moral ambiguity. If humans desire certainty, it is easy to recognize why the presence of co-workers of the other sex so complicates the social life of work.

Being "one of the boys" is a position that is perfectly congruent for some women, whereas for others it is a strain, an offense, or an impossibility. In considering this problem we must not stereotype the behaviors of either men or women into gender types, but acknowledge informal occupational structures—expectations based upon the conditions of work in that occupation, rather than on the gender of those who do the work.

REFERENCES

Collins, E.G.C. (1983). Managers and lovers. *Harvard Business Review, 61,* 142-153.

Easterday, L., Papademas D., Schorr, L., & Valentine, C. (1977). The making of a female researcher: Role problems in field work. *Urban Life, 6,* 333-348.

Epstein, C. F. (1970). Encountering the male establishment: Sex-status limits on women's careers in the professions. *American Journal of Sociology, 75,* 965-982.

Fine, G. A. (1976). Obscene joking across cultures. *Journal of Communication, 26,* 134-140.

Fine, G. A. (1981). Friends, impression management, and preadolescent behavior. In S. R. Asher & J. M. Gottman (Eds.), *The development of children's friendships* (pp. 29-52). Cambridge: Cambridge University Press.

Garfinkel, H. (1967). *Studies in ethnomethodology.* Englewood Cliffs, NJ: Prentice-Hall.

Gurney, J. N. (1985). Not one of the guys: The female researcher in a male-dominated setting. *Qualitative Sociology, 8,* 42-62.

Haas, J. (1972). Binging: Educational control among high steel workers. *American Behavioral Scientist, 16,* 27-34.

Harragan, B. L. (1977). *Games mother never taught you.* New York: Warner.

Hughes, E. C. (1971). Dilemmas and contradictions of status. In E. C. Hughes (Ed.), *The sociological eye* (pp. 141-150). Chicago: Aldine-Atherton.

Hunt, J. (1984). The development of rapport through the negotiation of gender in field work among police. *Human Organization, 43,* 283-296.

Kanter, R. M. (1977). *Men and women of the corporation.* New York: Basic Books.

Kirkpatrick, J. (1974). *Political woman*. New York: Basic Books.

Lipman-Blumen, J. (1976). Toward a homosocial theory of sex roles: An explanation of the sex segregation of social institutions. In M. Blaxall & B. Reagan (Eds.), *Women and the workplace* (pp. 15-31). Chicago: University of Chicago Press.

Lorber, J. (1984). Trust, loyalty, and the place of women in the informal organization of work. In J. Freeman (Ed.), *Women: A feminist perspective* (3rd ed., pp. 370-378). Palo Alto: Mayfield.

Martin, S. E. (1978). Sexual politics in the workplace: The interactional world of policewomen. *Symbolic Interaction, 1,* 44-60.

Mechling, E., & Mechling, J. (1986). Shock talk: From consensual to contractual joking relationships in the bureaucratic workplace. *Human Organization.*

Remmington, P. W. (1983). Women in the police: Integration or separation? *Qualitative Sociology, 6,* 118-35.

Skeen, R., & Nielson, J. M. (1983). Student-faculty sexual relationships: An empirical test of two explanatory models. *Qualitative Sociology, 6,* 118-35.

Valentine, C. G. (1985). *Female players and masculine-typed instruments: Barriers to women "making it" in the art music world.* Paper presented at the annual meeting of the American Sociological Association, Washington, DC.

Wax, R. H. (1979). Gender and age in fieldwork and fieldwork education: No good thing is done by any man alone. *Social Problems, 26,* 509-522.

Weston, K. M., & Rofel, L. B. (1984). Sexuality, class, and conflict in a lesbian workplace. *Signs, 9,* 623-646.

10

The Fraternal Bond
as a Joking Relationship

A Case Study of the Role of
Sexist Jokes in Male Group Bonding

PETER LYMAN

One evening during dinner, 45 fraternity men suddenly broke into the dining room of a nearby campus sorority, surrounded the 30 women residents, and forced them to watch while one pledge gave a speech on Freud's theory of penis envy as another demonstrated various techniques of masturbation with a rubber penis. The women sat silently, staring downward at their plates, and listened for about 10 minutes, until a woman law student who was the graduate resident in charge of the house walked in, surveyed the scene and demanded, "Please leave immediately!" As she later described that moment, "There was a mocking roar from the men, 'It's tradition.' I said, 'That's no reason to do something like this, please leave!' And they left. I was surprised. Then the women in the house started to get angry. And the guy who made the penis-envy speech came back and said to us, 'That was funny to me. If that's not funny to you I don't know what kind of sense of humor you have, but I'm sorry.' "

That night the women sat around the stairwell of their house

AUTHOR'S NOTE: This description of the original ritual joke is reconstructed from interviews with many of the participants. The event occurred at a private college with a predominantly white, upper-class student body; I am grateful to the men and women involved for their cooperation. Many thanks to Barrie Thorne, Jane Flax, Nancy Chodorow, Teresa Bernardez, and Mercedes Carter for their comments on this chapter.

discussing the event, some angry and others simply wanting to forget the whole thing. They finally decided to ask the university to require that the men return to discuss the event. When university officials threatened to take action, the men agreed to the meeting. I had served as a faculty resident in student housing for two years and had given several talks in the dorm about humor and gender, and was asked by both the men and the women involved to attend the discussion as a facilitator, and was given permission to take notes and interview the participants later, provided I concealed their identities.

The penis-envy ritual had been considered a successful joke in previous years by both "the guys and the girls," but this year it failed, causing great tension between two groups that historically had enjoyed a friendly joking relationship. In the women's view, the joke had not failed because of its subject; they considered sexual jokes to be a normal part of the erotic joking relationship between men and women. They thought it had failed because of its emotional structure, the mixture of sexuality with aggression and the atmosphere of physical intimidation in the room that signified that the women were the object of a joking relationship between the men. A few women argued that the failed joke exposed the latent domination in men's relation to women, but this view was labelled "feminist" because it endangered the possibility of reconstituting the erotic joking relationship with the men. Although many of the men individually regretted the damage to their relationship with women friends in the group, they argued that the special male bond created by sexist humor is a unique form of intimacy that justified the inconvenience caused the women. In reinterpreting these stories as social constructions of gender, I will focus upon the way the joke form and joking relationships reveal the emotional currents underlying gender in this situation.

The Sociology of Jokes

Although we conventionally think of jokes as a meaningless part of the dramaturgy of everyday life, this convention is part of the way that the social function of jokes is concealed and is necessary if jokes are to "work." It is when jokes fail that the social conflicts that the joke was to reconstruct or "negotiate" are uncovered, and the tensions and emotions that underlie the conventional order of everyday social relations are revealed.

Joking is a special kind of social relationship that suspends the rules of everyday life in order to preserve them. Jokes indirectly express the emotions and tensions that may disrupt everyday life by "negotiating" them (Emerson, 1969, 1970), reconstituting group solidarity by shared aggression and cathartic laughter. The ordinary consequences of forbidden words are suspended by meta-linguistic gestures (tones of voice, facial expressions, catch phrases) that send the message "this is a joke," and emotions that would ordinarily endanger a social relationship can be spoken safely within the micro-world created by "the joke form" (Bateson, 1955).

Yet jokes are not just stories, they are a theater of domination in everyday life, and the success or failure of a joke marks the boundary within which power and aggression may be used in a relationship. Nearly all jokes have an aggressive content, indeed shared aggression toward an outsider is one of the primary ways by which a group may overcome internal tension and assert its solidarity (Freud, 1960, p. 102). Jokes both require and renew social bonds; thus Radcliffe-Brown pointed out that "joking relationships" between mothers-in-law and their sons-in-law provide a release for tension for people structurally bound to each other but at the same time feeling structural conflict with each other (Radcliffe-Brown, 1959). Joking relationships in medicine, for example, are a medium for the indirect expression of latent emotions or taboo topics that if directly expressed would challenge the physician's authority or disrupt the need to treat life and death situations as ordinary work (see Coser, 1959; Emerson, 1969, 1970).

In each of the studies cited above, the primary focus of the analysis was upon the social function of the joke, not gender, yet in each case the joke either functioned through a joking relationship between men and women, such as in Freud's or Radcliffe-Brown's analysis of mother-in-law jokes, or through the joking relationship between men and women. For example, Coser describes the role of nurses as a safe target of jokes: as a surrogate for the male doctor in patient jokes challenging medical authority; or as a surrogate for the patient in the jokes with which doctors expressed anxiety. Sexist jokes, therefore, should be analyzed not only in general terms of the function of jokes as a means of defending social order, but in specific terms as the mechanism by which the order of gender domination is sustained in everyday life. From this perspective, jokes reveal the way social organizations are gendered, namely, built around the emotional rules of male bonding. In this case study, gender is not only the primary content of men's jokes, but the emotional structure of the male bond is built upon a joking relationship that "negotiates" the tension men feel about their relationship with each other, and with women.

Male bonding in everyday life frequently takes the form of a group joking relationship by which men create a serial kind of intimacy to "negotiate" the latent tension and aggression they feel toward each other. The humor of male bonding relationships generally is sexual and aggressive, and frequently consists of sexist or racist jokes. As Freud (1960, p. 99) observed, the jokes that individual men direct toward women are generally erotic, tend to clever forms (like the double entendre), and have a seductive purpose. The jokes that men tell about women in the presence of other men are sexual and aggressive rather than erotic and use hostile rather than clever verbal forms; and, this paper will argue, have the creation of male group bonding as their purpose. While Freud analyzed jokes in order to reveal the unconscious, in this chapter, relationships will be analyzed to uncover the emotional dynamics of male friendships.

The failed penis-envy joke reveals two kinds of joking relationships between college men and women. First, the attempted joke was part of an ongoing joking relationship between "the guys and the girls," as they called each other. The guys used the joking relationship to negotiate the tension they felt between sexual interest in the girls and fear of commitment to them. The guys contrasted their sense of independence and play in male friendships to the sense of dependence they felt in their relationships with women, and used hostile joking to negotiate their fear of the "loss of control" implied by intimacy. Second, the failure of the joke uncovered the use of sexist jokes in creating bonds between men; through their own joking relationships (which they called friendship), the guys negotiated the tension between their need for intimacy with other men and their fear of losing their autonomy as men to the authority of the work world.

The Girls' Story

The women frequently had been the target of fraternity initiation rites in the past, and generally enjoyed this joking relationship with the men, if with a certain ambivalence. "There was a naked Christmas Carol event, they were singing 'We wish you a Merry Christmas,' and 'Bring on the hasty pudding' was the big line they liked to yell out. And we had five or six pledges who had to strip in front of the house and do naked jumping jacks on the lawn, after all the women in the house were lined up on the steps to watch." The women did not think these events were hostile because they had been invited to watch, and the men stood with them watching, suggesting that the pledges, not the women, were the targets of the joke. This made the joke sexual, not sexist, and part of the normal erotic joking relation between the guys and girls. Still, these jokes were ritual events, not real social relationships; one woman said, "We were just supposed to watch, and the guys were watching us watch. The men set up the stage and the women are brought along to observe. They were the controlling force, then they jump into the car and take off."

At the meeting with the men, two of the women spoke for the group while 11 others sat silently in the center, surrounded by about 30 men. Each tried to explain to the men why the joke had not been funny. The first began, "I'm a feminist, but I'm not going to blame anyone for anything. I just want to talk about my feelings." When she said, "these guys pile in, I mean these huge guys," the men exploded in loud cathartic laughter, and the women joined in, releasing some of the tension of the meeting. She continued, "Your humor was pretty funny as long as it was sexual, but when it went beyond sexual to sexist, then it became painful. You were saying 'I'm better than you.' When you started using sex as a way of proving your superiority it hurt me and made me angry."

The second woman speaker criticized the imposition of the joke form itself, saying that the men's raid had the tone of a symbolic rape. "I admit we knew you were coming over, and we were whispering about it. But it went too far, and I felt afraid to say anything. Why do men always think about women in terms of violating them, in sexual imagery? You have to understand that the combination of a sexual topic with the physical threat of all of you standing around terrified me. I couldn't move. You have to realize that when men combine sexuality and force it's terrifying to women." This woman alluded to having been sexually assaulted in the past, but spoke in a nonthreatening tone that made the men listen silently.

The women spoke about feeling angry about the invasion of their space, about the coercion of being forced to listen to the speeches, and about being used as the object of a joke. But they reported their anger as a psychological fact, a statement about a past feeling, not an accusation. Many began by saying, "I'm not a feminist, but . . .," to reassure the men that although they felt angry, they were not challenging traditional gender relations. The women were caught in a double-bind; if they spoke angrily to the men they would violate the taboo against the expression of anger by women (Miller, 1976, p. 102). If they said nothing, they would internalize their anger, and traditional feminine culture would encourage them to feel guilty about feeling angry at all (Bernardez, 1978; Lerner,

1980). In part they resolved the issue by accepting the men's construction of the event as a joke, although a failed joke; accepting the joke form absolved the men of responsibility, and transformed a debate about gender into a debate about good and bad jokes.

To be accepted as a joke, a cue must be sent to establish a "frame" the latent hostility of the joke content in a safe context; the men sent such a cue when they stood next to the women during the naked jumping jacks. If the cue "this is a joke" is ambiguous, or is not accepted, the aggressive content of the joke is revealed and generally is responded to with anger or aggression, endangering the relation. In part the women were pointing out to the men that the the cue "this is a joke" had not been given in this case, and the aggressive content of the joke hurt them. If the cue is given properly and accepted, the everyday rules of social order are suspended and the rule "this is fun" is imposed on the expression of hostility.

Verbal aggression mediated by the joke form generally will be without later consequences in the everyday world, and will be judged in terms of the formal intention of jokes, shared play marked by laughter in the interest of social order. By complaining to the university, the women had suspended the rules of joke culture, and attempted to renegotiate them by bringing in an observer; even this turned out to be too aggressive, and the women retreated to traditional gender relationships. The men had formally accepted this shift of rules in order to avoid punishment from the university, however their defense of the joke form was tacitly a defense of traditional gender rules that would define male sexist jokes toward women as erotic, not hostile.

In accepting the construction of the event as "just a joke" the women absolved the men of responsibility for their actions by calling them "little boys." One woman said, "It's not wrong, they're just boys playing a prank. They're little boys, they don't know what they're doing. It was unpleasant, but we shouldn't make a big deal out of it." In appealing to the rules of the joke form the men were willing to sacrifice their relationship to the women to protect the rules. In calling the men "little boys" the women were bending the rules trying to preserve the relationship through a patient nurturing role (see Gilligan, 1982, p. 44).

In calling the guys "little boys," the girls had also created a kind of linguistic symmetry between "the boys and the girls." With the exception of the law student, who called the girls "women," the students called the men "guys" and the women "girls." Earlier in the year the law student had started a discussion about this naming practice. The term "women" had sexual connotations that made "the girls" feel vulnerable, and "gals," the parallel to "guys," connoted "older women" to them.

While the term "girls" refers to children, it was adopted because it avoided sexual connotations. Thus the women had no term like "the guys," which is a bonding term that refers to a group of friends as equals; the women often used the term "the guys" to refer to themselves in a group. As the men's speeches were to make clear, the term "guys" refers to a bond that is exclusively male, which is founded upon the emotional structure of the joke form, and which justifies it.

The Guys' Story

Aside from the roar of laughter when a woman referred to their intimidating size, the men interrupted the women only once. When a woman began to say that the men obviously intended to intimidate them, the men loudly protested that the women couldn't possibly judge their intentions, that they intended the whole event only as a joke, and the intention of a joke is, by definition, just fun.

At this point the two black men in the fraternity intervened to explain the rules of male joke culture to the women. The black men said that in a sense they understood what the women meant, it is painful being the object of aggressive jokes. In fact, they said, the collective talk of the fraternity at meals and group events was made up of nothing but jokes, including many racist jokes. One said, "I know what you mean. I've had to listen to things in the house that I'd have hit someone for saying if I'd heard them outside." There was again cathartic laughter among the guys, for the male group bond consisted almost entirely of aggressive words that were barely contained by the responsibility absolving rule of the joke form. A woman responded, "Maybe people should be hit for saying those things, maybe that's the right thing to do." But the black speaker was trying to explain the rules of male joke culture to the women, "if you'd just ignored us, it wouldn't have been any fun." To ignore a joke, even though it makes you feel hurt or angry, is to show strength or coolness, the two primary masculine ideals of the group.

Another man tried to explain the failure of the joke in terms of the difference between the degree of "crudeness" appropriate between the guys and between "guys and girls." He said, "As I was listening at the edge of the room, near the door, and when I looked at the guys I was laughing but when I looked at the girls I was embarrassed. I could see both sides at the same time. It was too crude for your sense of propriety. We have a sense of crudeness you don't have. That's a cultural aspect of the difference between girls and guys."

The other men laughed as he mentioned "how crude we are at the house," and one of the black men added, "you wouldn't believe how crude it gets." Many of the men said privately that while they individually found the jokes about women vulgar, the jokes were justified because they were necessary for the formation of the fraternal bond. These men thought the mistake had been to reveal their crudeness to the women, this was "in bad taste."

In its content, the fraternal bond was almost entirely a joking relationship. In part, the joking was a kind of "signifying" or "dozens," a ritual exchange of insults that functioned to create group solidarity. "If there's one theme that goes on, it's the emphasis on being able to take a lot of ridicule, of shit, and not getting upset about it. Most of the interaction we have is verbally abusing each other, making disgusting references to your mother's sexuality, or the women you were seen with, or your sex organ, the size of your sex organ. And you aren't cool unless you can take it without trying to get back." Being cool is an important male value in other settings as well, such as sports or work; the joke form is a kind of male pedagogy in that, in one guys' words, it teaches "how to keep in control of your emotions."

But the guys themselves would not have described their group as a joking relationship or even as a male bond; they called it friendship. One man said he had found perhaps a dozen guys in the house who were special friends, "guys I could cry in front of." Yet in interviews, no one could recall any of the guys actually crying in front of each other. One said, "I think the guys are very close, they would do nearly anything for each other, drive each other places, give each other money. I think when they have problems about school, their car, or something like that, they can talk to each other. I'm not sure they can talk to each other about problems with women though." The image of crying in front of the other guys was a moving symbol of intimacy to the guys, but in fact crying would be an admission of vulnerability, which would violate the ideals of "strength" and "being cool."

Although the fraternal bond was idealized as a unique kind of intimacy upon which genuine friendship was built, the content of the joking relationship was focused upon women, including much "signifying" talk about mothers. The women interpreted the sexist jokes as a sign of vulnerability. "The thing that struck me the most about our meeting together," one said, "was when the men said they were afraid of trusting women, afraid of being seen as jerks." According to her, this had been the women's main reaction to the meeting by the other women, "How do you tell men that they don't have to be afraid, and what do you do with women who abuse that kind of trust?" One of the men on the boundary of the group remarked that the most hostile misogynist jokes came from the men with the fewest intimate relationships with women. "I think down deep all these guys would love to have satisfying relationships with women. I think they're scared of failing, of having to break away from the group they've become comfortable with. I think being in a fraternity, having close friendships with men is a replacement for having close relationships with women. It'd be painful for them because they'd probably fail."

Joking mobilized the commitment of the men to the group by policing the individual men's commitments to women and minimized the possibility of dyadic withdrawal from the group (see Slater, 1963). "One of the guys just acquired a girlfriend a few weeks ago. He's someone I don't think has had a woman to be friends with, maybe ever, at least in a long time. Everybody has been ribbing him intensely the last few weeks. It's good natured in tone. Sitting at dinner they've invented a little song they sing to him. People yell questions about his girlfriend, the size of her vagina, does she have big breasts."

Since both the jokes and the descriptions of the parties have strong homoerotic overtones, including the exchange of women as sexual partners, jokes were also targeted at homosexuality, to draw an emotional line between the homosocial male bond and homosexual relationships. Being called "queer," however, did not require a sexual relationship with another man, but only visible signs of vulnerability or nurturing behavior.

Male Bonding as a Joking Relationship

Fraternal bonding is an intimate kind of male group friendship that suspends the ordinary rules and responsibilities of everyday life through joking relationships. To the guys, dyadic friendship with a woman implied "loss of control," namely, responsibility for work and family. In dealing with women, the group separated intimacy from sex, defining the male bond as intimate but not sexual (homosocial), and relationships with women as sexual but not intimate (heterosexual). The intimacy of group friendship was built upon shared spontaneous action, "having fun," rather than the self-disclosure that marks women's friendships (see Rubin, 1983, p. 13). One of the men had been inexpressive as he listened to the discussion, but spoke about fun in a voice filled with emotion, "The penis-envy speech was a hilarious idea, great college fun. That's what I joined the fraternity for, a good time. College is a stage in my life to do crazy and humorous things. In 10 years when I'm in the business world I won't be able to carry on like this [again cathartic laughter from the men]. The initiation was intended to be humorous. We didn't think through how sensitive you women were going to be."

This speech gives the fraternal bond a specific place in the life cycle. The joking relationship is a ritual bond that creates a male group bond in the transition between boyhood and manhood, after the separation from the family, where the authority of mothers limits fun, but before becoming subject to the authority of work. One man later commented on the transitional nature of the male bond, "I think a lot of us are really scared of losing total control over our own lives. Having to sacrifice our individuality. I think we're scared of work in the same way we're scared of women." In this sense individuality is associated with what the guys called "strength," both the emotional strength suggested by being cool, and the physical strength suggested by facing the risks of sports and the paramilitary games they liked to play.

The emotional structure of the joking relationship is built upon the guys' latent anger about the discipline that middle-class male roles imposed upon them, both marriage rules and work rules. The general relationship between organization of men's work and men's domination of women was noted by Max Weber (1958, pp. 345-346), who described "the vocational specialist" as a man mastered by the rules of organization that create an impersonal kind of dependence, and who therefore seeks to create a feeling of independence through the sexual conquest of women. In each of the epochs of Western history, Weber argues, the subordination of men at work has given rise to a male concept of freedom based upon the violation of women. Although Weber tied dependence upon rules to men's need for sexual conquest through seduction, this may also be a clue to the meaning of sexist jokes and joking relationships among men at work. Sexist jokes may not be simply a matter of recreation or a means of negotiating role stress, they may be a reflection of the emotional foundations of organizational life for men. In everyday work life, sexist jokes may function as a ritual suspension of the rules of responsibility for men, a withdrawal into a microworld in which their anger about dependence upon work and women may be safely expressed.

In analyzing the contradictions and vulnerabilities the guys felt about relationships with women and the responsibilities of work, I will focus upon three dimensions of the joking relationship: (1) the emotional content of the jokes; (2) the erotic of rule breaking created by the rules of the joke form; and (3) the image of strength and "being cool" they pitted against the dependence represented by both women and work.

The Emotional Dynamic of
Sexist Jokes

When confronted by the women, the men defended the joke by asserting the formal rule that the purpose of jokes is play, then by justifying the jokes as necessary in order to create a special male bond. The defense that jokes are play defines aggressive behavior as play. This defense was far more persuasive to the men than to the women, since many forms of male bonding play are rule-governed aggression, as in sports and games. The second defense, asserting the relation between sexist jokes and male bonds, points out the social function of sexist jokes among the guys, to control the threat that individual men might form intimate emotional bonds with women and withdraw from the group. Each defense poses a puzzle about the emotional dynamics of male group friendship, for in each case male group friendship seems more like a defense against vulnerability than a positive deal.

In each defense, intimacy is split from sexuality in order to eroticize the male bond, thereby creating an instrumental sexuality directed at women. The separation of intimacy from sexuality transforms women into "sexual objects," which both justifies aggression at women by suspending their relationships to the men and devalues sexuality itself, creating a disgust at women as the sexual "object" unworthy of intimate attention. What is the origin of this conjunction between the devaluation of sexuality and the appropriation of intimacy for the male bond?

Chodorow (1978, p. 182) argues that the sense of masculine identity is constructed by an early repression of the son's erotic bond with his mother; with this repression the son's capacity for intimacy and commitment is devalued as feminine behavior. Henceforth men feel ambivalent about intimate relationships with women, seeking to replicate the fusion of intimacy and sexuality that they had experienced in their primal relationships to their mothers, but at the same time fearing engulfment by women in heterosexual relationships, like the engulfment of their infant selves by their mothers (Chodorow, 1976). Certainly the content of the group's joke suggests this repression of the attachment to the mother, as well as hostility to her authority in the family. One man reported, "There're an awful lot of jokes about people's mothers. If any one topic of conversation dominates the conversation it's 'heard your mother was with Ray [one of the guys] last night.' The guys will say incredibly vulgar things about their mothers, or they'll talk about the anatomy of a guy's girlfriends, or women they'd like to sleep with." While the guys' signifying mother jokes suggest the repression Chodorow describes, the men realized that their view of women made it unlikely that marriage would be a positive experience. One said, "I think a lot of us expect to marry someone pretty enough that other men will think we got a good catch, someone who is at least marginally interesting to chat with, but not someone we'd view as a friend. But at the same time, a woman who will make sufficient demands that we won't be able to have any friends. So we'll be stuck for the rest of our lives without friends."

While the emotional dynamic of men's "heterosexual knots" may well begin in this primordial separation of infant sons from mothers, its structure is replicated in the guys' ambivalence about their fathers, and their anger about the dependence upon rules in the work world. Yet the guys themselves described the fraternal bond as a way of creating "strength" and overcoming dependence, which suggests a positive ideal of male identity. In order to explore the guys' sense of the value of the male bond, their conception of strength and its consequences for the way they related to each other and to women has to be taken seriously.

"Strength"

Ultimately the guys justified the penis-envy joke because it created a special kind of male intimacy, but while the male group is able to appropriate its members' needs for intimacy and commitment, it is not clear that it is able to satisfy those needs, because strength has been defined as the opposite of intimacy. "Strength" is a value that represents solidarity rather than intimacy, the solidarity of a shared risk in rule-governed aggressive competition; its value is suggested by the cathartic laughter when the first woman speaker said, "These guys poured in, these huge guys."

The eros detached from sexuality is attached to rules, not to male friends; the male bond consists of an erotic toward rules, and yet the penis-envy joke expresses most of all the guys' ambivalence about rules. Like "the lads," the male gangs who roam the English countryside, "getting in trouble" by enforcing social mores in unsocial ways (Peters, 1972), "the guys" break the rules in rule-governed ways. The joke form itself suggests this ambivalence about rules and acts as a kind of pedagogy about the relationship between rules and aggression in male work culture. The joke form expresses emotions and tensions that might endanger the order of the organization, but that must be spoken lest they damage social order. Jokes can create group solidarity only if they allow dangerous things to be said; allow a physical catharsis of tension through laughter; or create the solidarity of an "in group" through shared aggression against an "out group." In each case there is an erotic in joke forms: an erotic of shared aggression, of shared sexual feeling, or an erotic of rule breaking itself.

It has been suggested that male groups experience a high level of excitement and sexual arousal in public acts of rule breaking (Thorne & Luria, 1986). The penis-envy speech is precisely such an act, a breaking of conventional moral rules in the interest of group arousal. In each of the versions of the joking relationship in this group there is such an erotic quality: in the sexual content of the jokes, in the need for women to witness dirty talk or naked pledges, in the eros of aggression of the raid and jokes themselves. The penis-envy speech, a required event for all members of the group, is such a collective violation of the rules, and so is the content of their talk, a collective dirty talking that violates moral rules. The cathartic laughter that greeted the words, "You wouldn't believe what we say at the house," testifies to the emotional charge invested in dirty talk.

Because the intimacy of the guys' bond is built around an erotic of rule breaking, it has the serial structure of shared risk rather than the social structure of shared intimacy. In writing about the shared experience of suffering and danger of men at war, J. Glenn Gray (1959, pp. 89-90) distinguishes two kinds of male bonding, comradeship and friendship. Comradeship is based upon an erotic of shared danger, but is based upon the loss of an individual sense of self to a group identity, while friendship is based upon an individual's intellectual and emotional affinity to another individual. In the eros of friendship one's sense of self is heightened; in the eros of comradeship a sense of self is replaced by a sense of group membership. In this sense the guys were seeking comradeship, not friendship, hence the group constructed its bond through an erotic of shared activities with an element of risk, shared danger, or rule breaking: in sports, in paramilitary games, in wild parties, in joking relations. The guys called the performance of these activities "strength," being willing to take risks as a group and remaining cool.

Thus the behavior that the women defined as aggressive was seen by the men as a contest of strength governed by the rules of the joke form, to which the proper response would have been to remain "cool." To the guys, the masculine virtue of "strength" has a positive side, to discover oneself and to discover a sense of the other person through a contest of strength that is governed by rules. To the guys, "strength" is not the same as power or aggression because it is governed by rules, not anger; it is anger that is "uncool."

"Being Cool"

It is striking that the breaking of rules was not spontaneous, but controlled by the rules of the joke form: that aggressive talk replaces action; that talk is framed by a social form that requires the consent of others; that talk should not be taken seriously. This was the lesson that the black men tried to teach the women in the group session: In the male world, aggression is not defined as violent if it is rule governed rather than anger governed. The fraternal bond was built upon this emotional structure, for the life of the group centered upon the mobilization of aggressive energies in rule-governed activities (in sports, games, jokes, parties), in each arena aggression was highly valued (strength) only when it was rule governed (cool). Getting angry was called "losing control" and the guys thought they were most likely to lose control when they experienced themselves as personally dependent, as in relationships with women and at work.

Rule-governed aggression is a conduct that is very useful to organizations, in that it mobilizes aggressive energies but binds them to order by rules (see Benjamin, 1980, p. 154). The male sense of order is procedural rather than substantive because the male bond is formal (rule governed), rather than personal (based upon intimacy and commitment). Male groups in this sense are shame cultures, not guilt cultures, because the male bond is a group identity that subordinates the individual to the rules, and because social control is imposed through collective judgments about self-control, such as "strength" and "cool." The sense of order within such male groups is based upon the belief that all members are equally dependent upon the rules and that no personal dependence is created within the group. This is not true of the family or of relations with women, both of which are intimate, and, from the guys' point of view, are "out of control" because they are governed by emotion.

The guys face contradictory demands from work culture about the use of aggressive behavior. Aggressive conduct is highly valued in a competitive society when it serves the interests of the organization, but men also face a strong taboo against the expression of anger at work when it is not rule governed. "Competition" imposes certain rules upon aggressive group processes: Aggression must be calculated, not angry; it must be consistent with the power hierarchy of the organization, serving authority and not challenging it; if expressed, it must be indirect, as in jokes; it must serve the needs of group solidarity, not of individual autonomy. Masculine culture separates anger from aggression when it combines the value "strength" with the value "being cool." While masculine cultures often define the expression of anger as "violent" or "loss of control," anger, properly defined, is speech, not action; angry speech is the way we can defend our sense of integrity and assert our sense of justice. Thus it is anger that challenges the authority of the rules, not aggressive behavior in itself, because anger defends the self, not the organization.

The guys' joking relationship taught them a pedagogy for the controlled use of aggression in the work world, to be able to compete aggressively without feeling angry. The guys recognized the relationship between their male bond and the work world by claiming that "high officials of the university know about the way we act and they understand what we are doing." While this might be taken as evidence that the guys were internalizing their fathers' norms and thus inheriting the mantle of patriarchy, the guys described their fathers as slaves to work and women, not as patriarchs. The guys also asserted themselves against the authority of their fathers by acting out against the authority of rules in the performance of "strength."

The guys clearly benefited from the male authority that gave them the power to impose the penis-envy joke upon the women with essentially no consequences. Men are allowed to direct anger and aggression toward women because social norms governing the expression of anger or humor generally replicate the power order of the group. It is striking, however, that the guys would not accept the notion that men have more power than women do; to them it is not men who rule, but rules that govern men. These men had so internalized the governing of male emotions by rules that their anger itself could emerge only indirectly through rule-governed forms, such as jokes and joking relationships. In these forms their anger could serve only order, not their sense of self or justice.

REFERENCES

Bateson, G. (1972). A theory of play and fantasy. In *Steps toward an ecology of mind* (pp. 177-193). New York: Ballantine. (Original work published 1955)

Benjamin, J. (1978). Authority and the family revisited, or, A world without fathers. *New German Critique, 4*(3), 13, 35-57.

Benjamin, J. (1980). The bonds of love: Rational violence and erotic domination. *Feminist Studies, 6*(1), 144-174.

Berndardez, T. (1978). Women and anger. *Journal of the American Medical Women's Association, 33*(5), 215-219.

Bly, R. (1982). What men really want: An interview with Keith Thompson. *New Age,* pp. 30-37, 50-51.

Chodorow, N. (1976). Oedipal asymmetries, heterosexual knots. *Social Problems, 23,* 454-468.

Chodorow, N. (1978). *The reproduction of mothering.* Berkeley: University of California Press.

Coser, R. (1959). Some social functions of laughter: A study of humor in a hospital setting. *Human Relations, 12,* 171-182.

Emerson, J. (1969). Negotiating the serious import of humor. *Sociometry, 32,* 169-181.

Emerson, J.(1970). Behavior in private places. In H. P. Dreitzel (Ed.), *Recent sociology: Vol. 2. Patterns in communicative behavior.* New York: Macmillan.

Freud, S. (1960). *Jokes and their relation to the unconscious.* New York Norton.

Gilligan, C. (1982). *In a different voice.* Cambridge, MA: Harvard University Press.

Gray, G. J. (1959). *The warriors: Reflections on men in battle.* New York: Harper & Row.

Lerner, H. E. (1980). Internal prohibitions against female anger. *American Journal of Psychoanalysis, 40,* 137-148.

Miller, J. B. (1976). *Toward a new psychology of women.* Boston: Beacon.

Peters, E. L. (1972). Aspects of the control of moral ambiguities. In M. Gluckman (Ed.), *The allocation of responsibility* (pp. 109-162). Manchester: Manchester University Press.

Radcliffe-Brown, A. (1959). *Structure and function in primitive society.* Glencoe, IL: Free Press.

Rubin, L. (1983). *Intimate strangers.* New York: Harper & Row.

Slater, P. (1963). On social regression. *American Sociological Review, 28,* 339-364.

Thorne, B., & Luria, Z. (1986). Sexuality and gender in children's daily worlds. *Social Problems.*

Weber, M. (1958). Religions of the world and their directions. In H. Gerth & C. W. Mills (Eds.), *From Max Weber.* New York: Oxford University Press.

PART IV

Sexuality

11

In Pursuit of the Perfect Penis

The Medicalization of Male Sexuality

LEONORE TIEFER

Sexual virility—the ability to fulfill the conjugal duty, the ability to procreate, sexual power, potency—is everywhere a requirement of the male role, and, thus, "impotence" is everywhere a matter of concern. Although the term has been used for centuries to specifically refer to partial or complete loss of erectile ability, the first definition dictionaries give for impotence never mentions sex but refers to a general loss of vigor, strength, or power. Sex therapists, concerned about these demeaning connotations, have written about the stigmatizing impact of the label "impotent."

> The word impotent is used to describe the man who does not get an erection, not just his penis. When a man is told by his doctor that he is impotent or when the man turns to his partner and says he is impotent: they are saying a lot more than that the penis cannot become erect. (Kelley, 1981, p. 126)

Yet a recent survey of the psychological literature found that the frequency of articles with the term "impotence" in the title has risen dramatically since 1970, in contrast with the almost total disappearance of the term "frigidity," a term with comparable pejorative connotations and comparable frequency of use from 1940 to 1970. (Elliott, 1985)

In this article I would like to show how the persistence and increased use of the stigmatizing and stress-inducing label of impotence reflects a significant moment in the social construction of male sexuality. The factors that create this moment include the increasing importance of life-long sexual activity in one's life, the insatiability of mass media for appropriate sexual topics, the expansionist needs of specialty medicine and new medical technology, and the highly demanding male sexual script. I will show how these factors interact to produce a medicalization of male sexuality and sexual impotence, which limits many men even as it offers new options and hope to others. Let me begin with a discussion of men's sexuality, and then a discussion of what medicine has recently had to offer it.

Male Sexuality

Sexual competence is part—some would say the central part—of contemporary masculinity, whether we are discussing the traditional man, the modern man, or even the "new" man.

> What so stokes male sexuality that clinicians are impressed by the force of it? Not libido, but rather the curious phenomenon by which sexuality consolidates and confirms gender.... An impotent man always feels that his masculinity, and not just his sexuality, is threatened. In men, gender appears to "lean" on sexuality . . . the need for sexual performance is so great. . . . In women, gender identity and self-worth can be consolidated by other means. (Person, 1980, pp. 619, 626)

Gagnon and Simon (1973) explained how, during adolescent masturbation, genital sexuality (that is, erection and orgasm) acquires nonsexual motives such as the desire for power, achievement, and peer approval that have already become important during preadolescent gender role training. "The capacity for erection is an important sign element of masculinity and control" (Gagnon & Simon, 1973, p. 62) without which a man is not a man. Gross (1978) argues that by adulthood few men can accept other successful aspects of masculinity in lieu of adequate sexual performance.

Masculine sexuality assumes the ability for potent function, but the performances that earn acceptance and status often occur far from the bedroom. Tolson (1977) has described how working-class men engage in an endless performance of sexual stories, jokes, and routines:

As a topic on which most men could support a conversation and as a source of jokes, sexual talk and gesture were inexhaustible. In the machine noise, a gesture suggestive of masturbation, intercourse or homosexuality was enough to raise a conventional smile and re-establish a bond over distances too great for talking. (Marsden, quoted in Tolson, 1977, p. 60)

Tolson argues that this type of ritualized sexual exchange validates working men's bond of masculinity in a situation that otherwise emasculates them. This is an example of the enduring homosocial function of heterosexuality that develops from the adolescent experience (Gagnon & Simon, 1973).

Psychologically, then, male sexual performances may have as much or more to do with male gender role confirmation and homosocial status as with pleasure, intimacy, or tension release. This may explain why men express so many rules concerning proper sexual performance: Their agenda relates not merely to personal or couple satisfaction but to acting "like a man" in intercourse in order to qualify for the title elsewhere.

We can draw on the writings of several authorities to compile an outline of the 10 sexual beliefs to which many men subscribe (Doyle, 1983; Zilbergeld, 1978; LoPiccolo, 1985): (1) Men's sexual apparatus and needs are simple and straightforward, unlike women's. (2) Most men are ready, willing, and eager for as much sex as they can get. (3) There is suspicion that other men's sexual experiences approximate ecstatic explosiveness more closely and more often than does one's own. (4) It is the responsibility of the man to teach and lead his partner to experience pleasure and orgasm(s). (5) Sexual prowess is a serious, task-oriented business, with no place for experimentation, unpredictability, or play. (6) Women prefer intercourse to other sexual activities, particularly "hard-driving" intercourse. (7) All really good and normal sex must end in intercourse. (8) Any physical contact other than a light touch is meant as an invitation to foreplay and intercourse. (9) It is the responsibility of the man to satisfy both his partner and himself. (10) Sexual prowess is never permanently earned; each time it must be reproven.

Many of these demands directly require—and all of them indirectly require—an erection. Nelson (1985) pointed out that male sexuality is dominated by a genital focus in several ways: Sexuality is isolated from the rest of life as a unique experience with particular technical performance requirements; the subjective meaning for the man arises from genital sensations first practiced and familiar in adolescent masturbation and directly transferred without thought to the interpersonal situation; and the psychological meaning primarily depends on the confirmation of virility that comes from proper erection and ejaculation.

It is no surprise, then, that any difficulty in getting the penis to do what it "ought" can become a source of profound humiliation and despair, both in terms of immediate self-esteem and the destruction of one's masculine reputation, which, it is assumed, will follow.

> Few sexual problems are as devastating to a man as his inability to achieve or sustain an erection long enough for successful sexual intercourse. For many men the idea of not being able to "get it up" is a fate worse than death. (Doyle, 1983, p. 205)

> What's the worst thing that can happen? I ask myself. The worst thing that can happen is that I take one of these hip beautiful liberated women to bed and I can't get it up. I can't get it up! You hear me? She tells a few of her friends. Soon around every corner there's someone laughing at my failure. (Parent, 1977, p. 15)

Biomedical Approaches
to Male Sexual Problems

Within the last decade, both professional and popular discussion about male sexuality has emphasized physical causes and treatments for sexual problems. There is greater awareness and acceptance within the medical profession of clinical and research work on sexuality, and sexually dissatisfied men are increasingly willing to discuss their problem with a physician (Bancroft, 1983). The professional literature on erection problems has focused on methods of differentiating between organic and nonorganic causes (LoPiccolo, 1985). Recent reviews survey endocrine, neurological, medication-related, urological, surgery-related, congenital, and vascular causes and contrast them with psychological and relationship causes (Krane, Siroky, & Goldstein, 1983).

Although the psychological contributions to adequate sexual functioning theoretically can be specified in some detail, as yet few diagnostic tests exist that enable specific identification of one type of pathophysiological contribution versus another. Moreover, as yet few medical treatments are available for medically caused erectile disorders aside from changing medications (particularly in the case of hypertension) or correcting an underlying disease process. The most widely used medical approach is an extreme one: surgical implantation of a device into the penis that will permit intromission. This is the penile prosthesis.

The history of these devices is relatively short (Melman, 1978). Following unsuccessful attempts with bone and cartilage, the earliest synthetic implant (1948) was of a plastic tube placed in the middle of the penis of a patient who had had his urethra removed for other reasons. Today, several different manufacturers produce slightly different versions of two general types of implant.

One type is the "inflatable" prosthesis. Inflatable silicone cylinders are placed in the corpora cavernosa of the penis, the cylindrical bodies of erectile tissue that normally fill with blood during erection. The cylinders are connected to a pump placed in the scrotum that is connected to a small, saline-filled reservoir placed in the abdomen. "When the patient desires a tumescent phallus, the bulb is squeezed five or six times and fluid is forced from the reservoir into the cylinder chambers. When a flaccid penis is wanted, a deflation valve is pressed and the fluid returns to the reservoir" (Melman, 1978, p. 278).

The other type of prosthesis is a pair of semirigid rods, now made of silicone, with either a bendable silver core or a hinge to allow concealment of the erection by bending it down or up against the body when the man is dressed.

Because these devices have been implanted primarily by private practitioners, the only way to estimate the number of implant operations is from manufacturers' sales figures. However, many devices are sold that are not used. A French urologist estimated that 5,000 patients were given penile implants in 1977 alone (Subrini, 1980). It seems reasonable to guess that by the mid-1980s hundreds of thousands of men had received implants.

Needless to say, many articles have been written stressing the need to evaluate carefully men who might be candidates for the procedure. Surgeons are concerned to exclude:

> patients at risk of becoming psychotic or suicidal, developing chronic psychogenic pain, or initiating inappropriate malpractice suits. . . . A second important concern has been to rule out patients whose erectile dysfunction is psychogenic and could be cured without surgery . . . although several urologists have reported high patient satisfaction when carefully selected patients with psychogenic dysfunction received penile prostheses. (Schover & von Eschenbach, 1985, p. 58)

Postimplant follow-up studies typically have been conducted by surgeons interested in operative complications and global measures of patient satisfaction (Sotile, 1979). Past reports have encouraged the belief that the devices function mechanically, are adjusted to by the man and his partner without difficulty, and result in satisfactory sexual function and sensation. But recent papers are challenging these conclusions. One review of the postoperative follow-up literature was so critical of methodological weaknesses (brief follow-up periods, rare interviews with patients' sexual partners, few objective data or even cross validation of subjective questions about sexual functioning, among others), the authors could not summarize the results in any meaningful way (Collins & Kinder, 1984). Another recent summary criticized the implants' effectiveness:

> First, recent reports indicate that the percentage of surgical and mechanical complications from such prosthetic implants is much higher than might be considered acceptable. Second, despite claims to the contrary by some surgeons, it appears likely that whatever degree of naturally-occurring erection a man is capable of will be disrupted, and perhaps eliminated by the surgical procedures and scarring involved in prosthetic implants. Finally, it has been my experience that, although patients are typically rather eager to have a prosthesis implanted and report being very happy with it at short-term surgical follow-up, longer term behavioral assessment indicates poor sexual adjustment in some cases. (LoPiccolo, 1985, p. 222)

Three recent urological papers report high rates of postoperative infection and mechanical failure of the inflatable prosthesis, both necessitating removal of the device (Apte, Gregory, & Purcell, 1984; Joseph, Bruskewitz, & Benson, 1984; Fallon, Rosenberg, & Culp, 1984). In the first paper, 43% of patients required at least one repeat surgery; in the second paper, the device malfunctioned in 47% of 88 cases operated on since 1977; in the third, 48% of 95 patients have had their prosthesis malfunction in one way or another since 1977.

In perhaps the only paper reporting on the effectiveness of penile implants in gay men, a therapist who had worked with three such patients indicated that

> the implants were less successful with homosexuals than with heterosexuals because there tends to be much more direct penile contact in gay sexuality than in heterosexual sexuality. The person with the implant is aware of the difference, not his partner. (Paff, 1985, p. 15)

One of the patients had to have the implant removed because of a mechanical malfunction.

Public Information About
Penile Prostheses

Public sexual information is dominated by health and medical science in both language and substance. Newspapers present "new" discoveries. Magazines have "experts" with advanced health degrees outline "new" norms and ways to achieve them. Television and radio talk-show guests, health-degreed "experts," promote their latest book or therapeutic approach as "resources" are flashed on the screen or mentioned by the host. Sexuality is presented as a life problem—such as buying a house, having a good relationship, dealing with career choices—the "modern" approach is to be rational, orderly, careful, thorough, up-to-date, and in tune with the latest pronouncements of the experts.

The public accepts the assumption that scientific discoveries improve our ability to manage and control our lives and welcomes new biomedical developments in areas perceived to be dominated by the physical or by standards of health and illness. Sexual physiology has a tangibility, which "love" and "lust" lack, increasing its propriety as a language for public discourse. When biomedicine, health, and physiology are considered the appropriate sexual discourse, scientists and health care providers are the appropriate authorities.

The media have presented information about penile prostheses in the same straightforward, rational, scientific, informative way as other "news" about sexuality. One article in *The New York Times* in 1979 presented the findings of a urological paper that had appeared in the *Journal of the American Medical Association* the day before. It gave the address of the prothesis manufacturer as well as typical financial cost, length of hospital stay, and insurance coverage. A JAMA editorial, criticizing the study's inattention to the patients' sexual partners, was mentioned.

An article in *Vogue* discussed new medical/surgical approaches to impotence under a typically simple and optimistic title, "Curing Impotence: The Prognosis is Good." The financial cost of the devices is mentioned as well as a new item being developed, a "electrostimulatory device to be inserted in the anus before intercourse and controlled by a ring or wristwatch-like switch so that patients can signal appropriate nerves to produce an erection" (Hixson, 1985, p. 406). The style is technical and mechanical and so simple and cheerful, it is hardly amazing to read in a sentence following the anal electrode description, "While psychological impotence problems probably also require psychological treatment, the doctors feel that successful electronic intercourse may provide the confidence needed by some men" (p. 406).

Literature for patients has been developed by the major prosthesis manufacturers and is available at patient education centers, in doctors' waiting rooms, and through self-help groups such as *Impotents Anonymous.* A typical booklet is seven pages of high quality glossy paper, with photographs of healthy young couples in a garden, watching a beautiful sunset, sitting by the ocean (Mentor Corporation, 1984). Titled "Overcoming Impotence," the text reads:

> Impotence is a widespread problem that affects many millions of men. It can occur at any age and at any point in a man's life. The myth of impotence as an "old man's disease" has finally been shattered. Impotence is a problem of men but also affects couples and families. Now, as a result of recent medical advances, impotence need no longer cause frustration, embarrassment and tension. New solutions are now available for an age-old problem.

In the second section, on causes of impotence, the booklet reads as follows:

> The causes can be either physical or psychological. For many years, it was believed that 90 percent of impotent men had a psychological cause for their problem; but as a result of recent medical research, it is now known that at least half of the men suffering from impotence can actually trace its origin to a physical problem.

After a lengthy discussion of the methods used to distinguish between physical and psychological impotence, the booklet continues in its relentlessly upbeat way:

> For the majority of men who are physically impotent and for those who are psychologically impotent and do not respond to counseling, a penile implant offers the only complete, reliable solution. It offers new hope for a return to satisfactory sexual activity and for the disappearance of the anxieties and frustrations of impotence.

This, of course, seems to be merely a straightforward technological solution to a technical problem. No mention is made of individual differences in adjustment to the prosthesis, or even that adjustment will be necessary at all. The mechanical solution itself will solve the problem; the person becomes irrelevant.

Other patient information booklets are similar: informative about the device and reassuring about the outcome. In addition to lengthy and detailed discussion of specific physical causes of impotence, brief mention is made of psychogenic impotence.

Another group of patients have some type of mental barrier [sic] or problem. This latter group may account for as high as 50% of the people with impotence, but only a small number of these people are candidates for a penile implant. (Medical Engineering Corp., 1983)

Is it any wonder that men who "fail" the physical tests and are diagnosed as having psychogenic impotence cannot understand why they should be deprived of the device?

Urologists have begun in recent years to specialize in the diagnosis and surgical treatment of impotence. A quarterly publication from a prothesis manufacturer "for surgeons practicing prosthetic urology" recently devoted a front page to the subject "Impotence Clinics: Investments in the Future" (American Medical Systems, 1984). Newspaper advertisements have begun to appear from groups of urologists with such names as Potency Plus in California. Another California group calling itself Potential advertises "Impotence . . . there could be a medical reason and a medical solution." An ad in a New York newspaper is headlined "Potent Solution to Sexual Problem."

Another source of publicity about the physical causes and treatments for erectile difficulties has come from The Impotence Institute of America, an organization founded by a man who describes how his own search ended happily with an implanted penile prosthesis. Although the subhead on the not-for-profit institute's stationery is "Bringing a 'total-care' concept to overcoming impotency," the 10 men on the board of directors are all urologists.

In 1982 the institute created two consumer-oriented groups, Impotents Anonymous (IA) and I-Anon, based on the Alcoholics Anonymous models (both the institute's founder and his wife formerly had been members of Al-Anon). Recent correspondence from the institute indicates 70 chapters of IA operating and another 20 planned. A 1984 news article about IA, "Organization Helps Couples with Impotence as Problem," repeated the now familiar information that "until five years ago most physicians believed that up to 95% of all erectile impotence stemmed from psychological problems, [but that] medical experts now agree that about half of all impotence is caused by physical disorders" (New York Times, 1984). The IA brochure cites the same numbers.

Let us turn now to a critique of the biomedical approach to male sexuality, beginning with this question of organic and psychogenic etiology.

Critique of the Biomedical Approach

The frequent claim that psychogenic impotence has been oversold and organic causes are far more common than was realized has captivated the media and legitimated increased medical involvement in sexuality. An International Journal of Andrology editorial summarizes the shift:

> Medical fashions come and go and the treatment of erectile impotence is no exception. In the 20s and 30s, physicians and surgeons looked for physical causes and tried out methods of treatment, most of which now seem absurd. Since that time there has been a widely held view that 90-95% of cases of impotence are psychologically determined. Where this figure came from was never clear [some sources cite Havelock Ellis], but it has entered into medical folklore. In the past five years or so, the pendulum has been swinging back. Physical causes and methods of treatment are receiving increasing attention. (Bancroft, 1982, 353)

In the Center for Male Sexual Dysfunction in the Department of Urology, Beth Israel Medical Center, New York City, over 800 men have been seen since 1981 because of erectile problems. Very few who, on the basis of a simple history and physical, could be declared unambiguously "psychogenic" were referred immediately for sex therapy; the remainder underwent a complete medical and psychological workup. Over 90% of these patients believed their problem was completely or preponderantly physical in origin; yet we have found only about 45% of patients have exclusively or predominantly medically caused erectile problems, and 55% have exclusively or predominantly psychologically caused problems. This approximately 50/50 split is, in fact, what is being observed by the mass media. But it is based on a sample of men usually referred by their primary physicians (over 75%) because of their likely medical etiology and their need for a comprehensive workup.

A Chicago group found 43% of a group of men coming to a urology clinic for impotence evaluation had at least partly an organic basis for their problems, whereas only 11% of men coming to a psychiatry department sex clinic had organic contributing factors (Segraves, Schoenberg, Zarins, Camic, & Knopf, 1981). A review of all patients seen at the Johns Hopkins Sexual Behaviors Consultation Unit between 1972 and 1981 showed 105 men over 50 years old with a primary complaint of erectile dysfunction. Even in this age group, only 30% could be assigned an organic etiology (Wise, Rabins, & Gahnsley, 1984). After listing 66 possible physical causes of secondary impotence, Masters and Johnson (1970, pp. 184-185) reported that only seven of their 213 cases (3%) had an organic etiology.

Obviously, one cannot describe the actual rate of occurrence of any particular problems (e.g., "organic impotence") without describing the population from which the sample comes. The urology departments' findings that approximately half of the patients seen for erectile problems have a medical cause cannot be generalized to other groups (e.g., men in general practitioners' waiting rooms reading prosthesis manufacturers' literature, men watching a TV program about impotence) without further normative data collection. It is important to emphasize that even men with diabetes, a known cause of peripheral neural and vascular difficulties, which could result in impotence, are as often potent as not (Schiavi, Fisher, Quadland, & Glober, 1984; Fairburn, McCulloch, & Wu, 1982), a result that cannot be predicted from the duration of the diabetes or the presence of other physical complications.

An even more serious criticism of the biomedical trend is the common tendency to contrapose organic and psychogenic causes of impotence as mutually exclusive phenomena.

> Conceptually, most of the research suffers from the flaw of attempting to categorize the patients into discrete, nonoverlapping categories of organic or psychogenic erectile failure. Yet, many cases, and perhaps the majority of cases, involve both organic and psychogenic erectile factors in the genesis of erectile failure. (LoPiccolo, 1985, p. 221)

Schumacher & Lloyd (1981), in a review of 102 cases seen at two different medical school centers, conclude that "all patients reported psychological distress associated with their impotence [including] inhibitions, shame, avoidance, insecurity, inadequacy, guilt, hostility, fear of intimacy" (p. 46). One prominent urologist reviewed 388 cases and concluded:

> There are wholly organic bases and also totally psychological causes for impotency; yet the two generally coexist. It is most probable that in all cases of organic impotency a psychologic overlay develops. (Finkle & Finkle, 1984, p. 25)

It is not so much, I believe, that all cases involve a mixture of factors but that all cases involve psychological factors to some degree. The director of a New York sexuality clinic sums up her impressions similarly:

> We have found in our work . . . that, where organic determinants are diagnosed, inevitably there will also be psychological factors involved, either as co-determinants of the erectile dysfunction or as reactive to it. . . . A man's emotional reactions to his erectile failures may be such that it serves to maintain the erectile problem even when the initial physiological causes are resolved. (Schreiner-Engel, 1981, p. 116)

The consequences of this implication are particularly serious given that, as LoPiccolo (1985, p. 221) notes, "many physicians currently will perform surgery to implant a penile prosthesis if any organic abnormality is found." The effect of psychological factors is to make the dysfunction look worse than the medical problem alone would warrant. Altering the man's devastated attitudes will improve the picture, whatever else is going on.

Perelman (1984, p. 181) refers to "the omnipresent psychogenic component existing in any potency problem regardless of the degree of organicity," to describe his successful use of cognitive-behavioral psychotherapy to treat men diagnosed with organic impotence. He reminds us that physical sexual function has a psychosomatic complexity, which is not only poorly understood but which may have the "ability to successfully compensate for its own deficits." Thus the search for the etiology that characterizes so much of the biomedical approach to male sexual problems seems to have less to do with the nature of sexuality than it does to the nature of the medical enterprise.

The Allure of Medicalized Sexuality

Men are drawn to a technological solution such as the penile prosthesis for a variety of personal reasons which ultimately rest on the inflexible central place of sexual potency in the male sexual script. Those who assume that "normal" men must always be interested in sex and who believe male sexuality is a simple system wherein interest leads easily and directly to erection (Zilbergeld, 1978) are baffled by any erectile difficulties. Their belief that "their penis is an instrument immune from everyday problems, anxieties and fears" (Doyle, 1983, p. 207) conditions them to deny the contribution of psychological or interpersonal factors to male sexual responsiveness. This denial, in turn, results from fundamental male gender role prescriptions for self-reliance and emotional control (Brannon, 1976).

Medicalized discourse offers an explanation of impotence which removes control, and therefore responsibility and blame, for sexual failure from the man and places it on his physiology. Talcott Parsons (1951) originally argued that an organic diagnosis confers a particular social role, the "sick role," which has three aspects: (1) The individual is not held responsible for his or her condition; (2) illnesses are legitimate bases for exemption from normal social responsibilities; and (3) the exemptions are contingent on the sick person recognizing that sickness is undesirable and seeking appropriate (medical) help. A medical explanation for erectile difficulties relieves men of blame and thus permits them to maintain some masculine self-esteem even in the presence of impotence.

> Understandably, for many years the pattern of the human male has been to blame sexual dysfunction on specific physical distresses. Every sexually inadequate male lunges toward any potential physical excuse for sexual malfunction. From point of ego support, would that it could be true. A cast for a leg or a sling for an arm provides socially acceptable evidence of physical dysfunction of these extremities. Unfortunately, the psychosocial causes of perpetual penile flaccidity cannot be explained or excused by devices for mechanical support. (Masters & Johnson, 1970, pp. 187-188)

Perhaps in 1970 "devices for mechanical support" of the penis were not in widespread access, but we now have available, ironically, precisely the type of medical vindication Masters and Johnson suggested would be the most effective deflection of the "blame" men feel for their inability to perform sexually.

Men's willingness to accept a self-protective, self-handicapping (that is, an illness label) attribution for "failure" has been demonstrated in studies of excuse making (Snyder, Ford, & Hunt, 1985). Reduced personal responsibility is most sought in those situations in which performance is related to self-esteem (Snyder & Smith, 1982). It may be that the frequent use of physical excuses for failure in athletic performance provides a model for men to use in sexuality. Medical treatments not only offer tangible evidence of nonblameworthiness, but they allow men to avoid psychological treatments such as marital or sex therapy, which threaten embarrassing self-disclosure and admissions of weakness men find aversive (Peplau & Gordon, 1985).

The final allure of a technological solution such as the penile prosthesis is its promise of permanent freedom from worry. One of Masters and Johnson's (1970) major insights was their description of the self-conscious self-monitoring, which men with erectile difficulties develop in sexual situations. "Performance anxiety" and "spectatoring," their two immediate causes of sexual impotence, generate a self-perpetuating cycle that undermines a man's confidence about the future even as he recovers from individual episodes. Technology seems to offer a simple and permanent solution to the problem of lost or threatened confidence, as doctors from *Vogue* to the *Journal of Urology* have already noted.

The Rising Importance of Sexuality in Personal Life

Even though we live in a time when the definition of masculinity is moving away from reliance on physical validation (Pleck, 1976), there seems no apparent reduction in the male sexual focus on physical performance. Part of the explanation for this must rest with the increasing importance of sexuality in contemporary relationships. Recent sociocultural analyses have suggested that sexual satisfaction grows in importance to the individual and couple as other sources of personal fulfillment and connection with others wither.

> I would say that with the collapse of other social values (those of religion, patriotism, the family, and so on), sex has been forced to take up the slack, to become our sole mode of transcendence and our only touchstone of authenticity. . . . In our present isolation we have few ways besides sex to feel connected with each other. (White, 1980, p. 282)

> People are being deprived more and more of opportunities to feel they are worth something to others, to experience what they are doing as something of significance, and to know that they are indispensable to the lives of their families or at least a few friends. The experience of powerlessness, dependency, inner emptiness, and one's own meaninglessness becomes radical and merciless; the vacuum left behind sucks in any experiences which make one at least temporarily aware of one's own importance. . . . A particularly important mode of compensation for narcissistic deprivation is the couple relationship or, more precisely, the emotions it can mobilize, such as falling in love and sexual desire and satisfaction. (Schmidt, 1983, p. 4-5)

The increasing pressure on intimate relationships to provide psychological support and gratification comes at the same time that traditional (that is, economic and family-raising) reasons for these relationships are declining. Both trends place more pressure on compatibility and companionship to maintain the relationship. Given that men have been raised "not to be emotionally sensitive to others or emotionally expressive or self-revealing" (Pleck, 1981, p. 140), much modern relationship success would seem to depend on sexual fulfillment. Although some contemporary research indicates that marriages and gay relationships can be rated successful despite the presence of sexual problems (Frank, Anderson, & Rubinstein, 1978; Bell & Weinberg, 1978), popular surveys suggest that the public believes sexual satisfaction is essential to relationship success.

The importance of sexuality also increases because of its use by consumption-oriented capitalism (Altman, 1982). The promise of increased sexual attractiveness is used to sell products to people of all ages. Commercial sexual meeting places and playgrounds are popular in both gay and heterosexual culture. A whole system of therapists, books, workshops, and magazines sells advice on improving sexual performance and enjoyment. Restraint and repression are inappropriate in a consumer culture in which the emphasis is on immediate gratification.

The expectation that sexuality will provide ever increasing rewards and personal meaning has also been a theme of the contemporary women's movement, and women's changing attitudes have affected many men, particularly widowed and divorced men returning to the sexual "market." Within the past decade, sexual advice manuals have changed their tone completely regarding the roles of men and women in sexual relations (Weinberg, Swenson, & Hammersmith, 1983). Women are advised to take more responsibility for their own pleasure, to possess sexual knowledge and self-knowledge, and to expect that improved sexual functioning will pay off in other aspects of life. Removing responsibility from the man for being the sexual teacher and leader reduces the definition of sexual masculinity to having excellent technique and equipment to meet the "new woman" on her "new" level.

Finally, the new importance of sexual performance has no upper age limit.

> The sexual myth most rampant in our culture today is the concept that the aging process per se will in time discourage or deny erective security in the older-age group male. As has been described previously, the aging male may be slower to erect and may even reach the plateau phase without full erective return, but the facility and ability to attain erection, presuming general good health and no psychological block, continues unopposed as a natural sequence well into the 80-year age group. (Masters & Johnson, 1970, p. 326)

Sex is a natural act, Masters and Johnson said over and over again, and there is no "natural" reason for ability to decline or disappear as one ages. Erectile difficulties, then, are "problems" that can be corrected with suitable treatment. Aging provides no escape from the male sexual role.

The Medicalization of Impotence:
Part of the Problem or
Part of the Solution?

The increased use of the term "impotence" that Elliott (1985) reported can now be seen as part of the process of medicalization of sexuality. Physicians view the medical system as a method for distributing technical expertise in the interest of improved health (Ehrenreich & Ehrenreich, 1978). Their economic interests, spurred by the profit orientation of medical technology manufacturers, lie in expanding the number and type of services they offer to more and more patients. Specialists, in particular, have increased their incomes and prestige dramatically during the postwar era by developing high-reimbursement relationships with hospitals and insurance companies (Starr, 1982). In the sexual sphere, all these goals are served by labelling impotence a biomedical disorder, common in men of all ages, best served by thorough evaluation and appropriate medical treatment when any evidence of organic disorder is identified.

There are many apparent advantages for men in the medicalization of male sexuality. As discussed earlier, men view physical explanations for their problems as less stigmatizing and are better able to maintain their sense of masculinity and self-esteem. Accepting medicine as a source of authority and help reassures men who feel under immense pressure from role expectations but are unable to consult with or confide in either other men or women because of pride, competitiveness, or defensiveness. That "inhibited sexual excitement . . . in males, partial or complete failure to attain or maintain erection until completion of the [sic] sexual act" is a genuine disorder (American Psychiatric Association, 1980, p. 279), makes legitimate an important aspect of life that physicians previously dismissed or made jokes about. And, as I have said, permanent mechanical solutions to sexual performance worries are seen as a gift from heaven in erasing, with one simple operation, a source of anxiety dating from adolescence about failing as a man.

The disadvantages to medicalizing male sexuality, however, are numerous and subtle. (My discussion here is informed by Riessman's 1983 analysis of the medicalization of many female roles and conditions.)

First, dependence on medical remedies for impotence has led to the escalating use of treatments whose long-term effects are not known and, in many cases, seem to be harmful. Iatrogenic ("doctor-caused") consequences of new technology and pharmacology are not uncommon and seem most worrisome when medical treatments are offered to men with no demonstrable organic disease. Second, the use of medical language mystifies human experience, increasing dependence on professionals and experts. If sexuality becomes fundamentally a matter of vasocongestion and myotonia (as in Masters & Johnson's famous claim, 1966, p. 7), personal experience requires expert interpretation and explanation. Third, medicalization spreads the moral neutrality of medicine and science over sexuality, and people no longer ask whether men "should" have erections. If the presence of erections is healthy and their absence (in whole or part) is pathological, then healthy behavior is correct behavior and vice versa, again increasing dependence on health authorities to define norms and standards for conduct.

The primary disadvantage of medicalization is that it denies, obscures, and ignores the social causes of whatever problem is under study. Impotence becomes the problem of an individual man. This effect seems particularly pertinent in the case of male sexuality in which the social demands of the male sexual role are so related to the meaning of erectile function and dysfunction. Recall the list of men's beliefs about sexuality, the evaluative criteria of conduct and performance. Being a man depends on sexual adequacy, which depends on potency. A rigid, reliable erection is necessary for full compliance with the script. The medicalization of male sexuality helps a man conform to the script rather than analyzing where the script comes from or challenging it. Research and technology are directed only toward better and better solutions. Yet the demands of the script are so formidable, and the pressures from the sociocultural changes we have outlined are so likely to increase, that no technical solution will ever work—certainly not for everyone.

Medicine attracts public resources out of proportion to its capacity for health enhancement, because it often categorizes problems fundamentally social in origin as biological or personal deficits, and in so doing smothers the impulse for social change that could offer the only serious resolution (Stark & Flitcraft, 1983, p. 4).

Preventive Medicine:
Changing the Male Sexual Script

Men will remain vulnerable to the expansion of the clinical domain so long as masculinity rests heavily on a particular type of physiological function. As more research uncovers subtle physiological correlates of genital functioning, more men will be "at risk" for impotence. Fluctuations of physical and emotional states will become cues for impending impotence in any man with, for example diabetes, hypertension, or a history of prescription medication usage.

One of the less well understood features of sex therapy is that it "treats" erectile dysfunction by changing the individual men's sexual script.

This approach is primarily educational—you are not curing an illness but learning new and more satisfactory ways of getting on with each other (Greenwood & Bancroft, 1983, p. 305).

Our thesis is that the rules and concepts we learn [about male sexuality] are destructive and a very inadequate preparation for a satisfying and pleasurable sex life.... Having a better sex life is in large measure dependent upon your willingness to examine how the male sexual mythology has trapped you (Zilbergeld, 1978, p. 9).

Sexuality can be transformed from a rigid standard for masculine adequacy to a way of being, a way of communicating, a hobby, a way of being in one's body—and being one's body—that does not impose control but rather affirms pleasure, movement, sensation, cooperation, playfulness, relating. Masculine confidence cannot be purchased, because there can never be perfect potency. Chasing its illusion may line a few pockets, but for most men it will only exchange one set of anxieties and limitations for another.

REFERENCES

Altman, D. (1982). *The homosexualization of America: The Americanization of the homosexual.* New York: St. Martin's.

American Psychiatric Association. (1980). *Diagnostic and statistical manual of mental disorders* (3rd ed.). Washington, DC: Author.

Apse, S. M., Gregory, J. G., & Purcell, M. H. (1984). The inflatable penile prosthesis, reoperation and patient satisfaction: A comparison of statistics obtained from patient record review with statistics obtained from intensive followup search. *Journal of Urology, 131,* 894-895.

Bancroft, J. (1982). Erectile impotence: Psyche or soma? *International Journal of Andrology, 5,* 353-355.

Bancroft, J. (1983). *Human sexuality and its problems.* Edinburgh: Churchill-Livingstone.

Bell, A. P., & Weinberg, M. S. (1978). *Homosexualities: A study of diversity among men and women.* New York: Simon & Schuster.

Brannon, R. (1976). The male sex role: Our culture's blueprint of manhood, and what it's done for us lately. In D. David & R. Brannon (Eds.), *The forty-nine percent majority: The male sex role.* Reading, MA: Addison-Wesley.

Collins, G. F., & Kinder, B. N. (1984). Adjustment following surgical implantation of a penile prosthesis: A critical review. *Journal of Sex and Marital Therapy, 10,* 255-271.

Doyle, J. A. (1983). *The male experience.* Dubuque, IA: William C. Brown.

Ehrenreich, B., & Ehrenreich, J. (1978). Medicine and social control. In J. Ehrenreich (Ed.), *The cultural crisis of modern medicine.* New York: Monthly Review Press.

Elliott, M. L. (1985). The use of "impotence" and "frigidity": Why has "impotence" survived? *Journal of Sex and Marital Therapy, 11,* 51-56.

Fairburn, C. G., McCulloch, D. K., & Wu, F. C. (1982). The effects of diabetes on male sexual function. *Clinics in Endocrinology and Metabolism, 11,* 749-767.

Fallon, B., Rosenberg, S., & Culp, D. A. (1984). Long-term follow-up in patients with an inflatable penile prosthesis. *Journal of Urology, 132,* 270-271.

Finkle, A. L., & Finkle, C. E. (1984). Sexual impotency: Counseling of 388 private patients by urologists from 1954-1982. *Urology, 23,* 25-30.

Frank, E., Anderson, C., & Rubinstein, D. (1978). Frequency of sexual dysfunction in "normal" couples. *New England Journal of Medicine, 299,* 111-115.

Gagnon, J. H., & Simon, W. (1973). *Sexual conduct: The social sources of human sexuality.* Chicago: Aldine.

Gross, A. E. (1978). The male role and heterosexual behavior. *Journal of Social Issues, 34,* 87-107.

Hixson, J. R. (1985, April). Curing impotence: The prognosis is good. *Vogue,* p. 406.

Impotence clinics: Investments in the future. (1984). *Colleagues in Urology Newsletter,* fourth quarter, p. 1.

Joseph, D. B., Bruskewitz, R. C., & Benson, R. C. (1984). Long-term evaluation of the inflatable penile prosthesis. *Journal of Urology, 131,* 670-673.

Kelley, S. (1981). Some social and psychological aspects of organic sexual dysfunction in men. *Sexuality and Disability, 4,* 123-128.

Krane, R. J., Siroky, M. B., & Goldstein, I. (1983). *Male sexual dysfunction.* Boston: Little, Brown.

LoPiccolo, J. (1985). Diagnosis and treatment of male sexual dysfunction. *Journal of Sex and Marital Therapy, 11,* 215-232.

Masters, W. H., & Johnson, V. E. (1966). *Human sexual response.* Boston: Little, Brown.

Masters, W. H., & Johnson, V. E. (1970). *Human sexual inadequacy.* Boston: Little, Brown.

Medical Engineering Corporation. (1983). *Patient information booklet discussing the surgical correction of impotency.* Racine, WI: Author.

Melman, A. (1978). Development of contemporary surgical management for erectile impotence. *Sexuality and Disability, 1,* 272-281.

Mentor Corporation. (1984). *Overcoming impotence.* Minneapolis, MN: Author.

Nelson, J. (1985). Male sexuality and masculine spirituality. *Siecus Report, 13,* 1-4.

Organization helps couples with impotence as problem. (1984, June 24). *New York Times,* Section 1, Pt. 2, p. 42.

Paff, B. (1985). Sexual dysfunction in gay men requesting treatment. *Journal of Sex and Marital Therapy, 11,* 3-18.

Parent, G. (1977). *David Meyer is a mother.* New York: Bantam.

Parsons, T. (1951). *The social system.* New York: Free Press.

Peplau, L. A., & Gordon, S. L. (1985). Women and men in love: Gender differences in close heterosexual relationships. In V. E. O'Leary, R. K. Unger, & B. S. Wallston (Eds.), *Women, gender and social psychology.* Hillsdale, NJ: Lawrence Erlbaum.

Perelman, M. (1984). Rehabilitative sex therapy for organic impotence. In R. T. Segraves & E. J. Haeberle (Eds.), *Emerging dimensions of sexology.* New York: Praeger.

Person, E. S. (1980). Sexuality as the mainstay of identity: Psychoanalytic perspectives. *Signs, 5,* 605-630.

Pleck, J. H. (1976). The male sex role: Definitions, problems and sources of change. *Journal of Social Issues, 32,* 155-164.

Pleck, J. H. (1981). *The myth of masculinity.* Cambridge: MIT Press.

Riessman, C. K. (1983). Women and medicalization: A new perspective. *Social Policy, 14,* 3-18.

Schiavi, R. C., Fisher, C., Quadland, M., & Glover, A. (1984). Erectile function in nonimpotent diabetics. In R. T. Segraves & E. J. Haeberle (Eds.), *Emerging dimensions of sexology.* New York: Praeger.

Schmidt, G. (1983). Introduction: Sexuality and relationships. In G. Arentewicz & G. Schmidt, *The treatment of sexual disorders.* New York: Basic Books.

Schover, L. R., & Von Eschenbach, A. C. (1985). Sex therapy and the penile prosthesis: A synthesis. *Journal of Sex and Marital Therapy, 11,* 57-66.

Schreiner-Engel, P. (1981). Therapy of psychogenic erectile disorders. *Sexuality and Disability, 4,* 115-122.

Schumacher, S., & Lloyd, C. W. (1981). Physiological and psychological factors in impotence. *Journal of Sex Research, 17,* 40-53.

Segraves, R. T., Schoenberg, H. W., Zarins, C., Camic, P., & Knopf, J. (1981). Characteristics of erectile dysfunction as a function of medical care system entry point. *Psychosomatic Medicine, 43,* 227-234.

Snyder, C. R., & Smith, T. W. (1982). Symptoms as self-handicapping strategies: The virtues of old wine in a new bottle. In G. Weary & H. L. Mirels (Eds.), *Integration of clinical and social psychology.* New York: Oxford University Press.

Snyder, C. R., Ford, C. E., & Hunt, H. A. (1985, August). *Excuse-making: A look at sex differences.* Paper presented at the annual meeting of the American Psychological Association, Los Angeles.

Sotile, W. M. (1979). The penile prosthesis: A review. *Journal of Sex and Marital Therapy, 5,* 90-102.

Starr, P. (1982). *The transformation of American medicine.* New York: Basic Books.

Subrini, L. P. (1980). Treatment of impotence using penile implants: Surgical, sexual, and psychological follow-up. In R. Forleo & W. Pasini (Eds.), *Medical sexology.* Littleton, MA: PSG.

Surgical implants correct impotence. (1979, June 12). *New York Times,* Section C, p. 3.

Tolson, A. (1977). *The limits of masculinity.* New York: Harper & Row.

Weinberg, M. S., Swensson, R. G., & Hammersmith, S. K. (1983). Sexual autonomy and the status of women: Models of female sexuality in U.S. sex manuals from 1950 to 1980. *Social Problems, 30,* 312-324.

White, E. (1980). *States of desire.* New York: E. P. Dutton.

Wise, T. N., Rabins, P. V., & Bahnsley, J. (1984). The older patient with a sexual dysfunction. *Journal of Sex and Marital Therapy, 10,* 117-121.

Zilbergeld, B. (1978). *Male sexuality.* Boston: Little, Brown.

12

Motivations of Abortion Clinic Waiting Room Males

"Bottled-Up" Roles and Unmet Needs

ARTHUR B. SHOSTAK

What can we learn about the contemporary male role from the motivations of men who accompany their sex partners to an abortion clinic? How do they feel about their participation, and how is their manhood challenged by it? Above all, is their current situation really in the best interest of males and females alike? Or does it warrant substantial reform, the better to help reduce the rate of undesired pregnancies and to enhance the meaning of modern manhood?

Background. Abortion clinic staffs estimate that about 85% of their female clients inform their male sex partner prior to the termination of their pregnancies (Bracken et al., 1974; Melamed, 1975; Shostak & McLouth, 1984). As approximately 1.5 million abortions were obtained in the United States in 1985, almost 1.3 million males were knowingly involved. Given estimates that three-fourths of all terminations occur in nonhospital clinics, about 1.1 million expectant fathers could have accompanied their sex partners to the nation's 500 or so abortion clinics (Ory et al., 1983, p. 23). Only about 50% of these males did so, however, and their experience reveals much about contemporary role definitions and clinic responses to these attendees.

This chapter is based upon a 1982-1983 study of 1,000 waiting room males at 30 clinics in 18 states. Their answers to a 102-item questionnaire

AUTHOR'S NOTE: An earlier version of this chapter was presented at both the annual meeting of the Eastern Sociological Society, Philadelphia, spring 1984, and the annual meeting of the Midwest Sociological Society, Chicago, April 1984.

are combined with related data from representatives of 26 of the 30 clinics and relevant material from eight clinic case studies available in the literature.

Literature Review

Although the literature on abortion is expanding rapidly, very little focuses on the expectant father. Of the 279 citations in *Sociological Abstracts* for 1963-1983, for example, some 239 (or 85%) dealt only with the female patient. And half of the 40 articles interested in males discussed males in other countries (Canada, India, Israel, Taiwan). Those few that focused on American males commonly relied on the female sex partner as respondents, rather than interviewing the males themselves: Only 4 of all 279 citations drew data from American males (and I was the author of two of these research reports; Shostak, 1983, pp. 66-85; 1979, pp. 569-574). Little wonder that Smith's (1979, p. 13) earlier review of this literature had him conclude that it "often totally disregarded the male role, reported it in an implicit or covert manner, or at best reported through the perceptions of the man's partner."

Methods

Sample. To obtain the data for this analysis, two requests for research cooperation were sent at six-month intervals to 243 abortion clinic addresses printed in the 1981-1982 and 1982-1983 directories of the National Abortion Federation, the nation's only all-purpose, prochoice alliance of abortion providers. This list was supplemented by 30 more addresses located in the Yellow Pages of the phone directories for Atlanta, Boston, Chicago, New York City, Los Angeles, and San Francisco.

Unfortunately, only 30 of the 273 clinics agreed to offer our questionnaire to males in their waiting rooms, and only 3 wrote to explain their reasons for declining to cooperate (for example, reluctance to "intrude" on the privacy of the males; hesitation about "stirring emotions" at this time).

To supplement the survey answers, we conducted nearly 50 interviews with both waiting room and non-waiting room "veterans" of the abortion experience. Numerous radio "call-in" talk shows and several TV talk show appearances generated offers to complete our survey from males in the listening audience. Finally, I was able to secure the cooperation of former adult students of mine at the AFL-CIO's George

Meany Center for Labor Studies in reaching blue-collar respondents, even as several sociologists on nearby campuses joined me in requesting the cooperation of campus males.[1]

Limitation of the sample. Since our sample of 30 clinics was drawn from an unknown universe it is impossible to make any claim for its representativeness. No publicly available list of the nation's estimated 500 or so abortion clinics exists. All abortion statistics, including our own, would therefore seem estimates subject to unknown error. Similarly, as our data come only from males inclined to cooperate, we have no way of knowing what the experience meant for others too indifferent, self-contained, embarrassed, embittered, or upset to complete the questionnaire.

Above all, given the glaring absence of substantial scientific knowledge of this statistical cohort, we were unable to pursue systematically a random or representative sample. Instead, my analysis of our data cautiously draws on a sample of convenience, an available sample of a previously unmeasured aggregate (Spade, 1984). Limited in this way, we can make no claim for the representativeness of our 1,000 respondents, and urge care in generalizing beyond this (largest-ever) research cohort.

Sample characteristics. The 1,000 males in our study closely resembled a 1980 profile of female clients of the nation's abortion clinics (Henshaw & O'Reilly, 1983, pp. 5-16). The largest number were unwed (82%, as were 79% of the female clients), though only 5% regarded their lovers merely as casual acquaintances. Instead, 12% were in "living together" relationships, 17% were engaged, and 37% were dating their partners on a steady basis (87% of the husbands claimed to be accompanying their wives).

One-third of the 1,000 males were under 20 years of age (as were 30% of the female clients). Another 30% were 21 to 25 years old, but only 8% were over 36. Not surprisingly, given their youthfulness, 27% were still in school, though 45% had already attended or graduated from college (as had 34% of the female clients). While 35% were blue-collar workers, 6% were professionals, 20% were white-collar workers, and 6% were unemployed.

A disproportionately large number of the males were Roman Catholic (33%), though the largest number were Protestant (45%); 15% claimed no religious identification, 2% were Jewish, and 1% Muslim. When asked how important their religious beliefs were to them, 21% answered "very," and 47%, "somewhat," while only 19% indicated "not very" or "not at all" (14%).

As for racial distribution, 87% were Caucasian (as contrasted to 70% of the 1980 female clients), 10% were black; 2%, Hispanic; and 1%, Asian. Discussions with clinic staffers at our 30 data collection centers have persuaded us that black males are underrepresented significantly among our 1,000 respondents.

Findings

Reasons for attendance. Prior to our research and lengthy interviews, the only two field reports that had asked attendees why they were there dwelled on obvious motivations. Attendance was represented first and foremost as an affirmation of love, as proof of commitment, and as clear-cut evidence of involvement. Not surprisingly, 73% of a third case-study bloc (91 attendees at an Iowa clinic) recalled wanting "very much" to go along on the appointed day, and only 9% felt coerced by their partners (Smith, 1979, pp. 166-167).

Like their counterparts elsewhere, our 1,000 attendees also ranked proving their love as their primary motivation, though interview explanations, as contrasted to terse questionnaire answers, hinted at far more complex motives:

> I sort of felt a little in over my head from the start, although I immediately offered to spend as much time with her, to do this with her, to pay for it, since I was working and no one else was, and to keep our parents out of it. (26-year-old white-collar worker)

> Mentally, it definitely drained us. We were worried about something going wrong. She was scared, so was I, but I tried not to show it, so I could make it easier for her. (24-year-old salesman)

Convinced that affirming love and/or doing "the manly thing" only began to explain attendee motivations, we identified four less obvious needs: to keep a secret, to relieve anxiety, to experience a form of punishment, and to bear witness.

Secrecy as a motivation. Three of four waiting room males had spoken to no one other than their partners about their situation, their reaction to news of an ill-timed pregnancy, their thoughts and feelings about this affirmation of virility, their thoughts and feelings about prospective fatherhood, and their utter lack of preparation for any of this. When we asked why they had discussed their response and quandary with no outsider, answers included the following:

> It was a moral issue I had to resolve myself . . . involving my Catholic upbringing. (23-year-old blue-collar worker)

> Was something you have to do for yourself. (19-year-old student)

TABLE 12.1
Comparison of Reasons Given for
Clinic Attendance

106 Males; California Clinic (1983)			*126 Males; Midwest Clinic (1980)*		
(1)	80%	to provide moral support and company	(1)	62% + 19%	to provide support from love and concern
(2)	31%	express belief in the decision	(2)	15%	mutual involvement
(3)	28%	being there if partner becomes ill	(3)	–	
(4)	13%	do not know how helpful I can be	(4)	11%	do not know; am along at partner's request

SOURCE: Hill-Falkenthal (1983, p. 32); Rotter (1980, p. 113).

I would have liked to go to a counseling center, but I did not know of any that existed. (36-year-old teacher)

These American males cited a lack of relevant confidants, a fear of parental disapproval, and pride in far-reaching self-reliance, before conceding that still another covert pressure was also operating on them.

Specifically, almost all attendees who had spoken to no one had been asked not to by their sex partners. Frightened that harm might be done to their reputations, many abortion seekers insisted on total secrecy. On learning that the clinics insisted that each patient have an adult companion to assist her in the postabortion journey home, a couple shrouded in secrecy had only each other to call on—and many males were present at the clinic both to protect their lovers' privacy and to help with that journey.

Relieving anxiety. Another major motivator involved fear of a medical mishap or even the female's death during the 15-minute ambulatory medical procedure. As many as 48% of the 1,000 attendees felt they did not know all they needed to know about abortion's medical risks, and many came along to the clinic hoping to get reassurances from clinic personnel. Accordingly, the vast majority of questions most men directed to clinic staffers concerned the physical well-being of their partners:

I remember everything about the day it happened. Even the minute details are still clear. I remember asking the doctor how the procedure was done. I wanted to know everything that was going to happen. I remember when the operation was going on, I was sick several times. I remember after the procedure was over the weight lifted off my chest when the doctor said everything was fine. That was my biggest fear, what if something happened. I remember going into her recovery area and sitting by her bed. I began to cry, thinking about what she was thinking, feeling, and how this would affect her. (31-year-old white-collar worker)

Many respondents echoed the sentiments of one man who told us that "sitting in the waiting room was really mind-boggling, because it's totally out of your control. All you can do is hope. It was hard for me to sit there and know we were both in it, but she was the only one who could get us out of it."

Seeking punishment. A small number felt the need to experience some type of meaningful punishment, some analog for the real risk and pain being experienced elsewhere in the clinic by their sex partners. These men commonly held themselves responsible for the unwanted pregnancy; as abortion counselor Roger Wade explains:

The man who believes he should protect his partner from all harm may feel like a total failure because "his woman" is pregnant and will have to run the risks of abortion. He may take all the blame for not using any birth control, or for having sex in the first place. (in Lincoln, 1980, p. 243)

Considerable guilt and self-recrimination came through in our interviews:

I can now understand the importance of birth control. I now have a deeper respect for being able to have sex with a woman. (20-year-old student)

I wish it wouldn't seem like we're doing something dirty. (30-year-old married white-collar worker)

We are picking among options, not all good, because there's nothing you can do to make it better. No way not to cause pain. It's just how much you cause. The whole idea of loving someone and having sex with them is supposed to be a joyful thing. And then, all of a sudden, you've got two people going crazy. (26-year-old stockbroker)

Much of the guilt could be traced to neglect of contraception, a "sin" of omission for 43% of the males in a 1983 California (single-clinic) sample (Hill-Falkenthal, 1983, p. 23); 57% of a 1980 Colorado (two-clinic) sample (Brosseau, 1980, p. 51); 53% of a 1979 Iowa (single-clinic) sample (Smith, 1979, p. 90); and 55% of a 1978 Massachusetts (single-clinic) sample (Finley, 1978, p. 3).

Clinic attendance was judged a (desirable) form of self-punishment, because of job-related hardships (loss of pay, loss of work); the strain of telling no one about your destination; and the keen embarrassment and humiliation felt by many males over their presence at "the last place I ever wanted to be." In clinics across the country, we found waiting rooms eerie in their anxious calm and the bleak isolation of attendees from one another.

Being there. A fourth less-than-obvious motivation for clinic attendance involved the need many males had to make their peace with what abortion counselor Peter Zelles calls "the tragic nature of abortion" (Shostak & McLouth, 1984, p. 148).

On the one hand, 85% of the attendees took much comfort in recalling that their abortion decision was the product of a *joint* agreement: Only 5% felt forced into the decision by the female, and only 6% ruefully reported neither partner really agreed with what they were doing. Accordingly, only 17% condemned abortion as immoral, and far fewer indicated they would vote to outlaw abortion (9%).

On the other hand, a majority of the males did *not* feel a woman should be able to obtain a legal abortion in 5 of 17 situations we put before them:

(1) Tests reveal that the sex of the fetus is not what the prospective parents want at this time. (87% opposed)
(2) The male, for any reason, wants the abortion. (82% opposed)
(3) The parents of a pregnant minor female want the abortion. (69% opposed)
(4) The couple is on the verge of breaking up. (63% opposed)
(5) The couple has just ended their relationship. (52% opposed)

Provided these five reasons were *not* involved, 65% of the waiting room males felt a couple should be able to request an abortion for *any* other reason.

A related sort of ambivalence and discernment was evident in male attitudes toward the fetus. Nearly two-thirds took a prochoice position on when life begins; to a question on when a fetus becomes human, the following responses were given:

(1) when it can survive outside the mother's womb (21%)
(2) it is actually born (15%)
(3) this cannot be determined, one way or the other (25%)

At least 20% of the 1,000 respondents claimed to have "never" thought about the fetus after helping to make the proabortion decision, and 42%

did not feel involved in the killing of a child (34% of the remaining attendees were "neutral" regarding this critical antiabortion contention). A small, but still significant, bloc of attendees took quite the opposite position, that a fetus becomes human when

(1) sperm meets egg; i.e., at conception (20%)
(2) the nervous system of the fetus begins to function (19%)

This bloc grew to 26% of the 1,000 attendees who agreed "abortion is the killing of a child," and was probably a large part of the 29% who had "frequent" thoughts or 52% who had "occasional" thoughts about the fetus.

Interviews were indispensable in clarifying the emotional volatility and ambivalence of this covert matter:

> You know, I didn't like it really, but I couldn't deal with the kid right now, anyway. I gotta car that I can't even get out of the driveway because I ain't got no money for insurance. I couldn't deal with the kid right now. (23-year-old blue-collar worker)

> Killing the fetus may be a crime, but child abuse and neglect is a bigger crime, I feel. (26-year-old engineer)

> I want the child, but she is too young to get married. (26-year-old student)

> How big is it? Or is it a baby? It has only been three and a half weeks. (22-year-old student)

> During an abortion, you're killing a fetus. If you have a child and can't bring it up well, you're killing the child indirectly. A lot of kids can't get out of their backgrounds. (26-year-old factory worker)

> I do not believe in fetus supremacy. (24-year-old white-collar worker)

Counselor Katherine B. Oettinger (1979, p. 18) notes that "opting for abortion often involves a ruthless shattering of romantic fantasies, the intrusions of the grimmest kind of reality into an uninformed view of life." Little wonder, accordingly, that many of the 1,000 males referred to their clinic stay as one of the hardest experiences of their lives, a "dark involvement with blood and birth and death" (Didion, 1972, p. 14).

Many felt obliged, nevertheless, to be there, to bear witness, to somehow solemnize this (ritual-bare) life-and-death drama, to attend to the loss of a unique fatherhood possibility. Only through clinic attendance could many begin the grieving or mourning process required for their postabortion recovery; only through clinic attendance could many affirm a vital sense of self-rehabilitation.

Discussion

Counselor insights. When we explored these five motivations—to help confirm love and commitment; to honor a female's insistance on confidentiality; to lower anxiety over medical risks; to "pay some dues" in the form of personal discomfort; and to bear witness—with abortion clinic counselors, we found most were convinced they warranted sensitive discussion during the three-hour wait. Typical was the insistence of a male counselor that "sadness and loss are feelings evident with any abortion decision, and to get beyond them, they must be expressed. It is natural and healthy to want to make a crisis 'history,' but not before it has been psychically processed" (Shostak & McLouth, 1984, p. 146). Another staffer warned that abortion was "undeniably a death experience, a loss experience, and a separation experience with immense reverberations for everybody. If all of that gets blocked, and is not resolved, it is bound to have a dramatic and destructive impact on the relationship" (Medvene, 1982, p. 44).

The fact remained that 80% of the 1,000 attendees ignored the counseling option available at almost all clinics. Puzzled by this lack of outreach we asked a representative subset of 505 of the 1,000 attendees to indicate their attitudes toward various clinic options:

74% said they *would* utilize a private counseling session, one involving the couple and a clinic staffer.

62% said they *would* utilize a one-on-one meeting with a clinic counselor.

54% said they *would* utilize a small-group "rap session" of attendees, guided by a clinic counselor.

As 47% were uncertain about the abortion's lasting impact on their relationship, and 91% were emphatic in their desire never again to be in this situation, the motivation for the high "would use" numbers seemed clear, though the fact remained that only 20%, at best, had acted on the motivation.

One reason given by counselors for neglect of services by attendees was the reluctance males had about asking for help, getting involved with "head shrinkers," and admitting they needed assistance with emotional turmoil, all of which conform to traditional male role strictures.

Another major reason concerned the inability of most clinics to allocate appropriate services for males. Hard-pressed by antiabortion protesters, often violent, and always impassioned, clinics were also taxed by legislative denial of funds for indigent females. Limited financial resources were directed toward bolstering the counseling tendered to patients and to the subsidization of abortions for those unable to pay a full share, leaving little to spend on male-focused services. Not surprisingly, therefore, very few of our 30 cooperating clinics had males among their counselors, assigned any counselors to the waiting room attendees, or went out of their way to inform these men that they could request some time themselves with clinic counselors.

Reform possibilities. Many of the men with whom we spoke, and most of the abortion counselors we interviewed, had clear-cut notions about reforms to help men make better use of their 3-hour clinic wait. Six ideas appear especially promising:

(1) Every female client could be offered a leaflet for her sex partner explaining in a friendly way the various options available to attendees (counseling, contraception education, attendance in the procedure room or recovery room, and so on).

(2) Every female client could learn about the value of drawing her sex partner into the abortion experience, and the special contribution possible from a male's processing of his own relevant thoughts and feelings.

(3) Every clinic could revamp its logo and public relations material to include a male in the design, thereby underlining the legitimacy of male involvement.

(4) Every clinic could try to hire one or more male counselors, whose very presence would provide a valuable role model for attendees.

(5) Clinic receptionists could provide every attendee on arrival with a one-page promotional leaflet urging male use of clinic options (counseling and the like).

(6) Clinics could indicate to couples that a male may remain with his partner during the procedure (which 70% of our sample desired) and/or in the recovery room (which 91% desired), both options available in only 4 of our 30 clinics.

Changes of this sort are affordable and feasible, provided, however, that male attendees are required to shoulder all or nearly all of any related clinic expense.

TABLE 12.2

The Male Partner's "Bill of Rights"

A male partner should have the right

- to be informed of the physical risks and mental stress his partner is going through (before, during, and after the abortion);
- to have access to a sensitive, supportive, and experienced counselor before and during an abortion;
- to accompany his partner during the procedure and in the recovery room, *provided* she gives her prior consent;
- to learn about the full range of family planning aids available to prevent another unwanted conception; and
- to learn about available counseling resources should he want to talk about the abortion afterward (clinic, clergy, men's groups, etc.).

NOTE: Adapted from "The Pregnant Patient's Bill of Rights," prepared by Doris Haire for the National Women's Health Network, and "The Pregnant Woman's Bill of Rights," *Ms.* (September 1984, p. 56).

Finally, reform advocates urged the sensitive redefining of male role ambiguities:

> I would suggest, in a circumspect manner, that even though it's difficult for them to express their feelings to the woman, it was manly to do those things which are difficult. . . . I would also say that one of the ways they could take care of the woman was to make sure she followed the aftercare instructions. Most men seemed glad to have me spell out specific ways they could be involved. (Shostak & McLouth, 1984, p. 151)

Most counselors agreed "involving the man is important. New avenues and opportunities for involvement of men in pregnancy counseling and abortion need to be adopted. Men will not be a part of what is, in essence, a no-win situation. Men—and women—need roles other than those of victims and villains" (Shostak & McLouth, 1984, p. 155).

Summary. Male motivations for attendance at abortion clinics range from the obvious (affirm love and commitment, relieve anxiety) to the less readily apparent (protect the female's privacy, secure discomfort as a form of self-punishment) to those barely recognized by the holders themselves (bear witness, attend to the end of a unique fatherhood possibility).

Unfortunately, emotion-constricting attributes of the male role and the neglect of the male by abortion clinics combine to discourage attendees from using clinic counseling services to explore their various motivations. Unless and until the clinics sensitively reach out to help waiting room men get beyond their "bottled-up" macho posturing, nearly a half million men every year will make far less of their three-hour clinic wait than may be possible. Unless and until the clinics take an assertive stance and draw males creatively into singles, couples, and/or group counseling options, a rare opportunity for birth control education, interpersonal skills education, and even grief counseling will remain unrealized. This is plainly not in the interest of either males or females. Finally, unless and until concerned men help raise male consciousness about this neglected matter, all of us will continue to take far less from abortion involvement than is good for our postabortion lives, love, and manhood.

NOTE

1. Research help in the circulation and collection of abortion experience questionnaires was generously provided by Ed Gondolf, Russ Kleinbach, Joe Ruane, Kay Snyder, and Dave Voight.

REFERENCES

Bracken, M., et al. (1974). The decision to abort and psychological sequel. *Journal of Nervous and Mental Disease, 158,* 157.

Brossean, K. D. (1980). *Utilizing male partners of adolescent abortion patients as change agents.* Unpublished doctoral dissertation, University of Colorado, Boulder, Department of Psychology.

Didion, J. (1972, July 30). The woman's movement. *New York Times Book Review,* p. 14.

Finley, M. C. (1978). *A male counseling component for aborting fathers at preterm.* Unpublished research paper, Preterm Clinic, Brookline, MA.

Henshaw, S. K., & O'Reilly, K. (1983). Characteristics of abortion patients in the United States, 1979-1980. *Family Planning Perspectives, 15,* 5-16.

Hill-Falkenthal, J. (1983). *Counseling needs of men about abortion.* Unpublished research paper, California State University, Sacramento, Department of Sociology.

Lincoln, J. C. (1980, February). Abortion: How Men Feel About One of the Biggest Issues in a Woman's Life.

Melamed, L. (1975). Therapeutic abortion in a midwestern city. *Psychological Reports 37,* 1144.

Oettinger, K. B. (1979). *Not my daughter: Facing up to adolescent pregnancy.* Englewood Cliffs, NJ: Prentice-Hall.

Ory, H. W., et al. (1983). *Making choices: Evaluating the health risks and benefits of birth control methods.* New York: Alan Guttmacher Institute.

Patterson, J. (1982). Whose freedom of choice? *Progressive, 4.*

Rotter, K. L. (1980). *Men and the abortion experience.* Unpublished doctoral dissertation, Southern Illinois University, Department of Health Education.

Shostak, A. (1979). Abortion and fatherhood lost: Problems and reforms. *Family Coordinator, 14,* 569-574.

Shostak, A. (1983). Men and abortion: Three neglected ethical aspects. *Humanity and Society, 7,* 66-85.

Shostak, A. (1984). Catholic men and abortion. *Conscience: The Voice of Pro-Choice Catholics, 1,* 5-6.

Shostak, A., & McLouth, G. (1984). *Men and abortion: Lessons, losses, and love.* New York: Praeger.

Smith, M. R. (1979). How men who accompany women to an abortion service perceive the impact of abortion upon their relationship and themselves. Unpublished doctoral dissertation, University of Iowa, Iowa City, Department of Education.

Spade, J. Z. (1984). Men and abortion in retrospect: A methodological evaluation. In A. Shostak & G. McLouth (Eds.), *Men and abortion* (pp. 275-283). New York: Praeger.

13

Mass-Media Sexual Violence and Male Viewers

Current Theory and Research

EDWARD DONNERSTEIN
DANIEL LINZ

The influence of pornography on male viewers has been a topic of concern for behavioral scientists for many years, as well as a recent volatile political and legal question. Often research on pornography and its effects on behavior or attitudes is concerned with sexual explicitness. But it is not an issue of sexual explicitness; rather, it is an issue of violence against women and the role of women in "pornography" that is of concern to us here. Research over the last decade has demonstrated that sexual images per se do not facilitate aggressive behavior, change rape-related attitudes, or influence other forms of antisocial behaviors or perceptions. It is the violent images in pornography that account for the various research effects. This will become clearer as the research on the effects of sexual violence in the media is discussed. It is for these and other reasons that the terms *aggressive pornography* and *sexually violent mass media images* are preferred. We will occasionally use the term *pornography* in this article for communication and convenience.

In this chapter we will examine both the research on aggressive pornography and the research that examines nonpornographic media images of violence against women—the major focus of recent research and the material that provokes negative reactions. Our final section will examine the research on nonviolent pornography. We will also refer to

AUTHORS' NOTE: This research was partially funded by National Science Foundation Grant BNS-8216772 to the first author and Steven Penrod.

various ways in which this research has been applied to the current political debate on pornography and offer suggestions to mitigate the negative effects from exposure to certain forms of pornography and sexually violent mass media.

Research on the Effects of Aggressive Pornography

Aggressive pornography, as used here, refers to X-rated images of sexual coercion in which force is used or implied against a woman in order to obtain certain sexual acts, as in scenes of rape and other forms of sexual assault. One unique feature of these images is their reliance upon "positive victim outcomes," in which rape and other sexual assaults are depicted as pleasurable, sexually arousing, and beneficial to the female victim. In contrast to other forms of media violence in which victims suffer, die, and do not enjoy their victimization, aggressive pornography paints a rosy picture of aggression. The myths regarding violence against women are central to the various influences this material has upon the viewer. This does not imply that there are not images of suffering, mutilation, and death—there are. The large majority of images, however, show violence against women as justified, positive, and sexually liberating. Even these more "realistic" images, however, can influence certain viewers under specific conditions. We will address this research later.

There is some evidence that these images increased through the 1970s (Malamuth & Spinner, 1980). However, more recent content analysis suggests that the increase has abated in the 1980s (Scott, 1985). The Presidential Commission on Obscenity and Pornography of 1970 did not examine the influence of aggressive pornography, mainly because of its low frequency. This is important to note, as it highlights differences between the commission and the position outlined in this chapter. The major difference is not in the findings but in the type of material being examined. (The Commission on Obscenity and Pornography was interested only in sexually explicit media images.)

In many aggressive pornographic depictions, as noted, the victim is portrayed as secretly desiring the assault and as eventually deriving sexual pleasure from it (Donnerstein & Berkowitz, 1982; Malamuth, Heim, & Feshbach, 1980). From a cognitive perspective, such information may suggest to the viewer that even if a woman seems repelled by a pursuer, eventually she will respond favorably to forceful advances, aggression, and overpowering by a male assailant (Brownmiller, 1975). The victim's pleasure could further heighten the aggressor's. Viewers might then come to think, at least for a short while, that their own sexual aggression would also be profitable, thus reducing restraints or inhibitions against aggression (Bandura, 1977). These views diminish the moral reprehensibility of any witnessed assault on a woman and, indeed, suggest that the sexual attack may have a highly desirable outcome for both victim and aggressor. Men having such beliefs might therefore be more likely to attack a woman after they see a supposedly "pleasurable" rape. Furthermore, as there is a substantial aggressive component in the sexual assault, it could be argued that the favorable outcome lowers the observers' restraints against aggression toward women. Empirical research in the last few years, which is examined below, as well as such cases as the New Bedford rape, in which onlookers are reported to have cheered the rape of a woman by several men, suggests that the above concerns may be warranted.

Aggressive Pornography and Sexual Arousal

Although it was once believed that only rapists show sexual arousal to depictions of rape and other forms of aggression against women (Abel, Barlow, Blanchard, & Guild, 1977), research by Malamuth and his colleagues (Malamuth, 1981b, 1984; Malamuth & Check, 1983; Malamuth & Donnerstein, 1982; Malamuth, Haber, & Feshbach, 1980; Malamuth, Heim, & Feshbach, 1980) indicates that a nonrapist population will show evidence of increased sexual arousal to media-presented images of rape. This increased arousal primarily occurs when the female victim shows signs of pleasure and arousal, the theme most commonly presented in aggressive pornography. In addition, male subjects who indicate that there is some likelihood that they themselves would rape display increased sexual arousal to all forms of rape depictions, similar to the reactions of known rapists (Malamuth, 1981a, 1981b; Malamuth & Donnerstein, 1982). Researchers have suggested that this sexual arousal measure serves as an objective index of a proclivity to rape. Using this index, an individual whose sexual arousal to rape themes was found to be similar to or greater than his arousal to nonaggressive depictions would be considered to have an inclination to rape (Abel et al., 1977; Malamuth, 1981a; Malamuth & Donnerstein, 1982).

Aggressive Pornography
and Attitudes Toward Rape

There are now considerable data indicating that exposure to aggressive pornography may alter the observer's perception of rape and the rape victim. For example, exposure to a sexually explicit rape scene in which the victim shows a "positive" reaction tends to produce a lessened sensitivity to rape (Malamuth & Check, 1983), increased acceptance of rape myths and interpersonal violence against women (Malamuth & Check, 1981), and increases in the self-reported possibility of raping (Malamuth, 1981a). This self-reported possibility of committing rape is highly correlated with (a) sexual arousal to rape stimuli, (b) aggressive behavior and a desire to hurt women, and (c) a belief that rape would be a sexually arousing experience for the rapist (see Malamuth, 1981a; Malamuth & Donnerstein, 1982). Exposure to aggressive pornography may also lead to self-generated rape fantasies (Malamuth, 1981b).

Aggressive Pornography and
Aggression Against Women

Recent research (Donnerstein, 1980a, 1980b, 1983, 1984; Donnerstein & Berkowitz, 1982) has found that exposure to aggressive pornography increases aggression against women in a laboratory context. The same exposure does not seem to influence aggression against other men. This increased aggression is most pronounced when the aggression is seen as positive for the victim and occurs for both angered and nonangered individuals.

Although this research suggests that aggressive pornography can influence the male viewer, the relative contribution of the sexual and the aggressive components of the material remains unclear. Is it the sexual nature of the material or the messages about violence that are crucial? This is an extremely important question. In many discussions of this research the fact that the material is aggressive is forgotten and it is assumed that the effects occur owing to the sexual nature of the material. As we noted earlier, the sexual nature of the material is not the major issue. Recent empirical studies shed some light on this issue.

The Influence of Nonpornographic
Depictions of Violence Against Women

It has been alleged that images of violence against women have increased not only in pornographic materials but also in more readily accessible mass media materials ("War Against Pornography," 1985). Scenes of rape and violence have appeared in daytime TV soap operas and R-rated movies shown on cable television. These images are sometimes accompanied by the theme, common in aggressive pornography, that women enjoy or benefit from sexual violence. For example, several episodes of the daytime drama *General Hospital* were devoted to a rape of one of the well-known female characters by an equally popular male character. At first the victim was humiliated; later the two characters were married. A similar theme was expressed in the popular film, *The Getaway*. In this film, described by Malamuth and Check (1981):

> Violence against women is carried out both by the hero and the antagonist. The hero, played by Steve McQueen, is portrayed in a very "macho" image. At one point, he slaps his wife several times causing her to cry from the pain. The wife, played by Ali McGraw, is portrayed as deserving this beating. As well, the antagonist in the movie kidnaps a woman (Sally Struthers) and her husband. He rapes the woman but the assault is portrayed in a manner such that the woman is depicted as a willing participant. She becomes the antagonist's girlfriend and they both taunt her husband until he commits suicide. The woman then willingly continues with the assailant and at one point frantically searches for him. (p. 439)

In a field experiment, Malamuth and Check (1981a) attempted to determine whether or not the depiction of sexual violence contained in *The Getaway* and in another film with similar content influenced the viewers' perceptions of attitudes toward women. A total of 271 male and female students participated in a study that they were led to believe focused on movie ratings. One group watched, on two different evenings, *The Getaway* and *Swept Away* (which also shows women as victims of aggression within erotic contexts). A group of control subjects watched neutral, feature-length movies. These movies were viewed in campus theaters as part of the Campus Film Program. The results of a "Sexual Attitudes Survey," conducted several days after the screenings, indicated that viewing the sexually aggressive films significantly increased male but not female acceptance of interpersonal violence and tended to increase rape myth acceptance. These effects occurred not with X-rated materials but with more "prime-time" materials.

A recent study by Donnerstein and Berkowitz (1985) sought to examine more systematically the relative contributions of aggressive and sexual components of aggressive pornography. In a series of studies, male subjects were shown one of four different films: (1) the standard aggressive pornography used in studies discussed earlier, (2) an X-rated film that contained no forms of aggression or coercion and was rated by subjects to be as sexual as the first; (3) a film that contained scenes of aggression against a woman but without any sexual content and was considered less sexual and also less arousing (physiologically) than were the previous two films; and (4) a neutral film. Although the aggressive pornographic film led to the highest aggression against women, the aggression-only film produced more aggressive behavior than did the sex-only film. In fact, the sex-only film produced no different results than did the neutral film. Subjects were also examined for their attitudes about rape and their willingness to say they might commit a rape. The most callous attitudes and the highest percentage indicating some likelihood to rape were found in the aggression-only conditions; the X-rated sex-only film was the lowest.

This research suggests that violence against women need not occur in a pornographic or sexually explicit context in order for the depictions to have an impact on both attitudes and behavior. Angered individuals became more aggressive toward a female target after exposure to films judged not to be sexually arousing but that depict a woman as a victim of aggression. This supports the claim by Malamuth and Check (1983) that sexual violence against women need not be portrayed in a pornographic fashion for greater acceptance of interpersonal violence and rape myths.

In the Malamuth and Check study the victim's reaction to sexual violence was always, in the end, a positive one. Presumably the individual viewer of nonsexually explicit rape depictions with a positive outcome comes to accept the view that aggression against women is permissible because women enjoy sexual violence. In the studies by Donnerstein and Berkowitz, however, several other processes may have been at work. Exposure to nonpornographic aggression against women resulted in the highest levels of aggressive behavior when subjects were first angered by a female confederate of the experimenter or when the victim of aggression in the film and the female confederate were linked by the same name. Presumably subjects did not come to perceive violence as acceptable because victims enjoy violence from this material. Instead, the cue value or association of women with the characters in the film (Berkowitz, 1974) and the possibility that the pain cues stimulated aggression in angry individuals might better account for the findings. When the individual is placed in a situation in which cues associated with aggressive responses are salient (for example, a situation involving a female victim) or one in which he is predisposed to aggression because he is angered, he will be more likely to respond aggressively both because of the stimulus-response connection previously built up through exposure to the films and/or because the pain and suffering of the victim reinforces already established aggressive tendencies.

An important element in the effects of exposure to aggressive pornography is violence against women. Because much commercially available media contain such images, researchers have begun to examine the impact of more popular film depictions of violence against women. Of particular interest have been R-rated "slasher" films, which combine graphic and brutal violence against women within a sexual context. These types of materials do not fit the general definition of pornography, but we believe their impact is stronger.

The Effects of Exposure to R-Rated Sexualized Violence

In a recent address before the International Conference on Film Classification and Regulation, Lord Harlech of the British Film Board noted the increase in R-rated sexually violent films and their "eroticizing" and "glorification" of rape and other forms of sexual violence. According to Harlech:

> Everyone knows that murder is wrong, but a strange myth has grown up, and been seized on by filmmakers, that rape is really not so bad, that it may even be a form of liberation for the victim, who may be acting out what she secretly desires—and perhaps needs—with no harm done. . . . Filmmakers in recent years have used rape as an exciting and titillating spectacle in pornographic films, which are always designed to appeal to men.

As depictions of sex and violence become increasingly graphic, especially in feature-length movies shown in theaters, officials at the National Institute of Mental Health are becoming concerned:

> Films had to be made more and more powerful in their arousal effects. Initially, strong excitatory reactions [may grow] weak or vanish entirely with repeated exposure to stimuli of a certain kind. This is known as "habituation." The possibility of habituation to sex and violence has significant social consequences. For one, it makes pointless the search for stronger and stronger arousers. But more important is its potential impact on real life behavior. If people become inured to violence from seeing much of it, they may be less likely to respond to real violence.

This loss of sensitivity to real violence after repeated exposure to films with sex and violence, or "the dilemma of the detached bystander in the presence of violence," is currently a concern of our research program. Although initial exposure to a violent rape scene may act to create anxiety and inhibitions about such behavior, researchers have suggested that repeated exposure to such material could counter these effects. The effects of long-term exposure to R-rated sexually violent mass media portrayals is the major focus of our ongoing research program investigating how massive exposure to commercially released violent and sexually violent films influence (1) viewer perceptions of violence, (2) judgments about rape and rape victims, (3) general physiological desensitization to violence, and (4) aggressive behavior.

This research presents a new approach to the study of mass media violence. First, unlike many previous studies in which individuals may have seen only 10-30 minutes of material, the current studies examine 10 hours of exposure. Second, we are able to monitor the process of subject's desensitization over a longer period of time than in previous experiments. Third, we examine perceptual and judgmental changes regarding violence, particularly violence against women.

In the program's first study, Linz, Donnerstein, and Penrod (1984) monitored desensitization of males to filmed violence against women to determine whether this desensitization "spilled over" into other kinds of decision making about victims. Male subjects watched nearly 10 hours (five commercially released feature-length films, one a day for five days) of R-rated or X-rated fare—either R-rated sexually violent films such as *Tool Box Murders, Vice Squad, I Spit on Your Grave, Texas Chainsaw Massacre*; X-rated movies that depicted sexual assault; or X-rated movies that depicted only consensual sex (nonviolent). The R-rated films were much more explicit with regard to violence than they were with regard to sexual content. After each movie the men completed a mood questionnaire and evaluated the films on several dimensions. The films were counterbalanced so that comparisons could be made of the same films being shown on the first and last day of viewing. Before participation in the study subjects were screened for levels of hostility, and only those with low hostility scores were included to help guard against the possibility of an overly hostile individual imitating the filmed violence during the week of the films. This is also theoretically important because it suggests that any effects we found would occur with a normal population. (It has been suggested by critics of media violence research that only those who are already predisposed toward violence are influenced by exposure to media violence. In this study, those individuals have been eliminated.) After the week of viewing the men watched yet another film. This time, however, they saw a videotaped reenactment of an actual rape trial. After the trial they were asked to render judgments about how responsible the victim was for her own rape and how much injury she had suffered.

Most interesting were the results from the men who had watched the R-rated films such as *Texas Chainsaw Massacre* or *Maniac*. Initially, after the first day of viewing, the men rated themselves significantly above the norm for depression, anxiety, and annoyance on a mood adjective checklist. After each subsequent day of viewing, these scores dropped until, on the fourth day of viewing, the males' levels of anxiety, depression, and annoyance were indistinguishable from baseline norms.

What happened to the viewers as they watched more and more violence? We believe they were becoming desensitized to violence, particularly against women, which entailed more than a simple lowering of arousal to the movie violence. The men actually began to perceive the films differently as time went on. On Day 1, for example, on the average, the men estimated that they had seen four "offensive scenes." By the fifth day, however, subjects reported only half as many offensive scenes (even though exactly the same movies, but in reverse order, were shown). Likewise, their ratings of the violence within the films receded from Day 1 to Day 5. By the last day the men rated the movies less graphic and less gory and estimated fewer violent scenes than they did on the first day of viewing. Most startling, by the last day of viewing graphic violence against women the men were rating the material as significantly less debasing and degrading to women, more humorous, and more enjoyable, and they claimed a greater willingness to see this type of film again. This change in perception due to repeated exposure was particularly evident in comparisons of reactions to two specific films—*I Spit on Your Grave* and *Vice Squad*. Both films contain sexual assault; however, rape is portrayed more graphically in *I Spit on Your Grave* and more ambiguously in *Vice Squad*. Men who were exposed first to *Vice Squad* and then to *I Spit on Your Grave* gave nearly identical ratings of sexual violence. However, subjects who had seen the more graphic movie first saw much less sexual violence (rape) in the more ambiguous film.

The subjects' evaluations of a rape victim after viewing a reenacted rape trial were also affected by the constant exposure to brutality against women. The victim of rape was rated as more worthless and her injury as significantly less severe by those exposed to filmed violence when compared to a control group of men who saw only the rape trial and did not view films. Desensitization to filmed violence on the last day was also significantly correlated with assignment of greater blame to the victim for her own rape. (These types of effects were not observed for subjects who were exposed to sexually explicit but nonviolent films.)

Mitigating the Effects of
Exposure to Sexual Violence

This research strongly suggests a potential harmful effect from exposure to certain forms of aggressive pornography and other forms of sexualized violence. There is now, however, some evidence that these negative changes in attitudes and perceptions regarding rape and violence against women not only can be eliminated but can be positively changed. Malamuth and Check (1983) found that if male subjects who had participated in such an experiment were later administered a carefully constructed debriefing, they actually would be less accepting of certain rape myths than were control subjects exposed to depictions of intercourse (without a debriefing). Donnerstein and Berkowitz (1981) showed that not only are the negative effects of previous exposure eliminated, but even up to four months later, debriefed subjects have more "sensitive" attitudes toward rape than do control subjects. These debriefings consisted of (1) cautioning subjects that the portrayal of the rape they had been exposed to is completely fictitious in nature, (2) educating subjects about the violent nature of rape, (3) pointing out to subjects that rape is illegal and punishable by imprisonment, and (4) dispelling the many rape myths that are perpetrated in the portrayal (e.g., in the majority of rapes, the victim is promiscuous or has a bad reputation, or that many women have an unconscious desire to be raped).

Surveys of the effectiveness of debriefings for male subjects with R-rated sexual violence have yielded similar positive results. Subjects who participated in the week-long film exposure study that was followed by a certain type of debriefing changed their attitudes in a positive direction. The debriefings emphasized the fallacious nature of movie portrayals that suggest that women deserve to be physically violated and emphasized that processes of desensitization may have occurred because of long-term exposure to violence. The results indicated an immediate effect for debriefing, with subjects scoring lower on rape myth acceptance after participation than they scored before participation in the film viewing sessions. These effects remained, for the most part, six weeks later. The effectiveness of the debriefing for the subjects who participated in two later experiments (one involving two weeks of exposure to R-rated violent films) indicated that even after seven months, subjects' attitudes about sexual violence showed significant positive change compared to the preparticipation levels.

This research suggests that if the callous attitudes about rape and violence presented in aggressive pornography and other media representations of violence against women are learned, they can likewise be "unlearned." Furthermore, if effective debriefings eliminate these negative effects, it would seem possible to develop effective "prebriefings" that would also counter the impact of such materials. Such programs could become part of sex education curricula for young males. Given the easy access and availability of many forms of sexual violence to young males today, such programs would go a long way toward countering the impact of such images.

The Impact of Nonaggressive Pornography

An examination of early research and reports in the area of nonaggressive pornography would have suggested that effects of exposure to erotica were, if anything, nonharmful. For instance:

> It is concluded that pornography is an innocuous stimulus which leads quickly to satiation and that the public concern over it is misplaced. (Howard, Liptzin, & Reifler, 1973, p. 133)

> Results . . . fail to support the position that viewing erotic films produces harmful social consequences. (Mann, Sidman, & Starr, 1971, p. 113)

> If a case is to be made against "pornography" in 1970, it will have to be made on grounds other than demonstrated effects of a damaging personal or social nature. (President's Commission on Obscenity and Pornography, 1970, p. 139)

A number of criticisms of these findings, however (such as Cline, 1974; Dienstbier, 1977; Wills, 1977), led to a reexamination of the issue of exposure to pornography and subsequent aggressive behavior. Some—for example, Cline (1974)—saw major methodological and interpretive problems with the Pornography Commission report; others (for example, Liebert & Schwartzberg, 1977) believed that the observations were premature. Certainly the relationship between exposure to pornography and subsequent aggressive behavior was more complex than first believed. For the most part, recent research has shown that exposure to nonaggressive pornography can have one of two effects.

A number of studies in which individuals have been predisposed to aggression and were later exposed to nonaggressive pornography have revealed increases in aggressive behavior (such as Baron & Bell, 1977; Donnerstein, Donnerstein, & Evans, 1975; Malamuth, Feshbach, & Jaffe, 1977; Meyer, 1972; Zillmann, 1971, 1979). Such findings have been interpreted in terms of a general arousal model, which states that under conditions in which aggression is a dominant response, any source of emotional arousal will tend to increase aggressive behavior in disinhibited subjects (for example, Bandura, 1977; Donnerstein, 1983). A second group of studies (Baron, 1977; Baron & Bell, 1973; Donnerstein et al., 1975; Frodi, 1977; Zillmann & Sapolsky, 1977) reports the opposite—that exposure to pornography of a nonaggressive nature can actually reduce subsequent aggressive behavior.

These results appear contradictory, but recent research (Baron, 1977; Donnerstein, 1983; Donnerstein et al., 1975; Zillmann, 1979) has begun to reconcile seeming inconsistencies. It is now believed that as porno-graphic stimuli become more arousing, they give rise to increases in aggression. At a low level of arousal, however, the stimuli distract individuals, and attention is directed away from previous anger. Acting in an aggressive manner toward a target is incompatible with the pleasant feelings associated with low-level arousal (see Baron, 1977; Donnerstein, 1983). There is also evidence that individuals who find the materials "displeasing" or "pornographic" will also increase their aggression after exposure, whereas those who have more positive reactions to the material will not increase their aggression even to highly arousing materials (Zillmann, 1979).

The research noted above was primarily concerned with same-sex aggression. The influence of nonaggressive pornography on aggression against women tends to produce mixed effects. Donnerstein and Barrett (1978) and Donnerstein and Hallam (1978) found that nonaggressive pornography had no effect on subsequent aggression unless constraints against aggressing were reduced. This was accomplished by both angering male subjects by women and giving subjects multiple chances to aggress. Donnerstein (1983) tried to reduce aggressive inhibitions through the use of an aggressive model but found no increase in aggression after exposure to an X-rated nonviolent film. It seems, therefore, that nonaggressive sexual material does not lead to aggression against women except under specific conditions (for example when inhibitions against aggression are lowered deliberately by the experi-menter).

Almost without exception, studies reporting the effects on nonviolent pornography have relied on short-term exposure; most subjects have been exposed to only a few minutes of pornographic material. More recently, Zillman and Bryant (1982, 1984) demonstrated that long-term exposure (4 hours and 48 minutes over a six-week period) to pornography that does not contain overt aggressiveness may cause male and female subjects to (1) become more tolerant of bizarre and violent forms of pornography, (2) become less supportive of statements about sexual equality, and (3) become more lenient in assigning punishment to a rapist whose crime is described in a newspaper account. Furthermore, extensive exposure to the nonaggressive pornography significantly increased males' sexual callousness toward women. This latter finding was evidenced by increased acceptance of statements such as, "A man should find them, fool them, fuck them, and forget them," "A woman doesn't mean 'no' until she slaps you," and "If they are old enough to bleed, they are old enough to butcher." Zillmann and others (such as Berkowitz, 1984) have offered several possible explanations for this effect, suggesting that certain viewer attitudes are strengthened through long-term exposure to nonviolent pornographic material.

A common scenario of the material used in the Zillmann research is that women are sexually insatiable by nature. Even though the films shown do not feature the infliction of pain or suffering, women are portrayed as extremely permissive and promiscuous, willing to accommodate any male sexual urge. Short-term exposure to this view of women (characteristic of early studies of nonviolent pornography) may not be sufficient to engender changes in viewers' attitudes congruent with these portrayals. However, attitudinal changes might be expected under conditions of long-term exposure. Continued exposure to the idea that women will do practically anything sexually may prime or encourage other thoughts regarding female promiscuity (Berkowitz, 1984). This increase in the availability of thoughts about female promiscuity or the ease with which viewers can imagine instances in which a female has been sexually insatiable may lead viewers to inflate their estimates of how willingly and frequently women engage in sexual behavior. The availability of thoughts about female insatiability may also affect judgments about sexual behavior such as rape, bestiality, and sado-masochistic sex. Further, these ideas may endure. Zillman and Bryant (1982), for example, found that male subjects still had a propensity to trivialize rape three weeks after exposure to nonviolent pornography. It is important to point out, however, that in these studies long-term exposure did not increase aggressive behavior but in fact decreased subsequent aggression.

Unfortunately, the role that images of female promiscuity and insatiability play in fostering callous perceptions of women can only be speculated upon at this point because no research has systematically manipulated film content in an experiment designed to facilitate or inhibit viewer cognitions. One cannot rule out the possibility, for example, that simple exposure to many sexually explicit depictions (regardless of their "insatiability" theme) accounts for the attitudinal changes found in their study. Sexual explicitness and themes of insatiability are experimentally confounded in this work.

Another emerging concern among political activists about pornography is its alleged tendency to degrade women (Dworkin, 1985; MacKinnon, 1985). This concern has been expressed recently in the form of municipal ordinances against pornography originally drafted by Catherine MacKinnon and Andrea Dworkin that have been introduced in a variety of communities, including Minneapolis and Indianapolis. One central feature of these ordinances is that pornography is the graphic "sexually explicit subordination of women" that also includes "women presented in scenarios of degradation, injury, abasement, torture, shown as filthy or inferior, bleeding, bruised, or hurt in a context that makes these conditions sexual" (City County general ordinance No. 35, City of Indianapolis, 1984). These ordinances have engendered a great deal of controversy, as some individuals have maintained that they are a broad form of censorship. A critique of these ordinances can be found in a number of publications (for example, Burstyn, 1985; Russ, 1985).

The framers of the ordinance suggest that after viewing such material, "a general pattern of discriminatory attitudes and behavior, both violent and non-violent, that has the capacity to stimulate various negative reactions against women will be found" (Defendants' memorandum, U.S. District Court for the Southern District of Indiana, Indianapolis Division, 1984, p. 8). Experimental evidence is clear with respect to the effects of pornography showing injury, torture, bleeding, bruised, or hurt women in sexual contexts. What has not been investigated is the effect of material showing women in scenarios of degradation, as inferior and abased.

No research has separated the effect of sexual explicitness from degradation, as was done with aggressive pornography, to determine whether the two interact to foster negative evaluations of women. Nearly all experiments conducted to date have confounded sexual explicitness with the presentation of women as a subordinate, objectified class. Only one investigation (Donnerstein, 1984) has attempted to disentangle sexual explicitness and violence. The results of this short-term exposure investigation, discussed above, revealed that although the combination of sexual explicitness and violence against a woman (the violent pornographic condition) resulted in the highest levels of subsequent aggression against a female target, the nonexplicit depiction that showed only violence resulted in aggression levels nearly as high and attitudes that were more callous than those that resulted from the combined exposure. The implication of this research is that long-term exposure to material that may not be explicitly sexual but that depicts women in scenes of degradation and subordination may have a negative impact on viewer attitudes. This is one area in which research is still needed.

Conclusions

Does pornography influence behaviors and attitudes toward women? The answer is difficult and centers on the definition of pornography. There is no evidence for any "harm"-related effects from sexually explicit materials. But research may support potential harmful effects from aggressive materials. Aggressive images are the issue, not sexual images. The message about violence and the sexualized nature of violence is crucial. Although these messages may be part of some forms of pornography, they are also pervasive media messages in general, from prime-time TV to popular films. Males in our society have callous attitudes about rape. But where do these attitudes come from? Are the media, and in particular pornography, the cause? We would be reluctant to place the blame on the media. If anything, the media act to reinforce already existing attitudes and values regarding women and violence. They do contribute, but are only part of the problem.

As social scientists we have devoted a great deal of time to searching for causes of violence against women. Perhaps it is time to look for ways to reduce this violence. This chapter has noted several studies that report techniques to mitigate the influence of exposure to sexual violence in the media, which involves changing attitudes about violence. The issue of pornography and its relationship to violence will continue for years, perhaps without any definitive answers. We may never know if there is any real casual influence. We do know, however, that rape and other forms of violence against women are pervasive. How we change this situation is of crucial importance, and our efforts need to be directed to this end.

REFERENCES

Abel, G., Barlow, D., Blanchard, E., & Guild, D. (1977). The components of rapists' sexual arousal. *Archives of General Psychiatry, 34,* 395-403, 895-903.

Bandura, A. (1977). *Social learning theory.* Englewood Cliffs, NJ: Prentice-Hall.

Baron, R. A. (1977). *Human aggression.* New York: Plenum.

Baron, R. A. (1984). The control of human aggression: A strategy based on incompatible responses. In R. Green & E. Donnerstein (Eds.), *Aggression: Theoretical and empirical reviews* (Vol. 2). New York: Academic Press.

Baron, R. A., & Bell, P. A. (1977). Sexual arousal and aggression by males: Effects of type of erotic stimuli and prior provocation. *Journal of Personality and Social Psychology, 35,* 79-87.

Berkowitz, L. (1974). Some determinants of impulsive aggression: Role of mediated associations with reinforcements for aggression. *Psychological Review, 81,* 165-179.

Berkowitz, L. (1984). Some effects of thoughts on anti- and prosocial influences of media events: A cognitive-neoassociation analysis. *Psychological Bulletin, 95,* 410-427.

Brownmiller, S. (1975). *Against our will: Men, women and rape.* New York: Simon & Schuster.

Burstyn, V. (1985). *Women against censorship.* Manchester, NH: Salem House.

Burt, M. R. (1980). Cultural myths and supports for rape. *Journal of Personality and Social Psychology, 38,* 217-230.

Check, J.V.P., & Malamuth, N. (1983). Violent pornography, feminism, and social learning theory. *Aggressive Behavior, 9,* 106-107.

Check, J.V.P., & Malamuth, N. (in press). Can participation in pornography experiments have positive effects? *Journal of Sex Research*

Cline, V. B. (Ed.). (1974). *Where do you draw the line?* Salt Lake City: Brigham Young University Press.

Dienstbier, R. A. (1977). Sex and violence: Can research have it both ways? *Journal of Communication, 27,* 176-188.

Donnerstein, E. (1980a). Pornography and violence against women. *Annals of the New York Academy of Sciences, 347,* 277-288.

Donnerstein, E. (1980b). Aggressive-erotica and violence against women. *Journal of Personality and Social Psychology, 39,* 269-277.

Donnerstein, E. (1983). Erotica and human aggression. In R. Geen & E. Donnerstein (Eds.), *Aggression: Theoretical and empirical reviews.* New York: Academic Press.

Donnerstein, E. (1984). Pornography: Its effect on violence against women. In N. Malamuth & E. Donnerstein (Eds.), *Pornography and sexual aggression.* Orlando, FL: Academic Press.

Donnerstein, E., & Barrett, G. (1978). The effects of erotic stimuli on male aggression toward females. *Journal of Personality and Social Psychology, 36,* 180-188.

Donnerstein, E., & Berkowitz, L. (1982). Victim reactions in aggressive-erotic films as a factor in violence against women. *Journal of Personality and Social Psychology, 41,* 710-724.

Donnerstein, E., & Berkowitz, L. (1985). *Role of aggressive and sexual images in violent pornography.* Manuscript submitted for publication.

Donnerstein, E., & Hallam, J. (1978). Facilitating effects of erotica on aggression against women. *Journal of Personality and Social Psychology, 36,* 1270-1277.

Donnerstein, E., & Linz, D. (1984, January). Sexual violence in the media, a warning. *Psychology Today,* pp. 14-15.

Donnerstein, E., Donnerstein, M., & Evans, R. (1975). Erotic stimuli and aggression: Facilitation or inhibition. *Journal of Personality and Social Psychology, 32,* 237-244.

Dworkin, A. (1985). Against the male flood: Censorship, pornography, and equality. *Harvard Women's Law Journal, 8.*

Frodi, A. (1977). Sexual arousal, situational restrictiveness, and aggressive behavior. *Journal of Research in Personality, 11,* 48-58.

Howard, J. L., Liptzin, M. B., & Reifler, C. B. (1973). Is pornography a problem? *Journal of Social Issues, 29,* 133-145.

Liebert, R. M., & Schwartzberg, N. S. (1977). Effects of mass media. *Annual Review of Psychology, 28,* 141-173.

Linz, D., Donnerstein, E., & Penrod, S. (1984). The effects of long-term exposure to filmed violence against women. *Journal of Communication, 34,* 130-147.

MacKinnon, C. A. (1985). Pornography, civil rights, and speech. *Harvard Civil Rights-Civil Liberty Law Review, 20(1).*

Malamuth, N. (1981a). Rape proclivity among males. *Journal of Social Issues, 37,* 138-157.

Malamuth, N. (1981b). Rape fantasies as a function of exposure to violent-sexual stimuli. *Archives of Sexual Behavior, 10,* 33-47.

Malamuth, N. (1984). Aggression against women: Cultural and individual causes. In N. Malamuth & E. Donnerstein (Eds.), *Pornography and sexual aggression.* Orlando, FL: Academic Press.

Malamuth N., Feshbach, S., & Jaffe, Y. (1977). Sexual arousal and aggression: Recent experiments and theoretical issues. *Journal of Social Issues, 33,* 110-133.

Malamuth, N. M., & Spinner, B. (1980). A longitudinal content analysis of sexual violence in the best-selling erotic magazines. *Journal of Sex Research, 16(3),* 116-237.

Malamuth, N., & Check, J.V.P. (1981). The effects of mass media exposure on acceptance of violence against women: A field experiment. *Journal of Research in Personality, 15,* 436-446.

Malamuth, N., & Check, J.V.P. (1983). Sexual arousal to rape depictions: Individual differences. *Journal of Abnormal Psychology, 92,* 55-67.

Malamuth, N., & Donnerstein E. (1982). The effects of aggressive pornographic mass media stimuli. In L. Berkowitz (Ed.), *Advances in experimental social psychology* (vol. 15). New York: Academic Press.

Malamuth, N., & Donnerstein, E. (Eds.), (1983). *Pornography and sexual aggression.* New York: Academic Press.

Malamuth, N., Haber, S., & Feshbach, S. (1980). The sexual responsiveness of college students to rape depictions: Inhibitory and disinhibitory effects. *Journal of Research in Personality,14,* 399-408.

Mann, J., Sidman, J., & Starr, S. (1971). Effects of erotic films on sexual behavior of married couples. In *Technical Report of the Commission on Obscenity and Pornography* (vol. 8.). Washington, DC: Government Printing Office.

Meyer, T. (1972). The effects of viewing justified and unjustified real film violence on aggressive behavior. *Journal of Personality and Social Psychology, 23,* 21-29.

President's Commission on Obscenity and Pornography (vol.8). Washington, DC: Government Printing Office.

Russ, J. (1985). *Magic mommas, trembling sisters, puritans and perverts.* New York: Crossing.

Scott, J. (1985). *Sexual violence in* Playboy *magazine: Longitudinal analysis.* Paper presented at the meeting of the American Society of Criminology.

The war against pornography. (1985, March 18). *Newsweek,* pp. 58-62, 65-67.

Wills, G. (1977, November). Measuring the impact of erotica. *Psychology Today,* pp. 30-34.

Zillman, D. (1971). Excitation transfer in communication-mediated aggressive behavior. *Journal of Experimental Social Psychology, 7,* 419-433.

Zillman, D. (1979). *Hostility and agression.* Hillsdale, NJ: Erlbaum.

Zillman, D. (1984) *Victimization of women through pornography.* Proposal to the National Science Foundation.

Zillman, D., & Bryant, J. (1982). Pornography, sexual callousness, and the trivialization of rape. *Journal of Communication,32,* 10-21.

Zillman, D., & Bryant, J. (1984). Effects of massive exposure to pornography. In N. Malamuth & E. Donnerstein (Eds.), *Pornography and sexual aggression,* New York: Academic Press.

Zillman, D., & Sapolsky, B. S. (1977). What mediates the effect of mild erotica on annoyance and hostile behavior in males? *Journal of Personality and Social Psychology,35* 587-596.

PART V

Race and Gender

14

Gender and Imperialism

Colonial Policy and
the Ideology of Moral Imperialism
in Late Nineteenth-Century Bengal

MRINALINI SINHA

This chapter draws a connection between imperialism and the ideal of manliness and shows how foreign domination was mediated through a set of gender relations and gender identities. My analysis focuses on Bengal, which in many ways was a paradigmatic colonial possession. As the economic and administrative heart of British India, it was the first province to experience the full impact of Western colonialism and it was also the first to offer a direct challenge to British rule in India (Ray, 1984, pp. 1-5). The British response to the political challenge from the Bengali middle class in the second half of the nineteenth century was

AUTHOR'S NOTE: This chapter was inspired by the publication of some ideas on gender and imperialism in *South Asia Research* (Vol. 5, No. 2, November 1985, pp. 147-165). This work was first presented at a seminar at the New York Institute of Humanities, New York, May 16, 1986. Much of the material presented here is based upon my earlier work: "The Age of Consent Act: The Ideal of Masculinity and Colonial Ideology in 19th Century Bengal."

reflected in the popularity of a series of racial and cultural stereotypes. The stereotype of the "effeminate Bengali" was ubiquitous in the colonial discourse of the period.

The gender ideology of masculinity was an important element in the rationalization of imperialism in the late nineteenth century (Field, 1982, pp. 25-26; Nandy, 1982, pp. 200-208). Arguments based on gender relations and gender identities were used to point to certain defects in Indian society, which made it unfit for self-rule and self-determination. The subordination of women in traditional Hindu society provided a useful rationale for the continuation of British rule in India. I will argue that the concern about the condition of Indian women did not arise from a general interest in the status of women; rather, it was motivated by the political necessity of demonstrating the inferiority of Indian, particularly Bengali, masculinity. The British questioned the masculinity of the Bengali male and these doubts were often used to justify their unwillingness to share political power and administrative control with the new Bengali middle class. The British policy toward Indian women was conditioned by a standard of "manliness" and therefore it did not challenge male dominance in general, but only the specific form of male dominance found in Hindu society (Liddle & Joshi, 1985, pp. 149, 163).

To make the analysis more meaningful it is necessary here to digress a little and examine the role of Indian gender relations in the claim of British moral superiority in the nineteenth century. The two greatest nineteenth-century ideologues of moral imperialism were Charles Grant and James Mill (Copley, 1983). The writings of Grant and Mill had profound influence in shaping the attitudes of generations of British officials in India. Both emphasized the depravity of Indian society and the duty of the British to bring the light of civilization to the degraded Hindus. For Grant and Mill, societal regard for women was crucial in determining the level of civilization. In his famous *History of India*, James Mill wrote:

> The condition of women is one of the most remarkable circumstances in the manner of nations. Among rude people the women are generally degraded, among civilized people they are exalted. (quoted in Copley, 1983, pp. 16-17)

Mill was shocked at the status of women in India compared to their status in Britain and saw it as proof of the uncivilized and barbaric nature of Hindu society. His analysis of the depraved nature of Hindu society emphasized equally the unmanliness or effeminacy of the Hindu male.

Following Grant and Mill, successive exponents of the inferiority of Hindu civilization in the late nineteenth century drew attention to the degraded condition of Hindu women and the effeminacy of the Hindu men. Most officials saw female subordination peculiar to Indian gender relations and failed to draw a connection between the forms of female subordination in India and the West. The colonial officials, who shared in the general enthusiasm for the Victorian ideal of masculinity, did not see any parallels between the different cultural forms of male dominance in English and Indian society. The British in India, or the Anglo-Indians, as they were called, used the abuses perpetrated on Indian women not to argue for the abolition of male privilege in India and in Britain, but to argue against political recognition of the allegedly unmanly and effeminate Hindu men.

The record of British administration in India with regard to the status of women demonstrates that although women featured prominently in the legislation initiatives of the nineteenth century, they were seldom the legislators' prime concern. The colonial government did undertake various measures to rescue women from the abuses of Hindu society: It legislated against *sati* or the self-immolation of widows, female infanticide, and child marriage, and it promoted widow remarriage. But the official policy toward women was often contradictory in nature because it could seldom be divorced from the dictates of the colonial situation. The government claimed to be the champions of female emancipation in India on the one hand, and reinforced the oppression of Indian women on the other.

In the guise of noninterference with the religious customs of the Hindus, the British government had imposed rigid proscriptions on women that went beyond those customarily imposed on them. Ever since the nineteenth century, the government in India had favored the coexistence of Hindu with Western law; but for the sake of administrative efficiency it had declared Brahmin law as the law for all Hindus (Liddle & Joshi, 1985, pp. 149-150). In traditional Hindu society the law differed according to different castes and different cultural boundaries. By declaring Brahmin law as the universal Hindu law, the legislators subjected lower-caste women to restrictions not customarily imposed on them. Brahmin law prescribed rules against divorce, remarriage, and female ownership of property, which did not exist for women of other castes. The Widows Remarriage Act of 1856 demonstrated the constraints imposed by such a situation. The act made a concession to Brahmin law by barring a remarried widow from claims to the deceased husband's property. The high courts of the country rigidly adhered to the provisions of this act and disinherited several lower-caste women who by custom were not exposed to any restriction in the event of remarriage (Carroll, 1983, pp. 363, 370-372).

The interest in the women's question was linked inextricably to the political and administrative exigencies of the colonial situation. This was clearly evident in the official policy toward native prostitutes in military cantonments. From early in the nineteenth century, colonial policy encouraged the separation of the European from the native Indian community. The officials frowned upon sexual liaisons between Europeans and Indians (Ballhatchet, 1980). The British elite were encouraged to marry their own countrywomen and set up respectable "English homes" in India. The English elite were expected to display "manly" reserve and self-control in their interaction with the native population. The presence of a sizable population of lower-class Englishmen in the Army posed a problem. The lower-class British soldiers in India led bachelor lives in military cantonments and could not be expected to exercise the "self-control" of their superiors; acceptable outlets were required to provide for the sexual needs of these men.

The military authorities in India sanctioned a system of licensed prostitution that allowed British soldiers access to "safe" native prostitutes. The system was legalized by the Indian Contagious Diseases Act of 1868. When the act was repealed, because of the campaign against a similar act in England, the incidence of venereal disease among British soldiers reached alarming proportions. The system of regulating prostitutes continued unofficially and there was a clamor in official circles to reintroduce the Contagious Diseases Act (Liddle & Joshi, 1985, pp. 151-152). The officials preferred a policy of harassing female prostitutes in favor of adopting other measures to combat the problem of venereal disease. The military authorities did not impose any restrictions on the soldiers for fear that it would encourage the "unnatural" vices of masturbation and homosexuality. They also would not incur the expense of allowing English soldiers to bring their wives to India, despite the fact that venereal disease was far less frequent among the Indian recruits who lived with wife and family. Instead, the authorities encouraged native women to supply sexual services to the soldiers, and then victimized the women on suspicion of infecting the men.

Thus far, I have pointed to certain underlying contradictions in the government's ostensible concern for the plight of Indian women. The official attitude toward female subordination and male domination was myopic and contradictory because it could not be dissociated from the constraints of colonial politics. The valorization of Victorian masculinity and the devaluation of Indian, particularly Bengali, masculinity featured prominently in the politics of the period. This perspective pervaded the colonial government's policy toward the subordination of women in Hindu society.

The politics of masculinity played a significant role in the colonial legislators' approach to the problem of child marriage in India. The British rightly opposed the practice of child marriage because it imposed severe restrictions on Hindu women. Yet the legislators in India compounded the hardships of the Indian child bride by importing from England suits for the restitution of conjugal rights based on English ecclesiastical law (Engels, 1983, pp. 108-109). In England feminists and liberal critics had drawn attention to the coercive element in suits that legally sanctioned the right of the husband to demand the company of his wife. The criticism forced the English courts to adopt a lenient view and to try to modify the legal support for the husband's privilege. However, the colonial legislators were reluctant to introduce any modifications, even though the context of nonconsensual child marriage in India only exacerbated the elements of force and coercion inherent in such suits. The government of India dragged its feet about taking action on this issue. In British India the impetus for women's reform stemmed more from a desire to demonstrate the barbaric practices of the Hindu male than from a purely humanitarian concern for the plight of the Hindu female.

The controversy over the Age of Consent Act of 1891 was, perhaps, the most dramatic indication that the legislators were motivated more by the Victorian ideal of masculinity and the corresponding ideal of femininity than they were by a commitment to female autonomy (Sinha, 1986). The abuses of child marriage had attracted the attention of Indian social reformers even before the passage of the Consent Act. The Parsi reformer from Bombay, Behramji Malabari, had initiated a long campaign against child marriage with the publication of his *Notes on Infant Marriage and Enforced Widowhood* in August 1884. His early efforts were polemical and they were easily frustrated in India. By 1890, however, he had tempered his position and had succeeded in winning the support of leading English public opinion. Despite the fact that Malabari had adopted a more moderate position, his Resolution to the secretary of state for India incorporated a comprehensive critique of child marriage. The Resolution of 1890 proposed the following: that all child marriages be subject to ratification by law; a higher age of consent for girls; the removal of suits for the restitution of conjugal rights; and government encouragement for the remarriage of widows. Even in Bengal, where the abuses of child marriage were most acute and where support for social reform had declined, the educated class favored a policy that was comprehensive in its attack against child marriage.

The government regarded such a policy as exceedingly dangerous because it involved an interference in the religious nature of the Hindu marriage ritual. Nonetheless, public pressure in England and in India forced the viceroy and his council to take some action. Lord Lansdowne's government decided to retain child marriage and to focus only on the premature consummation of child marriage. The Consent Act simply declared that sexual intercourse with unmarried or married girls below 12 years of age, with or without their consent, would be treated as rape. The colonial government, for the sake of political expediency, was willing to tolerate the anomalous situation of permitting children to contract marriage and then prohibiting them from consummating their marriage. The major preoccupation of the government was to maintain political stability in the country and to ensure the security of foreign rule in an alien country. The nature of the colonial state, therefore, imposed constraints that forced it to abdicate its traditional functions, not only to uphold religion and custom but also to modify or abrogate them when necessary (Copley, 1981, pp. 22-23).

The argument for interference in Hindu religious customs was suspect. When it suited the purpose of the government they were willing to disregard Hindu religion and custom on grounds of common decency and humanity. The Consent Act prohibited intercourse with married girls below 12 years of age, thereby contravening Bengali religious custom, which enjoined intercourse at the first menstruation of the child bride. At the outset the proponents of the act tried to prove that it did not go against Bengali religion by showing that most Bengali girls first menstruated at 12 years of age. When it became impossible to establish conclusively that Bengali Hindu girls reached puberty at 12 years, the legislators abandoned the claim of not interfering in the religious rites of the Hindus. In his final speech on the Consent Act in the Legislative Council, the Legal Member Sir Andrew Scoble, ignored the religious aspect and defended the act on humanitarian grounds.

The plea of noninterference in the religious practices of the Hindus served a political function that could be used when desired by the legislators. The Consent Act shied away from addressing the problem of child marriage, but the issue itself was kept alive for many years. In 1927 American author Katherine Mayo wrote *Mother India*, a violent diatribe against the perverse and degraded practice of child marriage that had persisted into the twentieth century. Mayo's analysis did not take into account the peculiar relationship between imperialism and the perpetuation of traditional forms of female oppression in India (Liddle

& Joshi, 1985, p. 148). An English contemporary of Mayo, Eleanor Rathbone, was moved to write *Child Marriage: The Indian Minotaur*, in which she criticized the British government for abandoning the moral principle of female emancipation after the First World War, in favor of a policy for the continuation of foreign rule and the defense of British financial interests in India. In 1929 the government finally passed the Child Marriage Restraint Act because it was no longer possible to defend its policy of noninterference.

The nature of the 1891 Consent Act made clear that the moral principle of female emancipation had never been the prime concern of the legislators; they were always willing to subordinate the women's question to the pursuit of colonial economic and political power. The advocates of the Consent Act saw the anomaly of their position in prohibiting consummation and permitting child marriage. They were convinced of the legislative insignificance of such an anomalous act and were aware that it could do little to ameliorate the lot of the child bride. They realized that it would be virtually impossible to police young couples to detect cases of marital intercourse with wives below 12 years of age. Yet the legislators were single-minded in their resolve to pass the Consent Act, which humiliated the Bengali husband without being of much use to the Bengali child bride.

The insult to the Bengali husband came from the fact that in no other country was marital intercourse described as rape. Even in England the legislators had not yet abandoned Lord Hale's opinion: "The husband cannot be guilty of rape committed by himself upon his lawful wife, for by their mutual matrimonial contract the wife hath given up herself in this kind unto her husband which she cannot retract." Since English legislators were still informed by a belief in the absolute sanctity of marriage and the privilege of the husband, the reiteration of the marital rape clause in the Indian Consent Act can be understood only in the light of the contempt and disregard of Bengali masculinity.

The Indian Consent Act, despite its liberal and humanitarian rhetoric, became the focus, on the one hand, of the colonial disdain of Bengali masculinity and, on the other, of the Bengali male's attempt to reclaim his masculinity. The Bengalis were extremely sensitive to the insinuations against their "honor," implicit in the attitude of the legislators. The popular vernacular newspapers of Bengal commented:

> The Government wishes to civilize us for it seems we are a people who are extremely uncivilized and barbarous, and steeped in superstition . . . who subject their women to gross ill usage, nay commit bestial oppression on their girls.

One newspaper feared that if the bill was passed Bengali *jamais* or sons-in-law would be impounded in barracks and allowed to visit their wives only with government permission.

The advocates of the act saw the Bengali male's support for early consummation as proof of the depraved nature of Indian gender relations. The legislators did not see early consummation as one expression of male control over female sexuality, which was equally entrenched in their own society, albeit in a different form. Consequently, the framers of the act were content to rescue women from one form of male dominance and subject them to another. It is true that the Consent Act gave Indian women a degree of control over their sexuality by prohibiting intercourse below 12 years. However, the relative control was undermined by the legal right given to the husband to demand the company of his wife.

The right of a woman to a say in her own sexuality was made even more ambiguous because of the underlying Victorian belief in female purity and passivity that motivated the reformers. The Consent Act, very like the age of consent regulations in England, portrayed an overly simplified picture of women as the helpless victims of male lust (Gorham, 1978, pp. 354-355). The legislators in India were influenced by the Victorian premise that women hardly ever desired sexual relations. In contrast, the traditional Bengali view of female sexuality portrayed women as "naturally libidinous" (Basham, 1964, p. 9).

The Bengali religious orthodoxy and the Anglo-Indian medical authority agreed that sexual intercourse should occur only after the puberty of the child bride. Yet the Select Committee of the Viceroy's Legislative Council rejected the substitution of "puberty" for "12 years" in the Consent Act. Though the substitution accorded with religious and medical opinion the legislators preferred the chronological criterion to determine the appropriate time for sexual intercourse for Bengali girls. The Calcutta Medical Society quite arbitrarily declared that "it is a pretty well ascertained fact that few native girls in the country menstruate *naturally* before the completion of the 12th year" (emphasis added). The examples of Bengali girls who menstruated below 12 years was declared "unnatural," and many doctors believed that "unaided menstruation is unfortunately a rare event in Bengal." The *Indian Medical Gazette* categorically stated that "little girls are ripened in this country for the early consummation of their marriage by excitation of their sexual instincts."

The opposing male perspectives on female sexuality became a major point of disagreement (Engels, 1983, p. 107). The Victorian Anglo-Indians favored the opinion of Major C.H. Jourbet, professor of midwifery, Medical College, Calcutta, that sexual intercourse should not be encouraged even after the first menstruation of the child bride. In contrast, the Bengali doctors accused the British of making "children out of mature girls" and argued that intercourse after menses was not fraught with the dangers that the "foreigners" tried to make out. The orthodox Bengalis painted the terrible scenario of "females in groups hurrying from door to door begging males to gratify their lust" if the Consent Act was passed (quoted in Engels, 1983, p. 123). The pro-Consent Act reformers were perceptive in pointing out the oppressive elements in the traditional society's contempt of female sexuality, but they never questioned the implications of their own denial of sexual agency to women. They did not see the Victorian doctrine of female "passionlessness" as in any way restrictive for women (Cott, 1978, pp. 219-220; Walkowitz, 1982, pp. 84-86).

The reformers propagated the view of female sexual asceticism despite the fact that many native women displayed enthusiasm in sexual matters. The men accused the female members of the Bengali household of encouraging sexual intimacy between immature children (Engels, 1983, p. 117). In an anonymous petition signed simply by "a woman," the petitioner bemoaned the fate of a wife who was not allowed to have intercourse with her husband even after puberty (quoted in Borthwick, 1984, p. 127).

The Victorian Anglo-Indians were easily appalled by the open attitude to sexuality in the Indian household. They directed their criticisms against the sexual licentiousness and brutality of the Indian male. In particular, the British accused the Bengali male of displaying a singular lack of "self-control." The Victorians considered "manly self-control" as a very important attribute of the civilized man (Cominos, 1963, pp. 31-33; Mosse, 1985, pp. 13-33). Sir R. C. Mitter, the only Bengali member in the Viceroy's Legislative Council, was virulently attacked in the Anglo-Indian press for his criticism of the "puritanical" attitude of the reformers. Mitter advocated a lenient treatment of young boys, especially of lower castes, who often lived alone with their child wives in one-room hovels. He was more sympathetic toward young husbands who were subject to a "temptation of the most trying description." The *Pioneer*, the voice of the Anglo-Indian community, condemned Mitter's views as the "selfish gratification of voluptuous men." In a scathing editorial the paper declared that "male persons are bound to exercise self restraint in this matter" and that all "truly civilized" men could not condone the sexual precocity excused by Mitter and his friends.

The sexually indulgent attitude of the Bengali male was condemned as unmanly or effeminate. The Anglo-Indians held that premature consummation occurred only among effeminate people. The martial races of the Punjab and the Northwest, who were reputed to be more "manly," did not consummate their marriages at an early age. Ethnologist H. H. Risley of the Bengal Civil Service contrasted the nonmartial Bengalis with the martial races of the North:

> As we leave the great recruiting ground of the Indian Army and travel south eastward along the plains of the Ganges, the healthy sense which bid the warrior races keep their girls at home until they are fit to bear the burden of maternity, seems to have been cast out by the demon of corrupt ceremonialism ever ready to sacrifice helpless women and children to the traditions of fancied orthodoxy.

The argument was circular: Not only were effeminate men more likely to indulge in premature consummation, but premature consummation was also the cause of the moral and physical effeminacy of men.

Early sexual experience was believed to corrupt the moral fiber of men. It was alleged that men's appetites were aroused by sexual knowledge and they easily succumbed to the debilitating sexual practice of masturbation. A. O. Hume, a retired British civil servant, wrote to the viceroy that the practice of masturbation among males was "universal in Lower Bengal" and that masturbation was "one of the reflex consequences of the premature sexuality engendered by the early marriage and consummation system." Premature sexuality was also held responsible for "sapping the vigor of the race" because it often resulted in premature maternity and the birth of "weak and sickly" offspring. The *Indian Medical Gazette* set the tone:

> As regards race, there can be equally little doubt that the marriage of children often with aged males tends to the physical deterioration of the human stock, and *physical deterioration implies effeminacy, mental imperfection and moral debility.* (emphasis added)

The proponents of the ideal of manliness believed that the perfectly "manly physique" reflected a "robust" and manly character (Haley, 1978, pp. 4-5). Charles Kingsley, a famous proponent of "muscular Christianity" in mid-nineteenth century England, summed up the visual stereotype of manliness: "God made Man in His Image and not in an imaginary Virgin Mary's image" (quoted in Newsome, 1967, p. 210).

The "puny" and diminutive physique of the Bengali male was a

constant source of mirth and derision. In fact, by the second half of the
century the self-perception of physical effeteness had become fairly
universal among the Bengali middle class (Rosselli, 1980, p. 121).
Although the Bengalis accepted the charge of physical weakness, they
resented attempts to apply the "laws of cattle breeding" to human
beings. An anti-Consent Act paper, the *Hope,* rejected the physiological
arguments, and reasoned that man was "more a spiritual and moral
being than an animal for purposes of exhibition." The British Indian
Association was even more skeptical:

> Accept the argument and the case will stand thus. . . . Europeans as a rule
> are of better physique and therefore heads of departments should always
> select them in preference to natives. Tall robust men are better in physique
> than thin lanky diminutive people, therefore tall men should be preferred
> to short men.

It is at first a little curious that an act ostensibly passed for the
protection of child brides devoted so much attention to the alleged
effeminacy of the Bengali male. Throughout the deliberations of the
Consent Act the British were not interested in the condition of women
per se, but with its implications on the evaluation of the Indian male.
The British called into question the "manliness" of the Bengali male.
Their overriding concern was to show the Bengali male's inadequacy by
the standards of the *fin de siecle* ideal of moral and physical manliness.

The Bengali male was constantly derided for not being adequately
"manly" and for displaying allegedly "feminine" characteristics. The
gender ideology of manliness rested on a devaluation of femininity,
especially femininity in men. The emphasis on female sexual asceticism
that arose as a corollary to the desire for male sexual continence
displayed an underlying belief that women, unlike men, were incapable
of exercising rational control over their appetites. The Englishmen's
much vaunted regard for women did not include a regard for femininity
because women were seen as helpless creatures dependent on the
protection of benevolent men. Hence the British in India could be the
proud protectors of Hindu females at the same time they derided the
femininity of Bengali males.

The contempt for Bengali manliness was implicit in the general
attitude of the Anglo-Indians toward members of the educated middle
class (Baxter, 1978, p. 193). It was reflected in their disdain of the
Bengali claims to political recognition in the administration of the
country. During the Consent Act controversy, the *Englishman,* the
notoriously anti-Bengali newspaper of Calcutta, observed that the

"chief opposition to the proposed reform came from the educated class in Bengal." It evinced "justifiable scorn of the Native leaders whom English education had failed to reclaim from semibarbarity." The hostility against the class of politically self-conscious Bengalis was mediated through the gender identities of masculinity and effeminacy. The *Pioneer* wrote that the "agitation which has been set on foot will not command the sympathy of the more manly races."

The British animus against Bengali effeminacy in this period recalled the ambiguous response to homosexuality in Victorian and Edwardian society. Homosexual behavior had always been contemptuously associated with effeminacy, but certain developments in the nineteenth century had given rise to a greater ambiguity regarding effeminacy and homosexuality. Jeffrey Weeks has argued (1977, p. 5; 1981, chap. 6) that the second half of the nineteenth century in Europe witnessed the development of a separate and distinct homosexual personality. In the past, certain sexual acts were stigmatized as homosexual but there was no fixed homosexual personality with distinct homosexual attributes. The line between the homosexual and the heterosexual was not so rigidly drawn prior to the emergence in Victorian society of rigid gender distinctions of masculinity and femininity. In fact, homosexual activity did not always entail a removal from heterosexual society. This was evident in examples from the English public schools, where early homosexual encounters did not preclude adult heterosexuality (Gathorne-Hardy, 1977, pp. 259-263). By the turn of the century, however, homosexuality increasingly was being defined as a pathological state quite distinct from normal adult behavior.

Even so, the worshipers at the altar of manliness could not be entirely unambiguous in their response to homosexuality. This can be understood if we look upon all forms of interaction between men as part of a single continuum, with male homosexuality at one end (see Sedgwick, 1985). The cult of manliness in the late nineteenth century promoted a male homosocial world of male bonding and male camaraderie, often in single-sex institutional settings. But the new homosexual personality created a radical discontinuity in the male homosocial-homosexual continuum. The rupture in the different forms of male interaction, between the strong emotional bonds of the male homosocial world and the strong emotional-sexual bonds of the male homosexual world, resulted in the aggressive assertion of hypermasculinity and the violent negation of effeminacy. J. A. Symonds gave the standard nineteenth-century description of the homosexual: "lusts written on his face . . . pale, languid, scented, *effeminate*, oblique in expression" (Weeks, 1981, p. 111; emphasis added).

The nonmanly stereotype used for the homosexual was often extended to include other groups. The virulence against the homosexual and the effeminate Bengali, therefore, had a common origin in the Victorian ideal of manliness. The stereotype of effeminacy made it possible to subsume the Bengali in the categories of "manliness" and "effeminacy" that had developed as a result of the gender relations of nineteenth-century Britain. Bengalis could not be judged by a set of standards that were used to judge the homosexual. The appropriation of the Bengali in Victorian gender ideology was important for colonial justification.

The power of colonial justification and the authority of colonial discourse did not rest simply on colonial power relations. Edward Said (1978), in his analysis of the discourse of "Orientalism," emphasizes the concentration of political power in the hands of the European creators of colonial discourse. Homi Bhabha (1983, pp. 23-25), however, perceives an indeterminacy or ambivalence that was central to the authority of colonial discourse, which did not arise simply from the possession of political power. However, to understand the role of such discourse in the process of colonial justification it is necessary to relate its ideological function to practices that ensured the perpetuation of imperial power relations.

The process of colonial justification was not a simple one. It entailed a dual approach: On the one hand it emphasized the radical difference of the native society, which made necessary the alien control pattern of domination, and on the other, it posited a universality that opened up the possibility for the recuperation or redemption of the native. The latter was important to make sense of the colonial project as a "civilizing mission." The redemption of the native, however, could never be complete because of the need to justify continued foreign domination. The tension created between the possibility of redeeming the native and his irredeemable difference allowed for the complexity of colonial ideology.

For various political and tactical reasons, the British, in the early years of colonial rule, encouraged the possibility of redeeming the natives of India by promoting Western education and Western values. When westernized Indians began to prove an embarrassment to the still exclusive rule of the foreigners, the task of the redemption of the native was declared to be an impossible one (Gray, 1975: 104-118). The *Pioneer* posed the favorite imperialist question:

If Western education cannot bring the Bengali race into line with civilization, what force can possibly accomplish the desirable end?

The possibility of "educating" the native had to be kept open at the same time the "educated native" was condemned. The depiction of the westernized Bengali male as a "mimicry" of the white male was central to this process.

Since the stereotype of effeminacy drew its force from Victorian gender ideology, it was able to capture the element of mimicry in colonial justification (Bhabha, 1984, p. 126). The dichotomy of manliness and effeminacy did not refer simply to the discrimination between mother culture and alien culture, but rather to the mother culture and its bastards, the self and its doubles (Bhabha, 1985, pp. 153-154). Effeminacy was not the complete opposite but the bastardized or incomplete form of manliness. The effectiveness of the effeminate stereotype for the purpose of colonial justification, therefore, did not lie in a "duality of difference" but in a "perversion of similarity," a process that Bhabha (1985, pp. 154-155) calls "hybridization" or the "splitting of the Self."

In this chapter I have tried to show the importance of the gender identity of "effeminacy" for the ideology of moral imperialism in nineteenth-century Bengal. Most scholars who have examined the ideology of imperialism have emphasized the role of the degradation of Hindu females in the defense of the *Raj*. I have tried to demonstrate that the commitment to the Victorian ideal of manliness, and the belief in Bengali "unmanliness" were vital features for the rationalization of colonial rule. I have also pointed to the force of the effeminate stereotype in colonial justification by suggesting that the animus against Bengali effeminacy reflected the fear of homosexuality that was inherent in the Victorian ideal of manliness.

REFERENCES

Ballhatchet, K. (1980). *Race, sex and class under the Raj 1793-1905*. London: Weidenfield & Nicolson.

Basham, A. (1964). *The wonder that was India*. London: Sidgwick & Jackson.

Baxter, C. (1978). The genesis of the babu: Bhabanicharan Bannerji and Kalikatata Kamalalay. In P. Robb & D. Taylor (Eds.), *Rule, protest, identity: Aspects of modern South Asia* (pp. 193-206). London: Curzon.

Bhabha, H. (1983). The other question . . . *Screen, 24*(6), 18-36.

Bhabha, H. (1984). Of mimicry and man: The ambivalence of colonial discourse, *October, 28*, 125-133.

Bhabha, H. (1985). Signs taken for wonders: Questions of ambivalence and authority under a tree outside Delhi, May 1817. *Critical Inquiry, 12*(1), 144-165.

Borthwick, M. (1984). *The changing role of women in Bengal 1849-1905*. Princeton, NJ: Princeton University Press.

Carroll, L. (1983). Law, custom and statutory social reform: The Hindu Widows Remarriage Act of 1856. *Indian Economic & Social History Review, 20*(4), 363-388.

Cominos, P. (1963). Late Victorian sexual respectability and the social system, parts I & II. *International Review of Social History, 111* 18-48, 216-250.

Copley, A. (1981). Some reflections by a historian on attitudes towards women in traditional Indian society. *South Asia Research.*

Copley, A. (1983). Projection, displacement and distortion in 19th century moral imperialism: A re-examination of Charles Grant and James Mill. *Calcutta Historical Journal,* 1-27.

Cott, N. (1978). Passionlessness: An interpretation of Victorian sexual ideology 1790-1850. *Signs, 4*(2), 219-236.

Engels, D. (1983). The Age of Consent Act of 1891: Colonial ideology in Bengal. *South Asia Research, 3*(2), 107-132.

Field, J. H. (1982). *Towards a programme of imperial life: The British empire at the turn of the century.* Westport, CT: Greenwood.

Gathorne-Hardy, J. (1977). *The old school tie: The phenomenon of the English public school.* New York: Viking.

Gorham, D. (1978). The "Maiden tribute of modern Babylon" reexamined: Child prostitution and the idea of childhood in late Victorian England. *Victorian Studies, 21*(3), 353-379.

Gray, J. N. (1975). Bengal and Britain: Culture contact and the reinterpretation of Hinduism in the 19th century. In R. V. Baumer (Ed.), *Aspects of Bengali history and society* (pp. 99-131). Honolulu: Hawaii University Press.

Haley, B. (1978). 2The healthy body and Victorian culture. Cambridge, MA: Harvard University Press.

Liddle, J., & Joshi, R. (1985). Gender and imperialism in British India. *South Asia Research, 5*(2), 147-165.

Mosse, G. L. (1985). *Nationalism and sexuality: Respectability and abnormal sexuality in modern Europe.* New York: H. Fertig.

Nandy, A. (1982). The psychology of colonialism: Sex, age and ideology in British India. *Psychiatry: Journal for the Study of Interpersonal Processes, 45*(3), 197-219.

Newsome, D. (1967). *Godliness and goodlearning.* London: Murray.

Ray, R. K. (1984). *Social conflict and political unrest in Bengal 1875-1927.* New Delhi: Oxford University Press.

Rosselli, J. (1980). The self image of effeteness: Physical education and nationalism in 19th century Bengal. *Past & Present, 86,* 121-148.

Said, E. (1978). *Orientalism.* New York: Pantheon.

Sedgwick, E. K. (1985). *Between men: English literature and male homosocial desire.* New York: Columbia University Press.

Sinha, M. (1986). *The Age of Consent Act: The ideal of masculinity and colonial ideology in 19th century Bengal.* Paper presented at the Twentieth Annual Bengal Studies Conference, Lake Geneva, WI.

Walkowitz, J. R. (1982). Male vice and feminist virtue: Feminism and the politics of prostitution in 19th century British history. *History Workshop Journal, 13,* 77-93.

Weeks, J. (1977). *Coming out: Homosexual politics in Britain from 19th century to the present.* London: Quartet.

Weeks, J. (1981). *Sex, politics and society: The regulation of sexuality since 1800.* New York: Longman.

15

Predicting Interpersonal Conflict Between Men and Women

The Case of Black Men

LAWRENCE E. GARY

This chapter will explore how demographic and sociocultural factors predict interpersonal conflict between black men and women. To what extent do black men experience conflict with their spouses or mates? What demographic and sociocultural factors are the best predictors of conflict between the sexes in the black community? Is there a relationship between interpersonal conflict between the sexes and mental health outcomes?

In recent years writers have pointed to the precarious socioeconomic status of American black men and the consequences for their well-being. Racism continues to restrict systematically the opportunities and life chances of blacks in this society. An examination of social indicators such as income, education, employment, unemployment, and health demonstrates the high-risk status of black men (Gary, 1981; Gary & Leashore, 1982). For example, black men have higher rates of morbidity, mortality, incarceration, and criminal victimization than have white men and women and black women. In comparison to white men, black men experience greater underemployment, unemployment, and lower earning potential. These circumstances have important implications for the quality of relationships between black men and women.

AUTHOR'S NOTE: Ola M. Bell and Gayle D. Weaver assisted in the preparation of this chapter. In addition, the National Institute of Mental Health provided financial support for this research (Grant MH25551-04).

Relations Between Black Men and Women

Secondary data sources indicate that there are some serious problems in black male-female relationships. For example, census data for 1980 show that 40.3% of black family units are headed by women, compared to 11.6% for whites (U.S. Bureau of the Census, 1981b). Only 42.2% of black children under 18 years of age live with both parents, compared to 82.9% for whites. In other words, the majority (56.8%) of black children do not live in family units where both of their parents are present. Census data also suggest that an increasing number of blacks 18 years and older are not marrying, and those who do marry are dissolving their marriages through divorce or separation. For example, in 1970, 64.1% of black persons 18 years and older were married; but in 1980, only 51.9% were married. In 1980, 29.8% of black persons 18 years and older were single, compared to 20.6% in 1970 (U.S. Bureau of the Census, 1981a). In 1980, the majority of black males 15 years and older were not married (58%)—not the case for white males, of whom 37% were unmarried (U.S. Bureau of the Census, 1981a).

There is also a higher probability that blacks will get divorced. The divorce ratio (per 1,000 married persons with spouse present) in the black community was 203 in 1980, compared to 92 for whites. In 1970, the divorce ratio for black people was 83; it was 62 in 1960 (U.S. Bureau of the Census, 1981a). When one looks at the adult female population specifically, the difference is even more striking; a divorce ratio for black females in 1980 of 257, compared to 110 white females (U.S. Bureau of the Census, 1981a).

Furthermore, unwanted pregnancies, abortion, and family violence are also disproportionately high among black families. More than half (55%) of all black babies in the United States today are born out of wedlock, most to teenagers ("Births to the Unwed," 1981; Reid, 1982; U.S. Bureau of the Census, 1981a). In 1976, 25.8% of all births to black mothers between the ages of 15 and 44 years were from unwanted pregnancies, compared to 9.5% for white mothers (U.S. Bureau of the Census, 1981b). Moreover, the abortion rate (per 1,000 women) was 22.7 for white women in 1978 and 60.4 for nonwhite women. A black woman is twice as likely to have an abortion as a white woman (U.S. Bureau of the Census, 1981b).

Homicidal violence is also a major problem confronting black communities. Most homicides in the black community are committed by other blacks. (Note that 51% of the murders committed in 1980 were perpetrated by relatives or persons acquainted with the victims: 16% were within family relationships, one-half of which involved spouse killing spouse; U.S. Department of Justice, 1981.) Black women are about eight times as likely as white women to kill their mates. Violent crimes such as forcible rape, robbery, and aggravated assault make it difficult to establish and maintain functional and meaningful interpersonal relationships between the sexes. Moreover, alcoholism, drug addiction, and depression among blacks may contribute to problems in personal and family relationships.

Several writers have identified a range of factors that influence interpersonal relationships between men and women (Anderson, 1978; Braithwaite, 1981; Franklin, 1980; Hammond & Enoch, 1976; Jackson, 1978; Noble, 1978; Rodgers-Rose, 1980; Staples, 1981; Stewart, 1980; Turner & Turner, 1974; Wallace, 1979), including (1) white racism, (2) scarcity of black men, (3) black male chauvinism, (4) black female emasculation of black males, (5) black male-white female intimacy, (6) class and cultural differences, (7) the women's movement, and (8) different friendships and recreational networks. Yet there continues to be a lack of systematic information concerning this problem from the perspective of black men. A review of the literature on black male-female relationships reveals the following deficiencies: (1) Most of the research is based on what black women say about their relationships with men; (2) there is a tendency to rely too heavily on college students; (3) relatively small and unrepresentative samples of the black male population are used; (4) there is a tendency to rely on secondary data sources and institutionalized subjects; (5) researchers have used rather simple analytical (statistical) techniques; (6) a limited range of variables has been explored; and (7) little attention has been paid to the mental health consequences of interpersonal conflict between the sexes. This chapter will attempt to solve some of these problems and to expand our knowledge of factors that predict conflict.

Methods

Data for this study were collected from noninstitutionalized male subjects who lived in a large northeastern city in the United States. In view of the general problem of securing "noncaptive" black males for research purposes, the following sample procedures were used: (1) a list of computer-generated random telephone numbers, which yielded 24% of the respondents; (2) posted announcements in barbershops that had a largely adult black male clientele (13%); and (3) referral by community groups and other respondents (63%). The major concern was to obtain a heterogeneous sample of black adults that potentially would reflect a variety of life-styles.

Out of a pool of 150 respondents recruited for the study, a total of 142 agreed to participate. These subjects ranged in age from 18 to 65 years, with a median age of 33 years. Of the respondents, 33% were married, 21% were formerly married, and 46% were never married. Half of the sample had received more than 12 years of education, while one-fourth each had received either 12 years or fewer than 12 years of education. Of the respondents, 38% had annual family incomes below $10,000; 44% had incomes between $10,000 and $24,999; and 18% had family incomes of $25,000 and above. This distribution of incomes and educational levels, age, and marital status suggests that these men reflect the diversity of the black male population in this northeastern city.

Personal interviews were conducted using facilities located at Howard University. The interview schedule consisted of open-ended and forced-choice questions on a wide range of topics. The dependent variable, conflict between the sexes, was defined as the number of disagreements with mates during the past few weeks. These items were developed by the Mental Health Research and Development Center at the Institute for Urban Affairs and Research (Gary, Leashore, Howard, & Buckner-Dowell, 1983). The items used to obtain data on this measure were extracted from 13 questions addressing issues the respondents sometimes agreed or disagreed about with their spouses or partners. This set of questions was asked only of those respondents who were married or who indicated having partners. The specific wording on the interview was, "I am going to read you some things about which men and their mates (wives, women) sometimes agree and disagree. Would you tell me which ones were problems between you and your (wife) (Ms. _____) during the past few weeks?" A conflict index was developed from these items with 0 as the lowest possible score and 13 as the highest possible score. The mean score for the respondents on the conflict between the sexes index was 3.22. The item-to-index correlation coefficients for this measure ranged from 0.19 to 0.64 and were all significant ($p < .05$). The alpha reliability coefficient for this index was 0.60.

A number of independent variables were examined in this study. Age, marital status, educational status, family income, household size, and residential mobility provided a demographic profile. Sociocultural variables included family type, number of friends, racial ideology, religious involvement, community involvement, mate communication, and neighboring.

The final variable was depressive symptoms. The Center for Epidemiological Studies Depression Scale (CES-D) has developed 20 items to

TABLE 15.1

Frequency Distribution of Disagreements with Spouse or Mate

		Yes		No	
Problem		F	%	F	%
1.	Irritating personal habits	46	41	65	59
2.	How to spend leisure time	42	38	68	62
3.	Time spent with friends	41	37	71	63
4.	Your being away from home too much	39	40	58	60
5.	Your job	34	32	72	68
6.	Keep the house neat	27	28	70	72
7.	Not showing love	21	19	90	81
8.	Household expenses	21	22	76	78
9.	In-laws/her family	18	19	78	81
10.	Religion	14	12	98	88
11.	Disciplining children	13	14	82	86
12.	Time spent with her friends	11	10	101	90
13.	Her being away from home too much	8	8	91	92

monitor depressive symptomatology during the past week (Radloff, 1977). With a score range from 0 to 60, a high score on the CES-D scale means a high level of depressive symptoms. The alpha coefficient for the CES-D scale with this sample was 0.82. This measure was used to answer the question regarding the mental health aspects of conflict between the sexes.

The analytic strategy for this study involved examining the relationship between mean scores on the conflict between the sexes index and the independent variables. Analysis of variance was used to examine these relationships. Where appropriate, Pearson correlation was also used to examine these relationships. Using the *Statistical Package for Social Sciences* (SPSS), a stepwise regression was compared with dummy coding (0, 1) for marital status (not married, married), and family type (nuclear, extended; see Nie, Hull, Jenkins, Steinbrenner, & Bent, 1975).

Results

The Extent of Conflict
Between the Sexes

As shown in Table 15.1, these subjects did have some conflict with women, but it was not extensive. The data showed that 14 respondents scored 0, indicating no conflict with their spouses or partners. No subjects scored 13, although one subject scored 11 and one scored 9. Irritating personal habits, leisure time with friends, and being away from home and job were the major areas of conflict between black men and women. Disciplining the children, religion, and female friendships were not viewed by these men as major problem areas.

Predicting Conflict

Bivariate analysis showed no demographic variables significantly related to the conflict between the sexes index, although some trends were noticeable. For example, male subjects under 30 years of age tended to have more conflict than had those who were older. Married men experienced more conflict than did formerly married and never-married men who were involved in relationships. The mean conflict score for the married respondents was 4.24 compared to 2.16 for the formerly married and 3.13 for the never married. As the educational level increased, there was a tendency for the respondents to have less conflict with women. Men who had a family income of less than $8,000 a year had the lowest mean conflict score among the various income categories. In other words, low-income black men reported less conflict in their relationships than did high-income men. Residential mobility and household size also had some impact on conflict between the sexes. Those men who moved four or more times in the past five years had the highest mean conflict score among any of the demographic variables. Men who lived alone ($\overline{X}$ = 2.17) had less conflict with women than had those who lived with one person ($\overline{X}$ = 3.62) or with two or more persons ($\overline{X}$ = 3.56).

Only one of the seven sociocultural variables—mate communication—had a significant impact on conflict between the sexes. The data showed that mate communication was significantly related to the conflict index (F[2, 65] = 3.45, p < .05). Men who had positive communication with their spouses or mates tended to have less conflict with women than had men who had negative communication with their female friends.

Multiple regression was used to examine the independent effects of various demographic and sociocultural variables on conflict between the sexes scores. A three-stage analytic strategy was used to examine the predictors of interpersonal conflict. The first two strategies involved determining the best demographic and sociocultural predictors and entering those variables into a third regression model. The third strategy tested the bivariate relationship between interpersonal conflict and depressive symptoms. Among the demographic variables, age and marital status explained the highest proportion of the variance (12%) in the conflict between the sexes, as shown in Table 15.2. Demographic variables accounted for 15.6% of the explained variance ($F[5, 76] = 2.81$, $p < .05$). Age was the best predictor of conflict between men and women, accounting for 6.6% of the total variance. Marital status increased the explanation to about 12%. As indicated in Table 15.3, the sociocultural variables accounted for 18.2% of the variance in the dependent measure, but the equation was not significant. On the other hand, the betas indicate that community involvement and mate communication significantly contributed to predicting conflict between the sexes. As a final analysis, the measures from each group of independent variables were included in a regression model. As shown in Table 15.4, when all six variables were counted, 33% of the variance was explained with an F-ratio of 4.60 ($p < .01$). Of the six variables, age (11%) and household size (8.3%) explained the largest proportion of the variance. Although the other variables—mate communication, neighboring, and community involvement—were significant predictors, together they accounted for only 13.2% of the variance. The data suggest that black men who are younger (under age 30), live in somewhat large households (three or more persons), have negative mate communication style, and have little involvement with neighbors or community activities tended to experience more conflict with black women than did those men who did not possess these characteristics.

Conflict and Depressive Symptoms

A major research question for this chapter is whether there was a relationship between conflict with mates and depressive symptoms. The mean score of the CES-D score (depressive symptoms) was 12.15 and the standard deviation was 8.44 for the sample. Researchers generally have used a score of 16 and above to indicate the presence of serious depressive symptoms (Roberts, 1980; Weissman, Sholmskas, Pattenger, Porusoff, & Locke, 1977). Since 31% of the respondents had CES-D scores of 16 or more, about one-third of the black men in this study were suffering from depression. The data show that there was a significant relationship between scores on the CES-D scale and scores on the conflict index ($F[2, 75] = 8.07$, $p < .001$). The mean depression score for the black men who experienced low levels of conflict with mates was 6.72, compared to 14.21 and 12.23 for those in medium and high conflict categories. These data suggest that there is an important relationship between mental health and the quality of male-female relationships.

TABLE 15.2

Multiple Regression of Conflict Scores and
Selected Demographic Variables

Variables	Multiple R	R² Change	Simple R	Beta
Age	.256	.066	−.257	−.333*
Marital status	.349	.056	−.165	−.177
Household size	.375	.019	.216	.144
Educational status	.391	.012	−.067	−.127
Family income	.395	.003	.028	.063
Total R²		.156		

*Significant at the .01 level. $F_{(5, 76)} = 2.81$, $p < .05$.

TABLE 15.3

Multiple Regression of Conflict Scores and
Selected Sociocultural Variables

Variables	Multiple R	R² Change	Simple R	Beta
Community involvement	.234	.055	−.235	−.242*
Mate communication	.308	.040	−.204	−.282*
Neighboring	.346	.025	.048	.236
Racial ideology	.394	.036	−.179	−.261
Family type	.406	.009	−.031	−.127
Religious involvement	.413	.006	.004	−.125
Friends	.426	.011	.051	.114
Total R²		.182		

*Significant at the .05 level. $F_{(7, 37)} = 1.17$, not significant.

Discussion and Implications

The results of this investigation show that most of the black men in this sample did not perceive themselves as having a high level of conflict with black women. But some men did experience considerable conflict with their mates. Irritating personal habits, how to spend leisure time, being away from home too much, time spent with friends, and work were the major areas of conflict. These results are somewhat inconsistent with most of those reported in the literature. For example, Scanzoni (1970) found that 38% of his sample said that money-related matters were the major areas of contention in their marriages (see also Blood & Wolfe, 1960; Strong & DeVault, 1983). This was not the case here.

Both Blood and Wolfe and Scanzoni also found that disagreement over children constituted another area of conflict between men and women. This investigation did not find a large number of men indicating that child-related matters were problems for them. In fact, only 14% of

TABLE 15.4

Multiple Regression of Conflict Scores and

Selected Demographic and Sociocultural Variables

Variables	Multiple R	R^2 Change	Simple R	Beta
Age	.333	.111	−.333	−.296*
Household size	.442	.084	.267	.296*
Mate communication	.495	.050	−.275	−.253*
Neighboring	.538	.044	.140	.230
Community involvement	.573	.039	.223	−.195
Residential mobility	.574	.0021	.137	.051
Total R^2		.330		

*Significant at the .05 level. $F (6, 56) = .4.60, p < .01.$

the men who had children reported that disciplining children created a problem with their mates. Among areas of disagreement, these black men indicated that irritating personal habits (punctuality, cleanliness, preferences, etc.) were the most frequent source of conflict. This is in direct contrast to what Scanzoni (1970) found in his research: Only slightly more than 20% of his respondents cited such issues as a major area of conflict. The black men in this study tended to have a number of problems with their mates in the general areas of companionship, leisure time, and recreation. In fact, over 37% of the respondents indicated that these were areas of disagreement with their mates. By comparison, Blood and Wolfe (1960) found that 16% of their subjects had experienced conflict in these areas.

In the black community, social life has not been couple centered, but sex segregated. Hundreds spend more time with work colleagues, male friends in bars, or sporting activities, whereas wives or girlfriends interact with relatives, children, and female friends (Anderson, 1978; Gary, 1981; Liebow, 1967). Mate companionship is still considered a major goal toward which every couple is expected to aim. According to Scanzoni and Scanzoni (1981, p. 402), "husbands and wives are expected to accompany each other to most social occasions, to devote their leisure time to mutual activities and to enjoy simply being together as best friends." For the black men in this study, the companionship idea of a couple was not operative and this was a major source of disagreement between them and their mates. Scanzoni (1970) discovered that when compared with whites, blacks were less likely to be satisfied with the companionship received in marriage.

Demographic variables were not significant predictors of male-female conflict. Of the seven sociocultural variables, only one—mate communication—was significantly related to the conflict index. This chapter demonstrates the utility of using multiple regression to explain differences among black men in the conflict between sexes scores. Based on the grand multiple regression model (Table 15.3), the best predictors of conflict between the sexes were age, household size, mate communication style, neighboring, and community involvement.

Among those black men who experienced considerable conflict with their mates, there was a tendency for them to report a high level of depressive symptoms. Some antisocial or deviant behavior, such as excessive drinking, drug abuse, suicide attempts, and violence, which are prevalent in the black community, may be a manifestation of the level of interpersonal conflict with women that many black men are experiencing in their daily lives (Gary & Leashore, 1982; Staples, 1978; Stewart & Scott, 1978). There is some evidence that some black men are beginning to bring their interpersonal and family problems to the attention of mental health practitioners. For example, Jones and his colleagues (1982) found that the major presenting problems of black men included depression, work difficulties, problems relating to others, family difficulties, anxiety, and marital conflict, in that order. The data in this study seem to support their findings: that conflict between the sexes and depression were related significantly. According to Jones et al. (1982), the black male patients in psychotherapy typically were married.

To develop programs and policies for improving relationships between the sexes in the black community, conceptual clarity is needed to define the problem and its causes. As Franklin (1980, p. 47) stated,

> The familiar rationale offered for Black male-female (conflict), white racism, is deemed logically inadequate. . . . To be sure, not all Black males and females experience undue difficulty in social interaction. . . . It is suggested that the conflict stems from the diverse manner in which some Black males and females define situations, interpret each other's behaviors, and direct action toward each other.

One needs to recognize the diversity within the black community and to examine a range of factors that influence interpersonal relationships. Black community groups, voluntary associations, and churches need to develop projects to improve male-female relationships. Programs designed to build better interpersonal communication between black men and women will have an important impact on improving the mental health of the black community, and particularly of black men.

REFERENCES

Anderson, E. (1978). *A place on the corner.* Chicago: University of Chicago Press.
Births to the unwed found to have risen by 50% in 10 years. (1981). *New York Times.*

Blood, R. O., & Wolfe, D. M. (1960). *Husbands and wives.* New York: Free Press.

Braithwaite, R. (1981). Interpersonal relationships between black males and females. In L. Gary (Ed.), *Black men* (pp. 83-87). Newbury Park, CA: Sage.

Franklin, C. (1980). White racism as the cause of black male-female conflict: A critique. *Western Journal of Black Studies, 4,* 42-49.

Gary, L. (Ed.). (1981). *Black men.* Newbury Park, CA: Sage.

Gary, L., & Leashore, B. (1982). The high risk status of black men. *Social Work, 27,* 54-58.

Gary, L., Leashore, B., Howard, C., & Buckner-Dowell, R. (1983). Help-seeking behavior among black males. Washington, DC: Howard University, Mental Health Research and Development Center, Institute for Urban Affairs and Research.

Hammond, J., & Enoch, J. (1976). Conjugal power relations among Black working- class families. *Journal of Black Studies, 1,* 107-128.

Jackson, J. (1978). But where are the men? In R. Staples (Ed.), *The black family: Essays and studies.* Belmont, CA: Wadsworth.

Jackson, L. (1975). The attitudes of black females toward upper and lower class black males. *Journal of Black Psychology, 1,* 53-64.

Jones, B., Gray, B., & Jospitre, J. (1982). Survey of psychotherapy with black men. *American Journal of Black Psychiatry, 139,* 1174-1177.

Liebow, E. (1967). *Tally's corner.* Boston: Little, Brown.

Nie, N. H., Hull, C. H., Jenkins, J. G., Steinbrenner, K., & Bent, D. H. (1975). *Statistical package for the social sciences* (2nd ed.).

Noble, J. (1978). *Beautiful, also, are the souls of my black sisters: A history of black women in America.* Englewood Cliffs, NJ: Prentice-Hall.

Radloff, L. (1977). The CES-D scale. *Applied Psychological Measurements, 1*(3), 385-401.

Reid, J. (1982). Black America in the 1980's. *Population Bulletin, 37,* 11-13.

Roberts, R. (1980). Reliability of CES-D scale in different ethnic contexts. *Psychiatric Research, 2,* 125-134.

Rodgers-Rose, L. (1980). Dialectics of black male-female relationships. In L. Rodgers-Rose (Ed.), *The black woman* (pp. 251-263). Newbury Park, CA: Sage.

Scanzoni, J. (1970). *Opportunity and the family.* New York: Free Press.

Scanzoni, L. D., & Scanzoni, J. (1981). *Men, women and change* (2nd ed.). New York: McGraw-Hill.

Staples, R. (1978). Masculinity and race: The dual dilemma of black men. *Journal of Social Issues, 34*(1), 169-83.

Staples, R. (1981). Black manhood in the 1970's: A critical look back. *Black Scholar, 12*(3), 2-9.

Stewart, J. (1980). Relationships between black males and females in rhythm and blues music of the 1960's and 1970's. *Western Journal of Black Studies, 4,* 186-196.

Stewart, J., & Scott, J. (1978). The institutional decimation of black American males. *Western Journal of Black Studies, 2,* 82-92.

Strong, B., & DeVault, C. (1983). *The marriage and family experience* (2nd ed.). St. Paul, MN: West.

Turner, B., & Turner, C. (1974). Evaluations of women and men among black and white college students. *Sociological Quarterly, 15,* 442-456.

U.S. Bureau of the Census. (1981a). *Marital status and living arrangements, March 1980* (pp. 3, 8-9, 38). (Current Population Reports, Series P-20, No. 365). Washington, DC: Government Printing Office.

U.S. Bureau of the Census. (1981b). *Statistical abstract, 1981.* Washington, DC: Government Printing Office.

U.S. Department of Justice. (1981). *Uniform crime reports for the United States* (pp. 8, 11). Washington, DC: Government Printing office.

Wallace, M. (1979). *Black macho and the myth of the superwoman.* New York: Dial.

Weisman, M., Sholmskas, D., Pattenger, M., Porusoff, B., & Locke, B. (1977). Assessing depressive symptoms in five psychiatric populations: A validity study. *American Journal of Epidemiology, 106,* 203-214.

16

Men's Work and Family Roles and Characteristics

Race, Gender, and Class Perceptions of College Students

NOEL A. CAZENAVE
GEORGE H. LEON

Work and family role scripts are key determinants of both personal identity and social structure. Nowhere is this more evident than in the changing gender roles that are currently challenging American society. It has been on these two major fronts that women have advanced their opposition to the "feminine mystique" (Freidan, 1963), and have established that a "woman's place" is everywhere. Of course, such changes do not occur within a gender-specific social vacuum. As Lopata (1965) has found, the views of significant others of the opposite gender are crucial. In addition, these changes profoundly affect not only a "man's place" but his perception of masculinity as well. Without fundamental and reciprocal changes in male work and family roles and identities, women's quest for liberation will never be fully realized.

Unfortunately, the existing literature on work and family roles is limited in both its focus and its scope. Most of these studies have concentrated on the role conflict experienced by American women as

AUTHORS' NOTE: An earlier version of this chapter, "Race, Class and Gender: An Analysis of Male Work and Family Roles," was presented at the meeting of the Eastern Sociological Society, March 15, 1985, in Philadelphia. We wish to express our appreciation to Joseph H. Pleck for his helpful comments and suggestions on an earlier draft.

they adjust to the stress and strain of the modern "working" woman's role overload. There has been little analysis of the relationship between the two role systems for American men generally, much less for males of various races or socioeconomic statuses.

Most of the existing literature on male gender roles has continued to treat the worlds of work and family as distinct and competing sources of masculine identity rather than as isomorphic influences. The emphasis is still on whether men function primarily in the work sphere *or* in the family sphere. Gender roles tend to be treated in evaluative and mutually exclusive dichotomies, for example, work versus family (Pleck, 1977), instrumental versus expressive, traditional versus modern, or the breadwinner versus more emotionally expressive roles, with little analysis of work- and family-related masculine identities within a broader socioeconomic context (Cazenave, 1979, 1984).

Research on blacks and gender roles is particularly instructive, not only in regard to the limitations of commonly accepted gender-role dichotomies generally, but also in regard to the specific limitations as they apply to racial minorities. In their review of black gender-role research, Hatchett and Quick (1983) note the inconsistencies in research findings, with some results indicating that blacks are more egalitarian in their gender-role attitudes than are whites, other research finding more traditional attitudes for blacks, and still other studies revealing that gender-role attitudes are much more complex for blacks than is true for whites. Hatchett and Quick's (1983) conclusion about the complexity of gender roles for blacks and the inapplicability of existing gender-descriptive dichotomies to blacks is supported by Romer and Cherry (1980), who found, in a study of 360 black, Italian, and Jewish children from middle- and working-class families, that black children described both male and female gender roles as similar in expressiveness. Contrary to the highly criticized instrumental-male, expressive-female, work-family-related dichotomy proposed by Parsons and Bales (1955), Romer and Cherry suggest that black men may be unable to develop instrumental (for example, economic) forms of competence and, subsequently, will rely on more expressive and interpersonal types of masculine pursuits.

Finally, both Romer and Cherry (1980) and Ransford and Miller (1983) suggest that social class and SES operate differently for black and white respondents. For white respondents, being middle class and of a high SES are associated with less sex typing and more liberal gender roles. For black respondents these factors are correlated with greater sex typing and conservatism on gender-role items than they are for either white middle-class respondents or black working-class respondents.

These studies suggest that the black middle class appears to have an exaggerated need to accept the traditional view of gender roles, with its emphasis on competence (Romer & Cherry, 1980) and respectability (Ransford & Miller, 1983). In the quest for upward mobility, middle-class blacks may embrace traditional gender-role prescriptions, which more established and secure middle-class whites feel secure in relinquishing.

Pleck's (1975) analysis of changes occurring in male gender roles uses the traditional-modern dichotomy in a less evaluative way, attempting to place these changes within a sociohistoric context. While men traditionally have achieved masculinity in physical ways, modern forms of masculine achievement are based primarily in the work world, which requires increasing interpersonal and intellectual skills and the ability to manipulate one's social, as opposed to physical, environment. While the traditional male is reluctant to show his emotions and avoids emotional intimacy, the modern male is encouraged to express intimacy in heterosexual relationships while maintaining more functional, noninti-mate relationships with other men. Pleck also observes that the traditional male gender role is most reflective of contemporary working-class American culture, while the modern gender role is more indicative of the middle class, but sees *both* as being emotionally stifling and pathological to men and their relationships with others. The task, therefore, is not to move from traditional to modern masculine roles, but to move beyond both.

Cazenave (1979) also challenged the use of popular masculine role dichotomies. The dichotomy of breadwinner versus expressive-father roles set in opposition two nonantagonistic roles for middle-income black fathers, but the ability to provide adequately for one's family actually made the more expressive masculine familial roles possible. A more recent study (Cazenave, 1984) found that popular dichotomies were inadequate in analyzing the complexities of the gender-role ideologies of a sample of middle-class black men. An examination of the ideal traits chosen by the respondents revealed that what was being measured is much broader than gender-role ideologies, and that their choice of masculine ideals indicates how these men view their world and the appropriate strategies for operating within it.

Much of the so-called traditionalism of middle-class black men appears to be a result of the high achievement motivation and instrumental values of upwardly mobile minority group members, rather than of a desire to maintain gender-based privilege. These men's tendencies to place greater emphasis on work-related ideal character-istics (such as being competitive and aggressive), which have generally been perceived as traditional or instrumental gender-role orientations, as well as more familial-related traits (such as being warm and being gentle), which most closely fit the modern or expressive conceptualization, and still others that fit no clear pattern (such as "fights to protect family" and "stands up for beliefs") reflect their ethnic background, the effect of racism, strategies for upward mobility, and overall relationships to the status quo and power hierarchy of the dominant society. It should not be assumed that when black men reach what is apparently middle-class status they will develop into carbon copies of white middle-class males. Even when they appear similar it may be for different reasons and may reflect a significantly different set of meanings and circumstances.

Most existing studies of race and gender-role attitudes have used very limited measures of gender-role attitudes or very restricted samples. In the present study we also hope to delineate the ways in which, for racial minorities, masculine role attitudes and ideals may be reflecting strategic ideologies for upward mobility, while for some members of the dominant race or gender groups, views of appropriate masculine roles may be a part of ideologies conducive to maintaining the status quo. In some instances the effects of race or gender will be distinct. In other cases, race and gender will be additive in their impact. In still other situations, these two variables will interact in determining the phenomenology of masculine gender roles for white males, black males, white females, and black females. We propose a *majority status maintenance perspective* to explain the gender views of those white males for whom masculine ideologies are associated with maintaining the status quo and the inherent privilege of their race and gender positions. Other white males may be so secure in their dominant race-gender status that they can afford to be magnanimous about nonthreatening gender-role changes. At the other extreme are black males who, while appearing to be somewhat privileged because they are members of the dominant gender group, are actually faced with the "double bind" of not only being denied status as a racial minority, but also being expected to achieve at a level consistent with the ideals of American masculinity (Cazenave, 1981; Staples, 1978). The internalizing of unrealistic societal expectations and the impact of racial discrimination makes "masculinity" more a burden than a blessing. Black men may experience both minority status on the basis of their race and status inconsistency because of their gender. For upwardly mobile black male college students there may be a great deal of emphasis on masculine status-related pursuits. But for them, in contrast with white males, masculine ideologies may indicate their desire for *minority status attainment*.

As gender minorities, both white females and black females should conceptualize appropriate masculine gender roles somewhat differently than should their male counterparts. While white females benefit from racial dominance, they are likely to see status attainment or maintenance-related masculine roles as a threat to their own aspirations for gender-related changes in family and work roles. Since gender oppression is their chief obstacle to status attainment, white females should be the race-gender group that advocates gender-role change generally and, more specifically, that deemphasizes status-related masculine pursuits. Finally, as black feminists have observed, black females are faced with the "double jeopardy"(Beale, 1970) of both race and gender oppression. As a gender minority they may, like white females, desire fundamental change in the gender order that restricts their lives, but as a members of an oppressed racial group, they may be more supportive of masculine status-related pursuits as a mechanism for the collective advancement of their race.

The following is an analysis of the effects of race, gender, and class on the conceptualization of appropriate work- and family-related masculine gender-role attitudes and ideal characteristics of a sample of college students. It illustrates both minority-status attainment and majority-status maintenance perspectives by examining (1) the salience of various masculine roles of married men and appropriate work and provider roles, (2) ideal characteristics of men, and (3) an analysis of family- and work-related masculine-role scales and their correlates.

As Franklin and Walum (1972) observed, individuals in a particular society are members not only of the larger social structure, but also of societal substructures based on race and gender. The existence of these substructures is not only significant in understanding objective social phenomena such as social stratification, but also must be taken into account to comprehend how these different race-gender groups subjectively interpret the world they live in. For this reason, each analysis will include a description of the major findings for each of the four race-gender groups.

While a sample of college students limits generalization, it is nevertheless appropriate to the present study for several reasons. First, college students are still in the process of formulating the gender, work, and family views that will be retained through the remainder of their adult lives. Second, most are seeking either to achieve upward mobility (status attainment) or to maintain the status achieved by their parents (status maintenance) through obtaining the credentials needed in order to pursue professional careers. Finally, as college graduates, many of these respondents will hold important public policy positions through which they can develop and implement work- and family-related guidelines. Their views may be indicative of future public policy in this area.

Method

The Instrument

The instrument was designed to explore university students' perceptions of masculine gender roles and ideal masculine characteristics. The questionnaire consisted of 39 attitudinal items concerning masculinity and race-, class-, and gender-related beliefs about social status, stratification, and public policy proposals.

Most of the attitudinal items consisted of statements about which respondents were asked to identify a level of agreement or disagreement on a five-point Likert scale. In order to obtain perceptions of ideal masculine characteristics, the respondents were asked to rate 11 different characteristics on a four-point scale of importance. In a few instances, forced-choice questions were used to elicit the respondents' rankings of certain masculine roles or social issues (see Cazenave 1983a, 1983b, 1984).

In addition to the attitudinal items, the questionnaire contained 25 items designed to measure the students' demographic, life-cycle, socioeconomic, and scholastic characteristics. These included detailed questions about present and former residence, religion, family income, parents' employment, and so forth. There were also several questions concerned with voter registration status, political party affiliation, social class identification, and self-reported political liberalism or conservatism. Taken together, the questionnaire items allowed an examination of beliefs about masculinity within the context of broader views about social structure and stratification as well as respondents' actual positions within the stratification system.

Procedure

In December 1982, the questionnaire was pilot-tested on 60 undergraduate students enrolled in sociology courses taught by the authors. The purpose of the pilot test was to identify and resolve ambiguities in the wording of the questions and other problems that may have arisen during the construction of the instrument. After minor revisions, the questionnaire was administered in January 1983 to more than 500 undergraduates enrolled in lower-level sociology courses at Temple

University. Students were read a prepared statement that explained the purpose of the survey, solicited their participation, and assured confidentiality.

The Sample

Temple University is located in north-central Philadelphia and the student body is made up mainly of local middle- and working-class students. It is diverse with respect to ethnicity, socioeconomic status, and demographic characteristics. The historic mission of the university has been to provide education opportunities to the mainstream of the regional population, and many local community, political, and business leaders are Temple graduates. The overwhelming majority of students have permanent local residences and most were also raised in the area. While a university sample is never representative of the larger community, our sample does provide a rough characterization of the local, college-educated resident of the Philadelphia region's immediate future.

The sample originally consisted of 565 students, but was reduced to the 532 students who identified their race as either black or white. The limitation was imposed because the number of other minorities was too small in our sample for meaningful analysis.[1] The final sample consisted of 194 white males, 179 white females, 53 black males, and 106 black females. Relative to the universitywide figures on race and gender, it overrepresented blacks by about 10% and females by about 7%. Our sample was not drawn randomly from the university population, but consisted of a saturation sampling of lower-level sociology courses. Since a course of that type is mandatory for virtually all university students, the sample is highly diverse with respect to the students' demographic and scholastic characteristics.

Data Analysis

Percentage responses of different race-gender groups are presented with chi-square analysis of statistical significance. Chi-square analysis results are also presented for those items where statistically significant differences exist by race for the two gender groups (that is, white males versus black males and white females versus black females). Factor analysis was used to create scales. Data are presented showing the correlation between these scales, and multiple regression analysis is used to predict the scales with sociodemographic variables.

Findings and Discussion

Masculine Roles: Salience and Attitudes

Race-Gender Group Differences

Table 16.1 shows that there are notable race-gender differences in the selection of the most important activity for a married man. While the husband is chosen as more important by the largest percentage of each group, there appears to be a gender difference in the emphasis on the father role, with male respondents more likely to choose the father. There is a significant race difference in the choice of the provider role, with black respondents more likely to think it most important. Black females stressed the provider role much more than they did the father role. Finally, white females are the race-gender group most likely to pick career pursuits as the most important activity of a married man and are the least likely to emphasize the salience of the provider role.

An earlier study (Cazenave, 1979) noted that black male respondents did not seem to choose the provider role as an escape from more emotionally expressive paternal styles, but because it made the more emotionally involved fathering modes possible. Black males and females may differ substantially from the white respondents in the degree of their emphasis on the provider role for men because of a history many blacks have shared of difficulty in providing adequately for their families, even when they were fortunate enough to have regular employment. Since the black respondents tend to be of a lower SES status than are the white respondents, this may indicate an interaction effect of race and class. The provider role is more salient for the working classes compared to the middle classes—where economic provision can, relatively speaking, be taken for granted—with a concomitant emphasis on the noneconomic rewards of career pursuits (Cazenave, 1979, 1984).

As Table 16.2 shows, there are also statistically significant differences for race-gender groups for the two economic-provision-related masculine gender-role items: "A man who does not adequately provide for his family is less than a man," and "If a man's wife makes more money than he does, this should not bother him." For both of these items the black males are most likely to stress the role of economic provider and being the major provider in their conceptualization of appropriate strategies of masculine attainment. Consistent with our view that status attainment or maintenance dynamics are central to understanding the salience of various masculine roles and ideal characteristics, the overwhelming

TABLE 16.1

Most Important Activity for a Married-Man
Item for Race-Gender Groups

| | Race-Gender Groups | | | | | | | |
Choice	White Males %	N	Black Males %	N	White Females %	N	Black Females %	N
Husband	50.3	93	46.9	23	67.2	119	44.8	47
Father	29.2	54	26.5	13	16.4	29	16.2	17
Provider	16.2	30	22.4	11	6.2	11	34.3	36
Career pursuits	4.3	8	4.1	2	10.2	18	4.8	5
Total	100.0	185	99.9	49	100.0	177	100.1	105

$\chi^2 = 54.60$, 9 d.f., $p \leqslant .0000$

majority of all of the respondents, regardless of race-gender group, agreed or strongly agreed that "'Becoming someone' through working [and] making something of yourself" is the most essential component of manhood in modern society. That is, they seem to accept Pleck's (1975) work-oriented modern-man type.

For the "man who does not provide is less than a man" item, black females were more likely to agree or strongly agree than were white females ($\chi^2 = 15.83$, 2 d.f., $p \leq .0004$). For this item it is black males who were most likely to agree or strongly agree, followed by black females, white males, then white females. Again, this seems to reflect the salience of the provider role for the black respondents.

However, gender is the best predictor of agreement with the "if a man's wife makes more money, this should not bother him" item. While the overwhelming majority of all respondents agree with this statement, black males are the race-gender group least likely to agree, followed by white males, white females, and black females, in that order. With black females most likely to agree that such an arrangement should not bother a man and black males least likely to agree, the relative amount of the wife's earnings may constitute an important relationship issue for a substantial minority of black men and black women.

Ideal Characteristics of Men
and Minority Status Attainment

Table 16.3 provides some insights as to the nature, and possibly the origin, of black males placing more emphasis on work-related mascu-line-role ideologies. These findings suggest that racial minorities adopt

TABLE 16.2
Work-Related Masculine Gender-Role Items for Race-Gender Groups

Items and Response Categories	White Males %	White Males N	Black Males %	Black Males N	White Females %	White Females N	Black Females %	Black Females N
Not provide, not a man								
agree or strongly agree	32.5	63	37.7	20	14.0	25	34.0	36
undecided	17.5	34	9.4	5	16.8	30	13.2	14
disagree or strongly disagree	50.0	97	52.8	28	69.3	124	52.8	56
totals	100.0	194	99.9	53	100.1	179	100.0	106

$\chi^2 = 26.67$, 6 d.f., $p \leq .0002$

Items and Response Categories	White Males %	White Males N	Black Males %	Black Males N	White Females %	White Females N	Black Females %	Black Females N
Become someone through work essential to manhood								
agree or strongly agree	67.9	131	71.7	38	61.5	100	77.1	81
undecided	14.0	27	7.5	4	14.5	26	8.6	9
disagree or strongly disagree	18.1	35	20.8	11	24.0	43	14.3	15
totals	100.9	193	100.0	53	100.0	179	100.0	105

$\chi^2 = 9.35$, 6 d.f., $p \leq .155$

Items and Response Categories	White Males %	White Males N	Black Males %	Black Males N	White Females %	White Females N	Black Females %	Black Females N
Wife earns more money; should not bother husband								
agree or strongly agree	79.1	151	68.6	35	89.3	158	90.5	95
undecided	9.9	19	19.6	10	4.0	7	6.7	7
disagree or strongly disagree	11.0	21	1.8	6	6.8	12	2.9	3
totals	100.0	191	100.0	51	100.1	177	100.1	105

$\chi^2 = 22.93$, 6 d.f., $p \leq .0008$

TABLE 16.3

Statistically Significant Differences for Competitive and Aggressive Ideal Characteristics of a Man and Career Success Most Important Aspects of Life for Race-Gender Groups

	Race-Gender Groups							
	White Males		Black Males		White Females		Black Females	
Items and Response Categories	%	N	%	N	%	N	%	N
Competitive								
Not important or somewhat important	54.2	104	53.8	28	76.0	136	66.0	70.
Very important or essential	45.8	88	46.2	24	24.0	43	34.0	36
Totals	100.0	192	100.0	52	100.0	179	100.0	106
			$\chi^2 = 21.69$, 3 d.f., $p \leq .0001$					
Aggressive								
Not important or somewhat important	71.0	137	56.6	30	76.5	137	69.8	74
Very important or essential	29.0	56	43.4	23	23.5	42	30.2	32
Totals	100.0	193	100.0	53	100.0	179	100.0	106
			$\chi^2 = 8.09$, 3 d.f., $p \leq .0441$					
Career Success Most Important Aspect of One's Life								
Agree or strongly agree	18.6	36	36.5	19	20.2	36	38.7	41
Undecided	14.4	28	13.5	7	14.6	26	9.4	10
Disagree or strongly disagree	67.0	130	50.0	26	65.2	116	51.9	55
Totals	100.0	194	100.0	52	100.0	178	100.0	106
			$\chi^2 = 21.24$, 6 d.f., $p \leq .0017$					

gender ideologies consistent with their motivation and strategies for upward mobility (see also Cazenave, 1984).

For example, race is the major predictor of those who agree or strongly agree that "successfully climbing the career ladder is the most important aspect of one's life." Ironically (and perhaps tragically), black students are the most likely to accept this view of the overall significance of success in their lives, though they are not as likely to achieve it. For both races, females are slightly more likely to stress success than are males. This supports the view that, for minorities, status attainment is a key motivating factor at work.

Consistent with this minority status-attainment perspective, it might be expected that racial minorities should stress being competitive and being aggressive as ideal characteristics for men, while gender minorities, who generally stress greater gender-role liberalism, would not. We should expect that there will be a gender effect, with males tending to be more competitive and aggressive than are females.

The gender perspective seems most applicable to the acceptance of the view that being competitive is very important or essential as an ideal characteristic of a man. Black males and white males are virtually identical in their emphasis of this ideal. However, consistent with the minority status-attainment perspective, black females are more likely to emphasize being competitive than are white females, although these differences are not statistically significant.

Finally, the aggressive-ideal characteristic item is better explained by race than by gender. This is consistent with the view that being aggressive may be an ideal for racial minorities who have been denied traditional means through which to obtain status. While white males appear to make a conceptual distinction between being competitive and being aggressive, the black respondents do not. Black males (as the minority status-attainment perspective suggests) are most likely to choose being aggressive as a masculine ideal. Black females and white males are virtually identical, and white females are the least likely of any of the race-gender groups to support this masculine ideal.

Characteristics of an ideal man, such as being warm and gentle, being emotionally expressive, and being comfortable with children, are generally viewed as being indicative of a modern, versus traditional, gender-role orientation. It is assumed that, typically, the more modern race-gender groups would stress these characteristics while the more traditional groups would not. Contrary to this view, our study does not reveal any clear and consistent pattern in this area.

For example, while gender provides a better predictor of respondents who chose the warm and gentle and emotionally expressive ideal characteristics, race is more highly correlated with those choosing the "comfortable with children" ideal (see Table 16.4).

White females are most likely to identify both being warm and gentle and being emotionally expressive as very important or essential characteristics of an ideal man, followed by black women (warm and gentle, corrected χ^2 = 5.90, 1 d.f., p ≤ .0152; emotionally expressive, corrected χ^2 = 15.49, 1 d.f., p ≤ .0001). However, while white males are more likely to indicate that being warm and gentle is a very important or essential characteristic of an ideal man than are black males and black males are slightly more likely to stress being emotionally expressive than are white males. In neither case, however, are these differences statistically significant.

Finally, black males are most likely to identify being comfortable with children as an ideal characteristic, followed, in order, by black females, white females, and white males. There is a statistically significant difference between black males and white males for this item (corrected χ^2 = 3.75, 1 d.f., p ≤ .0527). This question best illustrates the difficulties associated with the use of ideal-characteristic items in gender-role research. As Pleck (1981) notes, the more abstract items are often difficult to interpret. For example, does this finding mean that children are more highly valued (Staples, 1978) or more central (Cazenave, 1981) in black intimacy, marriage, and family relationships than in those of whites? Or does it suggest that this ideal is more heavily stressed because male-child relationships are perceived to be more problematic by black Americans than they are by their white counterparts?

Family- and Work-Related Scales and Correlates

In order to better explain why different groups of respondents answered the gender-ideology questions as they did, a principal-components factor analysis with oblique rotations was performed on all of the variables included in the study. The Family-Man and Careerist scales were derived from that analysis. The Family-Man scale reflects emphasis on these ideal characteristics of a man: standing up for beliefs, being warm and gentle, fighting to protect one's family, being comfortable with children, and being emotionally expressive. The Careerist scale consists of these ideal characteristics: being self-confident, competitive, worldly and experienced, aggressive, and ambitious.

It was suggested earlier that different race-gender groups may seem to

TABLE 16.4
Statistically Significant Differences for More Emotionally Expressive Ideal Characteristics of a Man for Race-Gender Groups

Items and Response Categories	White Males		Black Males		White Females		Black Females	
	%	N	%	N	%	N	%	N
Warm and Gentle								
Not important or somewhat important	20.2	39	26.4	14	3.9	7	12.3	13
Very important or essential	79.8	154	73.6	39	96.1	172	87.7	93
Totals	100.0	193	100.0	53	100.0	179	100.0	106
			$\chi^2 = 28.77$, 3 d.f., $p \leqslant .0000$					
Emotionally Expressive								
Not important or somewhat important	44.0	85	41.5	22	12.8	23	33.0	35
Very important or essential	56.0	108	58.5	31	87.2	156	67.0	71
Totals	100.0	193	100.0	53	100.0	179	100.0	106
			$\chi^2 = 45.79$, 3 d.f., $p \leqslant .0000$					
Comfortable with Children								
Not important or somewhat important	225.4	49	11.5	6	15.6	28	14.2	15
Very important or essential	74.6	144	88.5	46	84.4	151	85.8	91
Totals	100.0	193	100.0	52	100.0	179	100.0	106
			$\chi^2 = 10.05$, 3 d.f., $p \leqslant .0182$					

be "traditional" or "modern" on gender-role items for reasons that go beyond gender roles. For example, racial minorities may choose certain ideal characteristics of men based on their desire for both individual and collective status attainment. Consistent with this view, it was reported in this study that blacks were more likely to stress career success than were white respondents. Table 16.5 provides additional support for the minority status-attainment perspective. In the first step of the regression equation predicting the Careerist scale we see that blacks, males, and the young and upper-income groups are more career oriented. When anticipated mobility is entered into the equation, the effect of race becomes insignificant, indicating that blacks adhere to the ideal characteristics of the Careerist scale only to the extent that they see themselves as being upwardly mobile. This suggests that blacks emphasize ideal characteristics such as competitiveness and aggressiveness because these are viewed as being essential ingredients of status attainment for minority members. In contrast, only gender significantly predicts the Family-Man scale.

Existing gender-role dichotomies assume that men are *either* family oriented *or* career oriented, but not *both*. If that assumption is true, we would expect those who score high on the Careerist scale to score low on the Family-Man scale and vice versa. Table 16.6 indicates just the opposite. Three of the four race-gender groups exhibit a positive correlation between Family-Man and Careerist characteristics. For example, men who stress the "stands up for beliefs," warm and gentle, fights to protect family, comfortable with children, and emotionally expressive ideal characteristics of a man, which constitute the Family-Man factor and scale, are more likely—not less likely—to stress the Careerist masculine ideals. That is, the Careerist and Family-Man ideal-characteristics factors are not mutually exclusive. Again it appears that dichotomies like traditional versus modern or breadwinner versus emotionally expressive do not apply. Instead, it seems that these Careerist ideals may be strategically related to the realization of the Family-Man ideals (see Cazenave, 1979).

These findings suggest that black-white differences in gender-role ideologies cannot be explained simply by the tendency of one race to be more or less traditional in its general life orientations than is another. What is being measured appears to be much more substantial than that and reflects fundamentally different locations in the social structure and different cognitive strategies as to how to maintain and/or obtain status within it.

TABLE 16.5

Regression Equations Predicting Family Man and
Careerist Scales with Structural and Attitudinal Items

Dependent Variable	Careerist Scale (N = 408)		Family Man Scale (N = 408)	
Independent variables				
Step 1				
Race	−.14	(.01)*	.02	(.73)
Sex	−.15	(.00)*	.22	(.00)*
Age	−.14	(.01)*	−.05	(.34)
Family income	.13	(.01)*	.02	(.72)
R^2	.06		.04	
Step 2				
Race	−.08	(.12)	−.01	(.81)
Sex	−.10	(.04)*	.22	(.00)*
Age	−.13	(.01)*	−.03	(.47)
Family income	.18	(.00)*	.03	(.51)
Anticipated mobility[a]	.24	(.00)*	.03	(.59)
R^2	.11		.05	

a. For this item respondents were asked, "How do you feel your social class level
will compare to that of your parents 10 years from now? Will it be: much lower,
slightly lower, about the same, slightly higher, much higher?"
*Significance level for statistically significant variables.

TABLE 16.6

Correlation Coefficients Between Family Man Scale and
Careerist Scale for Race-Gender Groups

	Race-Gender Groups			
Scales	White Males	Black Males	White Females	Black Females
Correlations between family man and careerist scales	.140*	.226*	.333***	N.S.

NOTE: Family Man Scale = ideal characteristics of a man, stands up for beliefs +
warm and gentle + fights to protect family + comfortable with children + emotionally expressive / 5. Careerist Scale = ideal characteristics of a man, self-confident +
competitive + worldly and experienced + aggressive + ambitious / 5.
*$p \leqslant .05$; **$p \leqslant .01$; ***$p \leqslant .001$.

Summary and Conclusions

A minority status-attainment/majority status-maintenance perspective has been advanced to explain race, gender, and SES differences in
masculine role ideologies. This perspective has been applied to help

interpret the phenomenology of appropriate masculine roles for white male, black male, white female, and black female college students. The minority status-attainment view of gender roles was supported, as was the phenomenological interpretative framework for the four race-gender groups. Black respondents in our study placed greater emphasis on the salience of the provider role for married men than did white respondents. White females were the race-gender group least likely to stress economic provision as a criterion for manhood, while black males were most likely to be concerned about a man not earning as much money as his wife does. The majority of all the respondents supported the view that becoming someone through working is the most important component of manhood. Black female respondents were most likely to agree that career success is the most important aspect of life, while males of both races tended to accept the masculine ideal characteristics of being competitive, and black males were most likely to stress being aggressive. Consistent with this perspective, we suggest that different race-gender groups may respond to gender-role items as they do for reasons that go beyond gender roles. For example, while white females may see a diminution of masculine status-related ideals as being best for their own aspirations for advancement, racial minorities may choose certain ideal characteristics of men based on their desire for both individual and collective status attainment. In addition, black males may be affected by the status inconsistency associated with being minority males, and black females may experience the cognitive dissonance of simultaneously desiring increased status for themselves, in a gender-specific way, and for their men, who are, like themselves, racially oppressed.

The majority status-maintenance perspective also receives support in the present analysis, although not as much as does the minority status-attainment perspective. The emphasis on becoming someone through working as the most important component of being a male supports both status-related perspectives. Consistent with the majority status-maintenance view, males and upper-income family groups are more likely to stress Careerist ideals for men than are females and lower-income family groups. The desire for upward mobility among the black respondents is the key factor in explaining the racial differences in emphasis on the Careerist scale. The Careerist and Family-Man scales are positively correlated. This suggests that there may be more of a symbiotic than an antagonistic relationship between male work-and family-related roles and ideal characteristics than is generally suggested in the existing literature. These findings suggest that to understand the gender-role ideologies of different race-gender groups, it is necessary to move beyond analyses that are limited to individuals and their subculture, to studies of the broader social system that produce both the structural and cultural processes behind these ideologies. This research indicates that a complete understanding of masculine work and family roles can come only from analyses that focus on how these ideologies are related to respondents' social location and strategies for status attainment or maintenance. Such research must be multidimensional in that it not only allows comparisons between different race, class, and gender groups, but provides adequate interpretations of why different groups respond the way they do. Future surveys should include not only questions related to gender roles, but a broad range of items that explore the major ideological issues affected by an individual's particular location in the social structure. Only through such research will it be possible to understand masculine work- and family-related roles within the broader social context, which determines both their salience and meaning.

NOTE

1. This low occurrence of other minorities is reflective of the demographics of the university and is not a weakness of our selection method. All nonblack and nonwhite minorities combined, as well as all nonresident foreign students, accounted for fewer than 900, or 5.8%, of the more than 15,000 undergraduates attending Temple University at the time of the study.

REFERENCES

Beale, F. (1970). Double jeopardy: To be black and female. In T. Cade (Ed.), *The black woman: An anthology* (pp.90-100). New York: Mentor.

Cazenave, N. A. (1979). Middle-income black fathers: An analysis of the provider role. *Family Coordinator, 28,* 583-593.

Cazenave, N. A. (1981). Black men in America: The quest for "manhood." In H. McAdoo (Ed.), *Black families* (pp. 175-185). Newbury Park, CA: Sage.

Cazenave, N. A. (1983a). Black male-black female relationships: The perceptions of 155 middle-class black men. *Family Relations, 32*(3), 341-350.

Cazenave, N. A. (1983b). A "woman's place": The attitudes of middle-class black men. *Phylon, 44*(1), 12-32.

Cazenave, N. A. (1984). Race, socioeconomic status, and age: The social context of American masculinity. *Sex Roles, 11,* 639-656.

Franklin, C. W., & Walum, L. R. (1972). Toward a paradigm of sub-structural relations: An application to sex and race in the United States. *Phylon, 33,* 242-253.

Freidan, B. (1963). *The feminine mystique.* New York: Dell.

Hatchett, S. J., & Quick, A. D. (1983). Correlates of sex-role attitudes among black men and women: Data from a national survey of black Americans. *Urban Research Review*, 9(2), 1-3, 11.

Hershey, M. R. (1978). Racial differences in sex-role identities and sex stereotyping: Evidence against a common assumption. *Social Science Quarterly*, 58(4), 583-596.

Lopata, H. Z. (1965). The secondary features of a primary relationship. *Human Organization*, 24, 116-123.

Parsons, T., & Bales, R. F. (1965). *Family, socialization and interaction process*. New York: Free Press.

Pleck, J. H. (1975). The male sex role: Definitions, problems, and sources of change. *Journal of Social Issues, 32*(3), 155-164.

Pleck, J. H. (1977). The work-family system. *Social Problems, 24*. 417-47.

Pleck, J. H. (1981). *The Myth of Masculinity*. Cambridge: M.I.T. Press.

Ransford, H. E., & Miller, J. (1983). Race, sex and feminist outlooks. *American Sociological Review*, 48(1), 46-59.

Romer, N., & Cherry, D. (1980). Ethnic and social class differences in children's sex-role concepts. *Sex Roles*, 6(2), 245-263.

Scanzoni, J. (1982). Sex roles, economic factors and marital solidarity in black and white marriages. *Journal of Marriage and Family, 37* 130-145.

Smith, M. D., & Fisher, L. J. (1982). Sex-role attitudes and social class: A reanalysis and clarification. *Journal of Comparative Family Studies, 33*(1), 77-88.

Staples, R. (1978). Masculinity and race: The dual dilemma of black men. *Journal of Social Issues, 34,* 169-183.

Tavris, C. (1977, January). Men and women report their views on masculinity. *Psychology Today*, pp. 35-38, 42, 82.

Turner, B. F., & Turner, C. B. (1975). Race, sex and perception of the occupational structure among college students. *Sociological Quarterly, 16*, 345-360.

PART VI

Toward Men's Studies

17

A Case for Men's Studies

HARRY BROD

The case for men's studies can best be made by demonstrating that men's studies perspectives are not only compatible with, but are essential to, the academic and political projects entailed by the feminist reconstruction of knowledge initiated by women's studies two decades ago. To that end, I shall propose a general theory of men's studies, consider some particularly illustrative examples of the manner in which men's studies challenges existing paradigms in intellectually and politically invigorating ways, and discuss the feminist politics of men's studies. I shall attempt to convey a sense of both the current status and future prospects of the field.

Defining Men's Studies

It would appear initially, at least, that men's studies represents an attempt to undermine feminist scholarship, since it seems to negate the fundamental premise of women's studies. Briefly, the rationale for

AUTHOR'S NOTE: I wish to acknowledge the comments of two anonymous reviewers and the editor on an earlier draft of this chapter.

women's studies rests on the proposition that traditional scholarship reflects a male-oriented or androcentric bias. The distortions resulting from this bias have resulted in women's experiences and perspectives being systematically written out of what has been taught as "knowledge." Traditional scholarship, therefore, has been a de facto program of "men's studies," despite its claim to objectivity and neutrality (Raymond, 1985, pp. 49-50; Shapiro, 1981, p. 111; Spender, 1981). Accordingly, women's studies has set itself the task of reconstituting knowledge to rectify these deficiencies, both by supplementing traditional scholarship with additional information about women and by forging fundamental revisions of academic disciplines where necessary. From this perspective, "men's studies" appears to be part of the problem, not part of the solution.

But the new men's studies is not simply a repetition of traditionally male-biased scholarship. Like women's studies, it too attempts to emasculate patriarchal ideology's masquerade as knowledge. Women's studies explores and corrects the effects on women and our understanding of them—of their exclusion from traditional learning caused by the androcentric elevation of "man" as male to "man" as generic human. Men's studies similarly looks into the, as yet, largely unrecognized effects of this fallacy on men and our understanding of them. Androcentric scholarship is only *seemingly* about men. In reality, it is, at best, only negatively about men, that is, it is about men only by virtue of not being about women. In a more important positive sense, its consideration of generic man as the human norm functions to exclude from consideration what is distinctive of men *qua* men. Its generalization from male to generic human experience not only distorts our understanding of what, if anything, is truly generic, it misdirects attention away from the study of masculinity as a *specifically male* experience, seeing it instead solely as a universal paradigm for *human* experience. Stated in its most general terms, therefore, the subject matter of men's studies is the study of masculinities and male experiences in their own right as specific and varying social, cultural, and historical formations.

From this perspective, men's studies can be seen as a necessary complement to women's studies, needed to bring to completion the feminist project, which motivates both. For no feminist vision can move women from the margin to the center (Hooks, 1984) by ignoring men. If men are to be removed from center stage and a feminist vision brought to fruition, that vision must be focused explicitly on men in a way that moves them from center to margin. Men's studies represents that vision. Without this focus, even new knowledge of women remains knowledge of the "Other," not on a par with knowledge of men. "The Woman

Question" cannot be studied properly unless "The Man Question" is also studied.

Men's studies raises new questions and demonstrates the inadequacies of existing paradigms and schools of thought. For example, we might ask why women are seen as "working mothers" even when they work in the paid public work force, while statistics on levels of fatherhood in the work force are generally uncollected. Insofar as the issue is one of the workplace itself, in answering this question, both men's and women's studies would focus on such factors as sex segregation in the labor market. Insofar as the question sheds light on the nature of parenting in our society, however, they would have a difficult focus, with men's studies looking not at the continuity in women's roles in and away from home in terms of "service" roles, but rather at the discontinuities in male socialization, which so severely divide work and home life.

To allude to other salient areas on inquiry, how much further along would we be in health science, for example, if gender bias had not prevented us from looking for sons affected by DES and miscarriages and birth defects among the offspring of males working with hazardous materials with the speed with which we moved to examine the supposedly weaker vessels of women's bodies? What concepts of men as citizen-warriors inform our political traditions (Stiehm, 1983, 1984)? How have images of the hero and the hero's mythological quest, with their distinctive rhythms of separation, conquest, and return, been shaped by the rhythms of male life cycles? What are society's male rites of passage? Is it possible to find the "moral equivalent of war"? What determines heterosexuality and homosexuality, both as activities and as identities? Can "womb envy" be an adequate explanatory concept for much of male behavior and attitudes (Kittay, 1984)? Questions like these form the core concerns of men's studies.

There are identifiable reasons—academic, social, and political—why such concerns attract attention at this particular time. Academically, women's studies has long since enlarged its scope, from adding supplemental or compensatory knowledge to the traditional curriculum to revising that curriculum fundamentally. Accompanying this change is a shift from simply questioning the status of women to questioning the fundamental nature of the gender division as it forms both women and men. As Hester Eisenstein (1983, p. 96) comments, "A women-centered perspective inevitably sheds new light on masculinity and maleness." Men's studies extends and highlights such trends.

Socially, numerous factors contribute to the interest in male role changes—forces specific to the male experience, as well as the more obvious demands for change in men occasioned by the women's movement. Several factors threaten the breadwinner role, traditionally seen as the core of male identity. Not only have women entered the paid work force in increasing numbers, but the nature of male work itself has changed, with greater emphasis on mental rather than manual labor. Such changes are accompanied by a shift from a work to a consumer ethic, creating a correspondingly greater emphasis on the satisfaction of personal desires rather than on the renunciation of those desires in the name of economic efficiency. This new ethic leads to a greater sensitivity to the psychological aspects of gender roles. Furthermore, the traditional heroism of the male warrior has been rendered obsolete by such developments as the advent of the electronic battlefield and nuclear weaponry. The women's and gay liberation movements, as well as other changes in sexual ethics brought about by the "sexual revolution" and its aftermaths, have also undermined the traditional use of heterosexual sexual conquest as a measuring rod of masculinity. The benchmarks of masculinity are thus conspicuously in transition, giving rise to widespread interest in an examination of male identity.

Politically, men's studies is rooted in the profeminist men's movement, roughly analogous to women's studies' being rooted in the feminist women's movement. A small but growing major national organization of the men's movement, the National Organization for Changing Men, has a Men's Studies Task Group that has been instrumental in organizing men's studies activities since 1983.

Knowledge, ultimately, cannot be severed from its social roots and repercussions. Therefore, in the discussion of men's studies research perspectives that follows, I shall intertwine the analysis of scholarly paradigm shifts with the analysis of the political implications of these developments.

Demystifying Masculinity

The new women's history that has developed since the 1960s has changed the understanding and writing of history, not primarily by elevating a few select women into the pantheon of the "great men" of male historiography, but rather by joining ranks with the social history that had emerged since the early twentieth century to change the manner in which historical narratives are constructed. The new women's social history focuses on the lives led by the majority of women in all strata of society, using material from a wide range of sources, from diaries to demographics. In the same vein, the new men's history practiced by men's studies is not a succession of biographies of great men or a tale of campaigns, military and political, won and lost. Rather, this new men's history deals with the daily lives led by the majority of men. And just as one of the leading questions raised by women's history has been the extent to which women acted self-consciously *as women*, so too men's history raises the question of how specific concepts and social forms of masculinity intersected in men's lives, either forming the basis of or emerging as reflections upon their actions. While the dominant trend in the new men's history lies in the social history tradition, some psychohistorical studies, informed by a more critical analysis of masculinity than that found in mainstream psychoanalytic literature, have also been incorporated.

Men's studies challenges the pervasive assumption that we live today in a period uniquely troubling and tumultuous for the beleaguered male ego. Men's history reveals that constructs of masculinity have always resulted from conflicting pressures. The nostalgic contemporary male eye that looks back longingly to the 1950s forgets that this was also a period of pervasive fears among the white middle class that men were being emasculated by being turned into faceless organization men in indistinguishable gray flannel suits. One of the most important films of apotheosis of that decade, *Rebel Without a Cause*, clearly attributes James Dean's character's juvenile delinquency to his father's wearing an apron. The 50s were also the era of the beatniks, and prefigured in Arthur Miller's tragic *Death of a Salesman*, arguably the most eloquent and profound single statement of mainstream contemporary American male dilemmas. All was not well in that kingdom.

To take a longer view, the 1890s were widely perceived as embodying an acute "crisis of masculinity." Articles abounded in the popular press of the time and instructional manuals aiming to solve male problems proliferated. Many factors contributed to the male malaise, among them the waning of Victorianism, the emergence of the "New Woman," the continuing impact of industrialization, urbanization, and the closing of the frontier. One cannot understand the politics and culture of this and the subsequent period without understanding much of it, including the rise of Teddy Roosevelt and the Progressive movement, as responses to the crisis (Dubbert, 1979; Filene, 1976).

There exists today an analogue to this earlier, specifically male shift in political consciousness, but it is obscured by precisely the kind of skewed vision men's studies aims to correct. Much has been written to explain the gender gap, a divergence of male and female voting patterns, which was first noted significantly in the 1980 presidential elections. While analysts have offered various explanations about the shift in women's political consciousness that produced the gap, males, as such, have not been addressed. Instead, male voting patterns have simply formed the norm against which female deviations must be explained. Such explanations of the gender gap must explain, often with great difficulty, the anomaly that the gap emerges most clearly not in regard to so-called women's issues—for example, ERA, abortion, child care—but rather in regard to the issues that are staples of male political discourse—for example, military spending and employment. Men's studies resolves this conundrum. The key to this gender gap lies in the study of men, not women. Closer analysis of voting patterns reveals that men have shifted to the right, rather than that women have shifted to the left.

> Women's votes in 1980 largely followed party lines and showed little change from 1976.... But *men* showed a significant shift *to* Reagan, and it was this change in male voting patterns that highlighted a gender gap.... One could make the argument that it was the men whose voting behavior really should be explained. (Elshtain, 1984, p. 22)

Recollecting the historical ambiguities of masculinity better enables men to face current and future male role change and challenges. Men are generally nostalgic for a past perceived as embodying a more stable and secure masculine identity. This nostalgia tends to act in immobilizing and conservative ways, leading men to be less responsive to contemporary demands, since they believe themselves to be justifiably defending a uniform continuous tradition against unique assaults on that tradition. Identifying the historical inaccuracies of this mythologizing of the past can free men's attentions to encounter present realities more directly. Even this mythologizing is not specific to the contemporary period. Our inherited mythology of western heroes, an important case in point, was a romanticizing of a vanished era even as it was being glorified. For example, the most famous gunfight in western history, the shoot-out at the OK Corral between the Earps and the Clantons, could be more accurately perceived in contemporary terms, not as a confrontation of law and order versus criminality, but as rival gang warfare.

Unfortunately, some attempts to encourage progressive change only perpetuate a monolithic, static view of the past by simply contrasting "modern" versus "traditional" male roles. Such an approach denies the complexities of historical change, as if the current wave of men questioning the meanings of masculinity arose *ex nihilo*. There is, however, a history of male gender-role nonconformity, as well as a history of explicitly profeminist, antisexist male political activism.

While women's studies has demonstrated how women have been written out of male history, profeminist men have as yet been insufficiently written into the new women's history:

> Where are the men in women's history? Are women historians perpetuating the same kinds of distortions perpetrated by those historians who wrote histories devoid of women? (Strauss, 1982, p. xv).

The history of male profeminist activism is an essential part of the history of feminism. In the nineteenth century, for example, many men, such as William Lloyd Garrison, Frederick Douglass, Thomas Wentworth Higginson, Parker Pillsbury, and Samuel Joseph May, significantly supported feminist demands, and many supportive husbands of suffrage leaders, such as Henry Blackwell and James Mott, were activists in their own right (Bradley, 1981-1982; Wagner, 1984-1985). Men's history has the task of not simply tracing and reinterpreting the history of patriarchal male bonding, but also the task of reclaiming those aspects of homosociality, the realm of male companionship, motivated by feminist or humanitarian concerns.

This project requires a comprehension of previous data, not merely an addition of information to what was previously known. In historical studies, much of the attention focused on such recomprehension is directed toward the question of reperiodization (Bell, 1981; Doyle, 1983; Franklin, 1984; Hoch, 1979; Pleck & Pleck, 1980). The level of sweeping generalization one sometimes finds at this level in recent men's history attests to men's studies still being in its relative infancy, as does the tendency to speak in the singular of *the* male sex role, rather than of different male sex roles, which vary by such categories as race, class, ethnicity, sexual orientation, and nationality. Even given this relative lack of sophistication, however, this new men's history is a far cry indeed from the men's history castigated by women's studies, and it has the clear potential to contribute a great deal to feminist historical understanding.

One other area in addition to historical scholarship is worth mentioning. The most dynamic component of the U.S. men's movement is its antiviolence wing. Dozens of men's groups are working with men who batter, rape, and commit other violent acts. Activities range from crisis-intervention hot lines and long-and short-term counseling programs to public education projects, legislative lobbying, and political demonstrations. New therapeutic techniques yield higher success rates than do standard treatments—techniques based on men's studies perspectives.

Men who are violent are seen conventionally as deviants or nonconformists, who have somehow failed to internalize society's condemnation of violence successfully. Accordingly, therapy is designed to apply, belatedly, the socialization that failed to take hold at earlier stages of life, thereby bringing these men into conformity with social norms. Men's studies, however, argues that one must critically examine specifically male socialization processes, rather than the socialization processes of a genderless "society." What emerges from such an examination is a picture of considerable socialization *toward* violence, learned in gangs, sports teams, military training, media images, at the hands (literally) of older males, and in putatively benign messages of acceptance that "boys will be boys" when they fight. This conveys tolerance and even approval of violence as an appropriately masculine means of conflict resolution or negation. From a men's studies perspective, then, violent men are not deviants or *non*conformists, but *over*conformists, men who have come too much under the domination of a particular aspect of male socialization. Consequently, the therapeutic task ought not be inculcation of society's mores, but personal empowerment of men to distance themselves from their socialization and more successfully become individuals. For men's studies, then, the question in relation to male violence is not the standard "What is wrong with these men and how can we bring them up to par?" but instead the more significant "How can we strengthen the mechanisms of resistance by which nonviolent men have avoided acting on society's prescriptions for male violence, and how can we stop society from prescribing and rewarding male violence?"

Specific counseling strategies, in addition to general goals of treatment, are also derived from investigations of the particulars of male socialization. For example, EMERGE: A Men's Counseling Service on Domestic Violence, a leading men's antiviolence group based in Boston, justifies its group-therapy mode in part on the grounds of specific aspects of male socialization, arguing that since so much of male role learning takes place in groups, its unlearning is also significantly facilitated by group interactions (Adams & Penn, 1981; EMERGE, 1980; Gondolf 1985). Groups have the positive virtue of allowing for the feeling of commonality with other men who share similar behavior patterns to emerge sufficiently for men to support each other in undertaking the kind of painful self-evaluation they would otherwise resist. Groups have the negative virtue of avoiding dyadic-counseling situations, which are often threatening to men because the intimate setting feels too feminine. Because of the intimacy of the setting, when domestic violence is treated in the usual couples-counseling context, men often become defensive because they feel that even the male therapist supports the women. Couples counseling treats domestic violence as a problem within the couple, often involving communication problems. This framework is often used by the male to blame the victim and avoid taking personal responsibility for his behavior, which is the prerequisite of change. These perspectives illustrate the significance of men's studies, in that they demonstrate how treating an issue like violence as a specifically male rather than a generic social problem proves most insightful and effective.

In more extensive analyses of male violence, several additional men's studies' themes emerge: the alienation of men from their emotions and bodies that underlies the mythology of violent men being overwhelmed by their passions or by drugs or alcohol, and performance pressures of all sorts. Some impetus to establish counseling programs for Vietnam veterans developed from reports that a disproportionate number of battered women seeking shelter were wives and lovers of veterans—a classic case of "bringing the war back home."

The treatment of male violence sketched above can be seen as a specific application of a more general, highly influential men's-studies paradigm developed by Pleck (1981) in *The Myth of Masculinity*. He articulates 11 propositions of the male sex-role identity paradigm (MSRI), which has dominated research on masculinity, and argues that it is fundamentally flawed and should be replaced by what he calls the sex-role strain paradigm (SRS). Although a summary of the work is beyond the scope of this chapter, I would like to point out that while one key element in the MSRI model is that a strong sense of oneself as masculine is essential to a male's mental health, the SRS model holds that such a self-conception may be harmful to his physical as well as his mental health. Stress in men's lives is caused not so much by the individual's failure to socialize properly as a male, but by the contradictory demands of the male sex role itself.

As the following example illustrates, clearly articulating the two paradigms can establish that many people who believe themselves to be allies in supporting male role changes actually are operating with fundamentally different and opposing assumptions and goals. Many people support proposals for men to be more actively involved in child rearing and early childhood education. Most frequently, such support is based on the contention that males have unique difficulties in establishing sex-role identification because of their relative lack of proximate role models, most child rearing being done by females. This position supports men's involvement with children so that young males can more easily and successfully achieve male sex-role identification. (Note that this argument supports the MSRI paradigm's contention that strong self-identification is desirable.) Others, however, support greater male child-rearing involvement because being nurturing is not part of traditional male roles, and men visibly functioning in this mode will therefore tend to diminish traditional sex-role expectations. On this line of reasoning, derived from the SRS paradigm, the goal of greater male child-rearing activities is to break down the rigid male identity being bolstered supposedly by this same activity on the MSRI line of reasoning. The seemingly mutually supportive arguments in favor of this male-role change are in truth mutually incompatible and contradictory.

The Politics of Men's Studies

Proponents of men's studies argue not only that it is intellectually valid, but also that its insights will be socially and politically beneficial. Such arguments, which speak largely to the consciousness-raising function of men's studies, depend on a particular variant of a theory of false consciousness, at least insofar as such arguments also lay claim to feminist consciousness. Most claims to have uncovered cases of false consciousness are made on behalf of oppressed groups who are said to believe falsely that their interests are being maintained or advanced by their society, when the satisfaction of these interests is, rather, being systematically thwarted. Feminism maintains, however, that men's interests are being advanced by patriarchy. A straightforward claim of the usual sort regarding false consciousness is therefore unavailable to those who wish to support men's studies with feminist arguments. The claim, rather, must be not that men's interests are not being advanced by society, but that the sort of men's interests being advanced are interests men would be better off without. Men's studies questions the *nature* of male interest, not the calculus of their satisfaction. Its claim is that the economic, legal, social, and political rewards patriarchy confers upon men as a group come at too high a personal, individual cost. Male sex roles are damaging to men, as demonstrated, in part, by disproportionately higher male rates of heart attacks, hypertension, ulcers, suicides, and early deaths (seven to eight years on average), as well as more subjectively felt dissatisfactions.

While many are in general agreement on the above, one can distinguish between male-oriented and female-oriented feminist lines of argument regarding the potential political efficacy of men's studies. These orientations differ principally on the question of whether men or women are more likely to bring men's studies' perspectives to bear in arenas of social and political action. The male orientation is the more common. On this line of argument it seems obvious that men's studies addresses men as a constituent interest group, just as women's studies addresses women. While not denying the realities of male privilege, this orientation argues that awareness of the disadvantages that necessarily accompany male advantages, awareness of the double-edged nature of power, will make men more willing, if not eager, to relinquish that power. Since these disadvantages are largely psychological in nature, this perspective accounts, at least in part, for the psychological orientation of much of men's studies.

In contrast, female-oriented feminist arguments for men's studies argues that as the oppressed group, women, inevitably, are more likely than are men to engage in political activism relating to gender issues. This line of argument emphasizes the advantages to women, rather than to men, of the development of men's studies, arguing that leaving men's lives unexamined leaves male privilege unexamined, and hence more powerful, precisely because it is more secretive. It attributes the lack of men's studies heretofore more to obfuscation than to ignorance, to the vested interest of the privileged in obscuring the roots of their privileges rather than to male false consciousness. The most important boon granted by men's studies is therefore female *empowerment*, reached through greater knowledge of the dominant group, rather than through male *enlightenment*, reached through self-examination. Men's studies appears, then, not as feminist outreach to enlightened men, but as female encroachment on previously male-occupied terrain.

The difference between the two orientations also emerges in programmatic difference regarding how specific themes should be treated. For example, in analyzing sex differences regarding emotions, the male orientation would focus on documenting how male-role constraints on emotional display inhibit and repress men, while the female orientation would add to this an analysis of how this restraint also functions to confer power upon men, in large part by effectively withholding information about oneself. Similarly, men's studies analyses of male sexuality would, on the female orientation, necessarily encompass more than the male orientation demonstration of how male sexuality is distorted or restricted by male roles, and also demonstrate how the social construction of male sexuality relates to various forms of domination. Taking its cue from the feminist thesis that much of Western culture reflects the analogy "Woman: Nature = Man: Culture," women's studies has seen much of its task as "enculturating" women. Analogously, men's studies would aim at "embodying" men (Davis,

1985), as its share of the task of overcoming the Western mind/body dualism that has often operated to the detriment of women. Men's studies' analyses of male sexuality would therefore have to be more than sophisticated self-help sex manuals, more than attempts simply to add greater sexual satisfaction to the list of male privileges (Brod, 1984).

I would like to conclude by discussing two controversial questions of a political nature regarding the future development of men's studies. The first question concerns competition over financial and other resources between women's and men's studies, and the second concerns the relative degree of autonomy and interdependence among women's, men's, and gay studies.

Feminist scholars who agree in principle with the sort of men's studies I have proposed above often worry that the results of implementing such programs may be to siphon off much-needed support from women's studies. They argue that in a male-dominated budget-trimming environment, men's studies may well edge out women's studies when they compete, inevitably, for shares of a shrinking pool.

A precedent for resolving such conflicts can be found in the relationship between women's and men's antiviolence groups discussed above. Similar conflicts arise in that context, where laudable programs for counseling violent men compete for funds with a variety of women's programs: shelters, hot lines, legal aid, counseling services, and so on. The problem can seem even more acute here, as one could argue that since many women's services largely treat women after the violence has occurred, while many men's programs are preventive in nature, funds would be allocated more efficiently to men's groups, an ounce of prevention being worth a pound of cure. Fortunately, the irony of giving support to the perpetrators rather than to the victims of crime usually prevents such arguments from being heeded. More important, leading men's movement organizations have coordinated measures with women's movement organizations to prevent such conflicts from arising, including the presence of appropriate women on the governing boards of men's antiviolence groups, agreement to submit funding proposals first to local feminist groups, and agreement on principle not to engage in competitive fund-raising practices. Should men's studies programs emerge, I envisage similar institutional arrangements between men's and women's studies.

Other questions remain as to how close the relationship should be between women's and men's studies. Some advocate incorporating both, under the new rubric of "gender studies." While this terminology has merit insofar as it acknowledges trends toward greater inclusiveness and comprehensiveness in feminist scholarship that led to the development of men's studies, as indicated earlier, its disqualifying drawback is that it connotes a false parity between the study of women and the study of men (Brod, 1986). It may suggest to some that men's studies arises as a corrective to women's studies under some sort of equal-time fairness doctrine. Such an approach bespeaks an antifeminist approach to men's studies, an approach that does characterize some men's studies work (Brod & August, 1986).

Even some women's studies scholars who accept the validity of men's studies still balk at recognizing it as an autonomous field. They argue that since men's studies itself acknowledges its debts to women's studies, one simply should recognize that women's studies already studies men. Hence there would be no need for a new men's studies field. This is reminiscent of initial defensive reactions against women's studies. Where the first line of defense is to deny the validity of studying women or men specifically, once this becomes no longer tenable one retreats to the second line of defense, which is to argue that to the extent that such studies have validity, they can be carried on under already existing rubrics with no need for new programs. But scattered insights, however significant or profound, are no substitute for consolidated analysis. Only men's studies can provide the requisite systematically focused study of masculinities.

Men's studies has a crucial relationship to gay studies, both substantively and methodologically. Gay studies has progressed from simply supplying supplemental information about gay men to questioning the nature of the dichotomous categories "heterosexual" versus "homosexual," in a manner analogous to the similar trend in women's studies discussed earlier. It is correspondingly more difficult to draw a clear distinction between gay and men's studies (Carrigan, Connell, & Lee, 1985). Gay studies also very importantly corrects the unfortunate tendency in men's studies to assume commonality among all men. Both because of its methodological commitment to specificity and its content, gay studies serves as a model to rectify this deficiency in other regards as well.

Finally, it may be objected that the arguments I have advanced prove too much. One could attempt to refute my arguments via *reductio ad absurdum,* positions analogous to those presented here for the establishment of such fields as white studies, straight studies, ruling-class studies, Gentile studies. My argument can be saved from these implications by adapting a fundamental contention of feminist theory to the effect that consideration of one's identity as specifically gendered, as male per se, is central to *any* real understanding. This is not to argue that masculinity is invariant. Rather, male identities may well consist of what philosophers following Wittgenstein refer to as "family resemblances." Just as members of a family may be said to resemble each other without having any single feature in common, so masculinities may form common patterns without sharing any single universal characteristic. The claim, which justifies men's studies, is that there is a sufficiently unified concept of "masculinity" to justify its study under one rubric. Such is not the case, at least in my present judgment, for whites, ruling classes, straights, Gentiles, and so on. I would have to reverse this stand and accept, for example, white studies, if a case were made successfully that whiteness was such a fundamental concept and not just an externally imposed overarching grouping of radically disparate national and ethnic identities. For now, men's studies remains situated uniquely in the academy.

REFERENCES

Adams, D., & Penn, I. (1981). *Men in groups: The socialization and resocialization of men who batter.* Paper presented at the annual meeting of the American Orthopsychiatric Association.

Bell, D. H. (1981). Up from patriarchy: The male role in historical perspective. In R. A. Lewis (Ed.), *Men in difficult times: Masculinity today and tomorrow.* Englewood Cliffs, NJ: Prentice-Hall.

Bradley, M. (1981-1982, Winter). Before us: A collage of feminist men. *M., 7.*

Brod, H. (1984). Eros thanatized: Pornography and male sexuality. *Humanities in Society, 7, 1-2.*

Brod, H. (1986). The new men's studies: From feminist theory to gender scholarship. *Hypatia: A Journal of Feminist Philosophy.*

Brod, H., & August, E. R. (1986). Dialogue on men's studies. *Changing Men: Issues in Gender, Sex and Politics, 16.*

Carrigan, T., Connell, T., & Lee, J. (1985). Toward a new sociology of masculinity. *Theory and Society, 5(14).*

Davis, T. (1985). *Men's studies: Defining its contents and boundaries.* Paper presented at the Tenth National Conference on Men and Masculinity, St. Louis, MO.

Doyle, J. A. (1983). *The male experience.* Dubuque, IA: Wm. C. Brown.

Dubbert, J. L. (1979). *A man's place: Masculinity in transition.* Englewood Cliffs, NJ: Prentice-Hall.

Eisenstein, H. (1983). *Contemporary feminist thought.* Boston: G. K. Hall.

Elshtain, J. B. (1984). The politics of gender: Why women sound a different note. *Progressive, 4(2).*

EMERGE (1980). *Organizing and implementing services for men who batter.* (Available from EMERGE, 25 Huntington Avenue, Boston, MA 02116.)

Filene, P. G. (1976). *Him/her/self: Sex roles in modern America.* New York: New American Library.

Franklin, C. W., II (1984). *The changing definition of masculinity.* New York: Plenum.

Gondolf, E. W. (1985). *Men who batter: An integrated approach for stopping wife abuse.* Holmes Beach, FL: Learning Publications.

Hoch, P. (1979). *White hero, black beast: Racism, sexism, and the mask of masculinity.* London: Pluto. (Available from Longwood Publishing Group Inc., Dover, NH 03820.)

Hooks, B. (1984). *Feminist theory: From margin to center.* Boston: South End.

Kittay, E. F. (1984). Womb envy: An explanatory concept. In J. Trebilcot. (Ed.), *Mothering: Essays in feminist theory.* Totowa, NJ: Rowan & Allenheld.

Men's Studies Task Group, National Organization for Changing Men. *Men's Studies Newsletter.* (Available from P. O. Box 32, Harriman, TN 37748-0032.)

Pleck, E. H., & Pleck, J. H. (Eds.). (1980). *The American man.* Englewood Cliffs, NJ: Prentice-Hall.

Pleck, J. (1981). *The myth of masculinity.* Cambridge: MIT Press.

Raymond, J. G. (1985). Women's studies: A knowledge of one's own. In M. Culley & C. Portuges (Eds.), *Gendered subjects: The dynamics of feminist teaching.* London: Routledge & Kegan Paul.

Shapiro, J. (1981). Anthropology and the study of gender. In E. Langland & W. Gove (Eds.), *A Feminist perspective in the academy: The difference it makes.* Chicago: University of Chicago Press.

Spender, D. (Ed.). (1981). *Men's studies modified: The impact of feminism on the academic disciplines.* Elmsford, NY: Pergamon.

Stiehm, J. K. (Ed.). (1983). *Women and men's wars.* Elmsford, NY: Pergamon.

Stiehm, J. K. (1984). *Women's views of the political world of men.* Ardsley-on-Hudson, NY: Transnational.

Strauss, S. (1982). *Traitors to the masculine cause: The men's campaigns for women's rights.* Westport, CT: Greenwood.

Wagner, S. R. (1984-1985). Before us (department). *Changing men: Issues in Gender, Sex and Politics.*

18

Teaching a Course on Men

Masculinist Reaction or "Gentlemen's Auxiliary"?

MICHAEL S. KIMMEL

When I first mentioned that I was preparing to teach a course on men and masculinity, my friends and colleagues were intrigued. "Why do you need a separate course on men?" many asked. "Aren't all courses that don't have the word 'woman' in the title implicitly 'about men'?" some wondered. "Isn't this just a way for men to jump on the sex-role bandwagon and, in effect, steal the area away from women?" remarked others, somewhat suspiciously.

Each of the statements contained within these questions is true, at least in part. Historically, nearly all university courses that have not addressed women deliberately have been about men. And the study of gender has all but completely superseded race and class as the intellectually trendy topic of the 1980s. Just about every major academic publisher currently boasts a women's studies list, and courses on women in sociology remain among the most popular on campus. Male academics notice this trend, and while we historically have relegated the sociology of women and marriage and the family to the intellectual margins of the discipline—pushing our female graduate students toward

AUTHOR'S NOTE: I am grateful to Harry Brod, Tom Mosmiller, Joseph Pleck, and Sarah Williams for comments on earlier drafts of this chapter; portions of an earlier version appeared in *National Association of Women Deans and College Administrators Quarterly*. Thanks also to the students enrolled in Sociology of the Male Experience for their enthusiasm and intellectual effort.

these "natural" interests while demoting those subfields to a virtual "ladies' auxiliary" of our weightier theoretical and methodological concerns—we also know a hot topic when we see one.

Yet there is also something serious and genuine about developing a new course on the sociology of the male experience. First, it recognizes that while all the courses not about women are about men, they are about men only by default. For example, we study men as historical actors—statesmen, soldiers, and the like—or as writers, psychological "personalities," as members of revolutionary mobs, classes, and status groups, filling occupational roles, or acting as economic producers or consumers. Rarely, if ever, are men discussed as men; rarely is the experience of being a man seen as analytically interesting. Of course, this has become evident only in recent years as a result of the exciting reexamination of gender and sexuality that has been occurring in universities, spurred by the intellectual branches of the women's and gay movements. In a sense, a course about men's experiences as men takes as a point of departure the efforts of feminist scholars in raising the issues of gender in the first place. Without the analyses of economic and political discrimination, social inequality, the social construction of sexuality, work, family, and intimacy that feminist and gay scholars have developed, the study of masculinity would have remained a hidden field. But now that these scholars have raised these issues, it is imperative that men begin to examine their own experiences, not as parasites or as intellectual bullies, but as committed social scientists for whom the intellectual task of deconstructing masculinity is vital and important.[1]

In this chapter, I shall describe the course I developed and taught: the Sociology of the Male Experience. In so doing, I shall have three concerns: to explain the logic and organization of the course itself, to analyze the composition (race, class, and gender) of the class and assess students' reactions to the course, and to detail the reactions to the course from the university community and the public at large. Finally, I shall raise some unanswered issues in the study of masculinity within sociology, and discuss several pedagogical issues that arose during the course.

The Male Experience
Through the Life Course

The overwhelming majority of both courses and studies of masculinity have been developed from within a framework of the social psychology of sex roles.[2] Brannon, for example, identifies the male sex role as composed of four elements that he states as commands: (1) "No Sissy Stuff"—avoid all behaviors that might be even remotely perceived as feminine, (2) "Be a Big Wheel"—be powerful, strong, competitive, since men must be admired in order to be "real," (3) "Be a Sturdy Oak"—show no emotion, be even tempered and steadily reliable, and (4) "Give 'em Hell"—exude an aura of daring and bravado, "go for it." This formulation is useful in marking the parameters of the male sex-role stereotype, but also evidences the limitations of the sex-role paradigm.

The sex-role paradigm is limited because it rarely develops an approach to the study of masculinity that is both comparative and historical, two dimensions that are crucial to the sociologist. We understand that the specific constellation of behaviors, which we might label "masculinity" or "femininity," develop over time and vary across cultures. A sex-role paradigm appears to posit temporally and spatially fixed behaviors as normative; the central concern to the sociologist of gender is the social construction of masculinity and femininity. (In addition, I make a distinction between "sex roles" and "gender," since roles suggest acting by behavioral scripts that can be easily discarded like parts in a play and not a socially constructed identity.) To posit a socially constructed, historically variable notion of gender implies a potential for change that is, I hope, not lost upon students in sociology courses.

In order to examine the male experience, the course was organized to follow men in America over the span of their lives. We began with a discussion of the "crisis" of masculinity, with students exploring the meaning of masculinity in modern society, the various demands made upon them, and the ways in which they believe they are supposed to behave. Having read Bruce Fierstein's affectionately satiric gloss, *Real Men Don't Eat Quiche*, the class posed questions about how one knows what it is to be a "real man" in modern society.

Interestingly, as the class discovered, the 1980s is not the first historical era in which this crisis of masculinity has been evident. The issue was a powerful organizing concept in the late nineteenth century, the crucible in which our contemporary understanding of masculinity and femininity were forged. The words *heterosexual* and *homosexual* came into popular use only after Krafft-Ebing's *Psychopathia Sexualis* was reviewed in the *New York Times* in 1886 (Katz, 1983).[3] Changes in the nature of work following the late-century rapid industrialization, the closing of the frontier, and the perceived "feminization" of American culture (as socialization—home, school, and Sunday school—increasingly became the domain of women) led to a crisis of masculinity. Between 1880 and 1920, manuals advising young men on the perils of femininity and counseling the proper behavior of a real man proliferated. The founding of the Boy Scouts of America in 1910 and the establishment of the YMCA were also deliberate attempts to reverse the enervating trends in American society.[4] To discover another era of the "crisis" of masculinity was intellectually puzzling. In our class discussions, we explored the ways in which the character of work had changed in recent years, as the rise of multinational corporations and the shift to a service economy, themselves phenomena of the globalization of production and the "deindustrialization" of advanced countries, have reshaped both the American economy and the ways in which individuals relate to their work. Again, in the late twentieth century, we experience the closing of the frontier as movements of national liberation and decolonization in the Third World seek to remove those nations from the American orbit. The solution to the earlier frontier closing— expanding geographic boundaries to create new frontiers—has itself reached its limits. And finally, there is renewed concern about the "feminization" of America, a nation grown slothful and indolent as a result of political-economic hegemony, a nation gone "soft" on communism, in which the gains of the women's movement (and, not coincidentally, the rise of a visible gay culture, at least part of which challenges traditional definitions of masculinity) are seen as sapping the masculine strength of the nation.

These large-scale structural shifts—changes in the character of work, the closing of the global frontier, and the rise of a visible women's movement—directly bear on our experience of masculinity and femininity and the constellation of behaviors that we feel is expected of us. This type of analysis may not be of interest to some psychologists of sex roles, but to the sociologist of gender they are of great importance because they link macrolevel, structural shifts to the immediate, microlevel of personal interactions, linking, as C. Wright Mills would have it, history and biography, itself the chief task of the sociological imagination. To the sociologist of gender, then, it is of significance (but not a surprise) that the late nineteenth and late twentieth centuries have been the eras in which we observe profound confusion about the meaning of masculinity, evidenced, in part, by a strident antifeminist backlash (antisuffrage and anti-ERA), a spate of manuals advising how to be a real man, organizations devoted to redesigning the male role (Boy Scouts and National Organization for Changing Men), and, finally, courses on the male experience.

This setting of historical and social contexts was followed by a set of class sessions that followed men developmentally through the life course. Like a photograph album, we paused at various pivotal moments—early childhood socialization, education, peer socialization in adolescence, sports, the military, the construction of sexuality, relationships with women and men, marriage (for straight men) and fatherhood, and aging—to observe how social scientists, historians, and writers and poets had understood those issues. It was also crucial to understand how these experiences vary by class, race, and age, as well as by gender. A final session was devoted to questions of strategies for transforming those components of masculinity that we felt were constraining men's development as healthy and fully responsive people; here we discussed personal transformation and political organization and social movements as different strategies.

Course Organization

If the Sociology of the Male Experience was to avoid adopting a static paradigm, it seemed necessary to address issues of both content and context, that is, to develop an interdisciplinary approach to the social construction of masculinity through history (both personal and structural) and to allow students to interact with the course materials in intellectual as well as personal ways. I sought, therefore, to develop course materials from a wide array of sources and to organize the course so that students would be intellectually challenged without losing personal interest in the subject or, conversely, becoming personally engaged without a loss of intellectual content.

An additional motivation—to use the class as an experiment-in-process, to use class sessions to explore masculinity not only intellectually but in the class experience itself—was important in the development of the class. I saw this class, in part, as an object lesson in concretely confronting those issues about which we would be intellectually concerned—especially issues of competition among men, homophobia, intimacy, nurturance. At every level of course organization, then, these three organizing principles were central: (1) to have course materials engage students both personally and intellectually, (2) to organize assignments and presentations to engage these two levels simultaneously, and (3) to structure each class session as both an intellectual discussion about an issue and an object lesson directly confronting that issue in our own process.

Readings ranged from standard social scientific treatments of various aspects of the social construction of masculinity, to historical studies of the interaction of masculinity and other historical events, to poetry and excerpts from fiction, and interviews with men about the issues we raised. We also used lyrics from popular songs, newspaper articles, diaries, letters, and a large number of printed advertisements in our discussions. (The use of advertisements was a pleasant surprise suggested by the students' reactions to a slide show on media images of men.[5] After viewing the slide show, there was not one class session in which several students did not bring in examples of advertisements in magazines or discuss other ads that had resonated with themes raised in a previous class session or fit with the topic of that week.)

Unfortunately, there is no text or edited collection that both presents this range of topics and uses this broad range of course readings; we were therefore obligated to use a large amount of photocopied materials in the library.[6] Some topics were covered more easily with journal articles and readily available books. Selections, for example, from Freud's *General Introduction to Psychoanalysis* (1968) and "Femininity" from *New Introductory Lectures on Psychoanalysis* (1962) were very useful in explicating one crucial paradigm in development of gender identity; likewise, excerpts from his *Three Contributions to the Theory of Sex* (1964) were valuable points of departure in the discussion of the construction of homosexuality. Studs Terkel's masterful collection of interviews, *Working*, provided a set of narratives that allowed an important set of discussions about men and work; the book's last section, on fathers, was an extremely valuable textual counterpart to sociological analyses of the ways in which class, work, and nurturance are interwoven. Also, Tim Beneke's (1982) fine collection of interviews with men on the subject of rape, *Men on Rape,* presented a provocative beginning for a discussion of the ways in which men come to view women in contemporary society. Finally, Martin Duberman's (1982) essay, "Gay in the Fifties," interweaves diary entries of the author's painful realization of his sexual orientation with a recent commentary on those difficult years, in a way that is simultaneously personal, immediate, and carefully reflective.

Organized as a seminar, class discussion about the issues was a central feature of the course. And yet, even in seminars, students in large public universities do not experience the classroom as a safe place in which to take either personal or intellectual risks. These risks, though, seemed to be both symptomatic of the issues we were raising and essential for the success of the course. Consequently, each class session was organized by the students working together in groups, who decided how best to approach the assigned readings, raise issues with the class to generate and sustain a high-level discussion, and manage the flow of the class session. By inviting them to prepare together, I hoped they would combat the intellectual isolation they frequently described and begin to see one another as colleagues; at the same time, I hoped they would dig more deeply into their chosen areas, and feel increasingly comfortable believing that they had something to contribute.

These concerns were also evident in the class assignments. Students were required to write three papers in the course, as well as prepare and co-lead one class session. The first essay used literature and film as texts, as meditations on the construct of masculinity. Students analyzed one film or recent novel, focusing on how masculinity was understood, whether it was portrayed positively or negatively, how men related to each other and to women. Students chose a range of films from *Mr. Mom* and *Kramer vs. Kramer* to *The Godfather* and *Annie Hall,* and novels such as *Catch-22, Portnoy's Complaint, Rabbit, Run,* and *The Old Man and the Sea.*

The second and largest assignment was an interview. Students were asked to interview two men of different ages, one of them, if possible, their father, the other a friend or contemporary. This assignment allowed students to observe and analyze similarities and differences between generations in the construction of masculinity; the interview schedule included questions about who the men saw as heroes and role models when they were young boys, their relationship to work, to women, to other men, and to the ways they believe they were influenced by social definitions of masculinity. Predictably, about one-half of the students reported very little difference between the two men's construc-tions of masculinity, and came to the conclusion that the two generations had roughly equivalent notions of what constitutes a "real man" while the other half found profound and, they believed, decisive differences between the two men, leading them to conclude that the construction of masculinity was utterly different for men their age than for men their fathers' age. (This tended to fuel their optimism that masculinity is changing dramatically, and that they are not bound by the same constraints as were their parents.)

The cross-generational comparison was also intended to accompany the more personal agenda of raising these issues with their fathers and with male friends, providing a safe environment in which to begin to discuss these issues outside the classroom. Students frequently complain that even when they do get involved with a course, there is no one outside the classroom with whom to discuss it, and that neither family nor friends are really interested in what they are actually learning. Many of the students reported never having had such an intimate discussion with their fathers in their lives, and more than a few were disconcerted that this had been the case. One student was shaken that the father she had idealized had been so uneasy with the interview that he repeatedly failed to keep appointments for it and eventually declined to participate because it made him too uncomfortable to reveal those issues to anyone.

A final writing assignment asked students to respond both personally and intellectually to one class session, a session that they, themselves, did not co-organize and lead. The purpose of this exercise was to allow space for any unfinished or unresolved issues that students perceived and that they had felt uncomfortable about or simply been unable to raise at the time. At the same time, these essays would give the instructor some valuable feedback about which topics and which organizational strategies had been the most successful with the students.[7]

Class Composition

Rutgers University is a hybrid university, in which antithetical educational elements are joined. A large state university in the metropolitan New York/Philadelphia area, Rutgers draws its students from both the middle-class suburbs and from working-class urban centers such as Newark and Trenton. The three undergraduate colleges coexist in a tense symbiosis. Social life appears to revolve around fraternities and sororities. Racial tension is ubiquitous—many white students, for example, indicate that they are afraid to take courses at Livingston College because of the "danger." Fraternities routinely show pornographic films to raise money for parties, and their verbal and occasional physical harassment of women is widely known.[8] All this in the midst of a substantial minority and feminist population.

The time was obviously right for such a class, if judged by the heavy demand. Generally, seminars are limited to 25 students, but by the end of the first day of registration, 36 students had signed up for the course. Of these, 10 were men and 26 were women. While on the surface this might seem like a disproportionately low number of men, it actually is somewhat higher than expected. (An adage, mentioned to me by a colleague when I described the course, has it that courses on the sociology of women will draw 95% women and courses in the sociology of men will draw 90% women. Obviously, "real men" don't study the sociology of gender!) Of the men, 4 were black, 1 was Hispanic, and 5 were white; of the women, 5 were black and 21 were white. Almost half were sociology majors, almost all were juniors or seniors. It was clear at the outset that three subtexts to our discussions would be the different sets of experiences and expectations of white and nonwhite students, of male and female students, and of straight and gay students. For example, the study group that ran the class discussion on homophobia was composed entirely of black men and women (whose sexual orientations were unknown, although many of the women mentioned their boyfriends). When the class commented on this, there followed an exciting discussion of the similarities and differences of oppression. The black women, especially, said they felt they understood how homophobia affected gay people and felt drawn to the topic, even though they were aware of significant differences between racism and heterosexism.

The variations in men's experiences—by race, ethnicity, age, class, and sexual orientation—became one of the most significant subtexts to each class discussion. As these differences became more evident, our capacity to make sweeping sociological generalizations diminished, but our understanding of diversity correspondingly increased. For example, men of color demurred from a glib condemnation of all "macho" behavior that was offered by one white male student and indicated the ways in which certain behaviors could be seen as powerful assertions of pride and identity within a racist society. (These men also suggested a goal of developing a "nonsexist machismo" that could challenge racist emasculation but not at women's expense.)

Another example of variation was in the relationship between class background and role modeling. Middle-class students assumed that their fathers viewed themselves as role models for their sons, hoping their sons would see their behaviors and life choices as exemplary, worthy of emulation. These middle-class students were surprised when students of working-class backgrounds disagreed and found support in Studs Terkel's interviews. "I told my sons," one steelworker told Terkel, "If you ever wind up in that steel mill like me, I'm gonna hit you right over the head. Don't be foolish. Get yourself a schooling. Stay out of the steel mill or you'll wind up the same way I did" (Terkel, 1977, p. 55). Such a statement provides concrete expression of Sennett and Cobb's (1975, p. 156) observation that

> working class fathers . . . see the whole point of sacrificing for their children to be that the children will become unlike themselves; through education and the right kind of peer associations, the kids will learn the arts of rational control and acquire the power to make wide choices which in sum should make the kids better armed, less vulnerable in coping with the world than their fathers are. . . . To call the pressure working-class fathers put on their kids "authoritarian" is misleading in that the father doesn't ask the child to take the parents' lives as a model but as a warning.

Reactions from Class, Campus, and Community

Both informally during the term and following the course, and in formal course evaluations, the students registered their intellectual and personal excitement with this course. Both male and female students noted the immediate relevance of the topics in the course to their daily lives, and reported that the issues raised in class sessions and in the readings had provoked many conversations and arguments with their friends and family. One student jokingly complained that the course had "made it impossible to read a book, see a movie, or look at a magazine without thinking about how it portrays men and gives subtle messages about appropriate masculine behavior." More than a few students indicated that this term was the first in which they discussed what happened in the class with their friends and families. One female student remarked that many of the women in her sorority had taken to reading the assigned readings together (although only she was in the class) and talking about them at dinner the evening before the class met. (This student felt, as a result, that she had already generated some useful information to share.)

Students also noted that the organization of the class, as well as its content, facilitated a level of discussion they had rarely, if ever, experienced. Participation was extensive, with almost every student joining in the discussion in each class session. (In other seminars, I have often found that a central organizational task is to invite and sustain a discussion, encouraging students to speak. Here I was more challenged to moderate the participation, to keep the conversation flowing, and to insure that every one who wanted to speak was given a chance. In fact, each group of class facilitators had to develop either a mental or a written "waiting list" of students who wanted to participate.) For several reasons, some idiosyncratic and others structural, the level of discussion in the class was also highly personal, as students took significant risks in describing their beliefs, attitudes, and behaviors and attempting to understand the origins of them. This springs partially from the fact that this was the first time the course had been offered anywhere in New Jersey; in addition, the students realized they were part of an experiment, so the future of the course was, to some degree, contingent on their efforts in this class. Few students were already friendly beforehand, although many had one friend in the class, which may have afforded a supportive blend of an ally in the midst of relative strangers and further facilitated the discussion. A number commented that the personal nature of discussion reduced their anxieties about being "right" or "smart" when they spoke, as if to speak personally about these issues made each participant equal, and also equally expert on the one topic each knew the most about: himself or herself.

This personal risk-taking in class discussions, however, has another, less copesetic side to it. Class discussions tended to overemphasize the personal at the expense of a serious intellectual grappling with theoretical issues. As long as students remained on the personal risk-taking ground of self-revelation, they avoided the equally risky realm of intellectual speculation. One student mentioned to me that as long as the conversation remained personal "no one will be able to know if I'm smart or not." At times, the personal nature of the discussion resulted in a type of antiintellectual relativism; individual biographies were recounted without any attempts at building theoretical linkages among them. Often, students appear "allergic" to sociological reasoning, constructing an evaluation of an empirical statement of social trends from "my own personal opinion" or "I know someone who isn't like that" as if their statements, with their N's of 1, negate empirical regularities. This makes teaching sociology challenging, however, and the task I set for myself was to bring together the various personal narratives into some tentative sociological observations, generalizations into which they could then plug other experiences. (I believe that my most frequent linguistic construction during class discussion was "What we all seem to be saying here is . . ." or "It seems, then, from these comments, that the following is true . . .") Students often resisted my efforts at pushing sociological generalizations, preferring to stay on apparently safer ground of existentially unique personal narrative.

Reactions to the class around campus ranged from support and excitement to bemused tolerance to derisive laughter and, in some cases, anger. Students reported that the course was not taken seriously by other students, seen as an easy course—a "gut"—without intellectual rigor. More than that, though, students reported that both other students and their families believed that a course on masculinity was, by definition, devoid of intellectual content; no matter what happened in class, there was nothing to talk about in the first place. Campus reaction may be based, in part, on the intellectual scorn that is reserved for social sciences in general, and sociology in particular, at many colleges and universities across the country. But I think that Sociology of the Male Experience came in for a greater share of suspicion and derision, even more perhaps than did courses in women's studies. One student mentioned that his fraternity brothers were quite suspicious of the course and hoped that he wouldn't become either a "libber lover" or a "faggot." Another student told me that his friends had commented angrily that the course was probably a course "for fags taught by a fag." This overtly homophobic response derives, in part, from a perceived "breaking ranks" with other men, refusing to silently abide by and challenging behaviors seen as sexist, racist, and homophobic. A course on men—taught from within an antisexist, profeminist perspective— will incite greater negative response than will other courses.[9] In addition, the instructor's visibility on campus, as a speaker at rallies and panel discussions on rape, violence against women, and developing new roles for men, probably increased the perception of breaking the male "code of silence" and exacerbated the negative response.

Students reported less anger but a more puzzled interest among their families. The students' families became intimately involved in the course because the students interviewed their fathers (or another close older relative). Some students reported that their families questioned the intellectual value of a course on men—"You mean that's what they're teaching you at college? That's what we're paying good money for?" one father is reported to have commented—while other students indicated that their parents simply didn't understand the value of such a course. A few students, however, found surprising support and encouragement from their families and friends. "I wish I had a course like that when I was in college," one father told his daughter, while another father confided that he "always knew that I should have gone to college because the things that you get to study are so interesting." One woman even invited her father to attend a class to see for himself what he was missing.

The reaction to the course outside the campus, both from colleagues who work on issues related to the sociology of gender and from the larger community, was surprisingly positive. (This was especially gratifying since the reaction from many colleagues who do not work in the field was, as I mentioned earlier, less than enthusiastic and because the immediate campus community had also manifested such strongly mixed reactions.) The growing number of courses in men's studies put me in touch with a handful of academics who have been developing such courses in many different disciplines.

After the campus newspaper ran two articles about the course, the Office of Public Information at Rutgers requested some course materials, which they forwarded to newspapers around the state. Articles about the course appeared in several statewide newspapers, which then spawned several articles in national magazines and news-papers. I was also interviewed by a major New York City radio station talk show. This unexpected publicity rippled further, with invitations to speak about the course and about "changing definitions of masculinity" at organizations as diverse as a local Rotary Club luncheon and the 92nd Street Y's (in New York City) evening lecture series for singles. (That the course was bathed in a media spotlight also, I imagine, increased the students' commitment to their work in the course.) While such national media attention is unlikely to be repeated for this particular course, it does indicate a growing interest in the larger community in men's issues, changing definitions of masculinity, and men's reactions to the women's movement.

Toward a Sociology of Men:
A Teaching and Research Agenda

The recent development of subfields in the sociology of gender in general and the sociology of women in particular has raised important questions for social scientists concerning the social construction of masculinity. In both preparing for and teaching this course on the sociology of the male experience, the need for further work in the area became increasingly evident. Just as a growing number of men have begun to challenge a social order based on systematic discrimination against women, a growing number of social scientists have begun to examine masculinity as a component of the sociology of gender and provide intellectual support for our colleagues who have been working in the area of gender. As it appears now, the sociology of men has four important and interrelated research and teaching tasks before it.

First, the content of the subdiscipline needs to be defined carefully so that new areas of research and teaching are available. Our intellectual net needs to be cast wide and far, and whole new areas need to be incorporated. For example, as feminist scholarship has indicated, the sociology of men permits a reexamination of recent and classic works of literature in order to develop how these works construct and organize the concept of masculinity, how they suggest the ways in which men relate to each other, to women, to a larger society, to themselves. Or, as another example, historical events and documents can be examined, not only for what they can tell us about "great men" and the events of which they were a part but about the everyday life experiences of men at other times, which can provide clues about how masculinity has changed and how it has remained the same. Qualitative and quantitative data from the social sciences will also generate new insights into the contemporary construction of masculinity.

Second, not only does the sociology of men press us to go beyond the confines of sex-role research for the sources we will use to understand gender, but it also demands that we will bring a wide set of methodological concerns to our work. I have argued that the sociology of gender must be historical and comparative, capable of understanding change over time and variation from one society to another that allows the theoretical possibility of further change and a fluidity in social constructions. The expansion of our data implies a wider assortment of methods. For example, various styles of literary criticism might be appropriate to understand literary or cinematic texts, while archival historical methods might be appropriate to discuss diaries, letters, and other historical records. Similarly, cross-cultural anthropological methods can provide needed comparative information about contemporaneous cultures. And, of course, the methods of the social sciences, both qualitative (depth interviews, participant observation) and quantitative (survey research, demographic methods), will remain especially useful. This methodological expansion of the range of techniques by which we come to understand masculinity has the additional advantage of viewing both personal narratives (historical records, cultural descriptions, interview reports, semiotics) with analytic methods, so that in our research we use both personal and analytic tools.

Third, the combination of personal and analytic will continue to remain a central feature of our teaching practice as well. The paucity of texts in the sociology of masculinity is matched only by the enormous volume of potential texts. We need, however, to generate them ourselves because the field is both so young and has gone so long ignored. The assignments in this course required the generation of texts; the analysis of the novel or film required the transformation of an "unrelated" text into a deliberation on the question of masculinity, while depth interviews with students' fathers and friends generated a text of 36 interviews. The combination of personal and analytic materials within the teaching of the course itself will permit the course to be more inviting (or, conversely, less threatening) to male students, so that the level of male involvement will increase, and the racial and ethnic composition of the students remains varied.

Finally, the sociology of men must remain politically sensitive to, and supportive of, the larger intellectual and political project of the sociology of women. It was, after all, academic women who first identified gender and femininity as areas of intellectual urgency and significance (as the women's and gay movements made the study of sexuality a vital issue also). The sociology of men is a way for sociologists to take seriously the concerns raised by these movements and these colleagues, to understand that the sociology of gender and the sociology of the family are no longer the "ladies' auxiliary" of the discipline, but raise issues that remain at the center of sociological inquiry. The sociology of men must acknowledge feminist scholarship's pioneering work, and remain sensitive to the leading role academic feminists have taken around the study of gender. The sociology of men may in fact be the "gentlemen's auxiliary" to women's studies, and in that sense, would never want to push to the background the dominant force that has placed the study of gender squarely at the center of academic inquiry.

Postscript

I offered Sociology of the Male Experience in Spring 1986 and again in Spring 1987. Now part of the regular curriculum, the course size has almost doubled each time I have taught it, from 36 in 1985 to 65 in 1986 to more than 120 in 1987. Each time, about 25% of the students were male. Earlier suspicions that were aroused in the academic community prior to the first time the course was offered have now subsided, and colleagues and the institution have been encouraging and supportive.

These suspicions have now surfaced among the national media, however. The course became the subject of articles in major newspapers and magazines, among them the *Wall Street Journal, Newsweek,* the *London Times,* and *Vogue.* A wire story on the class through the Associated Press led to articles in hundreds of newspapers across the country. In addition, several radio interviews and a segment on the *Today Show* increased our national visibility. The criticisms raised in a few of these features echoed earlier fears voiced among my colleagues and university administrators, most especially that the course was a reaction against the women's movement and against women's studies and that there would be no intellectual content to the course. In most cases, these initial concerns were allayed after reporters attended the class and interviewed the students, as well as discussed with me the intellectual perspective that the course presents. As courses about men continue to grow—courses in which masculinity is taken as the analytic subject rather than assumed as normative and unexamined—the agenda for men's studies will become more refined and elaborate. But one hopes that it will not not be forgotten that these courses owe their original inspiration and their continuing accountability to programs in women's studies and to feminist scholarship in general.

NOTES

1. Naturally, raising the issue of masculinity requires raising the issue of femininity. Yet a course devoted to masculinity deserves a place in a sociology curriculum, because it cannot simply be incorporated into a course on gender, although the rationale for a course on men would be different from the rationale for a course on women. Most important is the treatment of men as men and not in some other category. I suppose that this sounds like an analogue to a course on "the sociology of the white eperience." However absurd this might sound on the surface, I think it actually would be fascinating to examine how racism structures the experience of white people as white people.

2. See, for example, Brannon and David (1976), Constantinople (1979), Filene (1975), Grady, Brannon, and Pleck (1979), Pleck (1974, 1976, 1981), Pleck and Brannon (1978).

3. I am grateful to Jonathan Katz for permission to cite this research.

4. See, for example, Douglas (1977), Dubbert (1979), Macleod (1983) Pugh. Also see my review of Macleod and Pugh in the *Village Voice* (Literary Supplement), October 1984.

5. "Stale Roles and Tight Buns: Advertising's Image of Men" is available from OASIS, 33 Richdale Ave., Cambridge, MA 02140.

6. See Franklin (1984) for the most contemporary evaluation in a textbook.

7. Another professor who teaches courses on men asked his students to write long letters to their fathers as a vehicle for expressing their feelings and attempting to understand their fathers' experiences.

8. Poet and essayist Adrienne Rich (1979), for example, noted how women students at Rutgers, specifically, "traversing a street lined with fraternity houses . . . must run a gauntlet of male commentary and verbal abuse" (p. 242).

9. A course, for instance, on the sociology of sport dealt only with men, but was met with much praise from the same sources.

REFERENCES

Beneke, T. (1982). *Men on rape*. New York: St. Martin's.
Brannon, R., & David, D. (1976). *The forty-nine percent majority: The male sex-role*. Reading, MA: Addison-Wesley.
Constantinople, A. (1979). Sex-role acquisition: In search of the elephant. *Sex Roles, 5*.
Douglas, A. (1977). *The feminization of American culture*. New York: Knopf.
Dubbert, J. (1979). *A man's place*. Englewood Cliffs, NJ: Prentice-Hall.
Duberman, M. (1982). Gay in the 50's. *Salmagundi, 58-59*.
Fierstein, B. (1982). *Real men don't eat quiche*. New York: Pocket Books.
Filene, B. (1975). *Him/her/self: Sex roles in modern America*. Orlando, FL: Harcourt Brace Jovanovich.

Franklin, C. (1984). *The changing definition of masculinity.* New York: Plenum.

Freud, S. (1962). *New introductory lectures in psychoanalysis.* New York: Norton.

Freud, S. (1964). Three contributions to the theory of sex. In S. Freud, *General writings.* New York: Modern Library.

Freud, S. (1968). *A general introduction to psychoanalysis.* New York: Norton.

Grady, H., Brannon, R., & Pleck, J. (1979). *The male sex-role: An annotated bibliography.* Rockville, MD: National Institute of Mental Health.

Katz, J. (1983, May). *The invention of heterosexuality.* Paper presented at the New York Institute for the Humanities seminar on Sexuality and the Consumer Culture.

Kimmel, M. (1987). The cult of masculinity: American social character and the legacy of the cowboy. In M. Kaufman (ed.), *Beyond Patriarchy.* Toronto: Oxford University Press.

Macleod, D. (1983). *Building character in the American boy.* Madison: University of Wisconsin Press.

Pleck, J. (1974, April). My male sex-role—and ours. *WIN Magazine.*

Pleck, J. (1976). The male sex role: Definitions, problems, and sources of change. *Journal of Social Issues, 32*(3).

Pleck, J., & Brannon, R. (1978). Male roles and the male experience. *Journal of Social Issues, 34*(1).

Pugh, D. (1984). *Sons of liberty: The masculine mind in 19th century America.* Westport, CT: Greenwood.

Rich, A. (1979). *Of lies, secrets, and silence.* New York: Norton.

Sennett, R., & Cobb, J. (1975). *The hidden injuries of class.* New York: Random House.

Turkel, S. (1977). *Working.* New York: Pantheon.

19

The Men's Movement

An Exploratory Empirical Investigation

MICHAEL SHIFFMAN

Struggles for women's equality in the United States have included male activists from the very start. About one-third of the signatories at the 1848 Seneca Falls convention were men.[1] But these profeminist men have always been a small minority of the male population. It is only since the most recent wave of the women's movement that men have struggled independently, both in support of women's rights and for alternative forms of masculinity, in such a way as to constitute a social movement. And that social movement is the men's movement.

As the historical heir of the women's and gay liberation movements, the men's movement inherited various political and organizational concerns in addition to those specific to the conditions of men's lives and their own experience of themselves as men. The central issues of the women's movement have been adopted politically by segments of the men's movement. The current feminist agenda addressing reproductive rights (including the right of lesbians to bear children), violence against women, comparable worth, and gender relations has been generally adopted as fundamental movement concerns. As in the women's movement, there is a diversity of concern about the issues as well as differences on matters of strategy and tactics. Take the current debate on pornography as an example. While neither male nor female feminists

AUTHOR'S NOTE: An earlier version of this chapter was presented at the American Sociological Association annual meetings in Washington, D.C., 1985. I am grateful to Harry Brod, Michael Kimmel, Anne Peplau, Joseph Pleck, and Ralph Turner for their comments on an earlier draft. Melvin Oliver was especially helpful and supportive during the initial data analysis and final preparation. I would especially like to thank Hazel Johnson and Ella Kelly for their brutal but caring readings of the final draft.

have organized support for the production and distribution of pornography, there has been substantial debate about its social significance and the ways feminists might most appropriately express their concern. The debate in the men's movement has paralleled that of the women's movement precisely because of a shared fundamental critique.

The men's movement also adopted the women's movement's commitment to consciousness raising. This has taken hold structurally through the adoption of consciousness raising (CR) and men's support groups as a principal and often an initial mode of participation. CR groups are used by women and men to share experience and, in the process, to develop vocabularies by which to understand and express that experience. The CR process also links those experiences to the larger issues of sexism and heterosexism (and in some cases racism), thereby explicating the relations of domination that frame their experience of themselves as gendered persons while validating that experience as a legitimate source of social knowledge. CR groups have been especially helpful to men in developing intimacy with other men by providing a safe place where they can explore feelings and an environment where they can strive to shed the competitive male model.

The men's movement also has adopted largely what has been referred to as "feminist process." Feminist process is a way by which group members can engage in purposive activities while remaining connected to their feelings about how those activities are proceeding. Most important, it legitimates participants' experience of the process as a significant consideration in the completion of the tasks. A number of men's movement organizations use adapted versions of feminist process as the means by which they conduct their regular business meetings.[2]

A number of issues initially raised by the gay liberation movement are also of primary concern in the men's movement. Heterosexism, homophobia, gay rights (including the right of gay men to parent children), and more recently the disease, AIDS (acquired immunodeficiency syndrome), are among those spotlighted by segments of the movement. More general concerns of power and domination, discrimination and psychological violence are also articulated.

Additionally, the men's movement has raised a number of issues emerging directly from men's daily lives and from their experiences of themselves as men. Fathering, men's health, aging, gender roles, and job satisfaction are but a few. While many movement activists recognize that all of the issues raised by both the women's and gay movements are directly relevant to men's experience in some ways, the men's movement is still too young to address broadly more than the most central issues of concern.

This chapter will characterize the men's movement as a social movement and examine empirically the connection to its social movement parentage through attitudinal, demographic, and networking information about participants. It begins to fill a void in the literature by providing systematic empirical data about movement participants.

Movement Structure and Goals

The men's movement can be described structurally as consisting of a national profeminist organization, a number of men's centers, networks of activists engaging issues of violence against women, networks of academics working on issues of masculinity, men's support groups, an annual national conference on men and masculinity, and various local and regional events.

The National Organization for Changing Men (NOCM) is a nationwide organization consisting of local chapters, regional affiliate groups, and members at large.[3] NOCM identifies itself as profeminist, gay affirmative, and male supportive.[4] NOCM coordinates a number of issue-oriented task groups (see Note 21), maintains an archive of men's movement materials, and currently hosts an annual national conference on men and masculinity.

NOCM has made one of its most significant contributions through the development of its men's studies task group. The task group, founded in 1983, provides a network of over 100 academics, who share resources and are developing men's studies as a formal academic area.[5] It is preparing currently for the formation of a national men's studies association.

The men's centers tend to identify themselves principally as male supportive. These centers provide a variety of services including coordinating men's support groups, counseling, community education, and providing a supportive atmosphere for men to share experiences, feelings, and ideas.[6] They serve as one of the front lines of the men's movement by having contact with the widest variety of men. At the Tenth National Conference on Men and Masculinity in St. Louis in 1985, several activists from one of the southern states told me that while their activist core was sympathetic to NOCM's profeminist and gay affirmative principles, they would be unable to affiliate formally for fear they would scare off a number of the men who attend their programs and use their services. Their experience was that only after several months of contact with their organization did some men become more open toward feminism and begin to address issues of homophobia and gay rights.

The men's alternatives to violence network consists of individuals and local groups providing community education on rape prevention and domestic violence.[7] Many of these organizations are decisively profeminist in both their approach to the issues and their public presentations, often networking extensively with battered women's shelters.

In addition to the above organizational forms there are state and regional men's gatherings and a national conference on men and masculinity (which is sponsored currently by NOCM). The national conferences on men and masculinity are structured similarly to academic conferences, with planned panels, keynote speakers, presentations, and workshops on recent movement developments and related social science findings. The first national conference took place in 1975 at the University of Tennessee at Knoxville, and as of 1986 there had been 10 others. Gatherings tend to be regional or local in scope, more informal, organized with both structured and spontaneously emerging workshops focusing on personal growth and networking issues, and frequently serving as an introductory experience to the movement itself. Gross, Smith, and Wallston (1983) traced the first regional gatherings back as early as 1973. While conferences also include personal growth and networking concerns, they tend to emphasize broader concerns more than they do gatherings.

Given the above description, Gerlach and Hine's (1970) characterization of social movements as segmented, networked, cellular, and without a single center of authority is a useful way to understand the organization of the men's movement. Characterizing social movements in terms of their overall structural organization, they write:

> A social, political or religious movement is characterized by (a) segmented, organizational units linked together into a reticulate network by various personal, organizational, and ideological ties; (b) face-to-face recruitment along lines of pre-existing significant social relationships of positive effect; (c) personal commitment on the part of most, if not all, participants resulting from an identity-altering experience, a bridge-burning act or both; (d) an ideology which provides the basis for overall unity as well as segmentary diversity, which exploits the motive power of an ideal-real gap, and which constitutes a comprehensive conceptual framework by means of which events are interpreted and the opposition defined; (e) the perception of opposition from the established order within which the movement is spreading. (p. 199)

Other social movement theorists typically have classified social movements according to the nature of their goals into two, often considered mutually exclusive, categories: those that seek social structural change (instrumental or purposive movements), and those that seek personal transformation (expressive or solidarity movements). Movements oriented toward social structural change tend to seek revolutionary or reformist transformation of either specific social institutions or the structure of social formations.[8] Movements oriented toward personal transformation tend to seek worldly remedies for personal problems, alternatives for self-improvement, or spiritual salvation.[9]

Men's movement goals are oriented toward both personal transformation *and* structural change, and reject the traditional formulation of their separation. Like the women's movement, the men's movement challenges the separation of personal experience from conventional notions of politics. It redefines the personal *as* political and seeks to draw closer connections between the macropolitical sphere and personal life. Given that movements with instrumental goals oriented toward structural changes tend toward organizational forms with at least some degree of centralized structure, we might speculate that the absence of such structure in the men's movement may be the product of the movement's youthfulness and lack of recognized social or legal victories. Even self-help groups whose goals are oriented solely toward personal transformation, but which have existed much longer, have more substantially developed centralized structures.[10]

Movement Participants

Little systematic information is available about men's movement participants. An early paper written during the movement's gestation period depicts the men's movement as the white, middle-class progeny of the women's and lesbian/gay liberation movements (Snodgrass, 1975). Snodgrass argued that if the movement failed to solidify organic ties to its movement parentage, it would develop in isolation and become more and more prone to internal splits and schisms. Gross et al. (1983) observe that the men's movement must satisfy both instrumental and expressive needs in order for it to survive and grow. Citing a survey completed by a small sample (about 13%) of participants at the 1979 National Conference on Men and Masculinity, Gross et al. found that 87% of the respondents had participated in small men's support groups and that 64% indicated that they participated for both personal *and* political reasons. The researchers report, "The typical participant in the men's movement is a youngish, college educated, middle class, straight, white male who is sympathetic to feminist demands to eliminate male dominance" (pp. 75-76). Although this study described many salient features of the movement and provided the first data on participants' goals and motivations, more systematic empirical research is needed. Gross et al. (p. 80) conclude that the "feminist men's movement continues to exist but fails to achieve the impact of a mass movement. As long as support groups and national meetings continue to satisfy some personal needs, the movement is likely to continue, but until one or more national organizations or communications networks are effectively developed, the movement is unlikely to grow in numbers or influence."[11]

Both Snodgrass and Gross et al. address the political, ideological, and structural relations among the men's, women's, and gay movements, and both articles note that the men's movement must satisfy instrumental as well as expressive needs. Neither work presents demographic information describing movement participants nor analyzes participants' attitudes on substantive issues. If the men's movement constitutes one historical outgrowth of the women's and gay movements, we would expect movement participants to express relatively high levels of agreement on attitudinal issues central to feminist and gay liberation concerns. Furthermore, we would also expect significant levels of participation in women's and gay organizations.

If movement survival is predicated on satisfying both expressive and instrumental concerns, we would expect widespread CR group participation, and high levels of movement participation, movement organization membership, or both. On the one hand, if the movement's slow rate of growth is a consequence of not only "the many apolitical participants and the lack of short-range instrumental activities but of the supportive function of the small groups,"[12] as suggested by Gross et al. (p. 79), we would expect CR group membership to be negatively correlated with public-sphere political participation. On the other hand, if men's movement participants are heirs to the feminist women's movement and adopt the proposition that the "personal is political," we would expect both popular CR group membership and high levels of participation in movement events.[13]

A Pilot Study

A questionnaire was distributed at the Seventh Annual California Men's Gathering in Oak Glen, September 1984.[14] The Gathering was attended by 219 men and 4 women from throughout California, including about a dozen men from Oregon and Arizona. A total of 126 completed instruments (57% response), which contained 116 variables, were obtained. A cover letter indicated that the surveys were to be used to document the Gathering and that the results would be passed on to the National Organization for Changing Men. The survey solicited information in five main areas: (a) demographics, (b) consciousness raising/support group history, (c) conference attendance and networking, (d) organizational membership and participation in feminist women's, gay, and men's movements, and (e) attitudes on 16 issues stemming from women's, men's, and gay liberation movement concerns.

Demographics

Respondents' ages ranged from 19 to 75, with a median age of 35. While 25% were under 30, another 27% were over 43. In 1983 the median age for white men in the United States was 31.8 years, and while comparable figures for California were not readily available, historically they have been somewhat higher than the national average (U.S. Bureau of the Census, 1985, pp. 27, 29). These findings contradict the notion that participants were young. With only 25% of the respondents under 30, 75% were in their mid-teens or older during the rise and consolidation of the women's and gay liberation movements of the 1960s and 1970s. This might be suggestive of a generational effect indicating that Gathering participants may have had some significant exposure to the social movements of the 60s and 70s.

The evidence clearly supports the claim that the men's movement currently lacks significant numbers of minority men. Over 90% of the respondents were white, with about 2% each being Black, Asian, Hispanic, and Native Americans.

The sexual orientation composition was significantly different from the general population. Instead of heterosexual men being a clear majority, gay men constituted nearly half of the respondents and bisexual men accounted for nearly 20%. These findings qualify the Gross et al. data that "a significant minority have been gay" (p. 76), and may indicate that the movement was addressing issues relevant to gay and bisexual men's lives. It could also indicate that the Gathering was an emotionally safe place for men to share a common experience regardless of their sexual orientation. Two other factors may have contributed to the larger percentage of gay respondents in this sample. First, about a quarter of the participants were from San Francisco, Berkeley, or Oakland—geographic areas with large gay and bisexual populations.[15] Second, there were about 15 men from a gay men's conference held the preceding week. Discussions with participants and movement activists indicate that movement participation is related to a desire to work with men on a variety of issues without respect to their sexual orientation, occupation, or class background.

The consistent claim that participants are well educated was clearly substantiated by this study. A total of 98% of the respondents had attended some college, 31% had received bachelor's degrees, and 38% held postgraduate degrees. This is well beyond the national averages of 32% having completed some college and 16% having completed four or more years. Even though Californians' college attendance is higher than the national average, 42% complete some college and only 19.6% complete four or more years (U.S. Bureau of the Census, 1985, p. 135). Thus our respondents' college attendance was substantially higher than the average for either the state or the nation.

However, while education was found to be associated with income (r = .25),[16] 58% of the respondents earned $18,000 or less annually, and only 15% earned more than $24,000 annually. The national mean income for single white males was $23,000 in 1982 (U.S. Bureau of the Census, 1985, p. 448). The national median income for householders who have completed some college was $24,606, and for those who completed four or more years of college the median income was $34,709 (U.S. Bureau of the Census, 1985, p. 443). Thus it is evident that the respondents' incomes were substantially lower than the national averages, especially considering their educational attainment. Given the tendency for Californians' incomes to be higher than the national averages,[17] these national comparisons may be seen in an even more conservative light. Moreover, because income is not simply a consequence of one's education, these findings need to be placed in the context of the respondents' occupations in order to draw even tentative inferences concerning participants' class composition.

No occupational data have been reported previously on men's movement participants.[18] This study found respondents' occupations to range from temporary clerical workers to congressional aides. Because of the vagueness of 32% of the occupational titles, it was not possible to categorize all of the respondents reliably; however, 42% of the responses could be categorized as professional positions (for example, attorney, pharmacist, psychologist, or counselor), and 26% could be identified as working-class positions (for example, gardener, machinist, clerical worker).

These data suggest that respondents are a well-educated yet underpaid population with a strong professional presence, tending to indicate that the movement has a middle-class base. We might expect to find high educational attainment with a low income distribution among an activist population that defers income to hours volunteered in community projects, but it is not yet clear that this is such a population. Moreover, with at least a 26% working-class presence, in addition to the relatively low income distribution, a more detailed investigation of work-related issues may yield some very interesting results.

Consciousness Raising/Support Group History

Gross et al. (1983) note that the overwhelming majority of their respondents were members of men's support groups. The present study supported the Gross et al. data in finding that 82% of the respondents had been support group members, 55% had been in more than one group, and 35% were current members. Support group participation did not vary along the lines of sexual orientation. However, we found a tendency for sexual-orientation composition to change toward increased integration for those who participated in more than one support group. Cross-tabulations between respondents' sexual orientations and the composition of their first and last support groups were significant. For respondents participating in more than one support group, three general tendencies were found:

(1) For gay men, 32% of those whose first support group was exclusively gay changed to mixed groups.
(2) For heterosexual men, 75% of those whose first support group was exclusively heterosexual changed to mixed support groups.
(3) For bisexual men, all of those initially in heterosexual groups changed to mixed groups, while 36% of those initially in mixed groups changed to exclusively heterosexual groups.

These findings are significant in light of the important role support groups play in the men's movement. While they demonstrate widespread CR group participation, they also indicate a tendency toward greater integration of gay, heterosexual, and bisexual men within the movement.

State Gathering Attendance and Networking

There is some debate as to whether state and regional gatherings aid movement growth. Some movement activists argue that attendance at national conferences and state or regional gatherings serves to satisfy participants' needs for accomplishing instrumental goals. In conjunction with support group satisfaction of expressive needs, these events are thought to hinder movement growth. Others have characterized the same events as rejuvenating and energizing activists, sustaining the motivation needed for local organizing. We found that 43% of the respondents attended the preceding Gathering in 1983, while 27% and 12% were found to have attended the 1982 and 1981 Gatherings, respectively. Throughout this time period, Gathering size has remained about the same. If the Gathering is a significant point of entry to the movement in California, we would have expected a declining rate of return over time, with many of those who attend regularly to be part of the movement's committed activist core. Thus return rates may be misleading if used as an index of movement growth. Discussions with longstanding movement activists, in addition to our own data, suggest that somewhere between one-third and one-half of the current participants have not attended a previous Gathering and are very probably new to the movement. Given that the movement itself has been growing, as well as attracting increasing amounts of publicity over the past three years,[19] the presence of about 50% first-timers could be seen as a positive trend.

Related to Gathering attendance is the notion of networking. Gross et al. note that both a national organization and communication networks are necessary for movement growth. We found that over 90% of our respondents first learned about the men's movement either from friends or an organization (70% and 22%, respectively). This was not the case for the Seventh Gathering, however, where about 40% of our respondents were notified by friends, another 40% by direct mail from the planning committee, and about 17% by related organizations. Although unable to address multiple forms of notification, these findings tentatively indicate that friendship networks are the foremost means by which men are introduced to the movement, while institutional means of notification reached more than half of the participants at this regional Gathering. This could indicate that movement organization and organizational networking gradually replace word of mouth and interpersonal networks as the means through which participants are notified about movement events. In that discovering a social movement is different from being notified about a specific movement event, and because the percentage of those who found out about the Gathering from friends roughly corresponds to that of new participants, these data may be essentially useful in directing our attention to networking concerns in future research.[20]

Organizational Membership
and Participation

If Gross et al.'s contention that men's support group participation hinders public-sphere political participation is correct, we would expect to find support group membership to be negatively correlated with membership in men's, women's, and gay organizations. In fact our analysis revealed the opposite to be true. First, respondents were found to participate in men's, women's, and gay organizations (see Table 19.1). Membership in men's movement organizations was found to be highly correlated with membership in women's organizations (r = .42), but not with gay organizations. Second, support group membership was found to be significantly correlated with participation in both men's and women's organizations (r = .30 and r = .25, respectively). These findings indicate that our respondents are members and active participants in both women's and gay organizations. Discovering that 35% and 40% of the respondents are members of women's and gay organizations, respectively, alleviates the overarching concern that ideological separation from feminist women and isolation from sexual minorities will lead to movement decline.

Attitudinal Analysis

Some concern has been expressed that the presence of gay, bisexual, and heterosexual men in a single movement could lead potentially to ideological schisms along sexual orientation lines. Because of this concern, 16 attitudinal items were included to provide preliminary assessments of respondents' "degree of personal concern" for various women's, men's, and gay liberation movement issues. The 16 items also represent NOCM's national task groups, thereby providing both a measure of the respondents' degree of concern on the issues as well as a surrogate evaluative indicator of NOCM's representation of local movement participants concerns.[21] The issues were coded on a five-point Likert scale rated from "1 = low concern" to "5 = great concern." For subsequent analyses the 16 attitude items were recoded to a three-point scale (see Table 19.2).

The respondents demonstrated high levels of personal concern on each of the 16 issues. More than 65% of the respondents expressed greatest concern regarding gender roles, men's support groups, homophobia, and gay rights. More than half of the respondents expressed similarly pronounced concern with job satisfaction, sexual and domestic violence, racism, pornography, and the quality of male-female relations.

A factor analysis was performed that identified three dimensions along these 16 attitudinal items: Dominance, Gender, and Family (see Table 19.3). These dimensions reflect elements of the three central areas of inquiry and political struggle for both the women's and gay liberation movements.

TABLE 19.1

Organizational Participation (in percentages)

Mode of Participation	Men's Movement (N = 65; 51%)	Women's Movement (N = 44; 35%)	Gay Movement (N = 51; 40%)
Paid member only	27	39	37
Conference planning	47	25	35
Committee work	65	48	49
Public speaking	34	30	29
Write articles	31	30	33
Cultural work	20	14	43
Child care	32	20	6
Task groups	31	32	27
Attended public events	60	45	75
Attended demonstrations	62	55	57

NOTE: Within-category percentages are reported in terms of their frequency of occurrence within each movement. For example, 51% of the respondents reported membership in one or more men's movement organizations, of which 27% are paid members only.

Dominance and Gender were found to be strongly correlated with sexual orientation ($r = .49$ and $r = -.33$, respectively), while, interestingly enough, Family was not ($r = .03/.70$). Cross-tabulations were formulated between sexual orientation and the variables constituting Dominance and Gender to examine more closely their interactions. We found a significant relationship between sexual orientation and ratings of personal concern on eight variables. A closer look at these cross-tabulations gave the impression that gay men rated the various issues differently than heterosexual and bisexual men did, while the bisexuals appeared in many respects not unlike the heterosexuals.

To determine the differences among heterosexual, bisexual, and gay men on these three attitudinal dimensions, we conducted a series of MANOVAs in which sexual orientation was the independent variable and the attitudinal items were the dependent variables. The first set of ANOVAs looked at differences for the factor scores. Significant mean differences were found between gays and heterosexuals/bisexuals for Dominance and Gender ($F[2, 125] = 23.46$, with $R^2 = 0.276164$; and $F[2, 125] = 10.67$, with $R^2 = 0.147801$, respectively). The Family dimension was not differentiated by the model. A series of ANOVAs were performed, again using sexual orientation as the independent variable, but this time employing the component variables forming the factors Dominance, Gender, and Family. Significant mean differences between ratings by gay and heterosexual/bisexual men were found on nine variables (see Table 19.4).

TABLE 19.2

Attitudinal Items: Issues of Personal Concern

Variable	Ranking	Frequency	Percentage
Aging	0	3	2.381
	1	39	30.952
	3	47	37.302
	5	37	29.365
Domestic violence	0	3	2.381
	1	29	23.016
	3	30	23.810
	5	64	36.508
Child care	0	2	1.587
	1	55	43.561
	3	23	18.254
	5	80	36.508
Men's consciousness raising groups	0	2	1.587
	1	6	4.762
	3	25	19.841
	5	93	73.810
Fathering	0	2	1.587
	1	38	30.159
	3	33	26.190
	5	53	42.063
Gay rights	0	3	2.381
	1	9	7.143
	3	29	23.016
	5	85	67.460
Gender roles	0	3	2.381
	1	12	9.524
	3	15	11.905
	5	96	76.190
Homophobia	0	2	1.587
	1	11	8.730
	3	22	17.460
	5	91	72.222
Men's health	0	2	1.587
	1	19	15.079
	3	36	28.571
	5	69	54.762
Male/female relations	0	2	1.587
	1	30	23.810
	3	26	20.635
	5	68	53.968

(continued)

TABLE 19.2 Continued

Variable	Ranking	Frequency	Percentage
Pornography	0	2	1.587
	1	44	34.921
	3	36	28.571
	5	44	57.937
Racism	0	2	1.587
	1	24	19.048
	3	27	21.429
	5	73	57.937
Sexual violence	0	2	1.587
	1	24	19.048
	3	25	19.841
	5	75	59.524
Reproductive rights	0	3	2.381
	1	36	28.571
	3	36	28.571
	5	51	40.476
Gender research	0	4	3.175
	1	25	19.841
	3	34	26.984
	5	63	50.000
Job satisfaction	0	2	1.587
	1	19	15.079
	3	28	22.222
	5	77	61.111

The underlying dimension here appears related to the salience of respondents' experiences as sexually oriented persons in a social milieu that discriminates against sexual minorities. For example, because homophobia is a more salient feature of gay men's experience than it is of heterosexual or bisexual men, we might expect that gay men would rank their concern systematically higher than the others would. However, while bisexual men are a distinct sexual minority, their heterosexual identity appears to hold greater salience in the experience of their social environment.

These findings clearly illustrate our respondents' responsiveness to issues fundamental to the women's, gay, and men's movements. Moreover, as a surrogate evaluation of NOCM's responsiveness to concerns of local movement participants, the data suggest that not only do NOCM task groups represent an array of issues drawn from the three movements, but the issues they identify as most important are rated as such by a segment of their constituency. While the above analysis may indicate a differential relevance of the task groups by individuals' sexual

TABLE 19.3
Variance Explained by Each Factor

Variable	Factor 1	Factor 2	Factor 3	Dimension
Domestic violence	.81240	.16647	−.13647	Dominance
Sexual violence	.80276	.195131	.03908	Dominance
Pornography	.67785	.06245	.11497	Dominance
Reproductive rights	.59245	.35930	.08661	Dominance
Male/female relations	.67856	−.17507	.20486	Dominance
Racism	.51647	.31129	.02094	Dominance
Homophobia	−.00472	.83195	.02594	Gender
Gay rights	.05533	.77326	−.07241	Gender
Men's health issues	−.04041	.61077	.48746	Gender
Gender roles	.19079	.59589	.02548	Gender
Gender research	.23215	.45337	.35600	Gender
Aging	.07299	.46566	.09110	Gender
Job satisfaction	.01632	.24133	.73226	Family
Fathering	.47556	−.16473	.61749	Family
Child care	.63221	−.14353	.48803	Family
Men's consciousness raising groups	−.07042	.03319	.33295	Family

orientation, we must bear in mind that the diversity discovered exists within the context of high levels of agreement. That is, the level of agreement on the importance of the various issues is far more significant than the differences discovered among subgroupings.

Discussion

This study has suggested that men's movement participants are largely white, middle-class, college-educated men with lower than average incomes for their level of education attainment. We have shown that for a single movement event there was a significant mixture of gay, bisexual, and heterosexual men, with gay men's presence exceeding their representation in the general population. Exploratory evidence indicates that the overwhelming majority of respondents have belonged to men's support groups, and for those who have participated in more than one group, we found a tendency toward increased integration with men of different sexual orientations. Evidence was presented to show that there is both an ideological and a structural connection to the women's and gay liberation movements, but the men's movement was found somewhat more strongly associated with the women's movement. However, given the sample on which these findings were drawn, they

TABLE 19.4

Mean Ratings by Sexual Orientation

Variable	Duncan Category	Mean Ratings	N	Sexual Orientation
Domestic violence	A	4.25	24	bisexual
	A	3.77	24	heterosexual
	B	3.00	62	gay
Sexual violence	A	4.41	24	bisexual
	A	4.17	40	heterosexual
	B	3.24	62	gay
Pornography	A	3.83	24	bisexual
	A	3.43	40	heterosexual
	B	2.31	62	gay
Male/female relations	A	4.58	40	heterosexual
	A	4.33	24	bisexual
	B	2.60	62	gay
Homophobia	A	4.56	62	gay
	B	3.92	24	bisexual
	B	3.86	40	heterosexual
Gay rights	A	4.58	62	gay
	B	3.75	24	bisexual
	B	3.67	40	heterosexual
Men's health	A	4.27	62	gay
	B	3.28	40	heterosexual
	B	3.17	24	bisexual
Fathering	A	3.85	40	heterosexual
	A	3.58	24	bisexual
	B	2.61	62	gay
Child care	A	3.48	40	heterosexual
	A	3.42	24	bisexual
	B	2.15	62	gay

NOTE: All mean differences are significant at the .01 level or less.

cannot be reliably generalized to the national movement itself. They are, one might say, exploratory.

Several questions arise with respect to issues raised in this project that demand attention in future research. First and foremost, a comparative study of men's movement participants and the general male population must be conducted so as to determine the degree to which men's movement participants constitute a special population with respect to their attitudes, behaviors, and political associations. Second, factors that motivate movement participation must be identified and a predictive model developed to assess future leadership. Third, while evidence was presented to demonstrate that support group participation was associated positively with active movement participation, informal observations still resonate with the notion that many support group members do not participate in private-sphere activities, yet alone become active movement organizers. Are there significant differences between the men's support groups of the 80s and women's consciousness raising groups of the 60s and 70s? More important, could such differences account for differences in political activity? If so, are there ways for a national organization attempting to build a profeminist men's movement to affect the outcome of such groups?

Three additional questions must be raised. First, given the current absence of significant numbers of minority males, what must the men's movement do to transform its ethnic-cultural composition? Along these lines, what can sociologists and psychologists do to advance our understanding of the fundamental nature of power and domination both among ethnic-cultural minority men and between ethnic-cultural minority and white men? Finally, given that the longer it takes for the movement to establish publicly acknowledged social or legal goals, let alone victories, the more likely it will experience membership attrition and the less likely it will grow into a mass movement, what must be done strategically and tactically to create a recognized, positive public presence?

The men's movement promises to confront issues of power and domination between men, between women and men, and between men and children. As a movement, it raises fundamental questions about men's gender roles and their effect on men's social experience. As a movement composed of those in power it is unique in its participants' critical reflection on their positions of dominance and struggles in changing both themselves and the institutions and structures of their society. Will it form a set of radical social practices, or will it travel down the liberal abyss?

NOTES

1. This point was first brought to my attention by Harry Brod. It is developed further in his chapter in this volume.

2. The California Antisexist Men's Political Caucus (CAMP Caucus) has developed an excellent adaptation of feminist process by which they and numerous other organizations conduct their business. They have made it available in pamphlet form.

3. NOCM emerged in part in reaction to the formation of an antifeminist men's organization called the National Congress for Men. I would not consider NOCM as representing a countermovement in the sense that Mottl (1980) has used the term, but rather as a separate movement altogether. The National Congress for Men is considered to

represent what has been often referred to as the "men's rights" movement. Both NOCM and NCM responded to the same structural conditions and to the gains of the women's movement, but reacted in opposing directions. The ideological presence of the National Congress for Men, however, probably helped to solidify NOCM's profeminist identity (see Gerlach & Hine, 1970, chap. 7).

4. Much organizational discussion has transpired within NOCM on both the specific phrases to use and the implications of their presentational order. By *profeminist* NOCM means to indicate that it fundamentally supports the women's movement and the feminist critique, and is thereby decisively different from other national men's organizations. By *gay affirmative* NOCM both invites the participation of gay men and lesbians and indicates its commitment to making its environment a safe place for them. By *male supportive* NOCM indicates its support for men as they undertake the processes of change.

5. For a fully articulated argument in support of men's studies and its relations to women's studies, see the chapter by Harry Brod in this volume.

6. The New York Center for Men, Boston Men's Center, Madison Men's Center, and the Men's Resource Center in Portland are but a few of the many centers nationwide.

7. EMERGE in Boston, RAVEN in St. Louis, and AMEND in Denver are three longstanding and well-known men's movement groups providing direct services to men who batter. There are also a number of Men Against Rape and Men's Alternatives to Violence groups providing direct services and community education on rape and other forms of male violence.

8. There is a voluminous literature studying macrohistorical change, revolutionary movements, and movement organizations. Exemplary texts would include Tilly (1978), Touraine (1983), Lenin (1929), Gerlach and Hine (1970), and McCarthy and Zald (1977).

9. These studies have included literatures on cults, religious movements, personal growth movements, and self-help organizations such as Alcoholics Anonymous. Examples would include Cantril (1941), Wallace (1956), Katz and Bender (1976), and Johnson (1985).

10. I am grateful to Hazel Johnson for pointing out that while the various Alcoholics Anonymous (AA) groups are wholly independent of any central authority and were intentionally designed as such, AA still has central service boards that produce meeting guidelines and officially sanctioned literature and host national conferences. This is evidence of far more national coordination than there is in the men's movement.

11. I agree that the men's movement has not yet become a mass movement and that both support groups and national (and local) meetings are requisite for its survival. I believe, however, that Gross et al. are employing a static model of needs-satisfaction that fails to take into account the potential politicizing effect of support groups.

12. I believe Gross et al. are suggesting that there is a tendency among men's movement participants toward expressive rather than instrumental organizational activities and rewards. Many community-based organizations suffer not from the lack of available instrumental activities but rather from the pitfall of orienting their central organizing activities toward producing a series of events under the rhetorical guise of a recruitment and mobilization strategy. Producing instrumental activities *ad nauseam* outside of an integrated long-term organizing strategy often becomes the plague of community organizers.

13. The relationship between support group membership and public-sphere political participation might best be understood in light of a developmental model. This model would propose a dynamic conception of needs recognition and satisfaction over time. It would suggest that support group participation aids in making connections between

private and public domains by clarifying personal dissatisfaction and linking it to larger social issues. Over time, this may lead support group members to public participation or activist involvement. It would also suggest that as one experiences the benefits of the support group process, that process itself may become increasingly incorporated in other movement activities and events as a matter of course.

14. It is essential to emphasize that the data presented below, while representing the event sampled, are not purported to be a sampling of the men's movement or necessarily representative of men's movement participants as a whole. They must be viewed as both exploratory and peculiar to the specific event. Interpretations must be made in light of the local context, the geographic location, and the related events immediately preceding the sampling.

15. This figure was derived from registration materials provided by the Gathering planning committee.

16. All probabilities reported are at 0.01 or less.

17. Californians rank tenth or higher in wages earned when compared to other states (see U.S. Bureau of the Census, 1985, pp. 450, 451).

18. This is fundamentally owing to the limited amount of data thus far gathered, however, movement participants are informally discouraged from discussing their work at movement events. Because men traditionally discuss work-related topics in ways that avoid emotional disclosure and provide opportunities to display status and success, movement ideology and practice discourages such discussion altogether. Movement activists, however, have been well aware that a disproportionate number of participants work in the helping professions.

19. For example, regular columns about men and gender-role change now appear in the *Los Angeles Times* and the *New York Times Magazine*. Feature articles on masculinity, the men's movement, the National Conference on Men and Masculinity, or the California Men's Gathering have appeared in *California Magazine*, the *Los Angeles Weekly*, *L.A. Reader*, *American Way* (American airlines flight magazine), *Time*, and *TV Guide*. Short articles on the men's movement accompanying feature articles on related issues have appeared in *Newsweek* and the *Wall Street Journal*.

20. Additional data were to be gathered at the Ninth California Men's Gathering in October 1986, which may help clarify some of these issues.

21. At the time of the Gathering NOCM coordinated the following task groups: Men and Aging, Battering and Domestic Violence, Consciousness Raising, Equal Rights Amendment, Fathering, Gay Rights, Homophobia, Men's Health Issues, Male-Female Relationships, Men and the Military Experience, Pornography, Rape and Sexual Violence, Reproductive Rights, Work and Job Satisfaction, Men's Culture, Sports and Men, Racism and Sex Roles, Media Images of Men, Sexual Harassment, and Men's Studies.

REFERENCES

Cantril, H. (1941). *The psychology of social movements*. New York: John Wiley.
Gerlach, L. P., & Hine, V. H. (1970). *People, power change: Movements of social transformation*. Indianapolis: Bobbs-Merrill.
Gross, A. E., Smith, R., & Wallston, B. S. (1983). The men's movement: Personal versus political. In J. Freeman (Ed.), *Social movements of the sixties and seventies*. New York: Longman.

Interrante, J. (1981). Dancing on the precipice: The men's movement in the 80's. *Radical America, 15*(6), 53-71.

Johnson, H. (1985, August). *Values of AA members for Alcoholics Anonymous meetings.* Paper presented at the annual meetings of the Society for the Study of Social Problems, Washington, DC.

Katz, A. H., & Bender, E. I. (1976). The strength in us: Self help groups in the modern world. New York: Franklin-Watts,

Lenin, V. I. (1929). *What is to be done.* New York: International.

McCarthy, John D., & Zald, M. (1977). Resource mobilization and social movements. *American Journal of Sociology, 82*(6), 1212-1241.

Mottl, T. (1980). The analysis of countermovements. *Social Problems, 8*(5), 620-635.

Snodgrass, J. (1975, April). The women's liberation movement and the men. Paper presented at the annual meetings of the Pacific Sociological Society, Victoria, BC.

Tilly, C. (1978). *From mobilization to revolution.* Reading, MA: Addison-Wesley.

Touraine, A. (1983). *Solidarity: The analysis of a social movement, Poland.* Cambridge: Cambridge University Press.

U.S. Bureau of the Census. (1985). *Statistical abstract of the United States.* Washington, DC: Government Printing Office.

Wallace, A.F.C. (1956, April). Revitalization movements. *American Anthropologist, 58.*

About the Contributors

Harry Brod is a Fellow in Law and Philosophy at Harvard Law School, where he is working on men's reproductive rights. He is the editor of two books: *The Making of Masculinities: The New Men's Studies* (Allen & Unwin, 1987), and *A Mensch Among Men: Explorations in Jewish Masculinity* (forthcoming). He is also the editor of special issues on aspects of men's studies in *American Behavioral Scientist* (September 1987), and *Journal of the National Association for Women Deans, Administrators, and Counselors* (Summer 1986).

Noel A. Cazenave is an Associate Professor of Sociology at Temple University. He has published extensively on black families and on male sex roles. His current research interests include the professions; movements and organizations of social science research; advocacy research organizations; race-, class-, and gender-related inequality; and critical sociology.

Edward Donnerstein is Professor and Chair of the Communication Studies Program at the University of California, Santa Barbara. A social psychologist, he taught at Iowa State University and the University of Wisconsin prior to his position at the University of California. His major research interest is in mass-media violence and he has published widely in this area. His most recent books include *The Question of Pornography: Research Findings and Policy Implications,* with Dan Linz and Steve Penrod, and *Pornography and Sexual Aggression*, with Neil Malamuth.

Gary Alan Fine is Professor of Sociology at the University of Minnesota. His most recent book is *With the Boys: Little League Baseball and Preadolescent Culture* (University of Chicago Press, 1987). His current research deals with the restaurant industry, particularly with the ways that professional cooks develop a sense of aesthetics congruent with the industrial demands of their jobs.

Lawrence E. Gary, Ph.D., is the Director of the Institute for Urban Affairs and Research and Professor of Social Work and Urban Studies at Howard University. For the 1986-87 school year, he was the Henry and Lucy Moses Distinguished Visiting Professor, Hunter College, New York. The author of a number of books, including *Black Men* and *Mental Health: A Challenge to the Black Community*, he has also published research on mental health in a range of journals such as the *American Journal of Public Health, Community Mental Health Journal, Journal of Applied Behavioral Science, Public Health Reports, Social Work*, and *Social Work Research and Abstracts*. His research interests include mental health, substance abuse, and the family.

Kathleen Gerson is Assistant Professor of Sociology at New York University and a Visiting Scholar at the Russell Sage Foundation for the 1987-88 academic year. She is the author of *Hard Choices: How Women Decide About Work, Career, and Motherhood* (University of California Press, 1985) and a coauthor of *Networks and Places: Social Relations in the Urban Setting* (Free Press, 1977). She is currently writing a book on how and why men's family and work commitments are changing.

Linda Haas is Associate Professor of Sociology and Director of Women's Studies at Indiana University, Indianapolis. She has published articles on changing roles in the family in the United States and Sweden in *Journal of Marriage and the Family, Journal of Family Issues, Sex Roles*, and *Family Relations*. Her current project is a book on fathers' participation in parental leave in Sweden.

Gregory M. Herek received his Ph.D. in 1983 from the University of California at Davis. He is an Assistant Professor in Psychology at the Graduate Center of the City University of New York. He is also the past chairperson of the Committee on Lesbian and Gay Concerns of the American Psychological Association. He is currently conducting research on public opinion surrounding AIDS and on violence against lesbians and gay men.

Teresa L. Jump is an Assistant Professor and Co-Project Director of a *Women's Educational Equity Act Project* in the School of Education at Indiana University, Indianapolis. She was recently selected as a Lilly Fellow for her work in promoting children and youth and strong community leadership. Her research interests include dual-career families, parental roles, gender and race equity, and educational reform.

Michael S. Kimmel is Assistant Professor of Sociology at S.U.N.Y. at Stony Brook, where he teaches courses on gender, sexuality, social theory, and social movements. He is the author of *Absolutism and Its Discontents* (Transaction, 1987) and *Revolutions in the Sociological Imagination* (forthcoming, 1988). He is the editor of *Men Confronting Pornography* (forthcoming, Crown, 1988) and the coeditor of *Men's Lives* (forthcoming, Macmillan, 1988). His current research includes a study of the "engendering" of sexual desire (with John H. Gagnon) to be titled *Gender and Desire* (forthcoming, Basic Books, 1989) and co-editing a documentary history of pro-feminist men in America (with Tom Mosmiller) to be titled *Against the Tide* (forthcoming, Beacon Press, 1988). He is the co-editor (with Joseph Pleck) of a book series called *Men and Masculinity* with Beacon Press.

George H. Leon received his doctoral degree in sociology from Temple University, where he has taught several gender-related courses. He and Dr. Noel A. Cazenave have written a number of gender-related papers based on their survey of Temple University students. He has served as Senior Research Associate for the *Families of Divorce Project* at the Philadelphia Child Guidance Clinic, and is currently a Research Associate at the National Analysts Division of Booz, Allen & Hamilton, Inc., Philadelphia.

Daniel Linz received his doctoral degree in psychology from the University of Wisconsin—Madison. His research over the past several years has focused on the effects on males of exposure to various forms of media violence against women and other images of women. His research interests include the legal policy implications of social science research in this area. Currently, he teaches in the Department of Psychology at UCLA and is a Research Associate at the UCLA Center for the Study of Women.

Peter Lyman studies the relationship between anger and the social order which governs middle-class men's lives. He is currently doing research on the relationship between anger and the cultures embedded in computer technology. (Why do computers have "control" keys? Why do we construct our instructions to computers as "commands," a power relationship?) He is a Professor of Political Theory at Michigan State University, and is currently the Margaret Boaz Library Research Professor at the University of Southern California.

Michael Messner received his doctoral degree in sociology at the University of California, Berkeley, in 1985. He is currently Assistant Professor in the Program for the Study of Women and Men in Society at the University of Southern California. His current research interests include masculinity, ethnicity, sports, and public policy and men's parenting roles.

Marc E. Mishkind is a doctoral candidate in clinical psychology at Yale University. He currently resides in San Francisco. His interests include men's issues in psychotherapy and the interface of catharsis and psychological healing.

Joseph H. Pleck is Henry R. Luce Professor of Families, Change, and Society at Wheaton College, Norton, MA. He is the author of *The Myth of Masculinity* (MIT Press, 1981) and *Working Wives, Working Husbands* (Sage, 1985).

Judith Rodin is Phillip R. Allen Professor of Psychology and Professor of Medicine and Psychiatry at Yale University. Recipient of the Distinguished Scientific Award for an early career contribution to psychology and an award for outstanding contribution to health psychology, she has been elected to the Institute of Medicine (National Academy of Sciences) and the Connecticut Academy of Science and Engineering. She is a current recipient of a John Simon Guggenheim Fellowship. She has served as President of the Eastern Psychological Association, the Division of Health Psychology of the American Psychological Association, and the Yale chapter of Sigma Xi. She has been a member of the board of Scientific Affairs of the American Psychological Association and is currently editor of the journal *Appetite*. She is chair of the John D. and Catherine T. MacArthur Foundation Mental Health Research Network on the Determinants and Consequences of Health Promoting and Health Damaging Behavior. Her research interests include obesity, bulimia, and mechanisms of food intake and weight regulation; pregnancy; aging; and the effects of psychosocial variables on neuroendocrine and immune system variables.

Michael Shiffman is a sociology doctoral candidate at UCLA completing his dissertation on issues related to men and masculinity. He has been a long-time activist in the women's movement and more recently in the feminist men's movement. He is currently on the national council of the National Organization for Changing Men as well as working locally on issues of domestic violence. His primary concerns relate to matters of social justice and social transformation.

Arthur B. Shostak received his doctoral degree in sociology from Princeton University. He has taught on college campuses for the past 26 years, primarily as an applied sociologist. He now teaches at Drexel University, Philadelphia. His 13 books include *Men and Abortion, The Air Controllers' Controversy, Blue-Collar Stress, Sociology, and Student Life.* He has been a member of the World Future Society since its 1968 founding and is an organizer of its Philadelphia chapter. He has been a futurist consultant for Monsanto, Lever-Brothers, Proctor & Gamble, Johnson & Johnson, the George Meany Center (AFL-CIO), and various levels of federal, state, and local governments. His ideas about the future have appeared in the *Wall Street Journal,* the *New York Times, The Futurist, Phi Delta Kappan,* and elsewhere. In 1987 he was chosen for the Distinguished Scholarship Award of the Pennsylvania Sociological Society, the Distinguished Practitioner Award of the Section on Sociological Practice of the American Sociological Association, and the Outstanding Practitioner Award of the Clinical Sociological Society. He specializes in long-range forecasting, social reforms, and technology assessment. A participant in various national, regional, and state men's conferences, he is a strong supporter of the men's movement.

Lisa R. Silberstein is a Postdoctoral Associate in the Department of Psychology at Yale University and Clinical Director of the Yale Eating Disorders Clinic. Her research focuses on the psychology of gender, including men and women in dual-career marriages, body image and eating behavior in women and men, and risk factors for bulimia.

Mrinalini Sinha is a Ph.D. student at the Dept. of History at the State University of New York, Stony Brook. Her chapter is part of her dissertation titled "'Manliness': A Victorian Ideal and Colonial Policy in Bengal, 1883-1891." She has a B.A. in English literature from Delhi University, India (1980), and an M.A. in international politics from Jawaharlal Nehru University, Delhi (1982), and in history from S.U.N.Y. at Stony Brook (1983).

Ruth H. Striegel-Moore is Assistant Professor in the Department of Psychology at Wesleyan University. She also is a Visiting Research Scientist at Yale University. Her research activities focus on body image concerns, eating disorders, and women's health.

Edward H. Thompson, Jr., is Associate Professor of Sociology at Holy Cross College, Worcester, MA. He received his doctoral degree in family and medical sociology from Case Western Reserve University. Family burden, parenting, and men's roles are his major research interests. He is currently conducting a study of public policy and older men.

Leonore Tiefer received her doctoral degree in experimental psychology from the University of California in 1969. She has been engaged in clinical and research work on human sexuality for the last 10 years, most recently in the Urology Department of Beth Israel Medical Center, New York.